McGraw Hill Education

Bothell, WA • Chicago, IL • Columbus, OH • New York, NY

 TextEvaluator™

Cover and Title Pages: **Nathan Love**

www.mheonline.com/readingwonders C

The McGraw-Hill Companies

 **Education**

Send all inquiries to:
McGraw-Hill Education
Two Penn Plaza
New York, New York 10121

Printed in the United States of America.

8 9 RMN 17 16 15 14

CCSS Reading/Language Arts Program

Program Authors

Dr. Diane August
Managing Director,
American Institutes
for Research
Washington, D.C.

Dr. Donald Bear
Iowa State University
Ames, Iowa

Dr. Janice A. Dole
University of Utah
Salt Lake City, Utah

Dr. Jana Echevarria
California State University, Long Beach
Long Beach, California

Dr. Douglas Fisher
San Diego State University
San Diego, California

Dr. David J. Francis
University of Houston
Houston, Texas

Dr. Vicki Gibson
Educational Consultant
Gibson Hasbrouck and Associates
Wellesley, Massachusetts

Dr. Jan Hasbrouck
Educational Consultant
and Researcher
J.H. Consulting
Vancouver, Washington
Gibson Hasbrouck and Associates
Wellesley, Massachusetts

Margaret Kilgo
Educational Consultant
Kilgo Consulting, Inc.
Austin, Texas

Dr. Jay McTighe
Educational Consultant
Jay McTighe and Associates
Columbia, Maryland

Dr. Scott G. Paris
Vice President, Research
Educational Testing Service
Princeton, New Jersey

Dr. Timothy Shanahan
University of Illinois at Chicago
Chicago, Illinois

Dr. Josefina V. Tinajero
University of Texas at El Paso
El Paso, Texas

Bothell, WA • Chicago, IL • Columbus, OH • New York, NY

PROGRAM AUTHORS

Dr. Diane August

American Institutes for Research, Washington, D.C.

Managing Director focused on literacy and science for ELLs for the Education, Human Development and the Workforce Division

Dr. Donald R. Bear

Iowa State University

Professor, Iowa State University

Author of *Words Their Way, Words Their Way with English Learners, Vocabulary Their Way,* and *Words Their Way with Struggling Readers, 4–12*

Dr. Janice A. Dole

University of Utah

Professor, University of Utah

Director, Utah Center for Reading and Literacy

Content Facilitator, National Assessment of Educational Progress (NAEP)

CCSS Consultant to Literacy Coaches, Salt Lake City School District, Utah

Dr. Jana Echevarria

California State University, Long Beach

Professor Emerita of Education, California State University

Author of *Making Content Comprehensible for English Learners: The SIOP Model*

Dr. Douglas Fisher

San Diego State University

Co-Director, Center for the Advancement of Reading, California State University

Author of *Language Arts Workshop: Purposeful Reading and Writing Instruction* and *Reading for Information in Elementary School*

Dr. David J. Francis

University of Houston

Director of the Center for Research on Educational Achievement and Teaching of English Language Learners (CREATE)

Dr. Vicki Gibson

Educational Consultant
Gibson Hasbrouck and Associates

Author of *Differentiated Instruction: Grouping for Success, Differentiated Instruction: Guidelines for Implementation,* and *Managing Behaviors to Support Differentiated Instruction*

Dr. Jan Hasbrouck

J.H. Consulting
Gibson Hasbrouck and Associates

Developed Oral Reading Fluency Norms for Grades 1–8

Author of *The Reading Coach: A How-to Manual for Success* and *Educators as Physicians: Using RTI Assessments for Effective Decision-Making*

Margaret Kilgo

Educational Consultant
Kilgo Consulting, Inc., Austin, TX

Developed Data-Driven Decisions process for evaluating student performance by standard

Member of Common Core State Standards Anchor Standards Committee for Reading and Writing

Dr. Scott G. Paris
Educational Testing Service, Vice President, Research
Professor, Nanyang Technological University, Singapore, 2008–2011
Professor of Education and Psychology, University of Michigan, 1978–2008

Dr. Timothy Shanahan
University of Illinois at Chicago
Distinguished Professor, Urban Education
Director, UIC Center for Literacy
Chair, Department of Curriculum & Instruction
Member, English Language Arts Work Team and Writer of the Common Core State Standards
President, International Reading Association, 2006

Dr. Josefina V. Tinajero
University of Texas at El Paso
Dean of College of Education
President of TABE
Board of Directors for the American Association of Colleges for Teacher Education (AACTE)
Governing Board of the National Network for Educational Renewal (NNER)

Consulting Authors

Kathy R. Bumgardner
National Literacy Consultant
Strategies Unlimited, Inc.
Gastonia, NC

Jay McTighe
Jay McTighe and Associates
Author of *The Understanding by Design Guide to Creating High Quality Units* with G. Wiggins; *Schooling by Design: Mission, Action, Achievement* with G. Wiggins; and *Differentiated Instruction and Understanding By Design* with C. Tomlinson

Dr. Doris Walker-Dalhouse
Marquette University
Associate Professor, Department of Educational Policy & Leadership
Author of articles on multicultural literature, struggling readers, and reading instruction in urban schools

Dinah Zike
Educational Consultant
Dinah-Might Activities, Inc.
San Antonio, TX

Program Reviewers

Kelly Aeppli-Campbell
Escambia County School District
Pensacola, FL

Marjorie J. Archer
Broward County Public Schools
Davie, FL

Whitney Augustine
Brevard Public Schools
Melbourne, FL

Antonio C. Campbell
Washington County School District
Saint George, UT

Helen Dunne
Gilbert Public School District
Gilbert, AZ

David P. Frydman
Clark County School District
Las Vegas, NV

Fran Gregory
Metropolitan Nashville Public Schools
Nashville, TN

Veronica Allen Hunt
Clark County School District
Las Vegas, NV

Michele Jacobs
Dee-Mack CUSD #701
Mackinaw, IL

LaVita Johnson Spears
Broward County Public Schools
Pembroke Pines, FL

Randall B. Kincaid
Sevier County Schools
Sevierville, TN

Matt Melamed
Community Consolidated School District 46
Grayslake, IL

Angela L. Reese,
Bay District Schools
Panama City, FL

Eddie Thompson
Fairfield City School District
Fairfield Township, OH

Patricia Vasseur Sosa
Miami-Dade County Public Schools
Miami, FL

Dr. Elizabeth Watson
Hazelwood School District
Hazelwood, MO

TEACHING WITH McGraw-Hill Reading Wonders

INTRODUCE

Weekly Concept
Grade Appropriate Topics, including Science and Social Studies

Reading/Writing Workshop Big Book

- **Videos**
- **Photographs**

TEACH AND APPLY

Listening Comprehension
Complex Text

Shared Reading Minilessons
Comprehension Skills and Strategies, Genre, Phonics, High-Frequency Words, Writing, Grammar

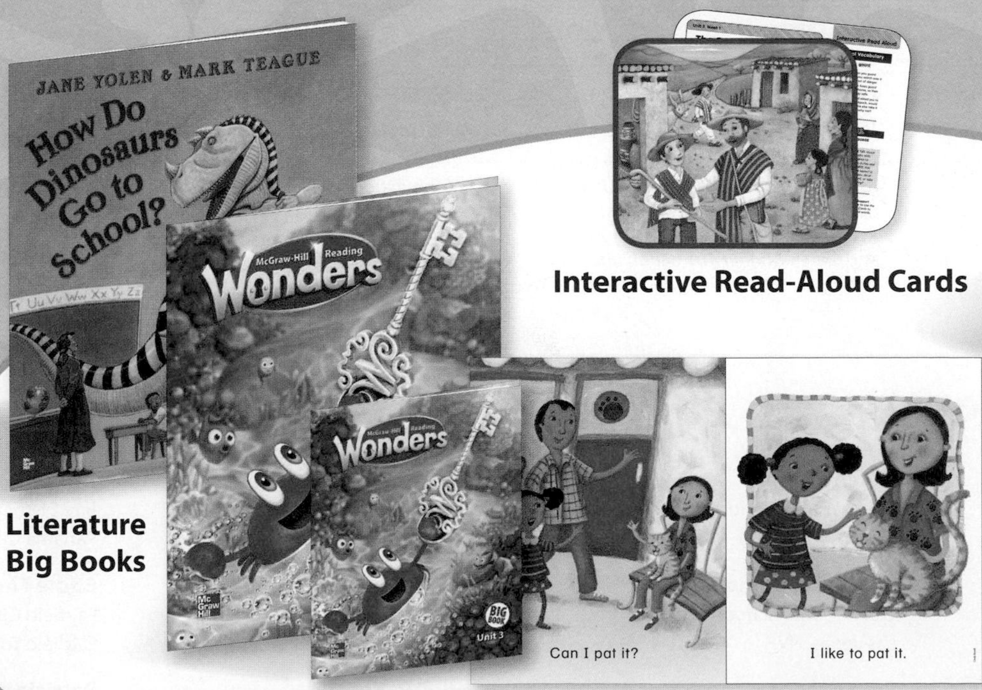

Literature Big Books

Interactive Read-Aloud Cards

Reading/Writing Workshop Big Book and Little Book

- **Visual Glossary**
- **eBooks**
- **Interactive Texts**
- **Listening Library**
- **English/Spanish Summaries**

Master the Common Core State Standards!

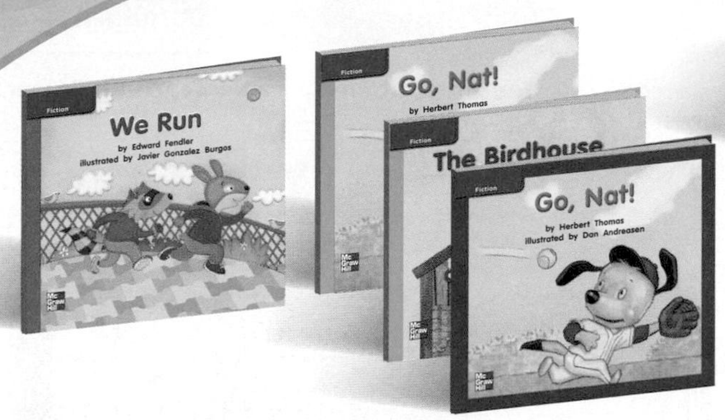

- eBooks
- Interactive Texts
- Level Reader Search
- Listening Library
- Interactive Activities

Leveled Readers

DIFFERENTIATE

Leveled Readers
Small Group Instruction with Differentiated Texts

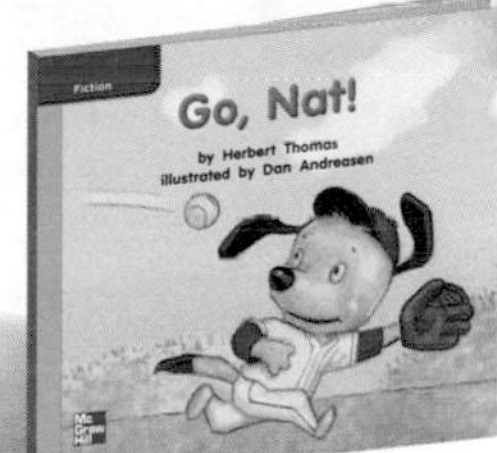

- Online Research
- Interactive Group Projects

Collection of Texts

INTEGRATE

Research and Inquiry
Research Projects

Text Connections
Reading Across Texts

Talk About Reading
Analytical Discussion

- Online Assessment
- Test Generator
- Reports

Unit Assessment

Benchmark Assessment

ASSESS

Unit Assessment

Benchmark Assessment

PROGRAM COMPONENTS

Big Book and Little Book of Reading/ Writing Workshop

Literature Big Books

Interactive Read-Aloud Cards

Teacher Editions

Teaching Posters

Puppet

Leveled Readers

Your Turn Practice Book

Visual Vocabulary Cards

Leveled Workstation Activity Cards

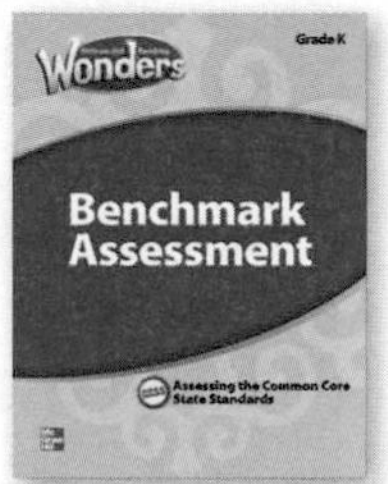

CCSS Assessing the Common Core State Standards

Retelling Cards

Photo Cards

High-Frequency Word Cards

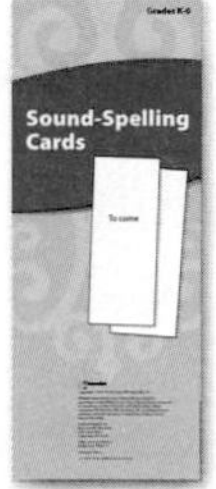
Sound-Spelling Cards

Response Board

Unit Assessment

Benchmark Assessment

Go Digital

For the Teacher

Plan
Customizable Lesson Plans

Assess
Online Assessments
Reports and Scoring

Professional Development
Lesson and CCSS Videos

Teach
Classroom Presentation Tools
Instructional Lessons

Collaborate
Online Class Conversations
Interactive Group Projects

Additional Online Resources
ELL Activities
Tier 2 Intervention
Interactive Games and Activities
Word-Building Cards
Sound-Spelling Songs
Sound Pronunciation Audio

Manage and Assign
Student Grouping and Assignments

School to Home
Digital Open House
Activities and Messages

For the Students

My To Do List
Assignments
Assessment

Words to Know
Build Vocabulary

Read
eBooks
Interactive Texts

Play
Interactive Games

Write
Interactive Writing

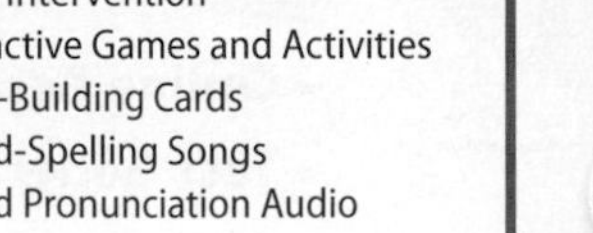

School to Home
Activities for Home
Messages from the Teacher
Class Wall of Student Work

www.connected.mcgraw-hill.com

UNIT 6 CONTENTS

Unit Planning

Weekly Lessons

Program Information

Nathan Love

UNIT 6 OVERVIEW

Week 1

THE FOUR SEASONS

READING

Oral Language
ESSENTIAL QUESTION
How are the seasons different?

Build Background

CCSS L.K.5c **Oral Vocabulary Words**
weather, seasons, migrate, active, spot

CCSS L.K.1b Category Words: Seasons

Comprehension
Genre: Fiction
Strategy: Visualize

CCSS RL.K.1 **Skill**
Key Details: Sequence

Word Work

CCSS RF.K.2d **Phonemic Awareness**
Phoneme Isolation
Phoneme Blending
Phoneme Segmentation

CCSS RF.K.3a **Phonics** /b/*b*, /l/*l* ♪
Handwriting: Bb, Ll

CCSS RF.K.3c **High-Frequency Words:** *is, little*

Fluency
Letter and Word Automaticity
Model Fluency

LANGUAGE ARTS

Writing
Trait: Voice
Express Your Feelings

CCSS W.K.1 Shared Writing
Write Opinion Sentences

Interactive Writing
Write Opinion Sentences

Independent Writing
Write Opinion Sentences

Grammar
Proper Nouns

Week 2

WHAT'S THE WEATHER?

READING

Oral Language
ESSENTIAL QUESTION
What happens in different kinds of weather?

Build Background

CCSS L.K.5c **Oral Vocabulary Words**
predict, temperature, storm, clever, drought

CCSS L.K.1b Category Words: Weather Words

Comprehension
Genre: Fantasy
Strategy: Visualize

CCSS RL.K.1 **Skill**
Key Details: Sequence

Word Work

CCSS RF.K.2d **Phonemic Awareness**
Phoneme Isolation
Phoneme Blending
Phoneme Segmentation

CCSS RF.K.3a **Phonics** /k/*k*, *ck* ♪
Handwriting: Kk

CCSS RF.K.3c **High-Frequency Words:** *she, was*

Fluency
Letter and Word Automaticity
Model Fluency

LANGUAGE ARTS

Writing
Trait: Voice
Show Your Personality

CCSS W.K.3 Shared Writing
Write a Personal Narrative

Interactive Writing
Write a Personal Narrative

Independent Writing
Write a Personal Narrative

Grammar
Nouns

UNIT 6

Week 3

STORMY WEATHER

Oral Language

ESSENTIAL QUESTION

How can you stay safe in bad weather?

Build Background

CCSS **Oral Vocabulary Words**

L.K.5c *safe, prepare, notice, celebration, enough*

CCSS Category Words: Question Words

L.K.1b

Comprehension

Genre: Fiction

Strategy: Visualize

CCSS **Skill**

RL.K.1 Key Details

Word Work

CCSS **Phonemic Awareness**

RF.K.2d Phoneme Identity

Phoneme Blending

Phoneme Addition

CCSS **Phonics Review** ♪

RF.K.3a **Handwriting:** Write Sentences with *h, e, f, r, b, l, k, ck*

CCSS **High-Frequency Words Review**

RF.K.3c

Fluency

Letter and Word Automaticity

Model Fluency

Reading Digitally, T248

Unit 6 Assessment

Unit Assessment Book

pages 71–84

Writing

Trait: Voice

Think About Audience

CCSS Shared Writing

W.K.2 Write a Weather Report

Interactive Writing

Write a Weather Report

Independent Writing

Write a Weather Report

Grammar

Nouns

Half Day Kindergarten

Use the chart below to help you plan your kindergarten schedule to focus on key instructional objectives for the week. Choose Small Group and Workstation Activities as your time allows during the day.

Oral Language

- **Essential Questions**
- **Build Background**
- **Oral Vocabulary**
- **Category Words**

Word Work

- **Phonemic Awareness**
- **Phonics**/b/b, /l/l, /k/k, *ck* ♪
- **High-Frequency Words:** *is, little, she, was*
- **Letter and Word Automaticity**

Reading/Comprehension

- **Reading/Writing Workshop**
  Is It Hot?; Kim and Nan; Mack and Ben
- **Big Books:**
  Mama, Is It Summer Yet?; Rain; Waiting Out the Storm
- **Interactive Read-Aloud Cards**
  "A Tour of the Seasons"; "The Frog and the Locust"; "Rainbow Crow"

Language Arts

- **Shared Writing**
- **Interactive Writing**
- **Independent Writing**

Independent Practice

- **Practice Book pages**
- **Workstation Activity Cards**

www.connected.mcgraw-hill.com

Interactive Games and Activities

UNIT 6 OPENER

READING/WRITING WORKSHOP BIG BOOK, pp. 4–5

The Big Idea *How do weather and seasons affect us?*

Talk About It

Ask children to consider what the weather is generally like during each of the four seasons. What kinds of things do they do outdoors during each season? How do they dress for the weather? Have children discuss how changes in the weather and the seasons affect both people and the environment. What do plants and animals do in very hot and very cold times? Can weather be dangerous? What should people do to stay safe in bad weather? As children discuss, encourage them to ask questions to clarify ideas they do not understand. Prompt them to wait after asking questions to give others a chance to respond. Help children answer questions with complete ideas, not one-word answers.

Sing the Song

Introduce the unit song: "What Shall We Do on a Rainy Day?" Read the lyrics of the song. Ask:

- → *What are some things that you like to do outdoors when the weather is sunny and warm?*
- → *Are there ways to enjoy those activities outside even when the weather is rainy? What about when the weather is snowy and cold?*
- → *If the weather is too bad to go outside, what can you do indoors instead?*

Play the song "What Shall We Do on a Rainy Day?" After listening to the song a few times, ask children to join in. Audio files of the song can be found in the Teacher Resources online at www.connected.mcgraw-hill.com.

UNIT 6

Research and Inquiry

Weekly Projects Each week students will be asked to find out more about the topic they are reading about. Children will be asked to work in pairs or small groups to complete their work. Children use what they learn from their reading and discussions as well as other sources to find additional information.

Shared Research Board You may wish to set up a Shared Research Board in the classroom. You can post illustrations and other information that children gather as they do their research.

WEEKLY PROJECTS

Students work in pairs or small groups.

Week 1 Seasons Chart

Week 2 Wind Chart

Week 3 Safety Book

Writing

Write about Reading Throughout the unit children will write in a variety of ways. Each week, writing is focused on a specific writing trait. Scaffolded instruction is provided through Shared Writing and Interactive Writing. Children review a student writing sample together and then write independently, practicing the trait.

WEEKLY WRITING

Week 1 Express Your Feelings

Week 2 Show Your Personality

Week 3 Think About Audience

Music Links

www.connected.mcgraw-hill.com Integrate music into your classroom using the downloadable audio files in the Teacher's Resources online. Song for this unit include:

WEEKLY SONGS

- → Rain, Rain, Go Away
- → Play Ball
- → I Licked a Lemon
- → Koala

HOLIDAY SONGS

- → O Hanukkah; We Wish You a Merry Christmas
- → All Who Born in January; Jolly Old Saint Nicholas
- → The More We Get Together; Turn Me 'Round
- → Bonhomme! Bonhomme!
- → The Year-Naming Race (story)

Celebration Posters

Celebrate Display the Winter Celebrations poster. Use it to remind students of important holidays during the season. Commemorate the holidays by selecting from the activity suggestions provided in the Teacher Resources found at www.connected.mcgraw-hill.com.

Teaching Posters are available for Fall, Winter, Spring, and Summer.

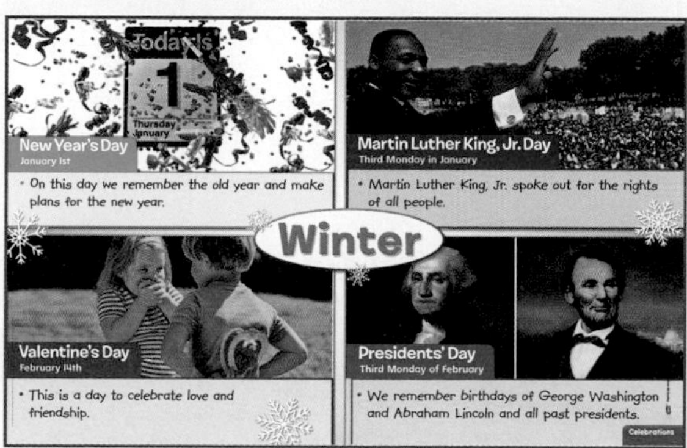

Teaching Posters, pp. 1–4

WEEKLY OVERVIEW

Listening Comprehension

Literature Big Book

Mama, Is It Summer Yet?, 4–33
Genre Fiction

Poetry, 34–42
Genre Poetry

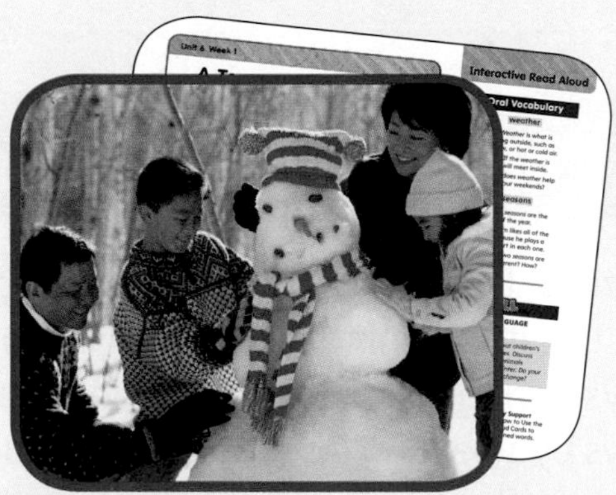

Interactive Read-Aloud Cards

"A Tour of the Seasons"
Genre Informational Text

Oral Vocabulary

active	spot
migrate	weather
seasons	

Minilessons

✓TESTED SKILLS CCSS

✓**Comprehension Strategy** .... Visualize, T13
✓**Comprehension Skill** .... Key Details, T22

Go Digital
www.connected.mcgraw-hill.com

Nathan Love

THE FOUR SEASONS

Essential Question
How are the seasons different?

WEEK 1

Big Book and Little Book
Reading/Writing Workshop

Shared Reading

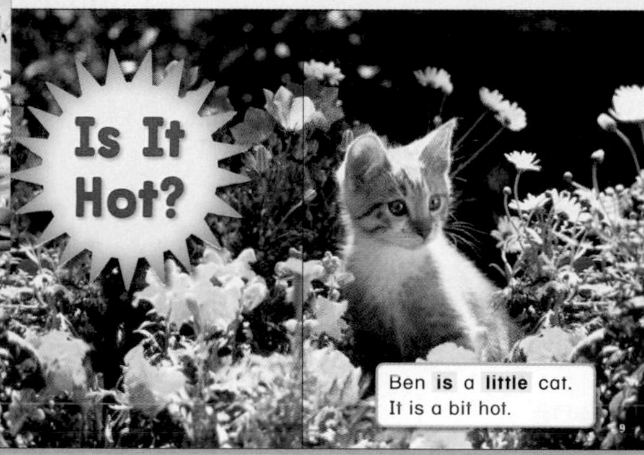

"Is It Hot?", 8–15
Genre Nonfiction

High-Frequency Words is, little, T17

Minilessons 

✓ **Phonics** .... /b/*b*, /l/*l*, T15
Writing Trait........................ Voice, T18
Grammar .... Proper Nouns, T19

Differentiated Text

Approaching

On Level

Beyond

ELL

TEACH AND MANAGE

What You Do

INTRODUCE

Weekly Concept

The Four Seasons

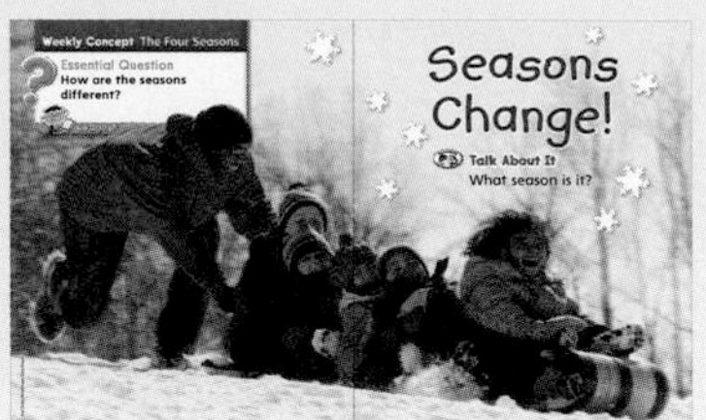

Reading/Writing Workshop Big Book, 6–7

TEACH AND APPLY

Listening Comprehension

Big Book
Mama, Is It Summer Yet?
Genre Fiction
Paired Read Poetry
Genre Poetry

Minilessons
Strategy: Visualize
Skill: Key Details (Sequence)

Shared Reading

Reading/Writing Workshop
"Is It Hot?"

Minilessons
/b/*b*, /l/*l*, High-Frequency Words: is, little, Writing, Grammar

Interactive Whiteboard

Interactive Whiteboard

Mobile

What Your Students Do

WEEKLY CONTRACT

PDF Online

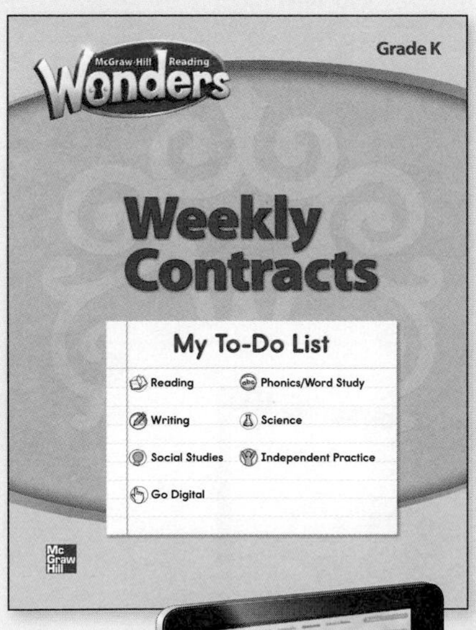

Online To-Do List

PRACTICE AND ONLINE ACTIVITIES

Your Turn Practice Book, pp. 153–162

Online Activities

Leveled Readers

Mobile

WEEK 1

DIFFERENTIATE

Small Group Instruction

Leveled Readers

Mobile

INTEGRATE

Research and Inquiry

Season Chart, pp. T52–T53

Text Connections

Compare Seasons, p. T54

Talk About Reading

Becoming Readers, p. T55

Online Research

WORKSTATION CARDS

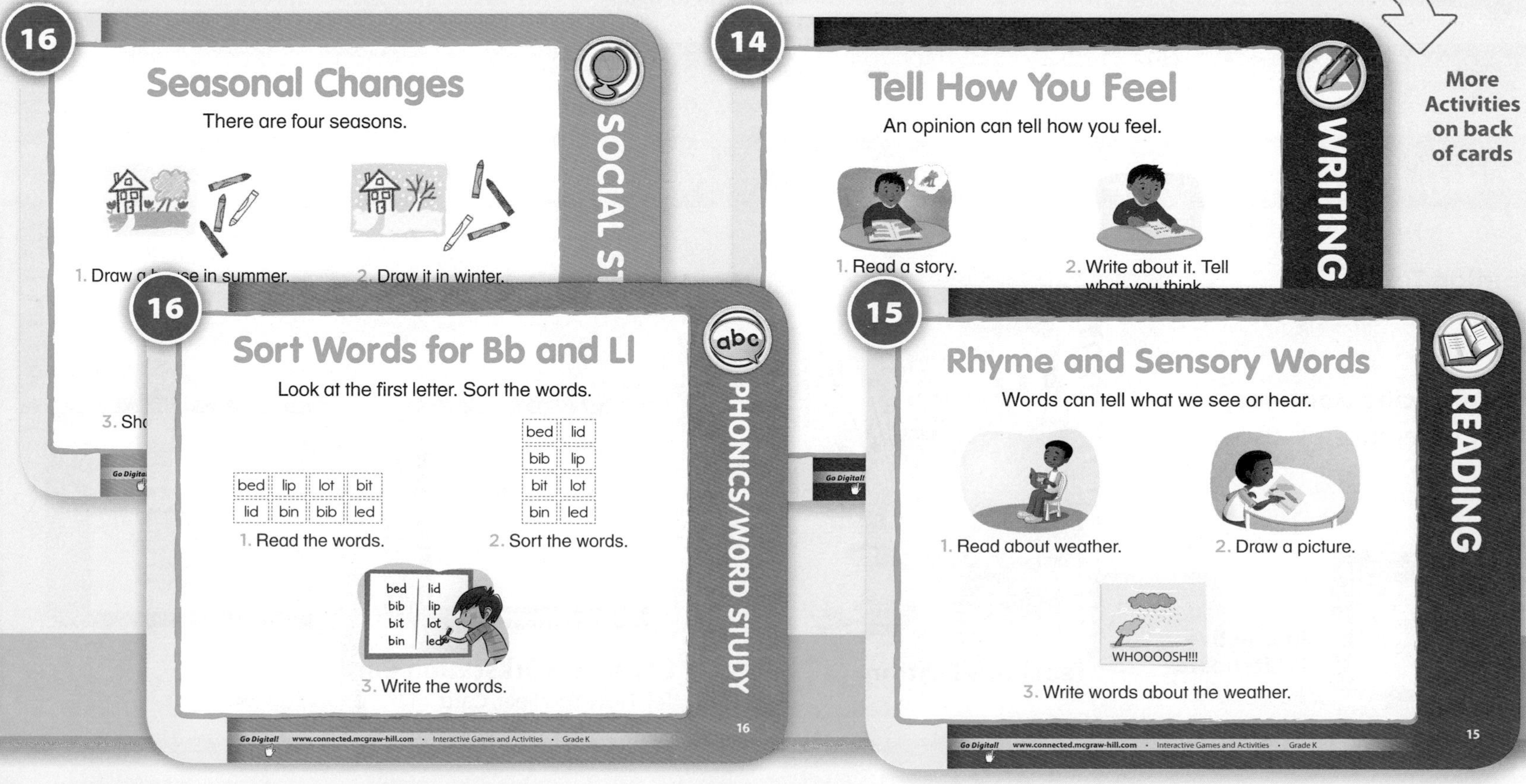

16

Seasonal Changes

There are four seasons.

1. Draw a h... se in summer. 2. Draw it in winter.

3. Sh...

SOCIAL ST...

14

Tell How You Feel

An opinion can tell how you feel.

1. Read a story. 2. Write about it. Tell what you think.

WRITING

16

Sort Words for Bb and Ll

Look at the first letter. Sort the words.

bed	lip	lot	bit
lid	bin	bib	led

bed	lid
bib	lip
bit	lot
bin	led

1. Read the words. 2. Sort the words.

3. Write the words.

PHONICS/WORD STUDY

Go Digital! www.connected.mcgraw-hill.com • Interactive Games and Activities • Grade K 16

15

Rhyme and Sensory Words

Words can tell what we see or hear.

1. Read about weather. 2. Draw a picture.

WHOOOOSH!!!

3. Write words about the weather.

READING

Go Digital! www.connected.mcgraw-hill.com • Interactive Games and Activities • Grade K 15

More Activities on back of cards

Nathan Love

DEVELOPING READERS AND WRITERS

Write About Reading • Analytical Writing

Write to Sources and Research

Respond to Reading, T13, T61, T69, T75, T79

Connect to Essential Question, T13, T45

Key Details, T27

Research and Inquiry, T52

Teacher's Edition

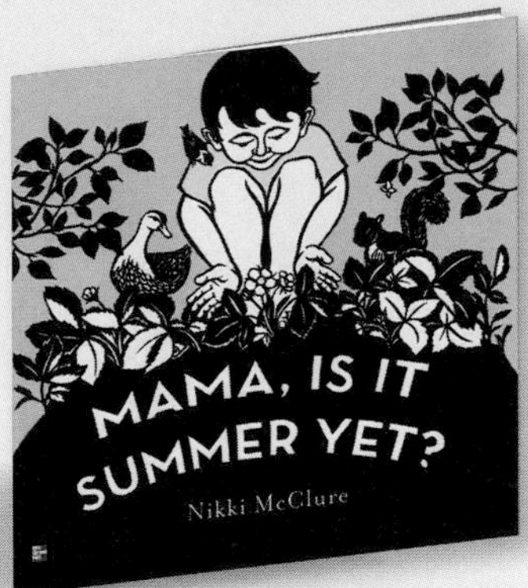

Literature Big Book
Mama, Is It Summer Yet?
Paired Read: *Poetry*

Interactive Whiteboard

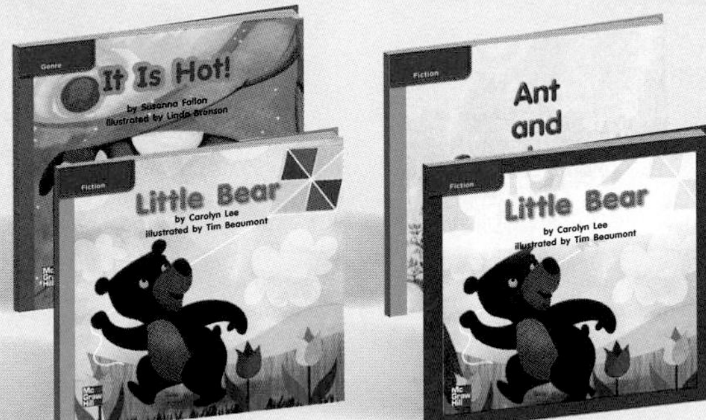

Leveled Readers
Responding to Texts

Writing Process • Independent Writing

Opinion Text
Opinion Sentences, T40–T41, T50, T58

Conferencing Routines
Peer Conferences, T50

Interactive Whiteboard

Teacher's Edition

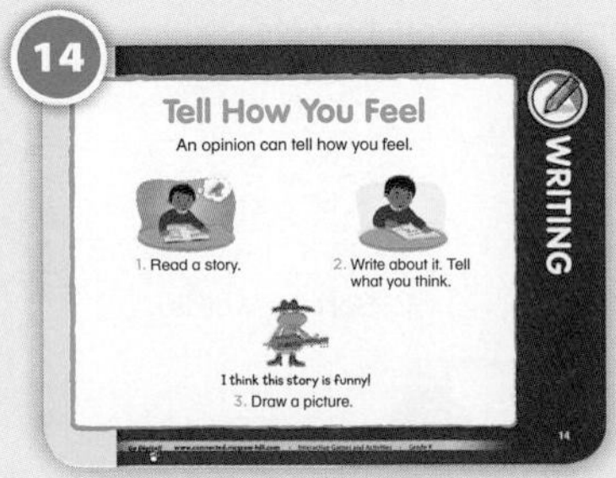

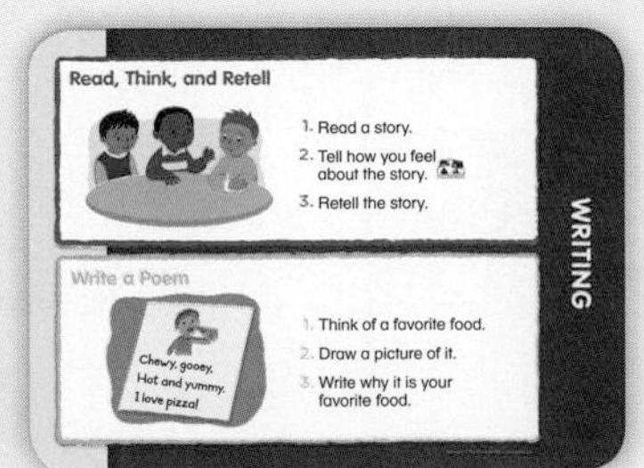

Leveled Workstation Card
Tell How You Feel, Card 14

WEEK 1

Writing Traits • Shared and Interactive Writing

Writing Trait:
Voice
Opinion Sentences, T18, T32

Teacher's Edition

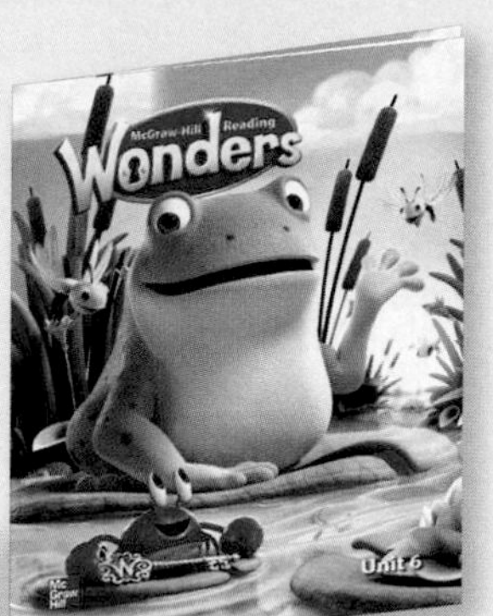

Voice, p. 18

Nouns, p. 19

Reading/Writing Workshop

Interactive Whiteboard

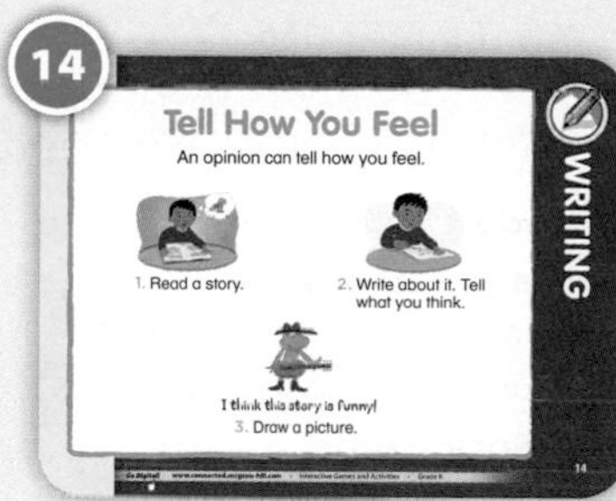

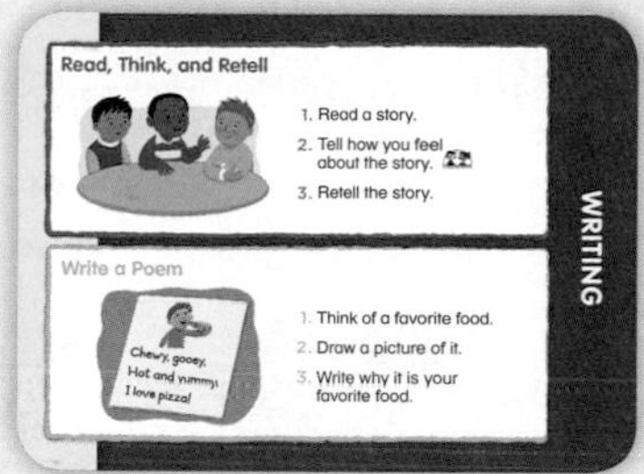

Leveled Workstation Card
Tell How You Feel, Card 14

Grammar and Spelling/Dictation

Grammar
Naming Words (Proper Nouns), T19

Spelling/Dictation
Words with *b, l* and *a, c, d, e, i, n, p, t*, T47, T57

Interactive Whiteboard

Teacher's Edition

Online Grammar Games

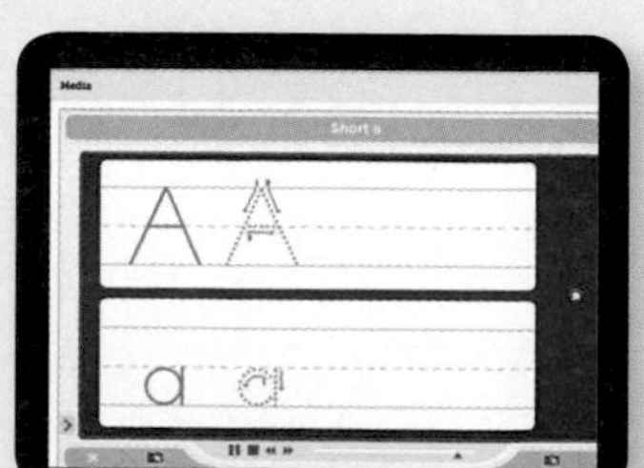

Handwriting

SUGGESTED LESSON PLAN

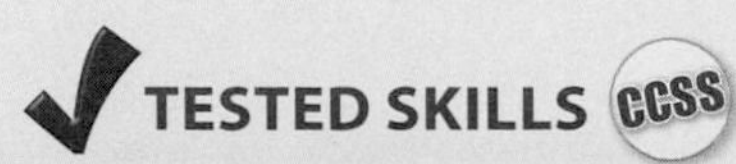

		DAY 1	DAY 2
Whole Group	**READING**		
	Teach and Model 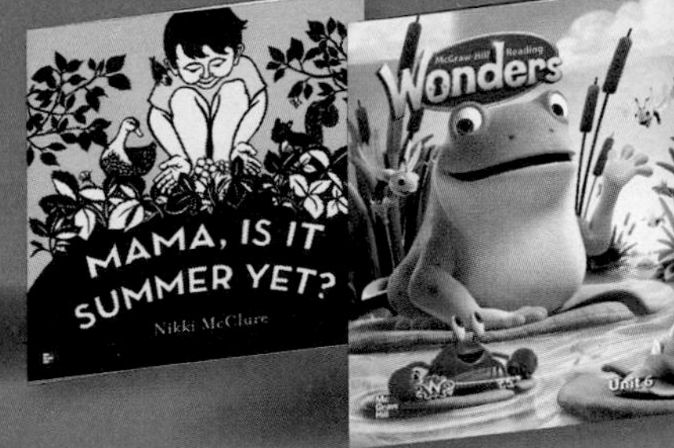 Literature Big Book Reading/ Writing Workshop	**Build Background** The Four Seasons, T10 **Oral Vocabulary Words** weather, seasons, T10 ✓**Listening Comprehension** • Genre: Fiction • Strategy: Visualize, T13 **Big Book** *Mama, Is It Summer Yet?* ✓**Word Work** **Phonemic Awareness:** • Phoneme Isolation, T14 **Phonics:** • Introduce /b/*b*, /l/*l*, T15 **Handwriting** Bb, Ll, T16 **High-Frequency Words** is, little, T17 **Practice** *Your Turn* 153–156	**Oral Language** The Four Seasons, T20 ✓**Category Words** Seasons, T21 ✓**Listening Comprehension** • Genre: Fiction • Strategy: Visualize, T22 • Skill: Key Details: Sequence • Guided Retelling, T27 • Model Fluency, T27 **Big Book** *Mama, Is It Summer Yet?* ✓**Word Work** **Phonemic Awareness** • Phoneme Isolation, T28 **Phonics** • Review /b/*b*, /l/*l*, T28 **High-Frequency Words** is, little, T29 **Shared Reading** "Is It Hot?" T30–T31 **Practice** *Your Turn* 157
Small Group	**DIFFERENTIATED INSTRUCTION** Choose across the week to meet your student's needs.		
	Approaching Level 	**Leveled Reader** *It Is Hot!* T60–T61 **Phonological Awareness** Onset and Rime Segmentation, T62 TIER 2 **Phonics** Sound-Spelling Review, T64 TIER 2 **High-Frequency Words** Reteach Words, T66 TIER 2	**Leveled Reader** *It Is Hot!* T60–T61 **Phonemic Awareness** Phoneme Isolation, T62 TIER 2 **Phonics** Connect *b* to /b/ and *l* to /l/, T64 TIER 2 **High-Frequency Words** Cumulative Reviews, T66
	On Level 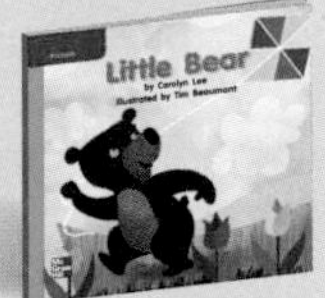	**Leveled Reader** *Little Bear,* T68–T69 **Phonemic Awareness** Phoneme Isolation, T70	**Leveled Reader** *Little Bear,* T68–T69 **Phoneme Awareness** Phoneme Blending, T70 **Phonics** Review Phonics, T71 **High-Frequency Words** Review Words, T73
	Beyond Level 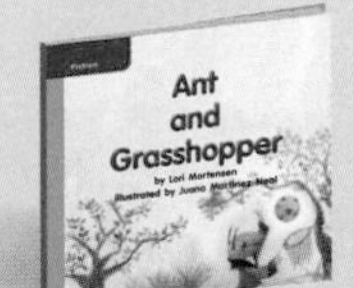	**Leveled Reader** *Ant and Grasshopper,* T74–T75 **Phonics** Review, T76	**Leveled Reader** *Ant and Grasshopper,* T74–T75 **High-Frequency Words** Review, T76
	English Language Learners 	**Leveled Reader** *Little Bear,* T78–T79 **Phonological Awareness** Onset and Rime Segmentation, T62 TIER 2 **Phonics** Sound-Spelling Review, T64 TIER 2 **Vocabulary** Preteach Oral Vocabulary, T80 **Writing** Shared Writing, T82	**Leveled Reader** *Little Bear,* T78–T79 **Phonemic Awareness** Phoneme Isolation, T62 TIER 2 **Phonics** Connect *b* to /b/ and *l* to /l/, T64 TIER 2 **Vocabulary** Preteach ELL Vocabulary, T80
Whole Group	**LANGUAGE ARTS**		
	Writing and Grammar	**Shared Writing** Writing Trait: Voice, T18 Write Opinion Sentences, T18 **Grammar** Naming Words (Proper Nouns), T19	**Interactive Writing** Writing Trait: Voice, T32 Write Opinion Sentences, T32 **Grammar** Naming Words (Nouns), T33

Nathan Love

Go Digital
CUSTOMIZE YOUR OWN LESSON PLAN
www.connected.mcgraw-hill.com

WEEK 1

DAY 3	DAY 4	DAY 5 Review and Assess
		READING
Oral Language The Four Seasons, T34 **Oral Vocabulary** migrate, active, spot, T34 ✓ **Listening Comprehension** • Genre: Informational Text • Strategy: Visualize, T35 • Make Connections, T35 **Interactive Read Aloud** "A Tour of the Seasons," T35 ✓ **Word Work** **Phonemic Awareness** • Phoneme Blending, T36 **Phonics** • Blend Words with *b, l* and *a, e, i, o,* T37 • Picture Sort, T38 **High-Frequency Words** is, little, T39 **Practice** *Your Turn* 158–160	**Oral Language** The Four Seasons, T42 ✓ **Category Words** Seasons, T43 ✓ **Listening Comprehension** • Genre: Poetry • Strategy: Visualize, T44 • Literary Element: Rhyme, T44 • Make Connections, T45 **Big Book** Paired Read: Poetry, T44 ✓ **Word Work** **Phonemic Awareness** • Phoneme Blending, T46 **Phonics** • Blend *b, l* and *e, i, n, t,* T46 **High-Frequency Words** is, little, T47 **Shared Reading** "Is It Hot?" T48–T49 **Integrate Ideas** Research and Inquiry, T52–T53 **Practice** *Your Turn* 161	**Integrate Ideas** • Text Connections, T54 • Talk About Reading, T55 • Research and Inquiry, T55 ✓ **Word Work** **Phonemic Awareness** • Phoneme Segmentation, T56 **Phonics** • Read Words with *b, l* and *a, c, d, e, i, p, t,* T56 **High-Frequency Words** is, little, T57  **Practice** *Your Turn* 162
		DIFFERENTIATED INSTRUCTION
Leveled Reader *It Is Hot!* T60–T61 **Phonemic Awareness** Phoneme Blending, T63 **Phonics** Reteach /b/*b*, /l/*l*, T64 **High-Frequency Words** Reteach Words, T66	**Leveled Reader** *It Is Hot!* T60–T61 **Phonemic Awareness** Phoneme Segmentation, T63 **Phonics** Blend Words with /b/*b* and /l/*l*, T65 **Oral Vocabulary** Review Words, T67	**Leveled Reader** Literacy Activities, T61 **Phonemic Awareness** Phoneme Segmentation, T63 **Phonics** Reread for Fluency, T65 Build Fluency with Phonics, T65 **Comprehension** Self-Selected Reading, T67
Leveled Reader *Little Bear,* T68–T69 **Phonemic Awareness** Phoneme Segmentation, T70 **Phonics** Picture Sort, T71	**Leveled Reader** *Little Bear,* T68–T69 **Phonics** Blend Words with /b/*b* and /l/*l*, T72 Reread for Fluency, T72	**Leveled Reader** Literacy Activities, T69 **Comprehension** Self-Selected Reading, T73
Leveled Reader *Ant and Grasshopper,* T74–T75 **Vocabulary** Oral Vocabulary: Synonyms, T77 	**Leveled Reader** *Ant and Grasshopper,* T74–T75 **Phonics** Innovate, T76	**Leveled Reader** Literacy Activities, T75 **Comprehension** Self-Selected Reading, T77 
Leveled Reader *Little Bear,* T78–T79 **Phonemic Awareness** Phoneme Blending, T63 **Phonics** Reteach /b/*b*, /l/*l*, T64 **High-Frequency Words** Review Words, T81 **Writing** Writing Trait: Voice, T82	**Leveled Reader** *Little Bear,* T78–T79 **Phonemic Awareness** Phoneme Segmentation, T63 **Phonics** Blend Words with /b/*b* and /l/*l*, T65 **High-Frequency Words** Review Category Words, T81 **Grammar** Nouns, T83	**Leveled Reader** Literacy Activities, T79 **Phonemic Awareness** Phoneme Segmentation, T63 **Phonics** Reread for Fluency, T65 Build Fluency with Phonics, T65
		LANGUAGE ARTS
Independent Writing Writing Trait: Voice, T40 Write Opinion Sentences Prewrite/Draft, T41 **Grammar** Naming Words (Nouns), T41	**Independent Writing** Writing Trait: Voice, T50 Write Opinion Sentences Revise/Final Draft, T50 **Grammar** Naming Words (Nouns), T51	**Independent Writing** Write an Opinion Sentence Prepare/Present/Evaluate/Publish, T58 **Grammar** Naming Words (Nouns), T59

DIFFERENTIATE TO ACCELERATE

ACT Scaffold to Access Complex Text

IF the text complexity of a particular section is too difficult for children

THEN see the references noted in the chart below for scaffolded instruction to help children Access Complex Text.

Qualitative / Quantitative / Reader and Task
TEXT COMPLEXITY

	Literature Big Book	Reading/Writing Workshop	Leveled Readers

Quantitative	*Mama, Is It Summer Yet?* **Lexile** 200 Paired Selection: Poetry **Lexile** NP	"Is It Hot?" **Lexile** 200	**Approaching Level** **Lexile** BR **On Level** **Lexile** 300 **Beyond Level** **Lexile** 280 **ELL** **Lexile** 300
Qualitative	What Makes the Text Complex? • **Organization** Questions and Answers, T22 ACT *See Scaffolded Instruction in Teacher's Edition, T22.*	What Makes the Text Complex? **Foundational Skills** • Decoding with *b, l*, T28–T29 • Identifying high-frequency words, T29	What Makes the Text Complex? **Foundational Skills** • Decoding with *b, l* • Identifying high-frequency words *is, little* *See Level Up lessons online for Leveled Readers.*
Reader and Task	The Introduce the Concept lesson on pages T10–T11 will help determine the reader's knowledge and engagement in the weekly concept. See pages T12–T13, T23–T27, T44–T45 and T52–T55 for questions and tasks for this text.	The Introduce the Concept lesson on pages T10–T11 will help determine the reader's knowledge and engagement in the weekly concept. See pages T30–T31, T48–T49 and T52–T55 for questions and tasks for this text.	The Introduce the Concept lesson on pages T10–T11 will help determine the reader's knowledge and engagement in the weekly concept. See pages T60–T61, T68–T69, T74–T75, T78–T79 and T52–T55 for questions and tasks for this text.

Nathan Love

BR = Epitome of a beginning reader NP = Non-Prose

WEEK 1

Monitor and *Differentiate*

IF you need to differentiate instruction

THEN use the Quick Checks to assess children's needs and select the appropriate small group instruction focus.

Quick Check

Comprehension Strategy Visualize, T35

Phonemic Awareness/Phonics /b/*b*, /l/*l*, T17, T29, T39, T47, T57

High-Frequency Words *is, little,* T17, T29, T39, T47, T57

If No → Approaching **Reteach,** pp. T60–T67

ELL **Develop,** pp. T78–T83

If Yes → On Level **Review,** pp. T68–T73

Beyond Level **Extend,** pp. T74–T77

Level Up with Leveled Readers

IF children can read their leveled text fluently and answer comprehension questions

THEN work with the next level up to accelerate children's reading with more complex text.

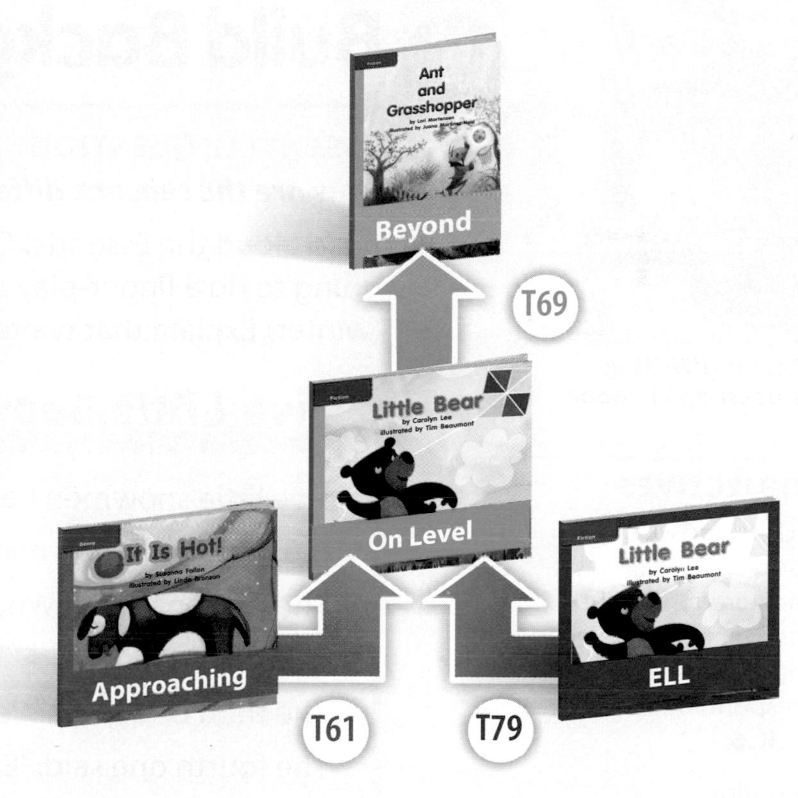

ENGLISH LANGUAGE LEARNERS SCAFFOLD

IF ELL students need additional support **THEN** scaffold instruction using the small group suggestions.

Reading-Writing Workshop T11 "Season's Change!" Integrate Ideas T53	Leveled Reader T78–T79 *Little Bear*	Phonological Awareness Onset and Rime Segmentation, T62 Phoneme Isolation, T62 Phoneme Blending, T63 Phoneme Segmentation, T63	Phonics, /b/*b*, /l/*l*, T64–T65	Oral Vocabulary, T80 weather, seasons, migrate, active, spot High-Frequency Words, T81 *is, little*	Writing Shared Writing, T82 Writing Trait: Voice, T82	Grammar T83 Nouns

Note: Include ELL Students in all small groups based on their needs.

WHOLE GROUP
DAY 1

Materials

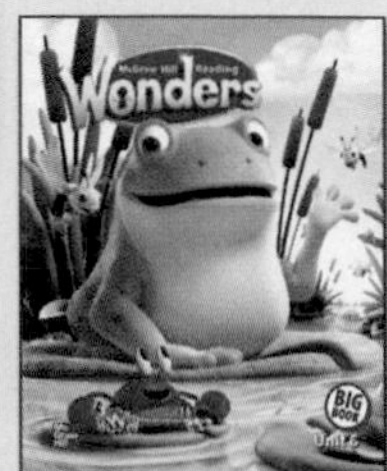
Reading/Writing Workshop Big Book
UNIT 6

Literature Big Book
Mama, Is It Summer Yet?

Visual Vocabulary Cards
weather
seasons

Photo Cards
balloon
bat
bike
boy
ladder
lamp
lemon
lock

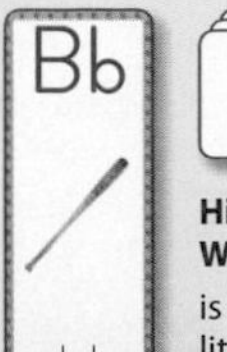

Sound-Spelling Cards
Bat
Lemon

High-Frequency Word Cards
is
little

Think Aloud Cloud

"Play Ball"

Introduce the Concept

Reading/Writing Workshop Big Book

OBJECTIVES

CCSS Use words and phrases acquired through conversations, reading and being read to, and responding to texts. **L.K.6**

CCSS Confirm understanding of a text read aloud or information presented orally or through other media by asking and answering questions about key details and requesting clarification if something is not understood. **SL.K.2**

MINILESSON 10 Mins

Build Background

ESSENTIAL QUESTION

How are the seasons different?

Read aloud the Essential Question. Then tell children that you are going to do a finger-play about snowmen. *When do we see snowmen?* (winter) Explain that winter is one of the four seasons.

Five Little Snowmen

Five little snowmen happy and gay,
(hold up five fingers and move one for each snowman)
The first one said, "What a nice day!"
The second one said, "We'll cry no tears."
The third one said, "We'll stay for years."
The fourth one said, "But what happens in May?"
The fifth one said, "Look, we're melting away!"
(hold hands out, gesturing "all gone")

Say "Five Little Snowmen" with children, encouraging them to mimic you as you perform the finger-play. *When are snowmen made?* (in the winter) *What are they made from?* (snow) *What happens to these snowmen?* (They melt.) Tell children that this week you will read to learn more about winter and the three other seasons.

Oral Vocabulary Words

Use the **Define/Example/Ask** routine to introduce the oral vocabulary words **weather** and **seasons**. To introduce the theme "The Four Seasons," explain that the seasons change throughout the year.

Go Digital

"The Four Seasons"

Video

Visual Glossary

Visual Vocabulary Cards

Oral Vocabulary Routine

Define: **Weather** is what is happening outside, such as rain, snow, or hot or cold air.

Example: The weather today is cool and breezy.

Ask: What type of weather do you like most? Why?

Define: The **seasons** are the four parts of the year.

Example: Two of the seasons are fall and spring.

Ask: In which season does school start every year?

Talk About It: The Four Seasons

COLLABORATE

Write the four seasons on the board. Have children describe the weather for each season and list their responses. Then display pages 6–7 of the **Reading/Writing Workshop Big Book** and have children do the **Talk About It** activity with a partner.

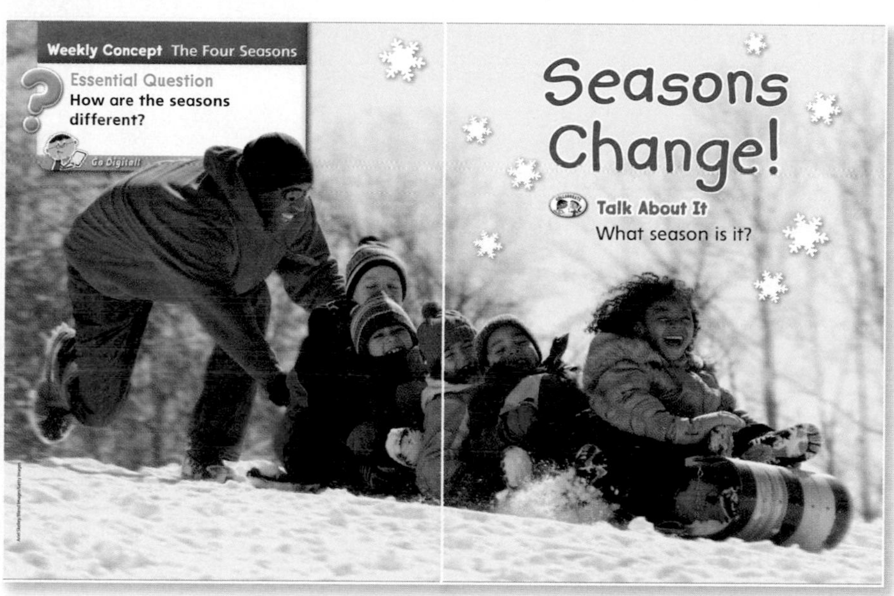

READING/WRITING WORKSHOP BIG BOOK, pp. 6–7

Collaborative Conversations

Ask and Answer Questions As children engage in partner, small group, and whole group discussions, encourage them to:

→ Ask questions to clarify ideas they do not understand.

→ Ask for help getting information.

→ Wait after asking a question to give others a chance to think.

→ Answer questions with complete ideas, not one-word answers.

ELL

ENGLISH LANGUAGE LEARNERS SCAFFOLD

Beginning

Comprehend Explain that the picture shows children having fun in the winter. Use the picture to review weather vocabulary, such as *hot* and *cold*. Ask: *Is winter cold?* (yes) Point to the fall image. Ask: *Does this picture show summer?* (no)

Intermediate

Describe Ask children to tell you about the season shown in the picture. Allow children ample time to provide their descriptions.

Advanced/Advanced High

Expand Have children use complete sentences to describe the season shown in the picture. Ask them to give details about winter, using one of the following prompts:

- *Winter is _______ and _______.*
- *In winter you can _______.*

Listening Comprehension

Literature Big Book

OBJECTIVES

 With prompting and support, name the author and illustrator of a story and define the role of each in telling the story. **RL.K.6**

CCSS Actively engage in group reading activities with purpose and understanding. **RL.K.10**

- Strategy: Visualize
- Connect Big Book to Weekly Concept

ACADEMIC LANGUAGE
characters, story

Read the Literature Big Book

Connect to Concept: The Four Seasons

Tell children that you will now read about a boy who is excited about summer. *What is your favorite season? Why?*

Concepts of Print

Boundaries Display the **Big Book** cover. Track the words from left to right with your finger as you read aloud the title. Point out that the words you say match the words on the cover. Explain that the title of this book is a sentence. The question mark at the end shows the end of a complete thought.

Genre: Fiction

Model *Mama, Is It Summer Yet?* is a fiction story. Remind them that fiction stories are made up. Share these characteristics of fiction:

→ Fiction stories have characters, people or animals who aren't real.

→ A fiction story has a beginning, a middle, and an end.

Story Words Preview these words before reading:
bud: a flower or leaf before it blossoms or opens
swelling: getting bigger
blossoming: opening up into a flower

Set a Purpose for Reading

→ Read aloud the title and the name of the author. Remind children that the author wrote the words in the story. Point out that for this story the author also drew the pictures.

→ Ask children to listen as you read aloud the Big Book to find out how plants, animals, and people get ready for summer.

Go Digital

Mama, Is It Summer Yet?

Model Think Aloud Cloud

Strategy: Visualize

Explain Tell children that they can use the words and pictures in a story to make pictures in their minds of what is happening.

Think Aloud As I read this book, I will pause every page or so to think about what is happening. I will picture the characters and events in my mind. This will help me to better understand what I'm reading.

Model As you read, use the **Think Aloud Cloud** to model the strategy.

Think Aloud On page 7, Mama says the buds are swelling. The tree will soon have new leaves that will unfold. I will close my eyes and make a picture in my mind. I see the leaf buds growing. I imagine how the leaves look as they unfold. This helps me to better understand what will happen to the tree in summer.

Respond to Reading

After reading, prompt children to share what they learned about spring and summer. Discuss what pictures they made in their minds as they listened to the story. Have children draw a picture of their favorite season. Help children to label their pictures with the appropriate season.

Make Connections

Use *Mama, Is It Summer Yet?* to discuss the ways the weather changes during the seasons. Revisit the concept behind the Essential Question *How are the seasons different?* by paging through the **Big Book** and having children describe what happens during spring and during summer.

Write About It Have children write about one of the things that Mama tells her little one will happen in the summer.

ENGLISH LANGUAGE LEARNERS SCAFFOLD

Beginning

Comprehend Point to the buds on page 7. Say: *Close your eyes. Make a picture of the buds in your mind. Now, imagine them growing. Are the buds getting bigger?* (yes) *The buds are* swelling. Have children repeat *swelling*. Restate their responses, adding details in order to develop their oral language.

Intermediate

Describe Point to the buds on page 7. Ask children to make a picture of the buds swelling in their minds and describe what happens. (They are getting bigger; growing; changing shape.) Elicit more details to support children's answers.

Advanced/Advanced High

Expand Point to the word *unfold* on page 7. Fold a piece of paper in half and then unfold it. Tell children to visualize other objects folding and unfolding. Ask: *What other things fold and unfold?* (hands, clothing, towels, letters, newspapers, magazines) Clarify children's responses as needed by providing vocabulary.

WHOLE GROUP

DAY 1

Word Work

Quick Review

Review /f/, /r/: Ask children to tell the initial sound of the *fish* and *rope* Photo Cards.

Build Fluency: Sound-Spellings: Display the following **Word-Building Cards:** *d, e, f, h, o, r*. Have children say each sound. Repeat and vary the pace.

MINILESSON 5 Mins

Phonemic Awareness

OBJECTIVES

CCSS Isolate and pronounce the initial sounds in three-phoneme words. **RF.K.2d**

CCSS Demonstrate basic knowledge of one-to-one letter-sound correspondences by producing the primary or many of the most frequent sounds for each consonant. **RF.K.3a**

Phoneme Isolation

Photo Cards

1 Model Display the **Photo Card** for *bat*. *Listen for the sound at the beginning of* bat. Bat *has the /b/ sound at the beginning. Say the sound with me: /b/.* Say *big, boy, bus* and have children repeat. Emphasize /b/.

Repeat with /l/ using the *lemon* Photo Card and the words *lip, lamp, log.*

Let's play a song. Listen for words with /b/ at the beginning. Play "Play Ball," and have children listen for /b/. *Let's listen to the song again and tap the top of our heads when we hear words that begin with /b/.* Play or sing the letter song again, encouraging children to join in. Have children tap the tops of their heads when they hear a word that begins with /b/.

Repeat with /l/ and "I Licked a Lemon."

2 Guided Practice/Practice Display and name the following Photo Cards: *bike, balloon, boy. Say each picture name with me. Tell me the sound at the beginning of the word.* Guide practice with the first word.

Repeat with /l/ and the *ladder, lamp,* and *lock* Photo Cards.

ARTICULATION SUPPORT

Demonstrate how to say /b/. Put your lips together, and push a little air behind them. Let the air push through as you open your mouth. Your throat will vibrate, or hum. Put your hand on your throat to feel it. Say *bed, bat, big* and have children repeat. Emphasize /b/.

Demonstrate how to say /l/. Open your mouth. Put just the tip of your tongue on the roof of your mouth, just behind your teeth. Use your voice. Let the air pass by both sides of your tongue. Hold your hand in front of your mouth. Can you feel the air on both sides? Say *lid, lap, let* and have children repeat. Stretch /l/.

ELL

ENGLISH LANGUAGE LEARNERS

Pronunciation
Have children name Photo Cards from this lesson to reinforce phonemic awareness and word meanings. Point to the *bat* Photo Card and ask: *What do you see? What is the sound at the beginning of the word* bat? Repeat using the *lemon* Photo Card. Reinforce the initial /b/ and /l/ sounds using the *ball, bike, light, leaf* Photo Cards.

Phonemic Awareness

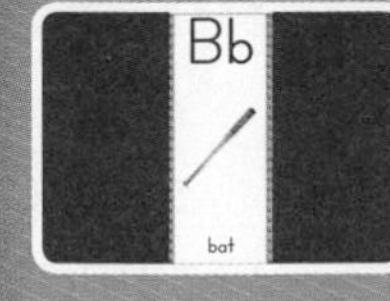

Phonics

Phonics

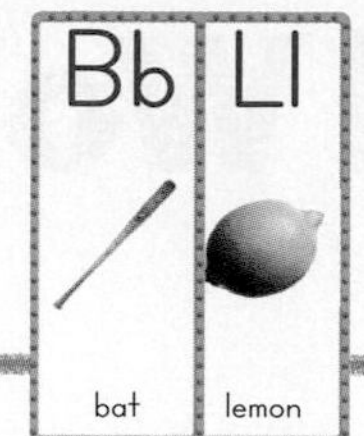

Sound-Spelling Cards

Introduce /b/*b*, /l/*l*

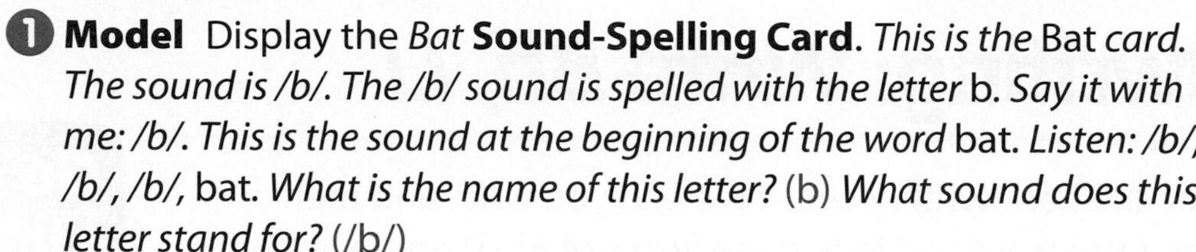

1 Model Display the *Bat* **Sound-Spelling Card.** *This is the* Bat *card. The sound is /b/. The /b/ sound is spelled with the letter* b. *Say it with me: /b/. This is the sound at the beginning of the word* bat. *Listen: /b/, /b/, /b/,* bat. *What is the name of this letter?* (b) *What sound does this letter stand for?* (/b/)

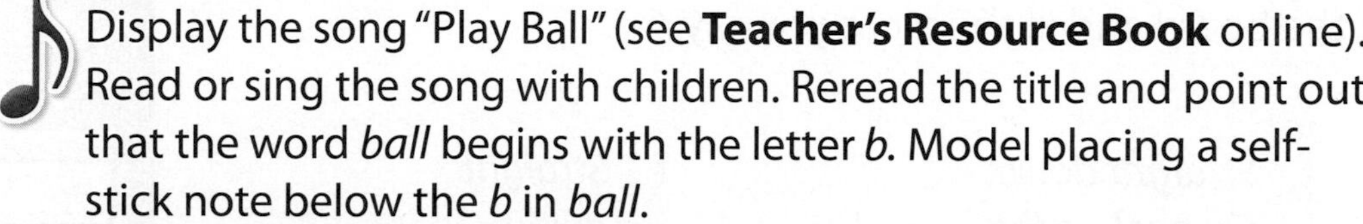

Display the song "Play Ball" (see **Teacher's Resource Book** online). Read or sing the song with children. Reread the title and point out that the word *ball* begins with the letter *b*. Model placing a self-stick note below the *b* in *ball*.

2 Guided Practice/Practice Read each line of the song. Stop after each line and ask children to place self-stick notes below words that begin with *B* or *b* and say the letter name.

Repeat Steps 1–2 with /l/*l*.

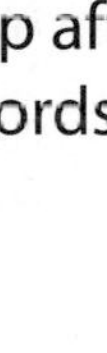

Play Ball!

You get the ball and I will get the bat.
You get the ball and I will get the bat.
You get the ball and I will get the bat.
Play ball!
Play ball!
Batter up!

I Licked a Lemon

I licked a lemon, and it had a sour taste.
I licked a lemon and I made a funny face.
I like lemon candy and I like lemonade,
and I like lemon cake and pie,
but a lemon I can't take!

ELL

ENGLISH LANGUAGE LEARNERS

Phonemic Awareness: Variations in Languages Speakers of Korean may have difficulty perceiving and pronouncing /b/ and /l/. Focus on articulation. Make the /b/ and /l/ sounds and point out your mouth positions. Have children repeat. Use the articulation photos.

Corrective Feedback

Sound Error Model initial /b/. Say: *My turn. Bat /b/ /b/ /b/. Now it's your turn.* Have children say the words *bit* and *bad* and isolate the initial sound. Repeat for /l/*l* with the words *laugh* and *look.*

YOUR TURN PRACTICE BOOK pp. 153–156

Word Work

MINILESSON 5 Mins

Handwriting: Write *Bb, Ll*

OBJECTIVES

CCSS Write a letter or letters for most consonant and short-vowel sounds. **L.K.2c**

CCSS Read common high-frequency words by sight. **RF.K.3c**

ACADEMIC LANGUAGE
uppercase, lowercase

1 Model Say the handwriting cues below as you write and then identify the uppercase and lowercase forms of *Bb*. Then trace the letters on the board and in the air as you say /b/.

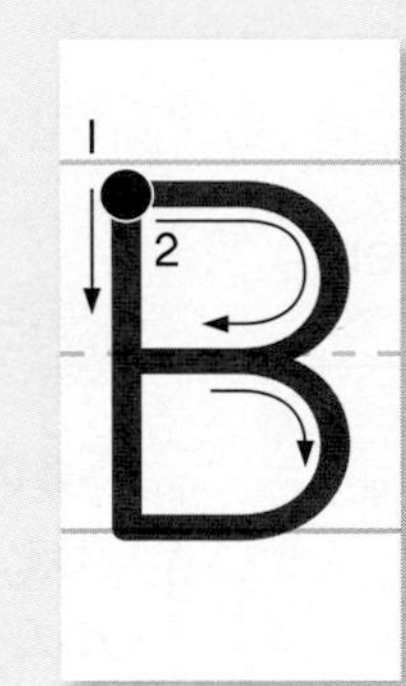

Straight down. Go back to the top. Around and in, around and in.

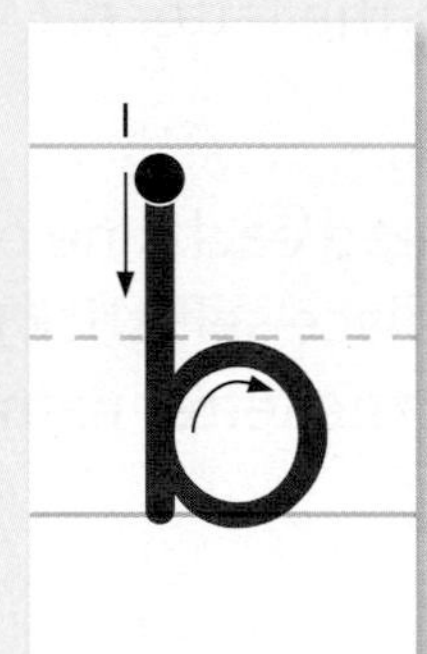

Straight down. Go to the dotted line. Around all the way.

2 Guided Practice/Practice

- Say the cues together as children trace the letter with their index finger. Have them identify the uppercase and lowercase forms of the letter.
- Have children write *B* and *b* in the air as they say /b/ multiple times.
- Distribute **Response Boards**. Observe children's pencil grip and paper position, and correct as necessary. Have children say /b/ every time they write the letter *Bb*.

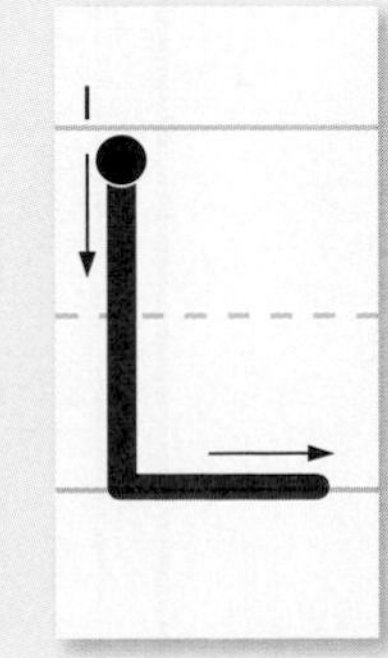

Straight down. Straight across the bottom line.

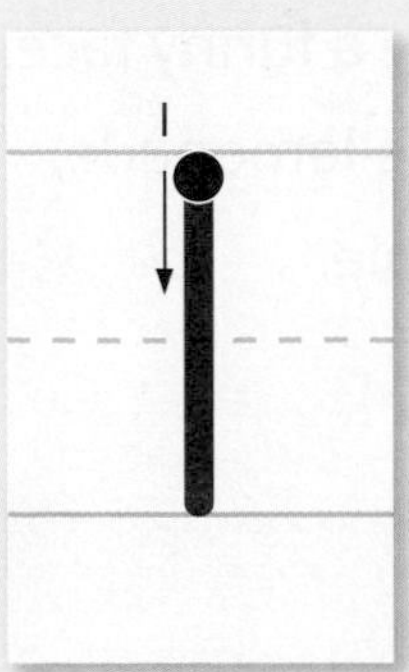

Straight down.

Repeat Steps 1–2 with *Ll*.

Daily Handwriting

Throughout the week teach *Bb* and *Ll* using the Handwriting models. At the end of the week, have children use **Your Turn Practice Book** page 162 to practice handwriting.

Go Digital

Handwriting

the | is | you | do

High-Frequency Word Routine

High-Frequency Words

is, little

is

High-Frequency Word Cards

1 Model Display the book *Mama, Is It Summer Yet?* Read the title. Point to the high-frequency word *Is*. Use the **Read/Spell/Write** routine to teach the words.

→ **Read** Point to the word *is* and say the word. *This is the word* is. *Say it with me:* is. *My hat* is *yellow.*

→ **Spell** *The word* is *is spelled i-s. Spell it with me.*

→ **Write** *Let's write the word in the air as we say each letter: i-s.*

→ Point out that the letter *s* in the word *is* has a /z/ sound.

COLLABORATE

→ Have partners create sentences using the word.

Then display page 7 of the book and read aloud the sentence: *Not yet, my little one.* Point to the high-frequency word *little*. Repeat the **Read/Spell/Write** routine with *little*. Point out that the /i/ and /t/ sounds in *little* are the same as in *it*.

2 Guided Practice/Practice Build sentences using **High-Frequency Word Cards**, **Photo Cards**, and teacher-made punctuation cards. Have children point to the high-frequency words *is* and *little*. Use these sentences.

Also online

The [photo] is little .

Is the [photo] little ?

High-Frequency Words Practice

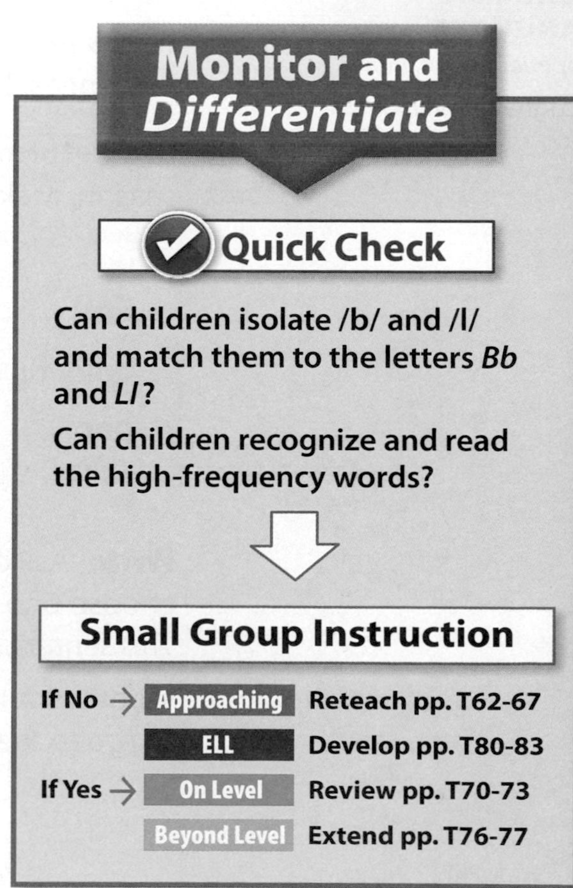

Monitor and *Differentiate*

Quick Check

Can children isolate /b/ and /l/ and match them to the letters *Bb* and *Ll*?

Can children recognize and read the high-frequency words?

Small Group Instruction

If No →	Approaching	Reteach pp. T62-67
	ELL	Develop pp. T80-83
If Yes →	On Level	Review pp. T70-73
	Beyond Level	Extend pp. T76-77

Language Arts

Shared Writing

OBJECTIVES

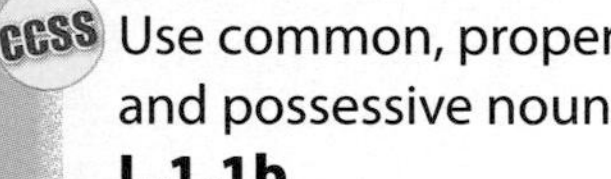

CCSS With guidance and support from adults, recall information from experiences or gather information from provided sources to answer a question. **W.K.8**

CCSS Use common, proper, and possessive nouns. **L.1.1b**

Form an opinion sentence

ACADEMIC LANGUAGE

- *opinion, noun, plural*
- Cognates: *opinión*

Writing Trait: Voice

1 Model Remind children that we can write how we feel about something. Some writers write sentences to give their opinions.

→ Write and read aloud these sentences: *I like playgrounds. Playgrounds are fun.*

Explain that both sentences are opinions that tell how the person feels about playgrounds.

2 Guided Practice/Practice Write: *I like* ______. Ask children to name games they like. Record responses on self-stick notes. Have children put their self-stick notes into the sentence frame. Help children read aloud the sentences they have formed.

Write Opinion Sentences

Focus and Plan Tell children that this week they will write opinion sentences. They will write how they feel about a season of the year.

Brainstorm Ask children to tell what they know about or do in each season. Make a chart to record responses.

Fall	Winter	Spring	Summer
colorful leaves	snow	pretty flowers	go to beach
cool	cold	gets warmer	hot

Write Ask children how they feel about each season. Have them choose one favorite season. Model making a sentence: *I like summer. This sentence tells how I feel about summer.*

Model writing sentences about summer, using ideas in the chart, such as *I go to the beach.* Read aloud the sentences with children.

Go Digital

Writing

Grammar

Grammar

Naming Words (Proper Nouns)

1 **Model** Explain to children that the names of people and places are called *proper nouns.* Write and read aloud: *I live on Main Street. Jay lives on Main Street, too. Which word tells the name of a person?* (Jay) *Which word tells the name of a place?* (Main Street) *The words* Main Street *and* Jay *are proper nouns.*

2 **Guided Practice/Practice** Write and read aloud: *Mary went to the market. She walked to Summer Street.*

Ask children which words give the names of a person and place. (Mary; Summer Street) Circle the words and read aloud with children. Have children say their names and the streets they live on.

Talk About It

Have children work with a partner to identify a naming word on a page of the **Big Book.** (trees, apples) Then have children generate sentences, using those words.

ELL

ENGLISH LANGUAGE LEARNERS SCAFFOLD

Beginning

Explain Help children recognize the plural form of nouns. Draw and label a picture of a single *apple* and a *tree*. Then draw and label the plural forms. Read the words with children as you point to the pictures. Encourage children to repeat each noun as they point to the picture that matches. Model correct pronunciation as needed.

Intermediate

Practice Have children draw a picture for a noun in its singular and plural forms (*tree/trees*). Have them create a phrase or short sentence about the noun, such as *a tall tree; I like the trees.* Correct the meaning of children's responses as needed.

Advanced/Advanced High

Practice Have children name some plural nouns and then say a sentence using each, such as *My friends play at recess.* Restate children's responses in order to develop their oral language proficiency.

Daily Wrap Up

- Review the Essential Question and encourage children to discuss it, using the new oral vocabulary words. *How are the seasons different?*
- Prompt children to share the skills they learned. How might they use those skills?

Materials

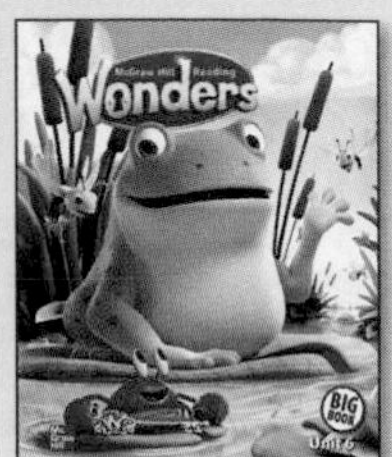
Reading/Writing Workshop Big Book
UNIT 6

Literature Big Book
Mama, Is It Summer Yet?

Visual Vocabulary Cards
weather
seasons

Photo Cards
bat
July
pumpkin
snow
umbrella

Response Board

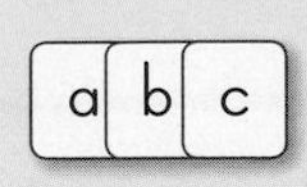
Word-Building Cards

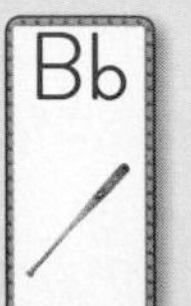
Sound-Spelling Cards
Bat
Lemon

High-Frequency Word Card
is
little

Retelling Cards

Build the Concept

Oral Language

OBJECTIVES

CCSS Blend and segment onsets and rimes of single-syllable spoken words. **RF.K.2c**

CCSS Sort common objects into categories (e.g., shapes, foods) to gain a sense of the concepts the categories represent. **L.K.5a**

Develop oral vocabulary

ACADEMIC LANGUAGE

- *pattern*
- Cognates: *patrón*

ESSENTIAL QUESTION

How are the seasons different?

Remind children that this week they are learning about how the weather changes throughout the year. Point out that the same seasons repeat every year—winter, spring, summer, fall, and then winter again. Ask children to name something they see or hear that reminds them of winter, of spring, of summer, and of fall.

Say with children "Five Little Snowmen" and do the finger-play.

Phonological Awareness

Onset/Rime Segmentation

To help children segment onset and rime, remind children of the finger-play "Five Little Snowmen" that they played on Day 1. Tell children that you are going to say some words from the finger-play. Tell them that you will say the very first sound and then the ending sounds in the words. Say the word *fifth*. Repeat the word, segmenting the onset and rime: /f/ /ifth/. Have children repeat. Then segment the word *years*, /y/ /ērz/. Have children repeat. Then say other words from the finger-play and have children segment the onset and rime in each one, such as: *five*, (/f/ /īv/); *day*, (/d/ /ā/); and *said*, (/s/ /ed/).

Review Oral Vocabulary

Use the **Define/Example/Ask** routine to review the oral vocabulary words **weather** and **seasons**. Prompt children to use the words in sentences.

Visual Vocabulary Cards

Go Digital

Visual Glossary

Category Words

Category Words: Seasons

1 Model Use the **Big Book** *Mama, Is It Summer Yet?* to discuss season words. Explain that there are four seasons in a year: *winter, spring, summer, fall*. Display page 5. *What season is it? What clues help you know?* (It is winter. There are no leaves on the trees. I see mittens and a scarf.) Repeat with other illustrations in the book.

Read the following poem. Ask children to listen for season words.

Winter, spring, summer, fall. Which season is the best of all?
Snow, rain, flowers, leaves. All four are great, I do believe.

→ Use a calendar to show when each season begins. Then have children discuss what they like about each season. (Possible answer: I like raking leaves in fall.)

2 Guided Practice/Practice Tell children that you will say some words. Have children identify a season that goes with each word.

rake	mittens	beach	planting seeds
flowers	pumpkin	sandals	snowballs

Vocabulary Strategy: Context Clues/Sentence Clues

1 Model Tell children that some words have more than one meaning. Use *Mama, Is It Summer Yet?* to model using sentence clues to determine the meaning of a multiple-meaning words and unfamiliar phrases.

Think Aloud I know the word *earth* has more than one meaning. In *Mama, Is It Summer Yet?* I can look for clues to understand what *earth* means here: *But the earth is soft. Soon the seeds will sprout and root.* I know that one meaning of *earth* is "the planet Earth." But the second sentence talks about seeds sprouting and rooting, so I know that *earth* means "soil" here.

2 Guided Practice Locate and discuss other multiple-meaning words in the book. Help children use clues from the sentences and illustrations to determine the meaning of the word.

*But the **swallows** are singing. Soon warmer winds will blow.*

3 Practice Talk about the different meanings of the word *seasons*. Model how to use *seasons* in different sentences to show the word's multiple meanings. Ask children which meaning of the word *seasons* would be used in *Mama, Is It Summer Yet?*

ENGLISH LANGUAGE LEARNERS

Describe Display **Photo Cards** for objects that can represent the seasons, such as *snow, umbrella, July,* and *pumpkin*. Say a season word that goes with each card and have children repeat the words with you.

LET'S MOVE!

Have children dramatize season-word sentences. As you say "We swim in summer," children should act out swimming in summer.

Listening Comprehension

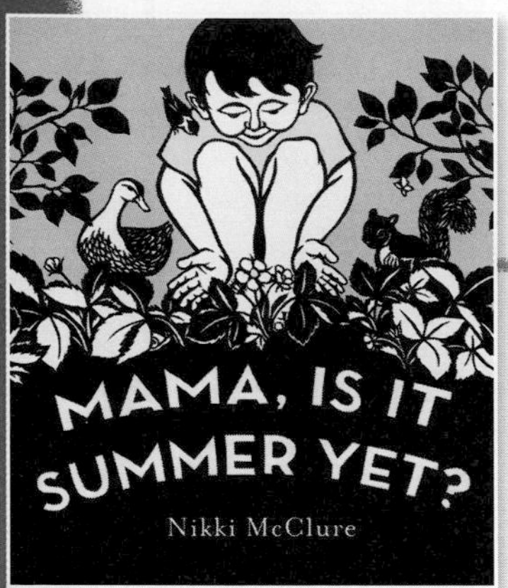

Literature Big Book

OBJECTIVE

 With prompting and support, ask and answer questions about key details in a text. **RL.K.1**

 With prompting and support, retell familiar stories, including key details. **RL.K.2**

- Strategy: Visualize
- Skill: Key Details

ACADEMIC LANGUAGE

- *sequence*
- Cognates: *secuencia*

MINILESSON 15 Mins

Reread Literature Big Book

Genre: Fiction

Display *Mama, Is It Summer Yet?* Remind children that fiction stories have characters. Some fiction contains events that could happen in real life, but the stories are made up. *What makes* Mama, Is It Summer Yet? *fiction?* (It's about a make-believe mother and her son.) Have children point to evidence in the text and the pictures to show that the story is fiction.

Strategy: Visualize

Remind children that good readers use the words and pictures in a story to make new pictures in their minds. *As we read, you can make pictures in your mind to understand what is changing in the story.*

Skill: Key Details: Sequence

Remind children that they can look for important details in the text and illustrations. Tell children that in fiction stories, it is also important to look for details about the sequence, or order in which things happen. *We can talk about the order of events by using words such as* first, then, next, *and* last. Model using sequence words after reading page 11 of *Mama, Is It Summer Yet? First, the squirrel will build its nest. Then the babies will be born.* As you read, have children listen for evidence in the text that tells about the sequence of the story. Use the prompts to fill out the sequencing graphic organizer.

Go Digital

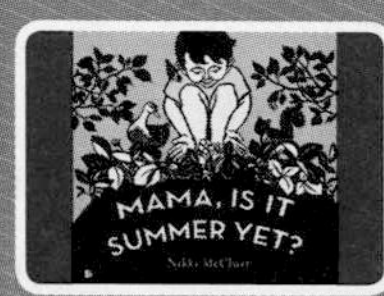

Mama, Is It Summer Yet?

Retelling Cards

ACT

Access Complex Text

Organization This book is composed of questions and answers.

→ Point out that the child is asking Mama questions on the pages to the left. The pages on the right show Mama's answers. Explain that this book includes dialogue even though there are no quotation marks or other dialogue indicators.

PAGES 4–5

KEY DETAILS: SEQUENCE

Think Aloud I read that the boy is asking his mother if it is summer. I see that they are looking out the window. I see a tree with no leaves. There are paper snowflakes taped to the window. I think it is winter. I will add this to my organizer.

pp. 4–5
Point out the question mark at the end of the sentence. Read the question aloud as you model how to slightly raise your voice at the end. Have children repeat. Ask another question, such as *How are you?* Have children mimic your intonation.

PAGES 6–7

VOCABULARY

Think Aloud I see the word *unfold.* I know that when I *fold* something, I close it up and make it smaller, such as folding a towel. I also know that the prefix *un-* means *not* or *to do the opposite of*. When the leaves *unfold*, it must mean that they will open up and get bigger.

pp. 6–7
swelling: Clasp your hands together. Slowly open them to make a large circular shape. Explain: *When something is swelling, it is getting bigger.* Have children open their hands as they say *swell.*

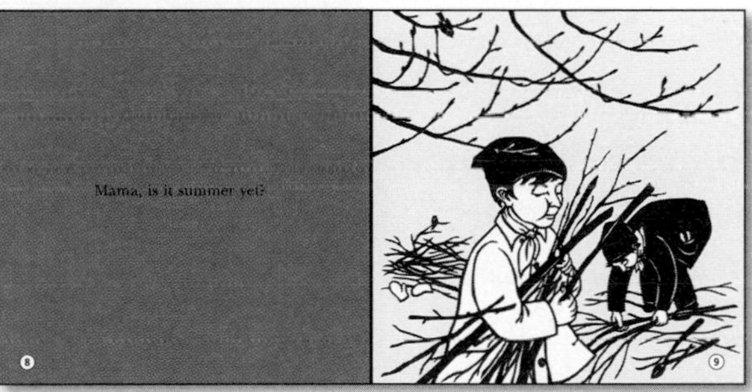

PAGES 8–9

VISUALIZE

Think Aloud I look at these pages and see bare trees, mittens, hats, coats, and broken branches. I can make a picture in my mind of people cleaning up after a long winter. This helps me to understand that winter is over, but summer has not started yet.

PAGES 10–11

HIGH-FREQUENCY WORDS

Have children identify and read the high-frequency words *little* and *is*.

pp. 10–11
my little one: Tell children that *my little one* is a special name that the mother calls her child. Ask children to list other names they know that show affection, such as *sweetie, honey,* or *dear*. Say the names aloud, and have children repeat.

Listening Comprehension

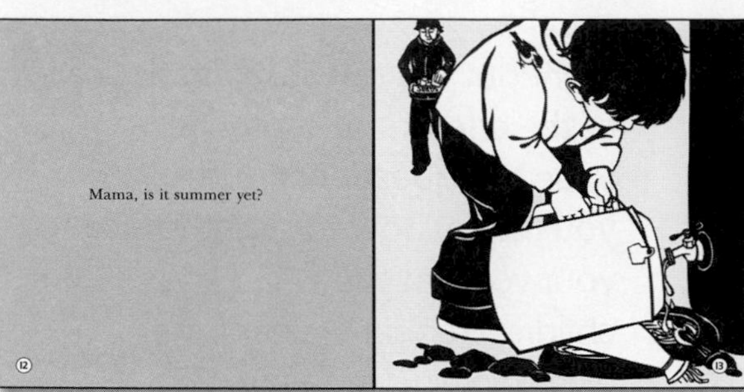

PAGES 12–13

CONCEPTS OF PRINT

Remind children that sentences begin with a capital letter and end with ending punctuation. Reread page 12. *What is the first letter of this sentence?* (capital *M*) *What is the ending punctuation?* (a question mark)

PAGES 14–15

KEY DETAILS: SEQUENCE

Remind children that the events in this story take place in a certain order. *What is happening in the story now?* (the earth is getting soft and the seeds are sprouting) Add children's answers to the organizer.

pp. 14–15

sprout and root: Draw a seed with roots growing down, a line to show the surface of the soil, and sprouts growing up out of the seed. Point to each part as you say: *The seeds will root and sprout*. Have children make gestures up and down to represent sprouts and roots.

PAGES 16–17

KEY DETAILS

How is the boy helping his mother? How do you know? (The boy is helping his mother hammer a nail. I can see his hand on the hammer in the illustration.)

PAGES 18–19

VISUALIZE

Think Aloud The text tells about swallows singing. The lines behind the birds show that they are flying. I will close my eyes and picture the swallows flying through the air. They go in circles. They fly quickly. This helps me understand what the swallows are doing.

pp. 18–19

swallow: Tell children that *swallow* has more than one meaning. It can be an action (demonstrate) or a type of bird. Say the word and have children repeat. Ask: *How many swallows are flying on these pages?* (seven)

PAGES 20–21

KEY DETAILS: SEQUENCE
What details do you see in the illustration that tell you what the boy and his mother might do next? (I think they might be going near mud or water because they are putting on rain boots.)

PAGES 22–23

VISUALIZE
Have children picture in their minds the little ducklings following the mother duck. *What else can you picture in your mind?*

pp. 22–23

bold: A person who grows bold becomes brave. When you are excited to try something new, you feel brave and bold. Ask: *How can you tell that a duckling feels bold?* (Possible answer: It tries new things all by itself.)

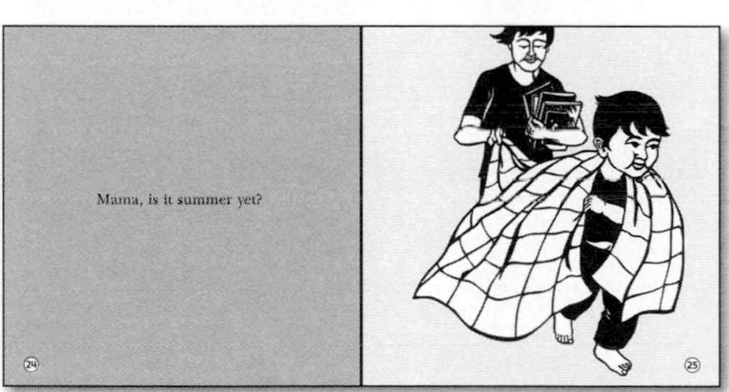

PAGES 24–25

VISUALIZE
Think Aloud I see the boy and his mother with books and a blanket. In my mind I can picture them curled up and reading together. I imagine that they are outside because the weather is getting warmer.

PAGES 26–27

KEY DETAILS: SEQUENCE
Think Aloud On the page before, the boy asked if it was summer yet. On this page I read that it is not summer, but now the trees are blossoming. I will add this to our organizer.

pp. 26–27

apples: Show a picture of an apple to confirm meaning for children. Explain that apples grow on trees.

Listening Comprehension

PAGES 28–29

VISUALIZE

Think Aloud The boy asks if it is summer yet. I close my eyes. I visualize a summer day. I see myself wearing shorts. I hear bugs making noises. I see and feel the hot sun. Close your eyes and try to picture a summer day.

PAGES 30–31

PHONICS

Reread the sentences on page 31 and have children identify the words with the initial /l/ and /b/ sounds. (little, belly, berries)

pp. 30–31

juicy: Tell children juicy means full of juice. *Berries are so juicy that the juice can drip down your chin when you eat them.* Ask children to name other fruits that are juicy. (oranges, watermelon)

PAGES 32–33

KEY DETAILS: SEQUENCE

When did summer happen in this story? (last; at the end) *Let's add this to our sequence organizer.*

Text Evidence

Explain Remind children that when they answer a question they need to show where in the story (both words and pictures) they found the answer.

Discuss *How do you know that summer has arrived at the end of the book?* (On page 33, Mama says it is summer. Pages 32 and 33 show summer things: swimming pool, ducklings that are grown up; summer clothing.)

Key Details: Sequence

Review Skill Remind children that when they read fiction stories, they can look for a sequence of events, or the order in which things happen. Discuss the order of events in *Mama, Is It Summer Yet?* using the completed graphic organizer.

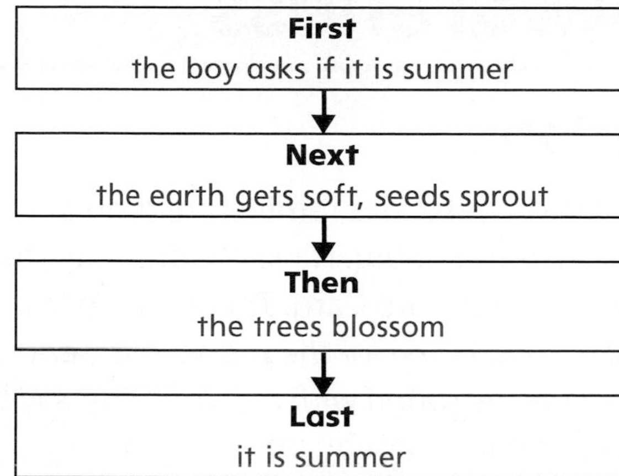
First
the boy asks if it is summer

Next
the earth gets soft, seeds sprout

Then
the trees blossom

Last
it is summer

Guided Retelling

Tell children that they will use the **Retelling Cards** to retell the story.

→ Show Retelling Card 1. Based on children's needs, use the Modeled, Guided or ELL retelling prompts. The ELL prompts contain support for English language learners based on levels of language acquisition. Repeat with cards 2–4, using the prompts as a guide.

Model Fluency

Remind children that exclamation points show strong feeling, such as excitement. Reread page 31 of *Mama, Is It Summer Yet?* emphasizing the expression used with exclamation points. Have children repeat the sentences with excitement and happiness in their voices.

Retelling Cards

YOUR TURN PRACTICE BOOK p. 157

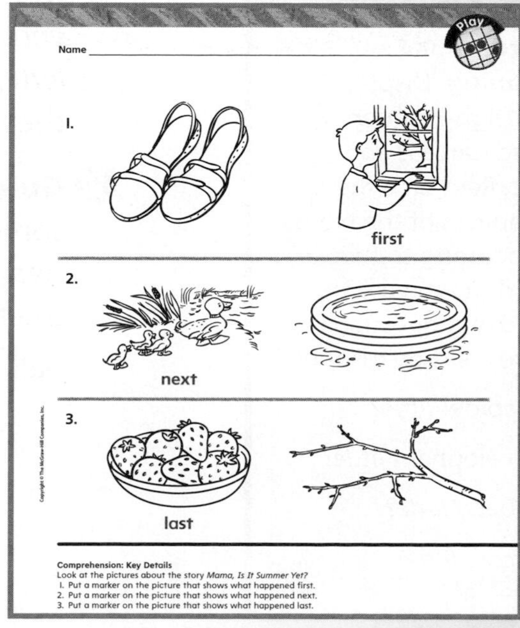
Name

1.
first

2.
next

3.
last

Comprehension: Key Details
Look at the pictures about the story *Mama, Is It Summer Yet?*
1. Put a marker on the picture that shows what happened first.
2. Put a marker on the picture that shows what happened next.
3. Put a marker on the picture that shows what happened last.

Word Work

Quick Review

Build Fluency: Sound-Spellings: Display the following **Word-Building Cards:** *b, d, e, f, h, l, o, r.* Have children say each sound. Repeat and vary the pace.

Phonemic Awareness

OBJECTIVES

CCSS Isolate and pronounce the initial sound in three-phoneme words. **RF.K.2d**

CCSS Demonstrate basic knowledge of one-to-one letter-sound correspondences by producing the primary or many of the most frequent sounds for each consonant. **RF.K.3a**

CCSS Read common high-frequency words by sight. **RF.K.3c**

Phoneme Isolation

1. **Model** Display the *bat* **Photo Card** and remind children of the /b/ sound heard at the beginning of *bat*. Have children say the sound /b/. Then display the *web* Photo Card. *The sound /b/ can also appear at the end of a word. Listen for the sound at the end of* web. Emphasize final /b/. *Say the sound with me: /b/.* Then say the following words and have children repeat: *job, cub, grab.*

2. **Practice** Say each of the following words and have children repeat. Have them say /b/ if they hear the sound at the end of the word. Guide children with the first word.

dab bad rub big tub ball crib

MINILESSON 5 Mins

Phonics

Review *b* and *l*

1. **Model** Display the *Bat* **Sound-Spelling Card**. *This is the letter* b. *The letter* b *can stand for the /b/ sound heard at the beginning of the word* bat. *The letter* b *can also stand for the /b/ sound heard at the end of* web. *What is the name of this letter?* (b) *What sound does this letter stand for?* (/b/) Repeat for the initial sound/letter /l/*l* using the *Lemon* Sound-Spelling Card.

2. **Guided Practice/Practice** Have children listen as you say some words. Ask them to write the letter *b* or the letter *l* on their **Response Boards** if the word begins with the sound /b/ or /l/. Do the first two words with children.

ball last bus boy leaf like back lock

ELL

ENGLISH LANGUAGE LEARNERS

High-Frequency Words: Build Meaning Display the High-Frequency Word Cards *is* and *little*. Reinforce the meanings of the words by pointing to the words as you ask the following questions. Have children respond.

Is a spider *little*?

Is an elephant *little*?

Is a baby *little*?

Is a cow *little*?

Go Digital

Phonemic Awareness

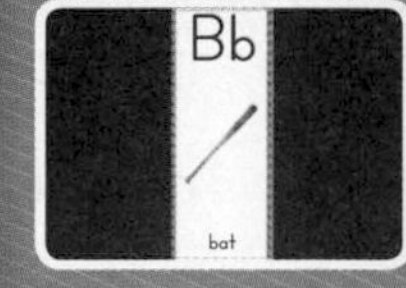

Phonics

High-Frequency Words

Handwriting

Blend Words with *b* and *l*

1 Model Place **Word-Building Cards** *b, e,* and *d* in a pocket chart. Point to the letter *b*. *This is the letter* b. *The letter* b *stands for /b/. Say /b/. This is the letter* e. *The letter* e *stands for /e/. Say /e/. This is the letter* d. *The letter* d *stands for /d/. Say /d/. Listen as I blend the three sounds together: /beeed/,* bed. *Let's blend the sounds to read the word.*

2 Guided Practice/Practice Change Word-Building Cards to *bet*. Point to the letter *b* and have children say /b/. Point to the letter *e* and have children say /e/. Point to the letter *t* and have children say /t/. Then move your hand from left to right under the word and have children blend and read the word *bet*. Repeat with *bat*.

Repeat Steps 1–2 with *l* using the words *let, lit,* and *lot*.

High-Frequency Words

is, little

is

little

High-Frequency Word Cards

1 Guided Practice Display the **High-Frequency Word Cards** *is* and *little*. Use the **Read/Spell/Write** routine to teach the words. Ask children to close their eyes, picture the words in their minds, and then write the words the way they see them. Have children self-correct by checking the High-Frequency Word Cards.

2 Practice Add high-frequency words *is* and *little* to the word bank.

→ Have partners create sentences using the words.

→ Have children count the number of letters in each word and then write *is* and *little* again.

Cumulative Review Review *he, with, are, my, to, and, go, you, do.*

Repeat the **Read/Spell/Write** routine. Mix the words and have children chorally say each one.

Monitor and *Differentiate*

Can children isolate /b/ and /l/ and match them to the letters *Bb* and *Ll*?

Can children read and recognize the high-frequency words?

Small Group Instruction

If No →	**Approaching**	**Reteach pp. T62-67**
	ELL	**Develop pp. T80-83**
If Yes →	**On Level**	**Review pp. T70-73**
	Beyond Level	**Extend pp. T76-77**

WHOLE GROUP
DAY 2

Shared Read

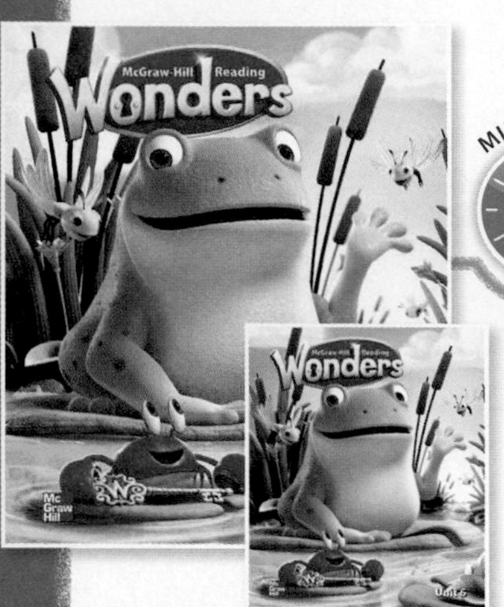

Reading/Writing Workshop Big Book and Reading/Writing Workshop

OBJECTIVES

CCSS Read common high-frequency words by sight. **RF.K.3c**

CCSS Read emergent-reader texts with purpose and understanding. **RF.K.4**

CCSS Recognize and name end punctuation. **L.K.2b**

ACADEMIC LANGUAGE

- *predict*
- Cognates: *predecir*

MINILESSON 10 Mins

Read "Is It Hot?"

Model Skills and Strategies

Model Concepts About Print Together, count the number of sentences on each page of the story. Then turn to page 10 and point to each sentence. *Notice that each sentence begins with a capital letter and ends with a punctuation mark. For example, the first sentence starts with a capital* I *and ends with a period. The second sentence begins with a capital* W *and ends with an exclamation point. This sentence should be read with more emotion because it ends with an exclamation point.* Read the sentence with expression. Then invite volunteers to come up to the **Big Book** and establish sentence boundaries by pointing first to the capital letter that begins the sentence and next to the ending punctuation mark.

Predict Read the title together and look at the photograph. Ask children to predict what the selection will be about.

Read Have children chorally read the story with you. Point to each word as you read it together. Help children sound out the decodable words and say the sight words. If children have difficulty, provide corrective feedback and guide them page by page using the student **Reading/Writing Workshop**.

Ask the following:

- *Look at page 8. Is it warm or cool out? How do you know?* (Possible answer: warm, hot; the sun is out and shining on the flowers)
- *Look at page 13. What is the girl doing? What season is it?* (playing hopscotch; fall)
- *Look at page 14. What season is this? How do you know?* (winter; there is a snowman)

Go Digital

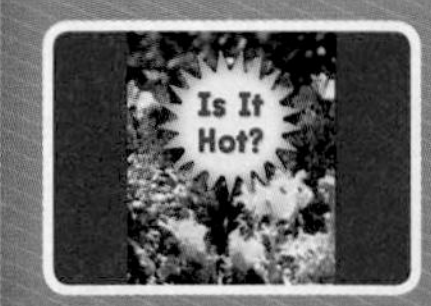

"Is It Hot?"

"Is It Hot?"

READING/WRITING WORKSHOP, pp. 8–15

Rereading

Have small groups use the **Reading/Writing Workshop** to reread "Is It Hot?" Then review the skills and strategies using the *Phonics* and *Words to Know* pages that come before the selection.

- → Have children visualize what it is like outside during each of the four seasons. Encourage them to describe what they might see and feel if they were outside. Then ask children to tell about each photograph in the selection, using details to describe them. Finally, have children look at each of the photographs and tell the sequence of the seasons that they see. (spring, summer, fall, and winter)
- → Have children use page 7 to review the high-frequency words *is* and *little*.
- → Have children use page 6 to review that the letters *b* and *l* can stand for the sounds /b/ and /l/, respectively. Have them identify and name each picture. Guide them to blend the sounds to read the words.

ENGLISH LANGUAGE LEARNERS

Reinforce Vocabulary Display the **High-Frequency Word Cards** *is, little, he, with*. Point to classroom objects and groups of children as you use the high-frequency words in sentences, such as the following: *Can you see the bulletin board?* (Yes, we can see the bulletin board.) *Does he have brown hair?* (Yes, he has brown hair.) *Is the big* L *with the little* l? (Yes, the big *L* is with the little *l*.)

Language Arts

Interactive Writing

OBJECTIVES

 Use a combination of drawing, dictating, and writing to compose opinion pieces in which they tell a reader the topic or the name of the book they are writing about and state an opinion or preference about the topic or book (e.g., *My favorite book is . . .*). **W.K.1**

 Form regular plural nouns orally by adding /s/ or /es/. **L.K.1c**

Form an opinion sentence

ACADEMIC LANGUAGE

- *opinion, sentence*
- Cognates: *opinión*

Writing Trait: Voice

Review Remind children that we can write an opinion that tells how we feel about something. Write: *I like rainy days. This sentence tells a reader how I feel about rainy days.*

Write Opinion Sentences

Discuss Display and read aloud the chart from Day 1. Guide children to pick a season to write about, such as fall.

Model/Apply Grammar Tell children that you will work together to write sentences that tell how you feel about fall.

Write the sentence frame: *I like* ______. Model how to choose a season to complete the sentence. Fill in the sentence frame and read the complete sentence aloud. Point out that the seasons are nouns because they name a thing; in this case, a time of year.

When we write to express our feelings, we should tell why we like something. What do you like about fall? Record children's responses. Use the chart and children's responses to write a sentence about fall, such as *The leaves are colorful.* Have children point to the naming words, such as *leaves,* and tell whether they name one thing or more than one thing.

Write Have children help you create more opinion sentences about a season, using the sentence frame: *I like* ______. Then guide them in forming sentences using the information in the chart, such as:

→ *I like winter. I play in the snow.*

→ *I like spring. I smell the flowers.*

Write and read aloud each sentence that children create. Share the pen with children and have them write the letters they know.

Point out that people may like the same season for a different reason. Also point out that people may like different seasons. Discuss how we can learn from different opinions.

Go Digital

Writing

I see a fish.

Grammar

Grammar

Naming Words (Nouns)

1 Review Remind children that naming words, also called nouns, tell the names of people, places, animals, and things. Explain to children that we can add *-s* to the end of naming words when we talk about more than one.

→ Write and read aloud the sentence: *The store sells clocks.*

Point out that *store* is a naming word that names one thing. *Store* is a singular noun. Point out that *clocks* is a naming word that names more than one thing. *Clocks* is a plural noun. Underline the *-s* at the end of *clocks*.

2 Guided Practice Write and read: *A man sells balloons.* Have children identify the naming words. (man, balloons) *Which word names one thing? Which word names more than one thing? How do you know* balloons *names more than one thing?* (the ending *-s*)

→ Write and read: *A girl sells red caps.*

Have children pick out the naming words. (girl, caps) Underline the naming words. Have them tell whether the words name one thing or more than one thing. Ask children to underline the *-s* that tells them a naming word is plural.

3 Practice Show children the **Photo Cards** for *bike, giraffe,* and *ladybug.* Write and read aloud: *The bike has two wheels. The giraffe stands on four legs. A ladybug has spots.*

Have partners identify the naming words in the sentences. Then ask them to write the word that names one thing and the word that names more than one thing.

Talk About It

Have children work with a partner to identify an object in the classroom. Ask children to say the word that names more than one of that object.

ENGLISH LANGUAGE LEARNERS

Demonstrate Comprehension Help children understand the meaning of plurals. Discuss pictures in the **Big Book** that provide plural words, such as the picture of the boy and his mother putting on their boots. Point to *boots, coats,* and *flowers*. Say the names as you point. Give children ample time to respond.

Daily Wrap Up

- Discuss the Essential Question and encourage children to use the oral vocabulary words. *How are the seasons different?*
- Prompt children to review and discuss the skills they used today. How do those skills help them?

Materials

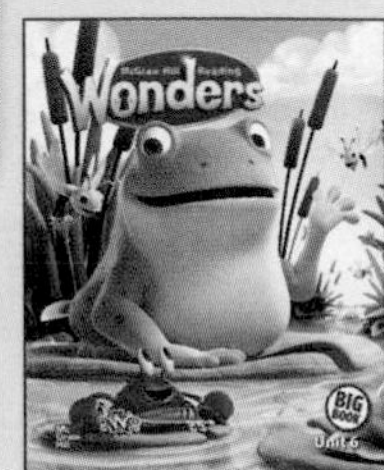

Reading/Writing Workshop Big Book
UNIT 6

Visual Vocabulary Cards
migrate
active
spot

Puppet

Word-Building Cards

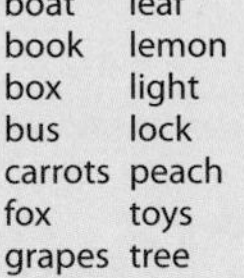

Interactive Read-Aloud Cards

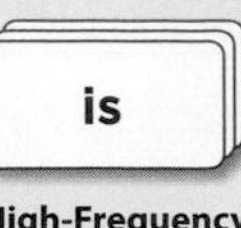

Photo Cards
bat, boat, book, box, bus, carrots, fox, grapes, inch, leaf, lemon, light, lock, peach, toys, tree

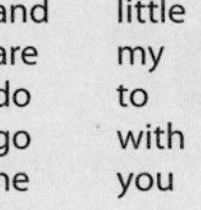

High-Frequency Word Cards
and, are, do, go, he, is, little, my, to, with, you

Think Aloud Cloud

Build the Concept

Oral Language

OBJECTIVES

CCSS Actively engage in group reading activities with purpose and understanding. **RI.K.10**

CCSS Identify real-life connections between words and their use. **L.K.5c**

Develop oral vocabulary

ACADEMIC LANGUAGE

- *informational text*
- Cognates: *texto informativo*

ESSENTIAL QUESTION

Remind children that this week they are talking and learning about how the seasons are different. Guide children to discuss the Essential Question using information from the **Big Book** and the weekly rhyme.

Remind children about what happens to the snowmen in May in "Five Little Snowmen." Say the rhyme and have children join in.

Oral Vocabulary

Review last week's oral vocabulary words, as well as *weather* and *seasons* from Day 1. Then use the **Define/Example/Ask** routine to introduce *migrate, active,* and *spot*.

Oral Vocabulary Routine

Define: To **migrate** means to move from one place to another, usually to a place that is warmer or colder.

Example: The birds migrate south to Florida every winter.

Ask: Why do many animals migrate to warmer places for the winter?

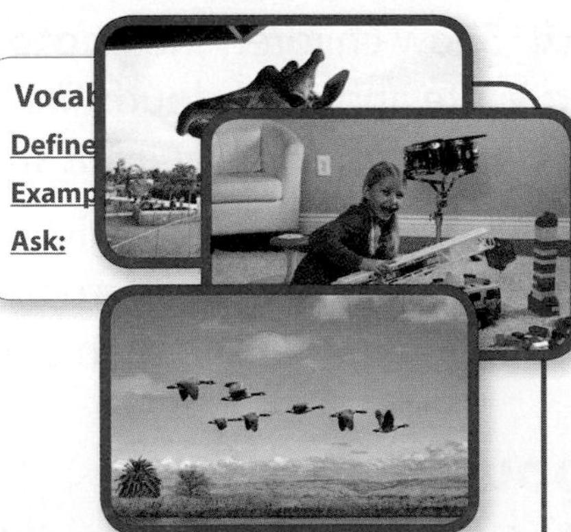

Visual Vocabulary Cards

Define: An **active** person is someone who is busy and moves around a lot.

Example: The active child played with every toy in the room.

Ask: Are you more active when you're watching television or when you're outside? Why?

Define: When you **spot** something, you notice it or find it.

Example: It's easy to spot a giraffe in the zoo because it's so tall.

Ask: What can you spot in the night sky?

Go Digital

Visual Glossary

"A Tour of the Seasons"

Think Aloud Cloud

Listening Comprehension

Read the Interactive Read Aloud

Genre: Informational Text

Tell children you will be reading an informational text. Remind them that *informational text* gives facts, or true information, about a topic. Display the **Interactive Read-Aloud Cards**.

Interactive Read-Aloud Cards

Read the title. Point out that a tour is like a trip. Tell children that they will go on a reading trip to learn about different seasons.

Strategy: Visualize

Remind children that they can use information from the pictures and the words to make pictures in their minds of what is happening. This can help them understand what is going on in the selection. Model the strategy using the **Think Aloud Cloud**.

Think Aloud I read that some children are riding down a hill on their sleds, and others are building snowmen. I can picture in my mind some children smiling and laughing as they ride down the hill. I picture other children rolling balls of snow to build snowmen. I can feel the cold air blow against my face. Visualizing helps me understand what the winter season is like as I read.

Read "A Tour of the Seasons," pausing occasionally to model the strategy of visualizing. As you read Card 3, help children understand the difference between the words *buzz* and *chirp* by having them act out the words.

Make Connections

Guide partners to connect "A Tour of the Seasons" with *Mama, Is It Summer Yet?* Discuss the ways both selections show how the seasons are different from one another.

ENGLISH LANGUAGE LEARNERS

Reinforce Meaning As you read "A Tour of the Seasons," help to make the meaning clear by pointing to specific people, places, or objects in the photographs, demonstrating word meanings, paraphrasing text, and asking children questions. For example, on Card 2, point to the family and say: *This family is having a picnic.*

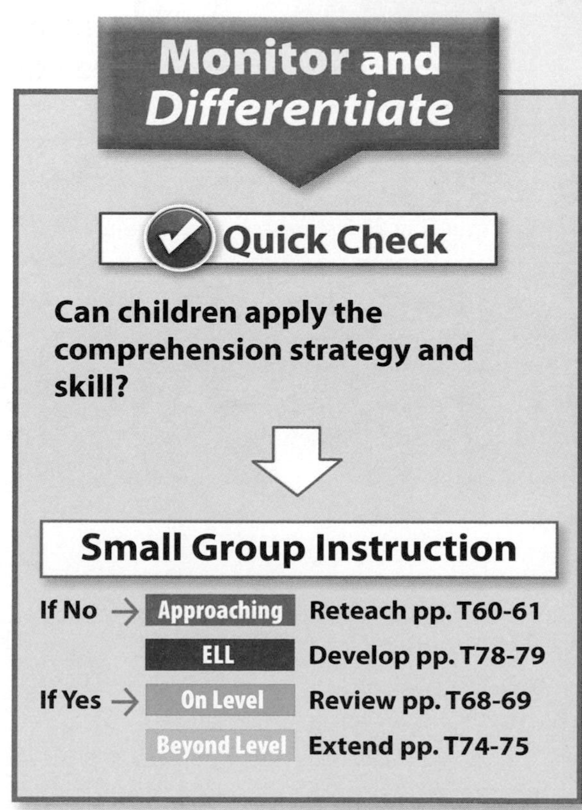

Word Work

Quick Review

Build Fluency: Sound-Spellings: Display the following **Word-Building Cards:** *b, d, e, f, h, l, o, r.* Have children say each sound. Repeat and vary the pace.

Phonemic Awareness

Puppet

OBJECTIVES

CCSS Demonstrate basic knowledge of one-to-one letter-sound correspondences by producing the primary or many of the most frequent sounds for each consonant. **RF.K.3a**

Orally blend sounds in words with /b/ and /l/

Phoneme Blending

1. **Model** *The puppet is going to say sounds in a word, /b/ /a/ /t/. It can blend those sounds to make a word: /baaat/,* bat. *When the puppet blends the sounds together, it makes the word* bat. *Listen as the puppet blends more sounds to make words.* Continue modeling phoneme blending with the following:

   /l/ /i/ /t/ lit   /t/ /u/ /b/ tub   /b/ /i/ /g/ big

2. **Guided Practice/Practice** Tell children that the puppet is going to say the sounds in a word. *Listen to the puppet as it says each sound. You will repeat the sounds, then blend them to say the word.* Guide practice with the first word.

   /b/ /e/ /d/ bed   /l/ /i/ /t/ lit   /r/ /u/ /b/ rub
   /b/ /e/ /l/ bell   /l/ /o/ /t/ lot   /b/ /e/ /t/ bet
   /l/ /e/ /t/ let   /t/ /u/ /b/ tub   /l/ /ē/ /f/ leaf

Review initial /b/ and /l/. Play and sing "Play Ball!" and "I Licked a Lemon." Have children clap when they hear initial /b/ or /l/. Demonstrate as you sing with children.

Go Digital

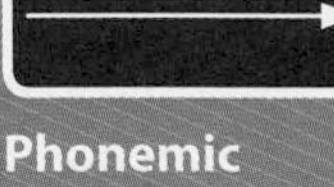

Phonemic Awareness

Phonics

Handwriting

Phonics

Review /b/*b*, /l/*l*

Word-Building Cards

1 Model Display **Word-Building Card** *b. This is the letter* b. *The letter* b *stands for /b/, the sound you hear at the beginning of* bat *and at the end of* web. *Say the sound with me: /b/. I will write the letter* b *because* bat *has the /b/ sound in the beginning and* web *has the /b/ sound at the end.* Repeat with initial sound /l/*l*, the sound heard at the beginning of *lemon*.

2 Guided Practice/Practice Tell children that you will say some words that have /b/ or /l/ at the beginning. Have children say /b/ and write the letter *b* on their **Response Boards** when they hear /b/ at the beginning of the word. Have them say /l/ and write the letter *l* on their boards when they hear /l/ at the beginning of the word. Guide practice with the first word.

bed lit lid bat Ben lid lip bug

Blend Words with *b, l* and *a, e, i, o*

1 Model Display Word-Building Cards *b, e, t. This is the letter* b. *It stands for /b/. This is the letter* e. *It stands for /e/. This is the letter* t. *It stands for /t/. Let's blend the three sounds together: /b/ /eee/ /t/, /beeet/. The word is* bet. Repeat with *bat, lad, lid.*

2 Guided Practice/Practice Write the following words. Have children read each word, blending the sounds. Guide practice with the first word.

bit rob lip let tab bad led

Write these sentences and prompt children to read the connected text, sounding out the decodable words: *Bob can bat and hit. Deb let him see the fat cat.*

Corrective Feedback

Sound Error Model the sound that children missed, then have them repeat. For example, for the word *bet,* say: *My turn.* Tap under the letter *b* and ask: *Sound? What's the sound?* Return to the beginning of the word. *Let's start over.* Blend the word with children again.

Extend the Lesson

Final Double Letters *ll*

Place the Word-Building Cards *b, e, l, l* in a pocket chart and model blending and reading the word.

Point out that the two letters, *ll,* stand for one sound /l/. Have children blend and read the word *bell*. Continue with the word *tell*.

YOUR TURN PRACTICE BOOK p. 158

Write

Name

bed bib lid

1. bed bed

2. bib bib

3. lid lid

Phonics: Blending /b/b, /l/l

Blend the sounds and say the word. Write the word. Repeat the word.

Copyright © The McGraw-Hill Companies, Inc.

Word Work

Phonics

Photo Cards

OBJECTIVES

CCSS Read common high-frequency words by sight.
RF.K.3c

Sort words by initial sound/letter

ACADEMIC LANGUAGE
sort

Picture Sort

1 Model Remind children that the letter *b* can stand for /b/. Place the **Word-Building Card** *b* on the left side of a pocket chart. *What is the letter?* (b) *What sound does it stand for?* (/b/) Continue the same routine for the letter *l*.

Hold up the **Photo Card** for *bat*. *Here is the picture for* bat. Bat *has the /b/ sound in the beginning. I will place* bat *under the letter* b *because the letter* b *stands for /b/.* Use the same routine for letter *l* and *lemon*.

2 Guided Practice/Practice Have children sort the Photo Cards *boat, book, bus, leaf, light, lock*. Have them say the sound at the beginning of the word and tell which letter the Photo Card should be placed under.

Photo Cards

Go Digital

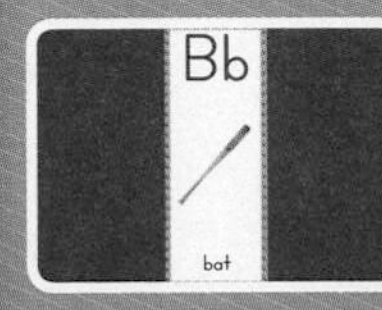

Phonics

High-Frequency Word Routine

High-Frequency Words

is, little

❶ **Guided Practice** Display the **High-Frequency Word Cards** *is, little.* Review the word using the **Read/Spell/Write** routine.

❷ **Practice** Point to the High-Frequency Word Card *is* and have children read it. Repeat with the word *little* and previous weeks' words *he, with, are, my, to, and, go, you, do.*

Build Fluency

Word Automaticity Write the following sentences and have children chorally read aloud as you track the print. Repeat several times.

Can Bob see the cat?
Ed can let the cat go.
Do you like a lot of ham?
I like to nap on the bed.

Read for Fluency Distribute pages 159–160 of **Your Turn Practice Book** and help children assemble their Take-Home Books. Chorally read the Take-Home Book with children. Then have children reread the books to review high-frequency words and build fluency.

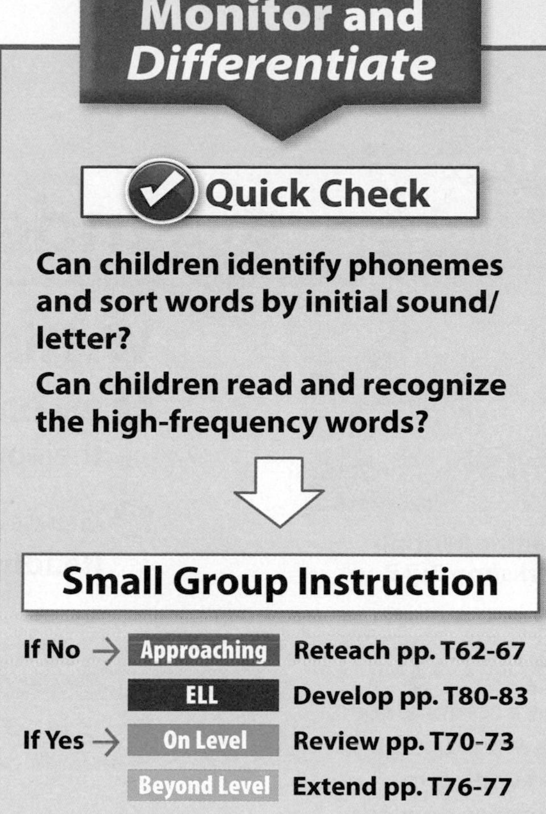

YOUR TURN PRACTICE BOOK pp. 159–160

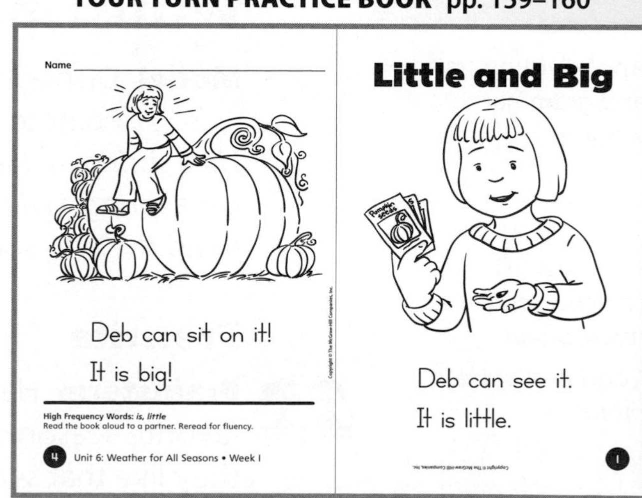
Name

Deb can sit on it!
It is big!

High Frequency Words: *is, little*
Read the book aloud to a partner. Reread for fluency.

4 Unit 6: Weather for All Seasons • Week 1

Little and Big

Deb can see it.
It is little.

1

WHOLE GROUP
DAY 3

Language Arts

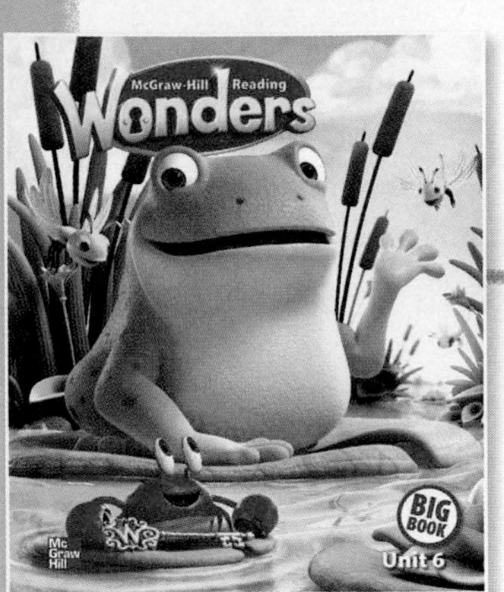

Reading/Writing Workshop Big Book

OBJECTIVES

 Use a combination of drawing, dictating, and writing to compose opinion pieces in which they tell a reader the topic or the name of the book they are writing about and state an opinion or preference about the topic or book (e.g., My favorite book is . . .). **W.K.1**

 Form regular plural nouns orally by adding /s/ or /es/. **L.K.1c**

- Write an opinion sentence
- Apply writing trait and grammar to writing

ACADEMIC LANGUAGE

- *sentence, opinion, noun, plural*
- Cognates: *opinión, plural*

Independent Writing

Writing Trait: Voice

1 Practice Tell children that today they will write sentences that tell their opinion about a season and explain why they like it.

2 Guided Practice Share the Readers to Writers page in the **Reading/Writing Workshop**. Read the model sentences aloud.

READING/WRITING WORKSHOP BIG BOOK, pp. 18–19

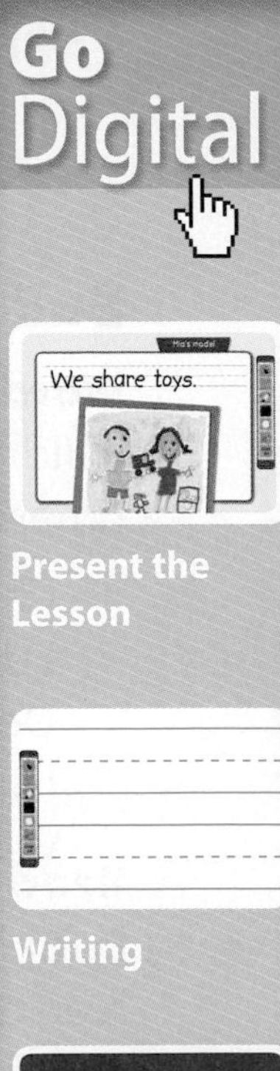

Write Opinion Sentences

Model Display the chart from Day 1. Write this sentence frame: *I like* ______. Point to the blank. *I will write my opinion about a season I like. I like spring, so I will write* spring *in the sentence. Now I need to tell why I like spring. I will use ideas from the chart.* Write: *I see beautiful flowers.* Read the two sentences aloud, tracking the print.

Prewrite

Brainstorm Have children work with a partner to choose their favorite season. Ask partners to help each other think of reasons why they like that season.

Draft

Ask children to draw a picture of their favorite season. Guide them in writing the sentence frame *I like* ______ below the picture. Then ask them to write a sentence that tells why this is their favorite season. Help children write the words to complete their sentences.

Apply Writing Trait As children write and draw, encourage them to write or dictate ideas that express their feelings.

Apply Grammar Tell children to point to the naming words in their sentences and tell whether they name one thing or more than one.

Grammar

Naming Words (Nouns)

1 Review Remind children that naming words, also called nouns, tell the names of people, places, animals, and things. Write and read: *I see the green bushes.*

Point out that *bushes* is a naming word that names more than one thing. It is a plural noun. Underline the *-es* ending at the end of *bushes*. Tell children we add *-es* to the end of some naming words when we talk about more than one.

2 Guided Practice/Practice Write and read: *Peaches grow on a tree. What are the naming words in this sentence?* (peaches, tree) Have children tell if each naming word names one thing or more than one thing. Ask them to tell you how they know peaches names more than one thing. (It ends in *-es*.)

Display and name the **Photo Cards** for *box, fox, grapes, inch, peach, toys, carrots.* Have children work in small groups. Distribute the Photo Cards, making sure each group gets a card with a plural that ends in *-es* (*box, fox, inch, peach*). Have groups say sentences about the photos using plural nouns, such as *We put the grapes in the boxes.*

Talk About It

Have children work with a partner to name things they eat. Ask them to say the naming word that tells there is more than one of that food.

ENGLISH LANGUAGE LEARNERS

Visual Support Use the Photo Cards for *peach* and *tree* for support. Have children draw a picture of one peach in a tree. Point to the peach in the drawing as you say *peach*. Have them say *peach*. Then ask children to draw more peaches on the tree. Point to several peaches in the drawing as you say *peaches*. Have children repeat *peaches* after you. Model correct pronunciation as needed.

Daily Wrap Up

- Review the Essential Question and encourage children to discuss it, using the oral vocabulary words *weather* and *seasons. How are the seasons different?*
- Prompt children to review and discuss the skills they used today. Guide them to give examples of how they used each skill.

WHOLE GROUP
DAY 4

Materials

Reading/Writing Workshop Big Book
UNIT 6

Literature Big Book
Mama, Is It Summer Yet?

Visual Vocabulary Cards
is
little

Puppet

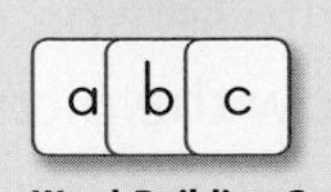

Word-Building Cards

Interactive Read-Aloud Cards

Photo Cards
August, carrots, fox, gate, grape, green, October, ostrich, rake, snow, toys, under, vegetables

Extend the Concept

Oral Language

OBJECTIVES

CCSS Use words and phrases acquired through conversations, reading and being read to, and responding to texts. **L.K.6**

CCSS Blend and segment onsets and rimes of single-syllable spoken words. **RF.K.2c**

Develop oral vocabulary

ESSENTIAL QUESTION

Remind children that this week they have been talking and reading about how the four seasons are different. Have them recite "Five Little Snowmen" and think about how the snowmen change as the seasons change. Then ask them to recall *Mama, Is It Summer Yet?* Ask how things change when summer arrives.

Phonological Awareness

Onset/Rime Segmentation

Remind children that a word can be divided into its beginning and ending sounds. Say: *The beginning sound in the word* day *is /d/. The ending sounds in the word* day *are /ā/.* Tell children that you will say other words from the finger-play, "Five Little Snowmen". Guide children to segment the following words and to say each word part aloud: *happy,* (/h/ /apē/); *little* (/l/ itə l/).

Review Oral Vocabulary

Reread the Interactive Read Aloud Use the **Define/Example/Ask** routine to review the oral vocabulary words *weather, seasons, migrate, active,* and *spot*. Then have children listen as you reread "A Tour of the Seasons."

- *In which season does a robin hop along in search of worms?* (spring)
- *In which season are insects active?* (summer)

Go Digital

Visual Glossary

"A Tour of the Seasons"

Category Words

Category Words: Seasons

1 Explain/Model Read aloud the following story. *Each time I say a season word, clap your hands.*

I play at the park all year. In winter, *I like to build snow castles. In* spring, *the rain makes puddles. I like to jump over them. In* summer, *I like to sit in the shade to cool off. In* fall, *the trees lose their leaves. I like to slide into a pile of them!*

→ Discuss what happens during each season. Encourage children to use season words in their responses.

2 Guided Practice Write the season words *winter, spring, summer,* and *fall* on the board. Next, display the **Photo Cards** *August, rake, green, October, under, fox, gate,* and *snow*. Have children name the season each Photo Card could show.

Vocabulary Strategy: Context Clues/Sentence Clues

1 Model Remind children to use clues in sentences and illustrations to determine the meaning of unfamiliar phrases.

Think Aloud In *Mama, Is It Summer Yet?*, I'm unsure of the meaning of this sentence: *But the buds are swelling.* I know that buds are small bumps on plants that flowers or leaves grow from. The other sentences and the illustration on the page talk about spring. I know that buds start out tiny and get bigger in spring. That helps me understand that buds are getting bigger during the spring.

2 Guided Practice Talk about the meaning of *unfold* in this sentence from *Mama, Is It Summer Yet?*: *Soon new leaves will unfold.* Ask children to name things that can be unfolded. (a piece of paper, a towel, a paper airplane) Reread the sentence and have children look at the illustration. Tell them to think about how buds grow into leaves. Ask them to close their eyes and picture how buds swell and *unfold* into leaves. Tell children that thinking about clues in the sentences and illustrations can help them understand the meaning of unfamiliar phrases.

3 Practice Talk about the different meanings of the word *sprout.* Model how to use *sprout* in different sentences to show the word's multiple meanings. Ask children which meaning of the word *sprout* would be used in *Mama, Is It Summer Yet?*

ENGLISH LANGUAGE LEARNERS

Distinguish Display several Photo Cards that children can associate with season words. Have children name the objects on the cards and then sort them by season. Say a sentence using a season word for each card, such as *Birds build their nests in the* spring.

LET'S MOVE!

Assign groups a season word. Then give simple directions that include season words. For example: *In winter, shovel snow. In spring, plant some seeds.*

YOUR TURN PRACTICE BOOK p. 161

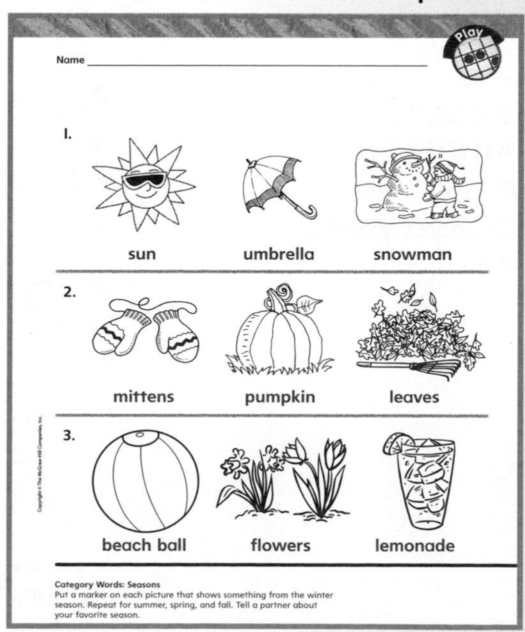
Name

1. sun, umbrella, snowman
2. mittens, pumpkin, leaves
3. beach ball, flowers, lemonade

Category Words: Seasons
Put a marker on each picture that shows something from the winter season. Repeat for summer, spring, and fall. Tell a partner about your favorite season.

Listening Comprehension

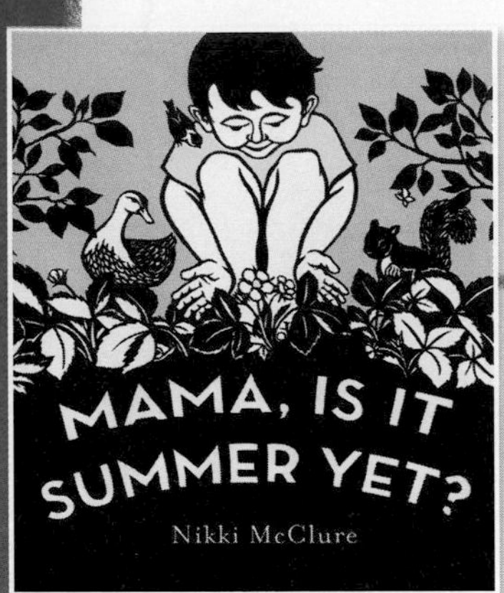

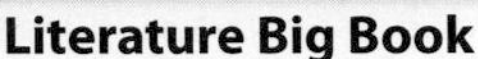

Literature Big Book

OBJECTIVES

CCSS Recognize common types of texts (e.g., storybooks, poems). **RL.K.5**

- Understand the characteristics of poetry
- Use the literary element rhyme to learn the features of poetry
- Apply the comprehension strategy: Visualize
- Make connections across texts

ACADEMIC LANGUAGE

- *poetry, rhyme*
- Cognates: *poesía, rima*

Read Poetry

Genre: Poetry

Display pages 34–40 of the **Big Book** and read aloud the title on page 34. Ask children what kind of text this is. (a poem) Remind children that poetry is creative writing that often includes rhyming words.

Set a Purpose for Reading

Read aloud page 34. Tell children to listen as you read aloud the other poems about the weather during different seasons.

Strategy: Visualize

Remind children that good readers sometimes use the text and illustrations to make pictures in their minds of what is happening in a story or poem. Have children look at page 34. *What pictures in your head do you have about what you would be doing on a day like the one in the picture?* (Possible answers: making a snowman; sledding)

Literary Element: Rhyme

Explain Tell children that many poems use words that rhyme. These words have the same ending sounds. Read aloud "Honey, I Love" on page 40. *Some of the rhyming words are* cool *and* pool.

Apply Read aloud the first two stanzas of "Covers" on page 38. *What are the rhyming words?* (away, day) *What kind of covers does this poet mention?* (glass, clouds, night, blankets)

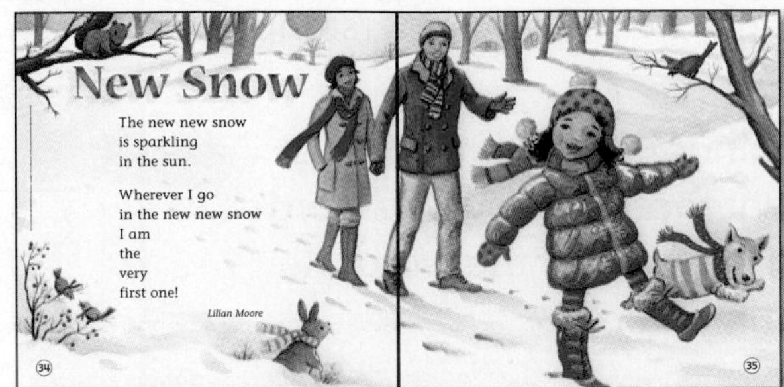

LITERATURE BIG BOOK PAGES 34–35

LITERARY ELEMENT

Read the second stanza. Have children identify rhyming words. (*go, snow*)

VOCABULARY

What is the opposite of new? (old)

Go Digital

Mama, Is It Summer Yet?

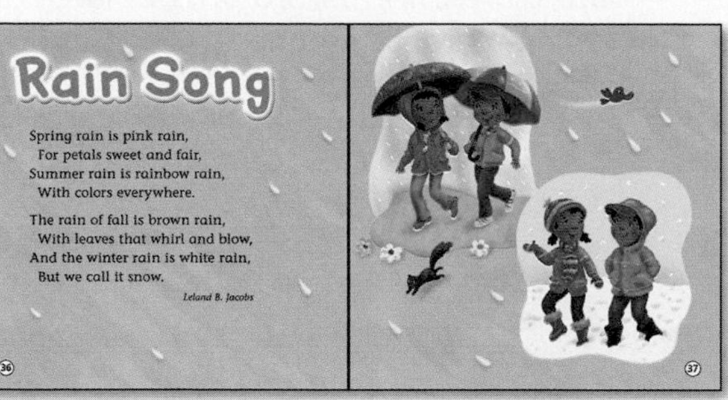

LITERATURE BIG BOOK PAGES 36–37

KEY DETAILS: SEQUENCE

What season is mentioned first in the poem? (spring) *Which season comes after the fall?* (winter)

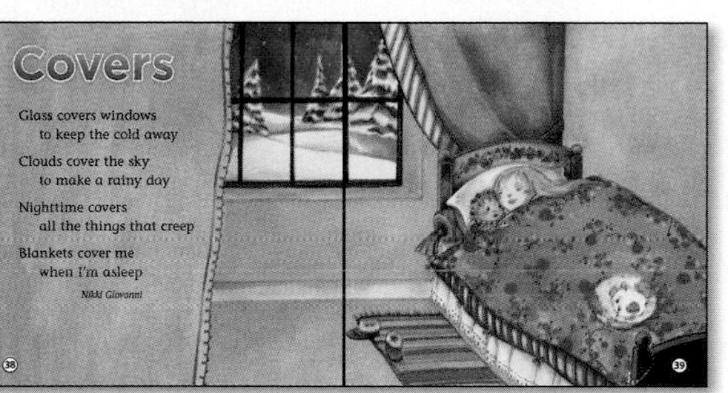

LITERATURE BIG BOOK PAGES 38–39

VISUALIZE

Have children visualize the various "covers" in the poem. Ask them to share the details they visualized that relate to the senses. Ask: *What do you picture in your mind when you hear the line,* "Nighttime covers/all the things that creep"*?*

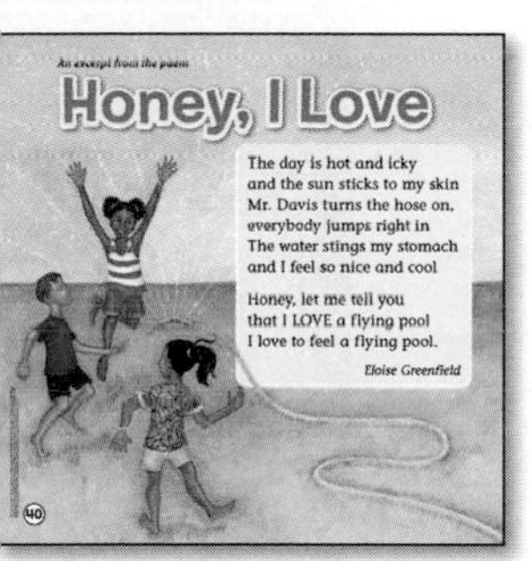

LITERATURE BIG BOOK PAGE 40

Remind children of the literary element rhyme. Ask: *Which words rhyme in this poem?* skin/in; cool/pool

ENGLISH LANGUAGE LEARNERS

Reinforce Meaning As you read aloud the text, make the meaning clear by pointing to details in the illustrations. Ask children questions and elicit language.

Retell and Respond

Have children discuss the poems by asking the following questions:

→ *Which poem tells about all four seasons?* ("Rain Song")

→ *What covers the sky on rainy days?* (clouds)

Make Connections

COLLABORATE

Have children recall the selections they read this week.

→ *What did the squirrels do to prepare for summer?* (make nests)

Write About It Write about two things that happen in autumn from "A Tour of the Seasons."

CONNECT TO CONTENT

The Seasons Review the different seasons mentioned in the poems (winter, spring, summer, autumn). Have partners look at the illustrations for each poem and discuss the different kinds of weather they experience in each season. Then have them discuss the activities they do during each season.

Word Work

Quick Review

Build Fluency: Sound-Spellings: Show the following **Word-Building Cards:** *a, b, c, d, e, f, h, i, l, m, n, o, p, r, s, t*. Have children say each sound. Repeat and vary the pace.

Phonemic Awareness

Puppet

OBJECTIVES

CCSS Distinguish between similarly spelled words by identifying the sounds of the letters that differ. **RF.K.3d**

CCSS Read common high-frequency words by sight. **RF.K.3c**

Blend phonemes to make words

Phoneme Blending

1 Model *The puppet is going to say sounds in a word, /l/ /o/ /t/. It can blend those sounds to make a word: /lllooot/* lot. *When the puppet blends the sounds together, it makes the word* lot. *Listen as the puppet blends more sounds to make words.* Continue modeling phoneme blending with the following:

/b/ /i/ /t/   /r/ /u/ /b/   /b/ /a/ /d/   /l/ /a/ /p/

2 Guided Practice/Practice Tell children that the puppet is going to say the sounds in a word. *Listen it says each sound. You will repeat the sounds, then blend them to say the word.*

/ b/ /e/ /t/ bet   /l/ /e/ /t/ let   /t/ /u/ /b/ tub

/b/ /e/ /d/ bed   /l/ /i/ /p/ lip   /b/ /e/ /l/ bell

Phonics

Blend Words with *b, l* and *e, i, n, t*

1 Guided Practice Display **Word-Building Cards** *b, i, n*. Point to the letter *b*. *This is the letter* b. *The letter* b *stands for /b/. Say /b/. This is the letter* i. *The letter* i *stands for /i/. Listen as I blend the two sounds together /biii/. Say /biii/. This is the letter* n. *The letter* n *stands for /n/. Listen as I blend the sounds /biiinnn/,* bin. *Now you say it. Let's change* n *to* t. Use the same routine to blend *bit* and *lit*.

2 Practice Write *bet, bit* and *let, lit*. Have children read the words. Point to *bet* and *bit*. *Which letters are the same?* (b, t) *Which letters are different?* (e and i) Discuss the sounds each letter stands for and how it changes the word. Repeat with *let* and *lit*.

Go Digital

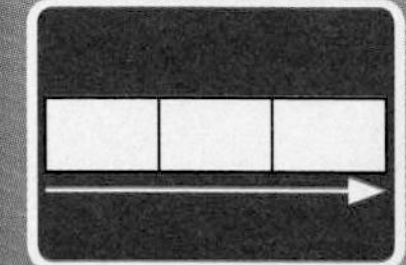

Phonemic Awareness

Phonics

Handwriting

Visual Glossary

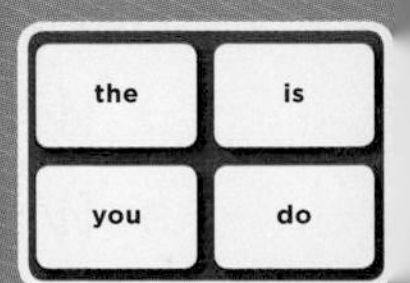

High-Frequency Word Routine

Dictation

Review Dictate each of the sounds for children to spell. Have them repeat the sound and then write the letter that stands for the sound.

/f/ /r/ /e/ /h/ /d/ /o/ /b/ /l/

Dictate the following words for children to spell: *bit, lid, bed, lap.* Model how to segment each word to scaffold the spelling.

When I say the word bit, *I hear three sounds: /b/ /i/ /t/. I know the letter* b *stands for /b/, the letter* i *stands for /i/, and the letter* t *stands for /t/. I will write the letters* b, i, t *to spell the word* bit.

When children finish, write the letters and words for them to self-correct.

Extend the Lesson

Final Double Letters *ll*
Use Word-Building Cards or write the word *hill*. Circle the *ll*. Point out that the two letters, *ll,* stand for one sound, /l/. Blend and read the word and have children repeat. Continue with *fill, fell, bell, tell.*

MINILESSON 5 Mins

High-Frequency Words

Visual Vocabulary Cards

Practice Say the words *is* and *little* and have children write them. Then display the **Visual Vocabulary Cards** for *is* and *little*. Follow the Teacher Talk routine on the back.

Build Fluency Build sentences in a pocket chart using **High-Frequency Word Cards** and **Photo Cards**. Use index cards to create punctuation cards for a period and a question mark. Have children chorally read the sentences as you track the print. Then have them identify the words *is* and *little*.

My apple is little.
Do you see the little ladybug?
The lemon is yellow.

Also online

High-Frequency Words Practice

COLLABORATE

Have partners create sentences using the words *is* and *little*.

Monitor and Differentiate

Quick Check

Can children blend words with /b/ and /l/ and match the sounds to the letters *Bb* and *Ll*?

Can children read and recognize high-frequency words?

Small Group Instruction

If No →	Approaching	Reteach pp. T62-67
	ELL	Develop pp. T80-83
If Yes →	On Level	Review pp. T70-73
	Beyond Level	Extend pp. T76-77

Shared Read

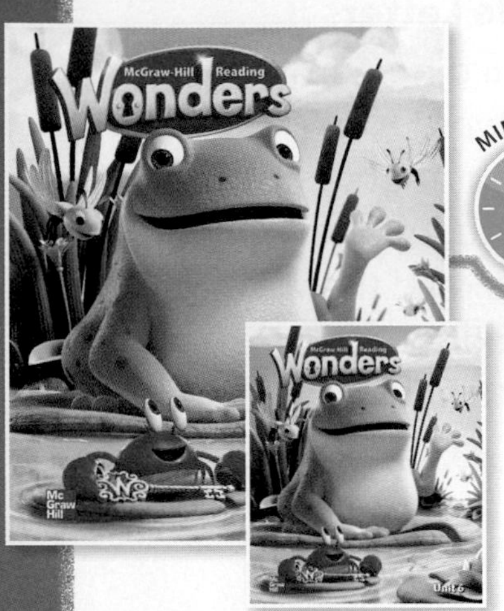

Reading/Writing Workshop Big Book and Reading/Writing Workshop

OBJECTIVES

CCSS Read common high-frequency words by sight. **RF.K.3c**

CCSS Read emergent-reader texts with purpose and understanding. **RF.K.4**

CCSS Recognize and name end punctuation. **L.K.2b**

MINILESSON 10 Mins

Read "Is It Hot?"

Model Skills and Strategies

Model Concepts About Print Reinforce sentence boundaries by turning to page 10 and discussing each sentence. *The first sentence begins with the word* It *and starts with a capital letter,* I. *This sentence makes a statement, so it ends with a period. The second sentence begins with the word* We *and starts with a capital letter,* W. *I will read it with feeling because it ends with an exclamation point.* Invite children to find sentence boundaries by pointing to the capital letters at the start of each sentence and the punctuation marks that come at the end of the sentences.

Reread Then have children chorally read the story. Children should sound out the decodable words and say the sight words. Offer support as needed using the student **Reading/Writing Workshop**.

Ask the following:

- *Look at page 9. Who is Ben?* (a little cat)
- *Look at page 10. What kind of animal has a fin?* (a dolphin)
- *Look at page 15. Is it hot or cold outside? How can you tell?* (It is cold outside because the children are wearing warm clothing. There is snow on the ground. The trees are bare.)

Go Digital

"Is It Hot?"

"Is It Hot?"

READING/WRITING WORKSHOP, pp. 8–15

Fluency: Expression

1. **Explain** Tell children that as you read the story, you will be reading with expression. Mention that as you read, you will look at the punctuation at the end of sentences to tell you how to change the tone of your voice.

2. **Model** Model reading the story "Is It Hot?" Read the text fluently and with emotion. Change your inflection as you read sentences that end with periods, question marks, and exclamation points.

3. **Guided Practice** Read each sentence and invite children to echo you, encouraging them to change their inflection as indicated by the punctuation. Then have them read the story chorally with expression.

Language Arts

Independent Writing

Write Opinion Sentences

OBJECTIVES

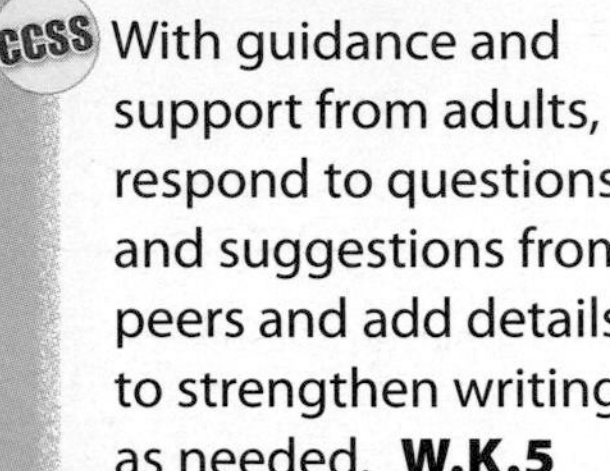
With guidance and support from adults, respond to questions and suggestions from peers and add details to strengthen writing as needed. **W.K.5**

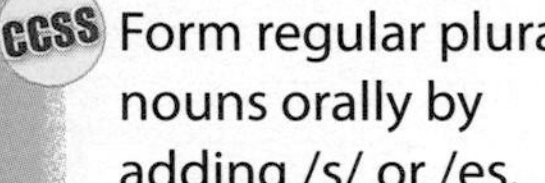
Form regular plural nouns orally by adding /s/ or /es. **L.K.1c**

Revise opinion sentences

ACADEMIC LANGUAGE

- *revise, draft, noun, plural*
- Cognates: *revisar, plural*

Revise

Distribute children's draft sentences and drawings from Day 3.

Apply Writing Trait: Voice Explain that as writers revise, they use sentences to express how they feel about something. Write and read: *I love winter. Winter is fun.* Explain that there are different ways to tell how you feel.

Help children decide which words best express how they feel about their favorite season. Then have children read the sentences they wrote on Day 3 and check for the following:

- → Does my first sentence tell how I feel about a season?
- → Is there a better way to say how I feel?
- → Does my drawing show why I like this season?

Apply Grammar Ask children to identify the naming words in these sentences: *Fall is great. I pick apples.* (fall, apples) Have children tell which naming word is plural, or names more than one thing. (apples)

Peer Edit Have children work in pairs to do a peer edit, in which they read their partner's draft. Partners can read the sentences aloud to see if they used the best words to express how they feel. Provide time for children to make revisions to their sentences.

Final Draft

After children have edited their own papers and finished their peer edits, have them write their final draft. Remind children that they should write neatly so that readers can read their writing. As children work, conference with them to provide guidance.

Go Digital

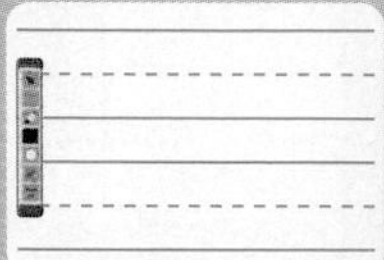
Writing

Grammar

Grammar

Naming Words (Nouns)

1 **Review** Remind children that naming words, also called nouns, tell the names of people, places, animals, and things. Write and read aloud: *desk. Does* desk *name a person, place, or thing?* (a thing) *How do we say the word for more than one desk?* (desks)

2 **Guided Practice** Display the **Photo Cards** for *grapes* and *ostrich*. Write and read aloud the following sentences:

The grapes look good.
The ostriches live at the zoo.

Ask children to identify a noun that names a place. (zoo) Ask them to identify naming words that talk about more than one thing. (grapes, ostriches) Then have children tell how they know the naming words are plural. (-s, -es)

Show the Photo Cards for *carrots, toys,* and *vegetables*. Ask children to say sentences for each word, such as *Carrots are crunchy.*

Ask children what the singular forms are of *carrots, toys,* and *vegetables*. Have children say sentences using *carrot, toy,* and *vegetable*.

3 **Practice** Ask children to name some vegetables. Write the singular form of each vegetable on the board. For example: carrot, potato, pea, corn, pepper, pumpkin. Draw a quick sketch of each vegetable next to its name. Point out that these are all naming words.

Write and read: *I have three* ______. Ask children to finish your sentence by choosing one of the vegetables you listed. As children say the plural nouns, write them next to the singular forms.

Talk About It

Have children work with a partner. Ask children to point and name one of the features on their face. Ask them to say the word that names more than one of that feature.

ENGLISH LANGUAGE LEARNERS

Photo Cards and Sentences Provide sentences that go with Photo Cards that show plural nouns, such as *The carrots are long.* As you say a sentence, point to the noun on the Photo Card. Point to and repeat the noun by itself emphasizing -*s* or -*es* at the end.

Daily Wrap Up

- Review the Essential Question and encourage children to discuss it, using the oral vocabulary words.
- Prompt children to discuss the skills they practiced and learned today. Guide them to share examples of each skill.

WHOLE GROUP
DAY 4

www.connected.mcgraw-hill.com
RESOURCES
Research and Inquiry

Wrap Up the Week
Integrate Ideas

RESEARCH AND INQUIRY

SCIENCE

The Four Seasons

OBJECTIVES

Participate in shared research and writing projects (e.g., explore a number of books by a favorite author and express opinions about them). **W.K.7**

With guidance and support from adults, explore a variety of digital tools to produce and publish writing, including in collaboration with peers. **W.K.6**

ACADEMIC LANGUAGE
research, inquiry

Make a Seasons Chart

Tell children that today, as part of a small group, they will do a research project to make a chart of information about the seasons. Review the steps in the research process.

STEP 1 **Choose a Topic**

Prompt children to name the four seasons. Discuss the characteristics of the seasons in your area. What makes one season different from the others? Divide the class into four groups, one for each season. Explain that each group will contribute information about their season to the chart.

STEP 2 **Find Resources**

Help children locate information in the library and on the Internet. Use a child-friendly search engine. Guide them to revisit selections from the week. Point out that children's own experiences are resources, too. Encourage them to think about their favorite activities during the season. Have children use the Research Process Checklist online.

STEP 3 **Keep Track of Ideas**

Help children note the information they find about the seasons by drawing pictures and writing words. Assist them with the names of sports, activities, and places, as needed.

Collaborative Conversations

Add New Ideas As children engage in partner, small-group, and whole-class discussions, encourage them to:

- stay on topic.
- connect their own ideas to things their classmates have said.
- connect their personal experiences or prior knowledge to the conversation.

STEM

STEP 4 Create the Project: Seasons Chart

Winter is cold. We go skating in winter.

Explain the characteristics of the project:

- **Information** Charts show categories of information. This chart is divided into four sections. Each section will give information about the characteristics of the different seasons.
- **Illustration** The drawings or photographs will show seasonal activities and weather changes.
- **Text** Provide these sentence frames for the captions:

  (Season) is _______. We _______ in (season).

Explain that each pair will choose one seasonal activity and create a page for the chart. When the chart is complete, discuss the differences and similarities between the seasons.

- Guide children to use the research from the Internet sources and digital tools to produce and publish their writing.
- Encourage children who can write more about their topic to do so.
- Encourage children to include details in their illustration.
- Conduct a class poll. Which season is the favorite? Which is second favorite? Which season is the least favorite?

ELL ENGLISH LANGUAGE LEARNERS SCAFFOLD

Beginning	Intermediate	Advanced/Advanced High
Identify As children create their illustrations, have them talk about the things they are showing in their picture. Provide these sentence frames: *We wear* _____. *We use* _____.	**Discuss** Prompt children to talk about their season. Ask prompting questions such as these: *What does a day during this season feel like? Can this activity be done during another season? Why or why not?*	**Describe** Ask children to describe their seasonal activity fully by describing where they do it, when they do it, what they wear, what they use, and so on.

WHOLE GROUP
DAY 5

Materials

Reading/Writing Workshop Big Book
UNIT 6

Literature Big Book
Mama, Is it Summer Yet?

Interactive Read-Aloud Cards

Response Board

High-Frequency Word Cards
are
he
is
little
my
with

Visual Vocabulary Cards
is
little

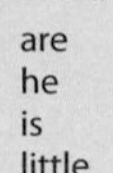

Integrate Ideas

TEXT CONNECTIONS

Connect to the Essential Question

OBJECTIVES

 Recognize common types of texts (e.g., storybooks, poems). **RL.K.5**

 With prompting and support, compare and contrast the adventures and experiences of characters in familiar stories). **RL.K.9**

 Participate in collaborative conversations with diverse partners about *kindergarten topics and texts* with peers and adults in small and larger groups. **SL.K.1**

- Make connections among texts
- Make connections to the world

Text to Text

Remind children that all week they have been reading different selections about the seasons. *What is a fiction story that we read this week? What is one poem that we read?* Tell them that now they will connect the texts, or think about how the selections are alike. Model comparing *Mama, Is it Summer Yet?* with another selection.

Think Aloud In *Mama, Is it Summer Yet?* I read about how the boy waited and waited throughout winter and spring for summer to come. In "A Tour of the Seasons," I read about the same order of seasons—winter, spring, and then summer. The illustrations and photos showed me how the outdoors changes as the seasons change.

Guide children to compare details about the seasons as those seasons appear in *Mama, Is it Summer Yet?* and in the poems "New Snow" and "Rain Song." Have them continue with other selections from the week.

Text to Self

Ask each child to name an activity that he or she can do during this season but would not want to do during other seasons.

Text to World

Talk about how the community changes during different seasons. *What is different about your neighborhood or town in summer and in winter? What about in spring and in fall?*

TALK ABOUT READING

Analyze and Explain

OBJECTIVES

CCSS Confirm understanding of a text read aloud or information presented orally or through other media by asking and answering questions about key details and requesting clarification if something is not understood. **SL.K.2**

Becoming Readers

Talk with children about the genres, strategy, and skill they have learned about this week. Prompt them to discuss how this knowledge helps them to read and understand selections.

- Remind children that one genre they learned about is fiction. Recall with them some characteristics of fiction.
- Discuss with children the strategy of visualizing. *How did making pictures in your mind help you understand the seasons in the different selections that we read? What are some things you pictured?*
- Talk about how the children learned to notice details about sequence, or the order of events. *What sequence did you notice in this week's selections? How did paying attention to details about the sequence help you understand the seasons?*

RESEARCH AND INQUIRY

SCIENCE

The Four Seasons

OBJECTIVES

CCSS Participate in shared research and writing projects (e.g. explore a number of books by a favorite author and express opinions about them). **W.K.7**

Wrap Up the Project

Guide groups to share information about their chosen season and to point out details in their pictures on the bulletin board. Encourage children to use words and phrases they learned this week. Have children use the Presenting and Listening checklists online.

WHOLE GROUP
DAY 5

Word Work

Quick Review

Build Fluency: Sound-Spellings: Display the following **Word-Building Cards:** *b, d, e, f, h, l, o, r*. Have children say each sound. Repeat and vary the pace.

Phonemic Awareness

OBJECTIVES

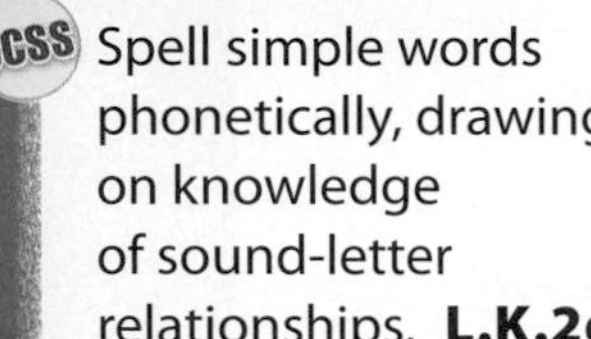

CCSS Spell simple words phonetically, drawing on knowledge of sound-letter relationships. **L.K.2d**

CCSS Read common high-frequency words by sight. **RF.K.3c**

- Segment words into phonemes
- Blend sounds to read words with /b/*b* and /l/*l*

Phoneme Segmentation

1 Model Use **Sound Boxes** and markers. *Listen to this word:* lip. *There are three sounds in* lip. *Say the sounds in* lip *with me: /l/ /i/ /p/. Let's place one marker for each sound in a Sound Box: /l/ /i/ /p/.* Repeat for *bet*.

2 Guided Practice/Practice Distribute Sound Boxes and markers. Have children say each sound in the word as they place a marker in a box. Then have them say the word and tell the number of sounds in the word. Guide children with the first word.

bed, /b/ /e/ /d/ bat, /b/ /a/ /t/ fill, /f/ /i/ /l/
lid, /l/ /i/ /d/ led, /l/ /e/ /d/ lot, /l/ /o/ /t/

Phonics

Read Words with *b, l* and *a, c, d, e, i, p, t*

1 Guided Practice Remind children that the letter *b* stands for /b/ and the letter *l* stands for /l/. Display **Word-Building Cards** *l, e, t*. Point to the letter *l*. *The letter* l *stands for /l/. Say /lll/. The letter* e *stands for /e/. Say /eee/. The letter* t *stands for /t/. Say /t/. Let's blend the sounds to make the word: /llleeet/,* let. *Now let's change the* l *to* b. Blend and read the word *bet* with children.

2 Practice Write these words and sentences for children to read:

lip bat led cab bed

I nap on my bed. The cat sat on my lap.
Bob had a bat. Ben and Deb like my pet cat.

Remove words from view before dictation.

Review initial /b/*b* and /l/*l*. Have children write *b* on their **Response Boards**. Play and sing "Play Ball!" Have children hold up and show the letter *b* on their boards when they hear initial /b/. Demonstrate as you sing with children. Repeat with /l/*l* and "I Licked a Lemon."

Go Digital

Phonemic Awareness

Phonics

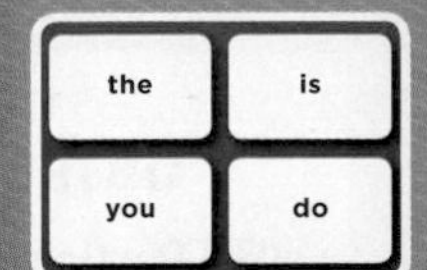

High-Frequency Word Routine

Handwriting

Dictation

Review Dictate the following sounds for children to spell. As you say each sound, have children repeat it and then write the letter that stands for the sound.

/f/ /r/ /e/ /h/ /d/ /o/ /b/ /l/

Dictate the following words for children to spell. Model for children how to use sound boxes to segment each word to scaffold the spelling. *I will say a word. You will repeat the word, then think about how many sounds are in the word. Use your Sound Boxes to count the sounds. Then write one letter for each sound you hear.*

bat led lot tab let bed

Then write the letters and words for children to self-correct.

High-Frequency Words

is, little

Visual Vocabulary Cards

1. **Review** Display **Visual Vocabulary Cards** *is* and *little*. Have children **Read/Spell/Write** the words. Then choose a Partner Talk activity.

   Distribute one of the following **High-Frequency Word Cards** to children: *are, he, is, little, my, with*. Tell children that you will say some sentences. *When you hear a word that is on your card, stand and hold up your word card.*

   He can go to the park.
   Mary and John *are* going, too.
   My sister can go to school.
   Is your brother coming to play?
   Mom says Jake can bring his *little* brother.
   Can I go *with* you?

2. **Build Fluency: Word Automaticity** Display High-Frequency Word Cards *is, little, he, with, are,* and *my*. Point to each card, at random, and have children read the word as quickly as they can.

Monitor and *Differentiate*

Quick Check

Can children segment words into sounds and read words with /b/*b* and /l/*l*?

Can children read and recognize high-frequency words?

Small Group Instruction

If No →	Approaching	**Reteach pp. T62-67**
	ELL	**Develop pp. T80-83**
If Yes →	On Level	**Review pp. T70-73**
	Beyond Level	**Extend pp. T76-77**

Language Arts

Independent Writing

OBJECTIVES

 Speak audibly and express thoughts, feelings, and ideas clearly **SL.K.6**

 Form regular plural nouns orally by adding /s/ or /es/. **L.K.1c**

- Make a presentation
- Listen to others

ACADEMIC LANGUAGE
- *present, publish, noun*
- Cognates: *presente*

Write an Opinion Sentence

Prepare

Tell children that they will present their finished sentences and drawings from Day 4 to the class. Hold up an example from Day 4 and read it aloud, tracking the print. *I read my sentence clearly so everyone can understand me. I read my sentences with feeling to show how I feel about the season I wrote about.*

Present

Have children take turns standing up and reading their sentences aloud. Remind children to read their sentences clearly so everyone can understand them and to read their sentences with feeling. Encourage the rest of the class to listen quietly and to wait until the presenter has finished before asking any questions.

Evaluate

Have children discuss their own presentations and evaluate their performances, using the presentation rubric. Use the teacher's rubric to evaluate children's writing.

Publish

After children have finished presenting, have children who have the same favorite season stand in groups and hold up their drawings for a group photo. After you take a photo for each season, collect their sentences with drawings and put them in a binder organized by season. Discuss the seasons children chose and the different reasons why they like those seasons.

Have children add their writing to their Writer's Portfolio. Then have them look back at their previous writing and discuss how they have changed as writers throughout the year.

Grammar

Naming Words (Nouns)

1 Review Remind children that nouns are called naming words and that these words tell the names of people, places, animals, and things. Review that plural nouns name more than one thing and can end in *-s* or *-es*.

→ On an index card, draw one dish. On another index card, draw three dishes. Have children say *dish* or *dishes* as you hold up each index card. Ask them to say sentences using the two words.

2 Review Practice Write and read aloud this sentence frame:

I have two _______.

Invite children to suggest words to complete the sentence. Tell them that the words they suggest are all naming words. As they say the plural nouns, repeat each word they say, stressing the *-s* or *-es* ending.

Have children work in pairs. Give each pair an index card with a noun written on it, such as *girl, boy, car, dish, dress, glass, hat*. Be sure the plural forms of these words end in *-s* or *-es*. Have children add the correct letters to make the word plural. On another index card, ask children to draw a picture of the plural noun.

Circulate to help children with their writing and drawing and to offer corrective feedback as needed.

Collect the cards. Have children work in small groups to play a game that involves matching nouns with pictures.

Wrap Up the Week

- Review blending words with initial/final /b/*b* and initial /l/*l*. Remind children that nouns tell the names of people, places, animals, and things, and that many plural nouns end in *-s* or *-es*.
- Use the High-Frequency Word Cards to review the Words to Know.
- Remind children that they can express their feelings in their writing.

Approaching Level

Leveled Reader

Leveled Reader: *It Is Hot!*

Leveled Reader

Before Reading

Preview and Predict

Read the title and the names of the author and illustrator. Discuss the illustration on the cover. Ask: *What season do you think the illustration shows? How do you know?* Preview each illustration and identify the rebus pictures on each page. Ask: *What do you think this story is about?*

Review Genre: Fiction

Tell children that although they have read a fantasy story this week now they will read a fiction story. Remind children that fiction stories are made-up stories with characters and the events in some fiction stories could happen in real life.

Model Concepts of Print

Provide children with more practice matching speech to print. As you read aloud slowly, ask children to try to match the words you say with the words on the page.

Review High-Frequency Words

Point to the high-frequency word *is* on each page of the story. Ask children to find the word on each page and say it aloud.

Essential Question

Remind children of the Essential Question: *How are the seasons different?* Set a purpose for reading: *Let's find out about the seasons and how they are different*.

During Reading

Guided Comprehension

As children whisper-read *It Is Hot!*, monitor and provide guidance by correcting blending and modeling the strategy and skill.

OBJECTIVES

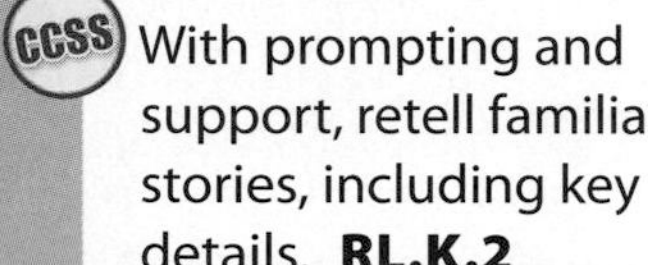

CCSS With prompting and support, ask and answer questions about key details in a text. **RL.K.1**

CCSS With prompting and support, retell familiar stories, including key details. **RL.K.2**

CCSS With prompting and support, describe the relationship between illustrations and the story in which they appear (e.g., what moment in a story an illustration depicts). **RL.K.7**

Strategy: Visualize

Review with children that as they read they can make pictures in their mind of what is happening in the story.

Skill: Key Details (Sequence)

Remind children that finding key details in the text and the illustrations will help them to understand the story. Explain that in this book, the illustrations provide key details about the sequence of the seasons.

Think Aloud On pages 2 and 3, the pictures show spring. The words don't tell me that, but I see buds on the tree and tulips and daffodils. On page 4 it is summer. The text tells me that the beach is hot and I see that the woman in the picture has suntan lotion. What these key details tell me is that the book shows the order of the seasons.

Guide children to talk about how the picture details show the sequence of the seasons. Discuss that the seasons change in the same order as they are shown in the book: *spring, summer, fall,* and *winter.*

After Reading

Respond to Reading

- *What are some things that are hot?* (Possible answers: tea, soup, mug)
- *What is the first season shown in the book?* (spring)
- *Look at page 4. In what season are people at the hot beach?* (summer)
- *In what season do people sit by a warm fire?* (winter)

Retell

Have children take turns retelling the story. Help them make a personal connection. Ask: *What things do you do in different seasons?*

Model Fluency

Read the story aloud, pointing to the rebus picture on each page as you say that word with extra emphasis.

Apply Have children practice reading aloud as they point to each word and rebus.

LITERACY ACTIVITIES

Have children complete the activities on the inside back cover of the reader.

Level Up

IF Children read *It Is Hot!* **Approaching Level** with fluency and correctly answer the Respond to Reading questions,

THEN Tell children that they will read another story about how the seasons are different.

- Have children page through *Little Bear* **On Level** to preview the story and make connections to what they know about the seasons.
- Have children read the story, monitoring their comprehension and providing assistance as necessary.

Approaching Level

Phonological Awareness

ONSET AND RIME SEGMENTATION

TIER 2

OBJECTIVES

Blend and segment onsets and rimes of single-syllable spoken words. **RF.K.2c**

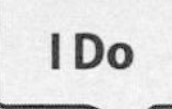

To help children segment onset and rime, remind them that words are made up of parts. Say that onset refers to the beginning sound in a word and that rime refers to the rest of the sounds in the word. Say the words *five, gay,* and *nice* from the fingerplay "Five Little Snowmen". Have children repeat the words. Segment the words into their onset and rimes: /f/ /īv/; /g/ /ā/; /n/ /īs/.

Say these words and guide children to segment the onset and rime of each word with you: stay, /st/ /ā/; away, /ə / /wā/; cry, /cr/ /ī/.

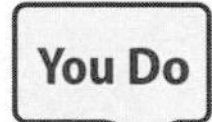

Say *day, men, snow, tray* and have children segment each word into its onset and rime. (/d/ /ā/; /m/ /en/; /sn/ /ō/; /tr/ /ā/)

PHONEME ISOLATION

OBJECTIVES

Isolate and pronounce the initial, medial vowel, and final sounds (phonemes) in three-phoneme words.

RF.K.2d

Display the *Bat* **Photo Card**. *This is a bat. The first sound I hear in* bat *is* /b/. *Say the word and the beginning sound with me:* bat, /b/. Repeat the routine for initial /l/ using the *Lemon* Photo Card.

Display the *Bike* Photo Card. *This is a bike. The first sound I hear in bike is /b/.* Have children repeat the word with you, emphasizing the initial sound. Then have children say the first sound with you: */b/.* Repeat using the *Butter* Photo Card. Repeat for /l/ using the *Leaf* and *Ladder* Photo Cards.

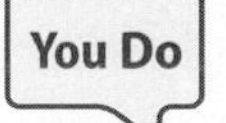

Display the *Boy* Photo Card. Have children name it and say the initial sound of the picture name. Repeat with the *Boot* Photo Card. Repeat for /l/ using the *Lightning* and *Lock* Photo Cards.

Repeat the routine in *I Do* for final /b/ using the *Web* Photo Card. Ask children to name the final sound. (/b/) In *We Do*, have children tell where they hear /b/ in *web*. (at the end) In *You Do*, have children say the following words and name the /b/ sound and its position in the words: *job, tab, big.*

You may wish to review Phonological Awareness and Phonemic Awareness with ELL using this section.

PHONEME BLENDING

OBJECTIVES

CCSS Isolate and pronounce the initial, medial vowel, and final sounds (phonemes) in three-phoneme words.
RF.K.2d

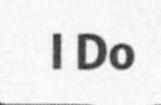

Listen as the puppet says the sounds in a word: /b/ /e/ /d/. *Now the puppet will blend the sounds to make a word:* /beeed/, bed. *The puppet blended the sounds /b/ /e/ /d/ to make the word* bed. Repeat with *big, tab*.

Listen as the puppet says the sounds in another word. Have the puppet say /b/ /i/ /t/. Have children repeat. *Let's blend the sounds and say the word with the puppet:* /b/ /i/ /t/, /biiit/, bit. Repeat with *bib*.

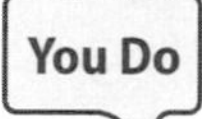

Have children blend sounds to form words. Practice together: /b/ /a/ /t/, *bat*. Then have children practice blending the following sounds to say words: /b/ /e/ /t/ bet; /k/ /a/ /b/ cab; /d/ /a/ /b/ dab.

Repeat the routine for /l/ and the sounds in the words /l/ /a/ /b/ lab; /l/ /i/ /p/ lip; /l/ /e/ /d/ led.

PHONEME SEGMENTATION

OBJECTIVES

CCSS Isolate and pronounce the initial, medial vowel, and final sounds (phonemes) in three-phoneme words.
RF.K.2d

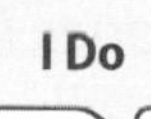

Use **Sound Boxes** and markers. *Listen as I say a word:* bid. *There are three sounds in* bid: /b/ /i/ /d/. *I'll place a marker in one box for each sound*. Repeat for the word *cab*.

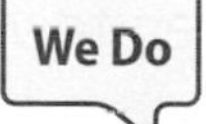

Distribute Sound Boxes and markers. *Let's listen for the number of sounds in more words. Listen as I say a word:* bee. *Say the word with me:* bee. *Say the sounds with me:* /b/ /ē/. *Let's place a marker in one box for each sound. There are two sounds in* bee. Repeat with *bet*.

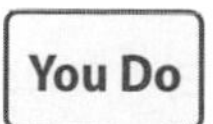

Repeat the routine with the following words: *bow*, /b/ /ō/; *bin*, /b/ /i/ /n/; *bag*, /b/ /a/ /g/.

Repeat the routine for /l/ using the sounds in these words: *lot*, /l/ /o/ /t/; *lie*, /l/ /ī/; *let*, /l/ /e/ /t/; *lab*, /l/ /a/ /b/.

ELL ENGLISH LANGUAGE LEARNERS

For the **ELLs** who need **phonics, decoding,** and **fluency** practice, use scaffolding methods as necessary to ensure children understand the meaning of the words. Refer to the Language Transfer Handbook for phonics elements that may not transfer in children's native languages.

Approaching Level

Phonics

SOUND-SPELLING REVIEW

TIER 2

OBJECTIVES

CCSS Demonstrate basic knowledge of one-to-one letter-sound correspondences by producing the sounds for each consonant. **RF.K.3a**

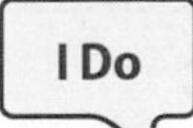

Display **Word-Building Card** *r.* Say the letter name and the sound it stands for: *r,* /r/. Repeat for *f, e, h, d.*

Display Word-Building Cards one at a time and together say the letter name and the sound that each letter stands for.

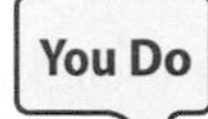

Display Word-Building Cards one at a time and have children say the letter name and the sound that each letter stands for.

CONNECT *b* TO /b/ AND *l* TO /l/

TIER 2

OBJECTIVES

Demonstrate basic knowledge of one-to-one letter-sound correspondences by producing the primary or many of the most frequent sounds for each consonant. **RF.K.3a**

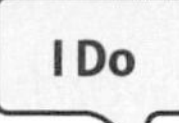

Display the *Bat* **Sound-Spelling Card**. *The letter* b *stands for* /b/ *at the beginning of* bat. *What is this letter? What sound does it stand for?* Repeat for final /b/ using the *Web* Photo Card. *I'll write* b *when I hear* /b/ *at the beginning or end of these words:* bone, rib, hint, crab, fix, band.

Beach *begins with /b/. Let's write* b. Guide children to write *b* when they hear a word that begins or ends with /b/: *best, song, bit, road, rub, tub, box.*

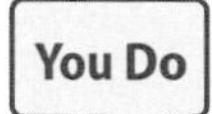

Have children write *b* if a word begins or ends with /b/: *jab, far, scrub, ball.*

Repeat for the initial sound/letter /l/*l* using the *Lemon* Sound-Spelling Card and the words *library, home, look, last, race, friend, link.*

RETEACH

OBJECTIVES

Know and apply grade-level phonics and word analysis skills in decoding words. **RF.K.3**

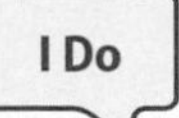

Display **Reading/Writing Workshop**, p. 6. Point to the *Bat* **Sound-Spelling Card**. *The letter* b *stands for the* /b/ *sound at the beginning of* bat. Emphasize /b/ and say *bat*. Repeat using the *Lemon* Sound-Spelling Card. Emphasize initial /l/.

Have children name each picture in row 1. Repeat the names, emphasizing initial /b/. Repeat for row 2, emphasizing initial /l/.

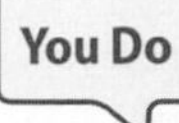

Guide children in reading the words in row 3. Then have them read the words in row 4, offering assistance as needed.

BLEND WORDS WITH /b/*b* AND /l/*l*

OBJECTIVES

CCSS Isolate and pronounce the initial, medial vowel, and final sounds (phonemes) in three-phoneme words. **RF.K.2d**

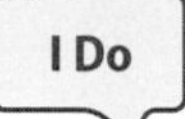

Display **Word-Building Cards** *b, i, n. This is the letter* b. *It stands for* /b/. *This is the letter* i. *It stands for* /i/. *This is the letter* n. *It stands for* /n/. *Listen as I blend all three sounds:* /biiinnn/, bin. *The word is* bin.

Let's blend more sounds to make words. Make the word *tab*. *Let's blend:* /taaab/, tab. Repeat with the word *bad*.

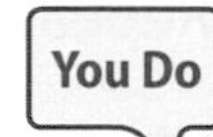

Distribute sets of Word-Building Cards with *b, e, a, i, o, d, l, p,* and *t*. Write: *bet, bad, Deb, bed*. Have children form the words and blend and read them.

Repeat the routine for /l/*l* using the words *lot, let, lip, lap, lid*.

REREAD FOR FLUENCY

OBJECTIVES

Read emergent-reader texts with purpose and understanding. **RF.K.4**

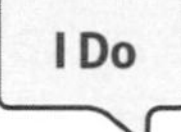

Turn to p. 8 of **Reading/Writing Workshop**, and read aloud the title, "Is It Hot?" *Let's read the title together*. Page through the book. Ask children what they see in each picture. Ask children to find the word *is* on the pages, and the word *little* on p. 9.

Then have children open their books and chorally read the story. Have children point to each word as they read. Provide corrective feedback as needed. After reading, ask children to answer the question *Is it hot?* for each season in the story.

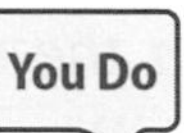

Have children reread "Is It Hot?" with a partner for fluency.

BUILD FLUENCY WITH PHONICS

Sound/Spelling Fluency

Display the following Word-Building Cards: *f, r, e, h, b,* and *l*. Have children chorally say each sound. Repeat and vary the pace.

Fluency in Connected Text

Write the following sentences. *Deb led a fat ram to the pen. Bob let the hen sit with him. Len set the big ham in the pot.* Have children read the sentences and identify the words with /b/ and /l/.

Approaching Level

High-Frequency Words

TIER 2

RETEACH WORDS

OBJECTIVES

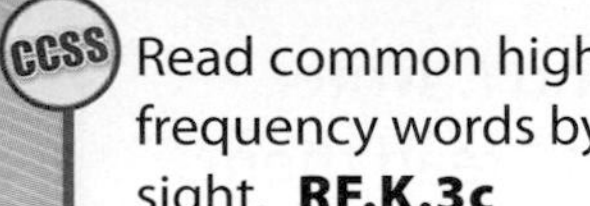

Read common high-frequency words by sight. **RF.K.3c**

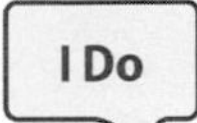

Display the **High-Frequency Word Card** *is* and use the **Read/Spell/Write** routine to reteach the high-frequency word *is*. Repeat for *little*.

Have children turn to p. 7 of **Reading/Writing Workshop** and discuss the first photograph. Then read aloud the first sentence. Reread the sentence with children. Distribute index cards with the word *is* written on them. Have children match their word card with the word *is* in the sentence. Use the same routine for *little* and the other sentence on the page.

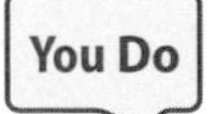

Write the sentence frame *The little cat is in a* ______. Have children copy the sentence frame on their **Response Boards**. Then have partners work together to read and orally complete the frame by talking about where the little cat is hiding. Reteach previously introduced high-frequency words using the **Read/Spell/Write** routine.

CUMULATIVE REVIEW

OBJECTIVES

Read common high-frequency words by sight. **RF.K.3c**

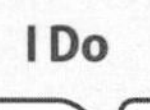

Display the **High-Frequency Word Cards** *I, can, the, we, see, a, like, to, and, go, you, do, my, are, he, with, is,* and *little*. Use the **Read/Spell/Write** routine to review words. Use both sets of cards to create sentences, such as *I like to go and see. Can you go?*

Use the High-Frequency Word Cards to create sentences such as: *Bob and I like to pet the red hen. Len can go with my Mom and Dad.* Have children identify the high-frequency words that are used in each sentence.

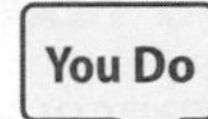

Have partners use the High-Frequency Word Cards and **Word-Building Cards** to create short sentences.

Oral Vocabulary

REVIEW WORDS

OBJECTIVES

Identify real-life connections between words and their use. **L.K.5c**

Develop oral vocabulary: *weather, seasons, migrate, active, spot*

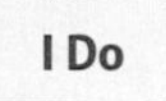

Use the **Define/Example/Ask** routine to review words. Use the following definitions and provide examples:

weather **Weather** is what is happening outside, such as rain or snow.

seasons The **seasons** are the four parts of the year.

migrate To **migrate** means to move from one place to another.

active An **active** person is someone who is busy and moves around a lot.

spot When you **spot** something, you notice it or find it.

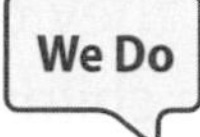

Ask questions to build understanding. *What should you wear in very cold weather? Which two seasons are warm? Why do birds migrate in the winter? What can we do to be more active? Why are grasshoppers hard to spot in grass?*

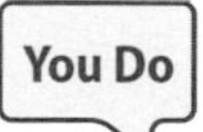

Have children complete these sentence frames: *Our weather today is ______. My favorite season is ______. Some animals migrate to ______. It is important to be active because ______. It would be easy to spot someone wearing a ______.*

Comprehension

SELF-SELECTED READING

OBJECTIVES

CCSS With prompting and support, ask and answer questions about key details in a text. **RL.K.1**

Apply the strategy and skill to reread the text.

Read Independently

Help children select an illustrated story for sustained silent reading. Remind them that figuring out what happens first, next, and last in a story can help them understand it better. They can make pictures in their minds to help them understand what is happening and how the characters feel.

Read Purposefully

Before reading, help children draw three boxes in a row on a piece of paper. Point to the first box and explain that they should draw a picture to tell what happens first in the story. Continue with *next* for the second box, and *last* for the last box. After reading, have children share their boxes and tell what happened first, next, and last. *How did making pictures in your mind help you understand the story?*

On Level

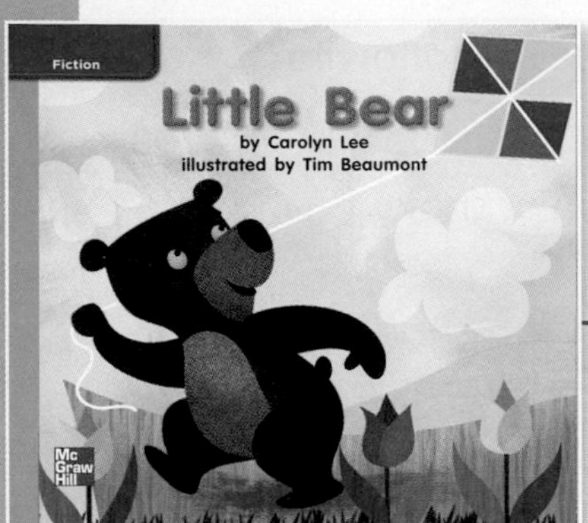

Leveled Reader

OBJECTIVES

With prompting and support, ask and answer questions about key details in a text. **RL.K.1**

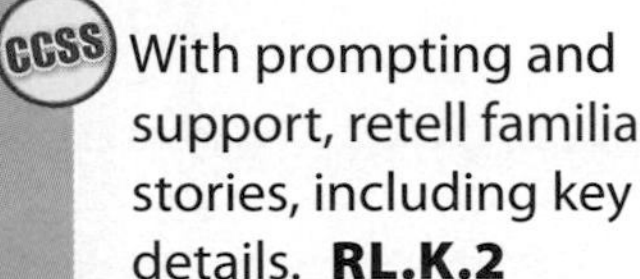

With prompting and support, retell familiar stories, including key details. **RL.K.2**

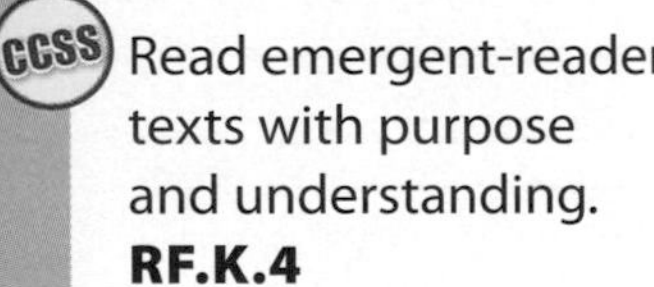

Read emergent-reader texts with purpose and understanding. **RF.K.4**

Leveled Reader: *Little Bear*

Leveled Reader

Before Reading

Preview and Predict

Read aloud the title and the names of the author and illustrator as children follow along in their books. Ask children what they think the story will be about. Preview each illustration and guide children to revise or confirm their predictions. Model the language pattern: *What does Little Bear like on this page? Yes, Little Bear likes a hat.*

Review Genre: Fantasy

Remind children that this week they have been reading fiction. Tell them that now they will read a fantasy story. Say: *Fantasy is a kind of fiction where things happen that could not happen in real life. How can you tell this is a fantasy story?* (Animals do not fly kites.)

Model Concepts of Print

Turn to page 2 and point to the sentence. Say: *The sentence begins with a capital letter. Who can tell me what it ends with?* (a period)

Review High-Frequency Words

Point out the word *little* on page 2. Have children go through the rest of the book and point to the word *little* on each page.

Essential Question

Set a purpose for reading: *Let's find out the different things Little Bear does in different seasons.* Remind children to use the illustrations to help them understand what is happening in the story.

During Reading

Guided Comprehension

As children whisper-read, monitor and provide guidance by correcting blending and modeling the strategy and skill.

Skill: Visualize

Remind children that as they read they can make pictures in their mind of what is happening in the story.

Skill: Key Details (Sequence)

Remind children to look for key details to find out more about the story. Explain that the details will tell them what the bear can do in different seasons and the order in which he does these things.

Think Aloud The pictures and text on pages 2 and 3 are about what Little Bear does. I can see from the details in the pictures that it's spring. I know tulips grow in spring and trees have new buds. Birds build their nests in spring too. I wonder if the next pages will be about what Little Bear does in summer. I'll read to find out.

Guide children to use the pictures and text to find details that tell what Little Bear does and what season it is. Help them to see that the story follows the sequence of the seasons.

After Reading

Respond to Reading

- → *What did Little Bear do in summer?* (ate berries and smelled flowers)
- → *What details in the picture tell you what season it is on pages 6 and 7?* (Bear's scarf, colored leaves; nuts)
- → *Why do we do different things in different seasons?* (Possible answer: Some things you can only do in certain weather, such as sledding.)

Retell

Have children take turns retelling the story. Help them make personal connections by asking: *What things do you like to do in each season?*

Model Fluency

Read the sentences one at a time and have children track the words with their fingers.

Apply Have children practice reading with partners. Encourage them to use picture clues to figure out the last word of each sentence.

LITERACY ACTIVITIES

Have children complete the activities on the inside back cover of the reader.

Level Up

IF Children read *Little Bear* **On Level** with fluency and correctly answer the Respond to Reading questions,

THEN Tell children that they will read another story about how the seasons are different.

- Have children page through *Ant and Grasshopper* **Beyond Level** as you talk about what we do to get ready for different seasons.
- Have children read the story, monitoring their comprehension and providing assistance as necessary.

On Level

Phonemic Awareness

PHONEME ISOLATION

OBJECTIVES

CCSS Isolate and pronounce the initial, medial vowel, and final sounds (phonemes) in three-phoneme words. **RF.K.2d**

Display the *Bat* **Photo Card**. *This is a* bat. *The first sound is* /b/. *Say it with me.* Repeat for final /b/ using the *Web* Photo Card and with initial /l/ using the *Lemon* Photo Card.

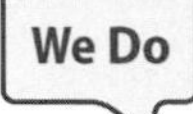

Say *bit* and have children repeat. *What is the first sound?* Say it together. Repeat for *bin, fit, set, bad*. Repeat for the final sound using *tub, lab, pin*, and /l/ using *lit, lap, bet, men*.

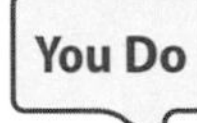

Say *bed, bin, cot, let, fed, ham, lot* and have children tell the initial sound in each word. Repeat for the ending sound in *cab, pit, web, hop, tub.*

PHONEME BLENDING

OBJECTIVES

CCSS Isolate and pronounce the initial, medial vowel, and final sounds (phonemes) in three-phoneme words. **RF.K.2d**

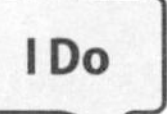

Listen as the puppet says the sounds: /t/ /a/ /b/. *Now the puppet will blend the sounds to make a word:* /taaab/, tab. Repeat with *bad, led*.

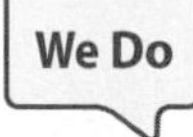

The puppet is going to say the sounds in a word. Listen: /l/ /a/ /p/. Have children repeat. *Now let's blend the sounds with the puppet and say the word:* /lll/ /aaa/ /p/, /lllaaap/, lap. Repeat with *bin* and *tub*.

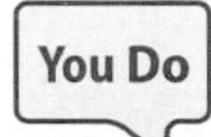

Say the following sounds. Ask children to blend the sounds and say the words: /l/ /o/ /t/, lot; /k/ /a/ /b/, cab; /b/ /e/ /d/, bed; /b/ /i/ /b/, bib.

PHONEME SEGMENTATION

OBJECTIVES

CCSS Isolate and pronounce the initial, medial vowel, and final sounds (phonemes) in three-phoneme words. **RF.K.2d**

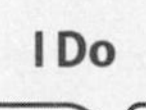

Use **Sound Boxes** and markers. *Listen as I say* bat. *There are three sounds in bat*: /b/ /a/ /t/. *I'll place a marker in one box for each sound*. Repeat for *low*.

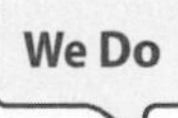

Distribute Sound Boxes and markers. *Listen as I say* let: */l/ /e/ /t/. There are three sounds in* let. *Place a marker in one box for each sound.* Repeat with *bin*.

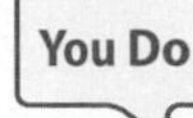

Use Sound Boxes and markers to repeat the practice with the words *lock, lie, by,* and *cab*.

Phonics

REVIEW PHONICS

OBJECTIVES

CCSS Know and apply grade-level phonics and word analysis skills in decoding words. **RF.K.3**

Display **Reading/Writing Workshop**, p. 6. Point to the *Bat* **Sound-Spelling Card**. *Which letter stands for the /b/ sound you hear at the beginning of* bat? *The letter is* b. Repeat for initial /l/ using the *Lemon* Sound-Spelling Card.

Have children say the name of each picture in rows 1 and 2. Then ask them to identify the words with /b/ at the beginning. Then have them identify the words with /l/ at the beginning.

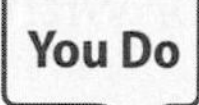

Have children read each word in rows 3 and 4, raising their hands if they hear /b/ at the beginning of a word. Repeat, having them raise their hands when they hear /b/ at the end of a word. Continue the routine, having children raise their hands when they hear /l/ at the beginning of a word.

PICTURE SORT

OBJECTIVES

Isolate and pronounce the initial, medial vowel, and final sounds (phonemes) in three-phoneme words. **RF.K.2d**

Display **Word-Building Cards** *b* and *l* in a pocket chart. Then show the *Bat* **Photo Card**. Say /b/ /a/ /t/, *bat. The sound at the beginning of* bat *is* /b/. *The letter* b *stands for* /b/. *I will put the bat under the letter* b. Show the *Lock* Photo Card. Say /l/ /o/ /k/, *lock. The sound at the beginning is* /l/. *The letter* l *stands for* /l/. *I will put the lock under the* l.

Show the *Bus* Photo Card and say *bus*, /b/ /u/ /s/. Have children repeat and say the sound they hear at the beginning of *bus*. Ask them if they should place the photo under the *b* or the *l*. (b)

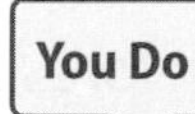

Continue the activity using the *Box, Leaf, Light,* and *Bike* Photo Cards. Have children say the picture name and the sounds in the name. Then have them place the card under the *b* or *l*.

On Level

Phonics

BLEND WORDS WITH /b/*b*, /l/*l*

OBJECTIVES

CCSS Isolate and pronounce the initial, medial vowel, and final sounds (phonemes) in three-phoneme words. **RF.K.2d**

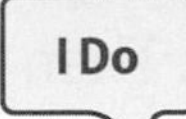

Use **Word-Building Cards** or write *l, i, t. This is the letter* l. *It stands for* /l/. *Say it with me: /lll/. This is the letter* i. *It stands for* /i/. *Say it with me: /iii/. This is the letter* t. *It stands for* /t/. *Say it with me:* /t/. *I'll blend the sounds together to read the word:* /lllit/, lit. Repeat with initial /b/ with *bad* and *bit,* and final /b/ with *cab* and *rib*.

Write *led* and *lab*. Guide children to blend the words sound by sound to read each word.

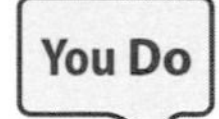

Write the following words and have children blend the words sound by sound to read each word.

bed lid bib lot

REREAD FOR FLUENCY

OBJECTIVES

Read emergent-reader texts with purpose and understanding. **RF.K.4**

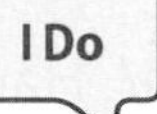

Point to the title "Is It Hot?" on p. 8 of **Reading/Writing Workshop**. Point to the question mark in the title. *When we read, we pay attention to the end marks. They tell us how to use our voices. This question mark tells us to raise our voices at the end*. Work with children to read for accuracy and expression. Model reading a page: *When I read,* "Ben is a little cat," *I read all the words in the sentence, then I pause before I read the next sentence on the page. This makes my reading sound smooth and natural.*

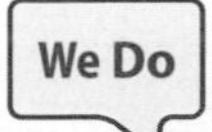

Reread page 9. Then have children chorally read the page with you. Continue choral reading the remainder of the pages.

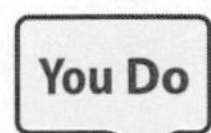

Have children reread "Is It Hot?" Provide time to listen as children read the pages. Comment on their accuracy and expression and provide corrective feedback by modeling proper fluency.

High-Frequency Words

REVIEW WORDS

OBJECTIVES

Read common high-frequency words by sight. **RF.K.3c**

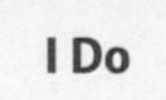

Use the **High-Frequency Word Card** *is* with the **Read/Spell/Write** routine to review the word. Repeat for *little.*

Have children turn to p. 7 of **Reading/Writing Workshop**. Discuss the photographs and read aloud the first sentence. Point to the word *is* and have children read it. Then chorally read the sentence. Have children frame and read the word *is* in the sentence. Repeat the routine with the word *little*.

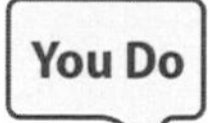

Say the word *is*. Ask children to close their eyes, picture the word, and write it as they see it. Have children self-correct. Repeat for *little*.

Reteach previously introduced high-frequency words using the **Read/Spell/Write** routine.

Fluency Point to the **High-Frequency Word Cards** *go, my, he, you, are, with, is,* and *little* in random order. Have children chorally read. Repeat at a faster pace.

Comprehension

SELF-SELECTED READING

OBJECTIVES

CCSS With prompting and support, ask and answer questions about key details in a text. **RL.K.1**

Apply the strategy and skill to reread the text

Read Independently

Have children select an illustrated story for sustained silent reading. Remind children that figuring out what happens first, next, and last in a story will help them better understand it. Visualizing as children read can help them figure out the order of events in the story.

Read Purposefully

Before reading, ask children to draw three boxes in a row. Then have them write *first, next,* and *last* above each box. Tell children that as they read, they should visualize what is happening and write a few words describing the story's events in each box. After reading, invite them to share their boxes with the class.

Beyond Level

Leveled Reader

OBJECTIVES

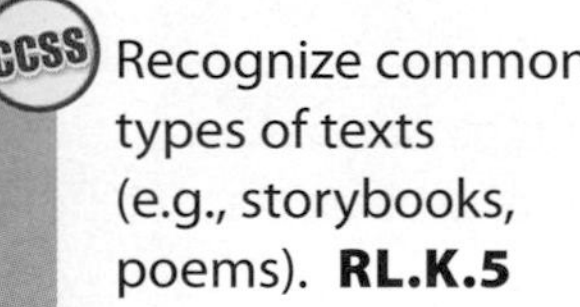

CCSS With prompting and support, ask and answer questions about key details in a text. **RL.K.1**

CCSS With prompting and support, retell familiar stories, including key details. **RL.K.2**

CCSS Recognize common types of texts (e.g., storybooks, poems). **RL.K.5**

Leveled Reader: *Ant and Grasshopper*

Leveled Reader

Before Reading

Preview and Predict

Ask children to point to the title and the names of the author and illustrator as you read them aloud. Ask children to describe what they see on the cover and to say what they think the book will be about. Ask: *Who do you think will be the characters in the story?*

Review Genre: Fantasy

Remind children that they have been reading fiction this week. Explain that now they will read fantasy, a kind of fiction where things happen that could never happen in real life. Ask: *How can you tell this story is fantasy*? (The ant and the grasshopper are wearing clothes. Ant has a garden and a house.)

Essential Question

Remind children of the Essential Question: *How are the seasons different?* Set a purpose for reading: *Let's read to find out how the seasons in this story are different and what the ant and grasshopper do in each season.*

During Reading

Guided Comprehension

As children whisper-read *Ant and Grasshopper*, monitor and provide guidance by correcting blending and modeling the strategy and skill. Stop periodically to ask open-ended questions, such as, *What do you think will happen next?*

Strategy: Visualize

Remind children that they will understand a story better if they visualize, or picture in their mind, what the characters are doing and feeling.

Skill: Key Details (Sequence)

Remind children that finding key details in the text and the illustrations will help them to understand the story. Explain that in this book, the illustrations and text provide key details about what Ant and Grasshopper do each season.

Think Aloud When I read pages 2 and 3, I learn from details in the text and the illustrations that it is spring and Ant is planting a garden. I also see that Grasshopper is playing with his ball while Ant is working. I think pages 4 and 5 will show them in the summer.

As children read the rest of the book, point out the sequence of the seasons in the story. Guide them to look for key details that tell them what Ant and Grasshopper do during the summer, fall, and winter. Have children point to evidence in the text and illustrations to support their statements.

After Reading

Respond to Reading

- Why do you think Ant is working so hard all summer and fall? (to get ready for the long, cold winter when it will be hard to find food.)
- Why doesn't Grasshopper do any work to get ready for winter? (Possible answers: He is not thinking ahead; he is being foolish.)
- What happened after the leaves fell from the trees? (Ant picked his beans while Grasshopper played in the leaves.)

Retell

Have children act out the story as they retell it. Help them make a personal connection by asking: *What do you do to get ready for winter?*

Gifted and Talented

EVALUATING Have children think about what they can do in summer to get ready for winter. Invite them to work in small groups to brainstorm ideas together.

HAVE children make a drawing to show how they can use the summer to get ready for the changes that come with the winter season.

LITERACY ACTIVITIES

Have children complete the activities on the inside back cover of the reader.

Beyond Level

Phonics

REVIEW

OBJECTIVES

Know and apply grade-level phonics and word analysis skills in decoding words. **RF.K.3**

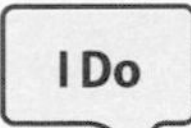
Display **Reading/Writing Workshop**, p. 6. Point to the *Bat* **Sound-Spelling Card**. *What is the sound at the beginning of* bat? *What letter can stand for* /b/? Repeat with the *Lemon* Sound-Spelling Card.

Have children say the name of each picture. Then ask children to share other words they know that begin with /b/ and /l/.

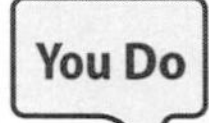
Have partners read each word. Ask them to write the words on their **Response Boards**, underlining the letter in each word that stands for initial /b/ and /l/ and final /b/.

Fluency Have children turn to p. 8 in **Reading/Writing Workshop** and reread "Is It Hot?" for fluency.

Innovate Have children create a new page for "Is It Hot?" by completing the sentence frame *We can* ______ *if it is not hot* and adding an action the children in the story can do when the weather is not hot.

High-Frequency Words

REVIEW

OBJECTIVES

Read common high-frequency words by sight. **RF.K.3c**

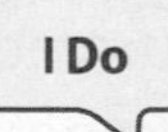
Create **High-Frequency Word Cards** for *know* and *her*. Introduce the words using the **Read/Spell/Write** routine.

Display the High-Frequency Word Cards for *I, we, like, the,* and *see*. Have children help you complete the following sentence frames using the High-Frequency Word Cards: *I know we like the* ______. *I see her* ______.

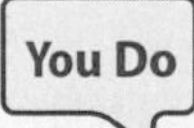
Have partners write sentences using the High-Frequency Words *know* and *her* on their Response Boards. Have them read their sentences.

Vocabulary

ORAL VOCABULARY: SYNONYMS

OBJECTIVES

CCSS With guidance and support from adults, explore word relationships and nuances in word meanings. **L.K.5**

Develop oral vocabulary: Synonyms

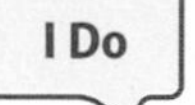

Review meanings of oral vocabulary words *spot* and *active*. Explain that a synonym is a word that means almost the same thing as another word.

A synonym for spot *is* notice. *You notice something when you pay attention to it.* I notice the loose dog running down the street.

A synonym for active *is* busy. *Someone who is busy is playing or doing work.* The child was busy doing a puzzle.

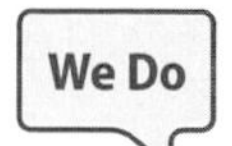

Write a few sentences together using the new words *notice* and *busy*. Read the sentences aloud.

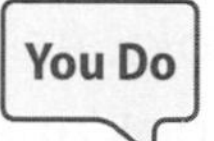

Have partners draw a picture and write a few sentences to tell about a trip to the market. Tell them to include the words *notice* and *busy* in their sentences. Ask them to share their pictures and sentences with the class.

Extend Challenge children to use new words *notice* and *busy* to interview a partner about the seasons of the year. Then ask children to share two facts they learned about their partner and the seasons.

Comprehension

SELF-SELECTED READING

OBJECTIVES

CCSS With prompting and support, ask and answer questions about key details in a text. **RL.K.1**

Apply the strategy and skill to reread the text.

Read Independently

Have children select an illustrated story for sustained silent reading. Remind them that visualizing while reading can help them better understand the order of story events and details.

Read Purposefully

Before reading, have children draw four boxes in a row. Use the boxes to write down what happens in story order. Remind them to visualize as they think about how to fill in the boxes. After reading, ask children to share their boxes. Have them explain how writing down the story events helped them better understand the story. Challenge them to come up with a new detail to add to the story that would make sense in one of the boxes.

Independent Study Have children create a poster illustrating a fact about each season that they learned this week. Challenge children to write a few sentences stating their opinion about one of this week's stories or poems.

English Language Learners

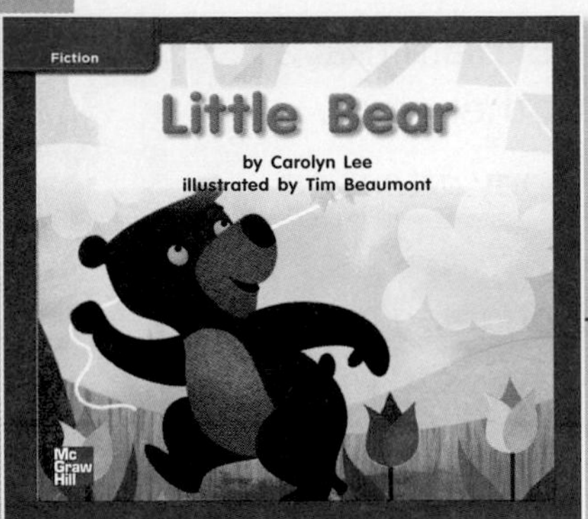

Leveled Reader

OBJECTIVES

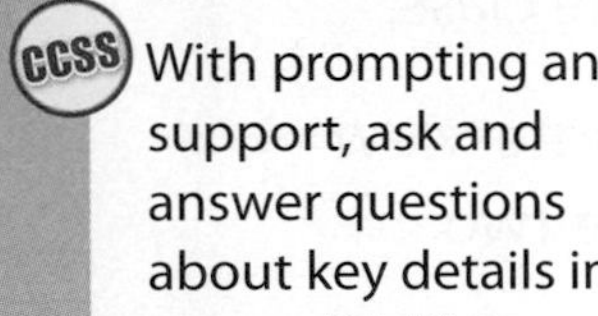
With prompting and support, ask and answer questions about key details in a text. **RL.K.1**

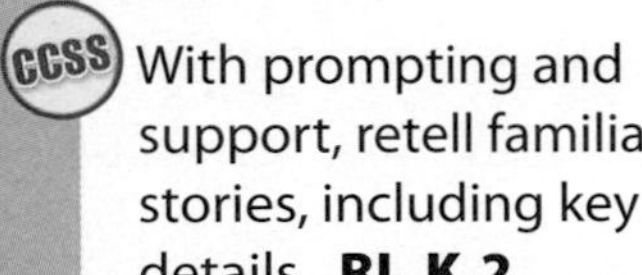
With prompting and support, retell familiar stories, including key details. **RL.K.2**

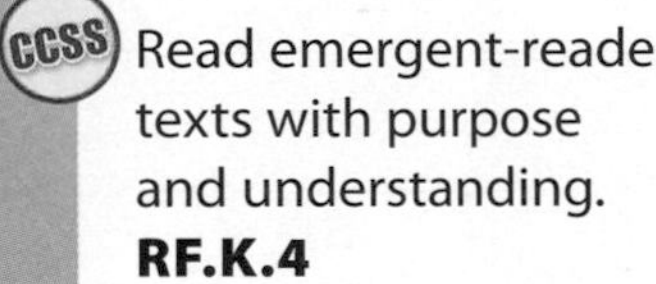
Read emergent-reader texts with purpose and understanding. **RF.K.4**

Shared Read: *Little Bear*

Go Digital

Leveled Reader

Before Reading

Preview and Predict

Show children the cover of the book. Read the title and say: *The name of this story is "Little Bear." Point to Little Bear on your books.* Ask children to name the things they see in the cover illustration. Look at each picture in the book with children. Point out the labels and ask children to repeat the words. Model the language pattern. Say: *What does Little Bear like?* Encourage children to respond using the pattern from the book: *Little Bear likes* ______. Make sure children are familiar with the English words for the different seasons.

Essential Question

Remind children of the Essential Question: *How are the seasons different?* Set a purpose for reading: *Let's find out what seasons the book talks about and what Little Bear does in each season.* Encourage children to ask questions about anything they do not understand.

During Reading

Interactive Question Response

Pages 2–3 As you talk about each spread with children, encourage them to use the language of the text to name what they see in the pictures. Point to the illustration and label on page 2. Ask: *What do you see?* (tree, nest, buds, rain) *What is on Little Bear's head?* (hat) *Let's read the sentence together.* Point to the illustration on page 3. Ask: *What do you see? What does Little Bear like in this picture?* (Little Bear likes a kite.) *What season is it on these pages?* (spring)

Pages 4–5 Point to the illustration and label on page 4. *What is this? Yes, it is a strawberry. Sometimes we call it a berry. What do you think Little Bear likes on this page?* (Little Bear likes a strawberry/berry.) *Let's read the sentence.* Point to page 5. Ask: *What does Little Bear like on this page?* (Little Bear likes a flower.) *What season is it?* (summer)

Pages 6–7 Point to the illustration and label on page 6. *What is the label pointing to?* (leaf) *What color is the leaf?* (yellow) *When are leaves yellow?* (fall) Point to page 7. *Which word says* nut? *What can Little Bear do with this nut?* (eat it) *Let's read the sentences on these pages.*

Page 8 Point to the illustration and the label. *This is where Little Bear lives. He is in his cave. It keeps him safe and warm in winter. Let's read the sentences on this page. Why does Little Bear nap in winter?* (It is cold; there is not much for him to do outside.)

After Reading

Respond to Reading

- → *What did Little Bear like in summer?* (strawberries/berries)
- → *What does Little Bear like in fall?* (leaves and nuts)
- → *Name the seasons that are shown in the book.* (spring, summer, fall, winter)

Retell

Say: *Let's retell the book together. Who likes things in different seasons?* (Little Bear) Begin to name each of the things Little Bear likes in each season: a hat and kite in spring, berry and flower in summer, leaf and nut in fall, and a nap in winter.

Model Fluency

As you read each sentence, track the print and have children chorally repeat it. Point to each picture label as you emphasize the word that corresponds to it.

Apply Ask small groups of children to read together. Encourage children to take turns reading a page aloud, pointing to the detail in the picture that helps them name the last word in each sentence.

LITERACY ACTIVITIES

Have children complete the activities on the inside back cover of the reader.

Level Up

IF Children read *Little Bear* **ELL Level** with fluency and correctly answer the Respond to Reading questions,

THEN Tell children that they will read a more detailed version of the story.

- Have children page through *Little Bear* **On Level** and describe what they see in each picture.
- Have children read the story, monitoring their comprehension and providing assistance as necessary.

English Language Learners

Vocabulary

PRETEACH ORAL VOCABULARY

OBJECTIVES

Speak audibly and express thoughts, feelings, and ideas clearly. **SL.K.6**

LANGUAGE OBJECTIVE

Preview vocabulary

I Do — Display the images from the **Visual Vocabulary Cards** and follow the routine to preteach the oral vocabulary words.

We Do — Display each image again and explain how it illustrates or demonstrates the word. Model using sentences to describe the image.

You Do — Display the word *weather* again and have children talk to a partner about what the weather today is like.

Beginning	Intermediate	Advanced/High
Ellicit language from children by asking about the weather.	Have partners talk about the weather in each season.	Ask children to use each of the words in a sentence of their own.

PRETEACH ELL VOCABULARY

OBJECTIVES

Speak audibly and express thoughts, feelings, and ideas clearly. **SL.K.6**

LANGUAGE OBJECTIVE

Preview ELL vocabulary

I Do — Display the images from the **Visual Vocabulary Cards** one at a time to preteach the ELL vocabulary words *hibernate* and *climate*. Follow the routine. Say the word, and have children repeat it. Define the word in English.

We Do — Display each image again and incorporate the words in a short discussion about the images. Model using sentences to describe the image.

You Do — Display the word *hibernate* again. Ask partners to talk about animals that hibernate.

Beginning	Intermediate	Advanced/High
Use the card to help children understand that some animals hibernate. Ask: *What are the bears doing?*	Have partners talk about animals that hibernate and draw a picture to illustrate the word.	Ask children to use each of the words in a sentence of their own.

High-Frequency Words

REVIEW WORDS

OBJECTIVES

CCSS Read common high-frequency words by sight (e.g., *the, of, to, you, she, my, is, are, do, does*). **RF.K.3c**

LANGUAGE OBJECTIVE

Review high-frequency words

I Do Display the **High-Frequency Word Cards** for *is* and *little*. Read the words. Use the **Read/Spell/Write** routine to teach the words. Have children write the words on their **Response Boards**.

We Do Write a sentence frame that uses the week's high-frequency words: *The ______ is little.* Track print as children read and complete the sentence. If necessary, model how to complete the sentence frame.

You Do Display a sentence that uses the high-frequency words *is* and *little*. Ask children to point to the words and say them aloud. Then work with children to read and say the entire sentence aloud.

Beginning	Intermediate	Advanced/High
Read the sentence aloud and have children repeat.	Ask partners to complete the following sentence frame: *The ____ is little.*	Ask children to use the words in a sentence.

REVIEW CATEGORY WORDS

OBJECTIVES

CCSS Identify real-life connections between words and their use (e.g., note places at school that are colorful). **L.K.5c**

LANGUAGE OBJECTIVE

Use category words

I Do Write the words *winter, spring, summer,* and *fall* and say the words aloud. Ask children to repeat each word after you. Define the words in English and then in Spanish, if appropriate, identifying any cognates.

We Do Ask children to help you describe and draw each season.

You Do Have children choose their favorite season and name one thing they do in that season.

Beginning	Intermediate	Advanced/High
Prompt children by asking them about their favorite seasons.	Have partners talk about what they like to do during each season.	Have children use the category words in sentences.

English Language Learners

Writing

SHARED WRITING

OBJECTIVES

CCSS Use a combination of drawing, dictating, and writing to narrate a single event or several loosely linked events, tell about the events in the order in which they occurred, and provide a reaction to what happened. **W.K.3**

LANGUAGE OBJECTIVE

Contribute to a shared writing project

Review the chart in the Whole Group Shared Writing project that names activities from each season. Model using the information in the chart to write a model opinion sentence: *I like summer because I like warm weather.*

We Do

With children, choose one of the seasons. Talk about it. Have children help you write a shared sentence: *We like* ______ *because* ______.

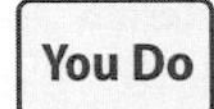

Help partners choose a season and talk about it. Provide them with a sentence frame to work on together: *We like* ______ *because* ______.

Beginning	Intermediate	Advanced/High
Ask children to tell you their opinion of a season. Help them say it in a complete sentence.	Help children complete the sentence frame with ideas from the chart in the Whole Group section.	Ask children to complete the sentence frame on their own and read their sentence to a partner.

WRITING TRAIT: VOICE

OBJECTIVES

Use a combination of drawing, dictating, and writing to narrate a single event or several loosely linked events, tell about the events in the order in which they occurred, and provide a reaction to what happened. **W.K.3**

LANGUAGE OBJECTIVE

Identify the importance of voice in writing

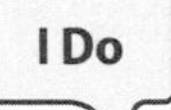

Explain that good writers allow their own voice to come through in their writing. Explain that a voice is the view of the person who is writing.

Point to the **Big Book** selection *Mama, Is It Summer Yet?* Explain that the writer's voice is a child waiting for summer. Ask children how to make their own voice show through in their writing: *How can I tell you are the author?*

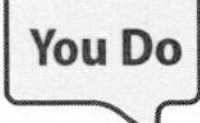

Have children think about things that happen in different seasons. Have them look back at the Big Book selection for ideas. Prompt them to write a sentence using *I* as the subject to show their voice as narrator.

Beginning	Intermediate	Advanced/High
Work with children to help them form a sentence about the seasons.	Ask children to work with a partner to form a sentence about the seasons.	Ask children to write their own sentence to describe a season, using *I* as the subject.

Grammar

NAMING WORDS (NOUNS)

OBJECTIVES

CCSS Use frequently occurring nouns and verbs. **L.K.1b**

LANGUAGE OBJECTIVE

Learn to use nouns correctly

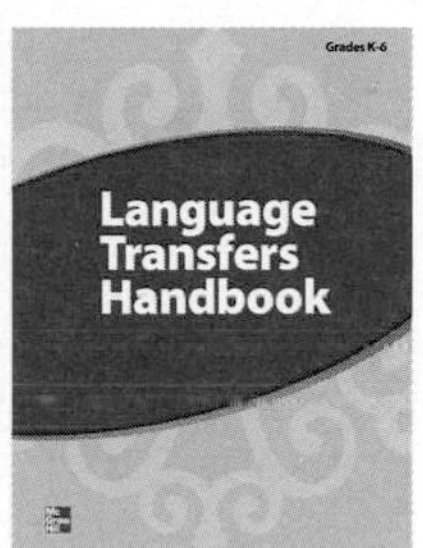

Language Transfers Handbook

In Spanish, nouns have feminine or masculine gender, so children may expect words to be masculine or feminine in English. Remind children that the word *the* or *a* used before nouns is gender neutral.

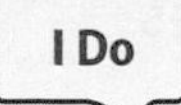

I Do Review with children that a noun names a person, place, or thing. Say the following sentence: *The snow is cold.* Explain that *snow* is a noun because it is a thing.

We Do Say the following sentences. Have children raise their hands when they hear the noun in each sentence. Have them say: *The naming word is* ______.

The rain falls.

The puddle is deep.

Now the sun is out.

You Do Say the following sentence frame about weather:

I like/don't like the ______ *because* ______.

Pair children and have them talk about types of weather they like or don't like and why (rain, wind, snow, sun, etc.). Have them use a noun to complete the first part of the sentence and then use details from this week's readings to complete the sentence. Circulate, listen in, and take note of each child's language use and proficiency.

Beginning	Intermediate	Advanced/High
Discuss the weather shown in the selections. Ask: *What is this weather like?* Guide children to complete the sentence frame.	Ask children to describe illustrations in the selections to help them complete the sentence frame.	Ask children to think about their personal experiences with weather to help them complete the sentence frame.

Weekly Assessment

Use your Quick Check observations and the assessment opportunities identified below to evaluate children's progress in key skill areas.

✓ TESTED SKILLS CCSS	Quick Check Observations	Pencil and Paper Assessment
PHONEMIC AWARENESS/ PHONICS b /b/, /l/ (initial/final b; initial l) **RF.K.3a**	Can children isolate /b/ and /l/ and match them to the letters *Bb* and *Ll*?	Practice Book, pp. 153–154, 155–156, 158
HIGH-FREQUENCY WORDS is *is, little* **RF.K.3c**	Can children recognize and read the high-frequency words?	Practice Book, pp. 159–160
COMPREHENSION Key Details: Sequence **RL.K.1**	As you read *Mama, Is It Summer Yet?* with children, can they identify key details and discuss the sequence in the text?	Practice Book, p. 157

Quick Check Rubric

Skills	1	2	3
PHONEMIC AWARENESS/ PHONICS	Does not connect the sounds /b/ and /l/ with the letters *Bb* and *Ll*.	Usually connects the sounds /b/ and /l/ with the letters *Bb* and *Ll*.	Consistently connects the sounds /b/ and /l/ with the letters *Bb* and *Ll*.
HIGH-FREQUENCY WORDS	Does not identify the high-frequency words.	Usually recognizes the high-frequency words with accuracy, but not speed.	Consistently recognizes the high-frequency words with speed and accuracy.
COMPREHENSION	Does not identify key details and their sequence in the text.	Usually identifies key details and their sequence in the text.	Consistently identifies key details and their sequence in the text.

Go Digital! www.connected.mcgraw-hill.com

Using Assessment Results

TESTED SKILLS	If ...	Then ...
PHONEMIC AWARENESS/ PHONICS	**Quick Check Rubric:** Children consistently score 1 or **Pencil and Paper Assessment:** Children get 0–2 items correct	... reteach tested Phonemic Awareness and Phonics skills using Lessons 16–17 and 27–29 in the ***Tier 2 Phonemic Awareness Intervention Online PDFs*** and Lessons 27–28 in the ***Tier 2 Phonics/Word Study Intervention Online PDFs.***
HIGH-FREQUENCY WORDS	**Quick Check Rubric:** Children consistently score 1	... reteach tested skills by using the High-Frequency Word Cards and asking children to read and spell the word. Point out any irregularities in sound-spellings.
COMPREHENSION	**Quick Check Rubric:** Children consistently score 1 or **Pencil and Paper Assessment:** Children get 0–1 items correct	... reteach tested skill using Lessons 10–12 in the ***Tier 2 Comprehension Intervention Online PDFs.***

Response to Intervention

Use the children's assessment results to assist you in identifying children who will benefit from focused intervention.

Use the appropriate sections of the ***Placement and Diagnostic Assessment*** to designate children requiring:

TIER 2 **Tier 2 Intervention Online PDFs**

TIER 3 **WonderWorks Intervention Program**

- → Phonemic Awareness
- → Phonics
- → Vocabulary
- → Comprehension
- → Fluency

WEEKLY OVERVIEW

Literature Big Book

Listening Comprehension

It was hot.
Everything was hot and dry.

The red soil was hot and dry and cracked.

Rain, 4–32
Genre Fantasy

"Cloud Watch," 33–36
Genre Informational Text

Interactive Read-Aloud Cards

"The Frog and the Locust"
Genre Folktale

Oral Vocabulary

clever
drought
predict
storm
temperature

Minilessons

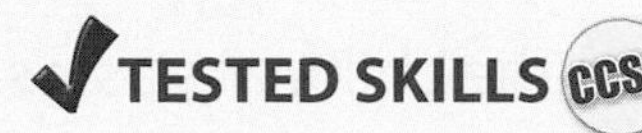
✓ TESTED SKILLS CCSS

✓ **Comprehension Strategy** .... Visualize, T95
✓ **Comprehension Skill** .... Key Details, T104

Go Digital
www.connected.mcgraw-hill.com

Nathan Love

Essential Question
What happens in different kinds of weather?

WEEK 2

Big Book and Little Book
Reading/Writing Workshop

Shared Reading

"Kim and Nan," 22–29
Genre Fiction

High-Frequency Words
she, was, T99

Minilessons

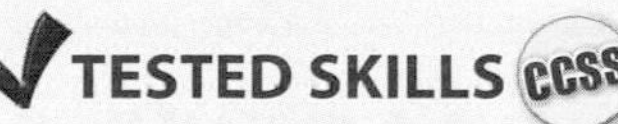

✓**Phonics** .... /k/*k*, T97
Writing Trait........................ Voice, T100
Grammar .... Nouns, T101

Differentiated Text

Approaching

On Level

Beyond

ELL

TEACH AND MANAGE

What You Do

INTRODUCE

Weekly Concept

What's the Weather?

Reading/Writing Workshop Big Book, 20–21

TEACH AND APPLY

Listening Comprehension

Big Book
Rain
Genre Fantasy
Paired Read "Cloud Watch"
Genre Informational Text

Minilessons
Strategy: Visualize
Skill: Key Details (Sequence)

Shared Reading

Reading/Writing Workshop
"Kim and Nan"

Minilessons
/k/k, High-Frequency Words: she, was
Writing, Grammar

Go Digital

Interactive Whiteboard

Interactive Whiteboard

Mobile

What Your Students Do

WEEKLY CONTRACT

PDF Online

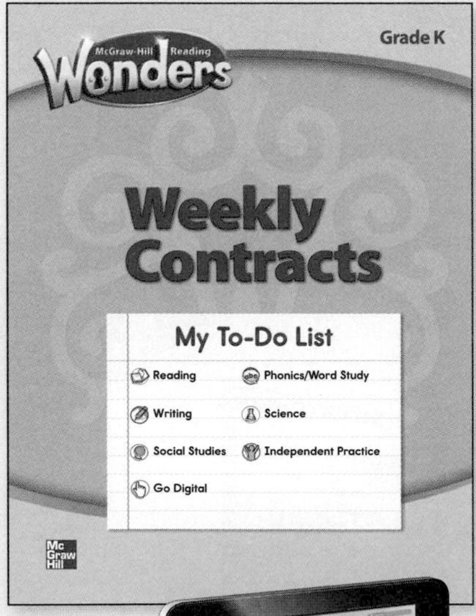

PRACTICE AND ONLINE ACTIVITIES

Your Turn Practice Book, pp. 163–172

Name ______

kite	key	ladder
kangaroo	banana	koala
king	feather	kayak

Phonemic Awareness: /k/
Say the name of each picture. Put a marker on each picture if its name begins with the /k/ sound.

Unit 6: Weather for All Seasons • Week 2 163

Leveled Readers

Go Digital

Online To-Do List

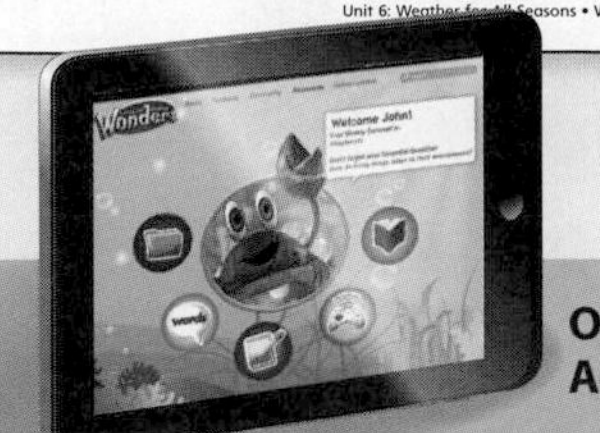

Online Activities

Mobile

WEEK 2

DIFFERENTIATE

Small Group Instruction

Leveled Readers

Mobile

INTEGRATE

Research and Inquiry

Wind Chart, pp. T134–T135

Text Connections

Compare Weather Conditions, p. T136

Talk About Reading

Becoming Readers, p. T137

Online Research

WORKSTATION CARDS

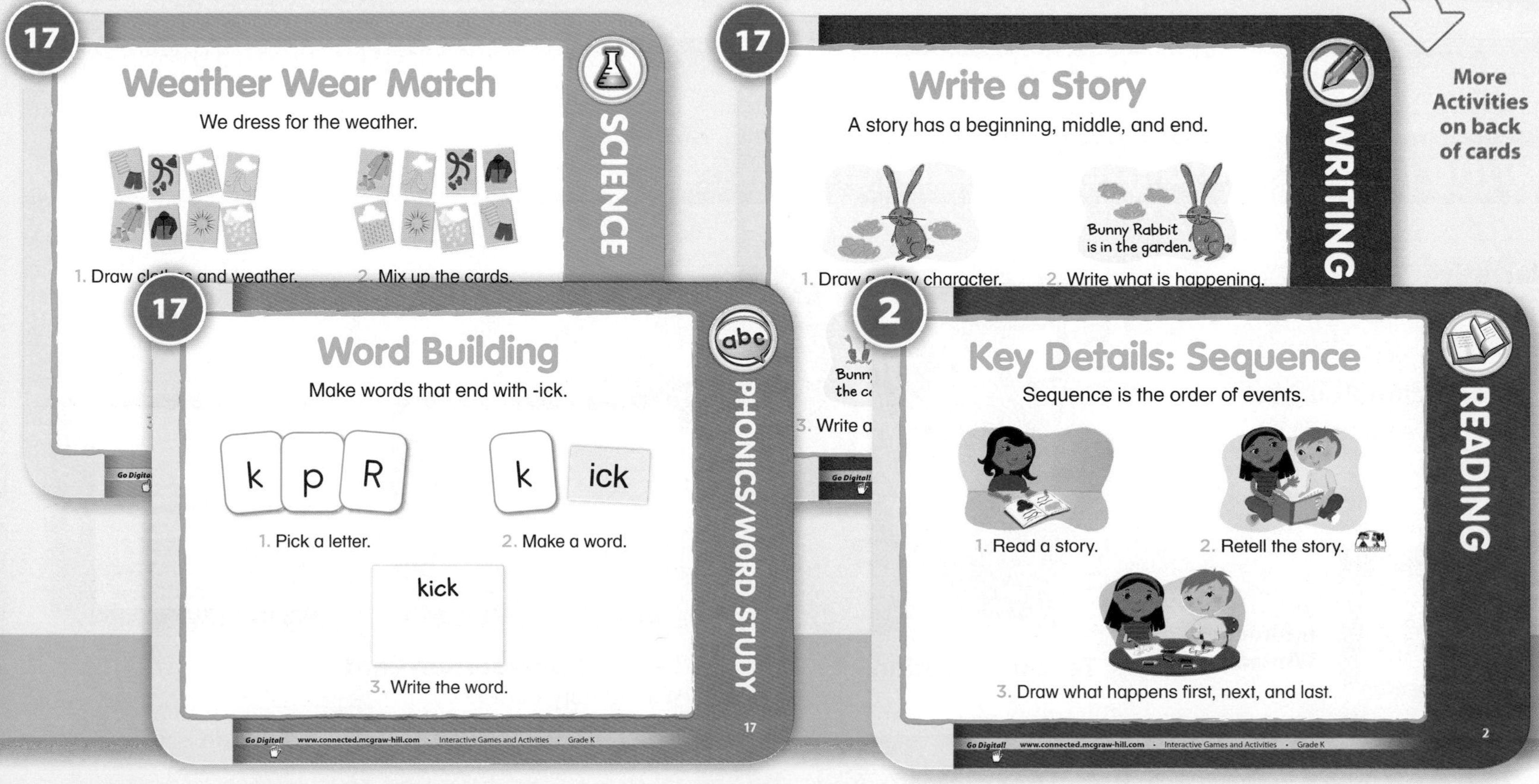

More Activities on back of cards

17 Weather Wear Match — SCIENCE

We dress for the weather.

1. Draw cl... and weather.
2. Mix up the cards.

17 Write a Story — WRITING

A story has a beginning, middle, and end.

Bunny Rabbit is in the garden.

1. Draw a ...y character.
2. Write what is happening.
3. Write a ...

17 Word Building — PHONICS/WORD STUDY

Make words that end with -ick.

k p R   k ick

1. Pick a letter.
2. Make a word.

kick

3. Write the word.

Go Digital! www.connected.mcgraw-hill.com • Interactive Games and Activities • Grade K

17

2 Key Details: Sequence — READING

Sequence is the order of events.

1. Read a story.
2. Retell the story.
3. Draw what happens first, next, and last.

Go Digital! www.connected.mcgraw-hill.com • Interactive Games and Activities • Grade K

2

Nathan Love

DEVELOPING READERS AND WRITERS

Write About Reading • Analytical Writing

Write to Sources and Research

Respond to Reading, T95, T143, T151, T157, T161

Connect to Essential Question, T95, T127

Key Details, T109

Research and Inquiry, T134

Teacher's Edition

Literature Big Book
Rain
Paired Read: *Cloud Watch*

Interactive Whiteboard

Leveled Readers
Responding to Texts

Writing Process • Independent Writing

Narrative Text
Personal Narrative, T122–T123, T132, T140

Conferencing Routines
Peer Conferences, T132

Interactive Whiteboard

Teacher's Edition

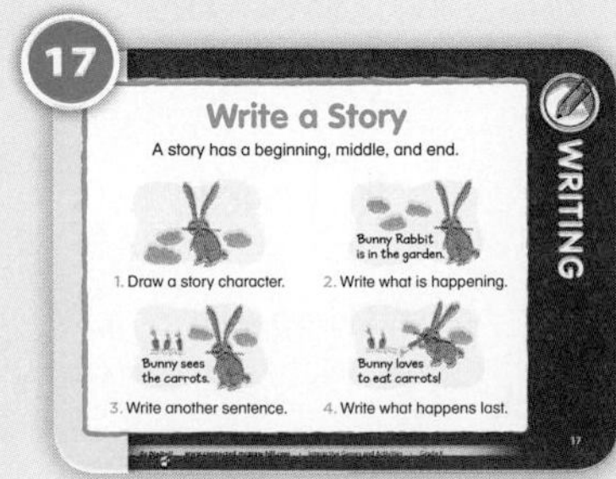

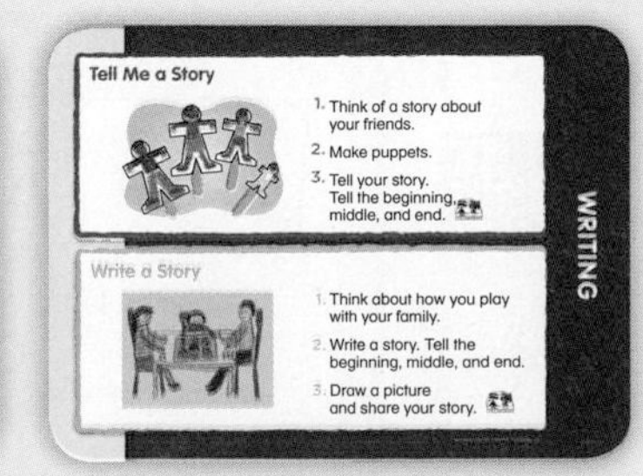

Leveled Workstation Card
Write a Story, Card 17

Writing Traits • Shared and Interactive Writing

Writing Trait:
Voice
Personal Narrative, T100, T114

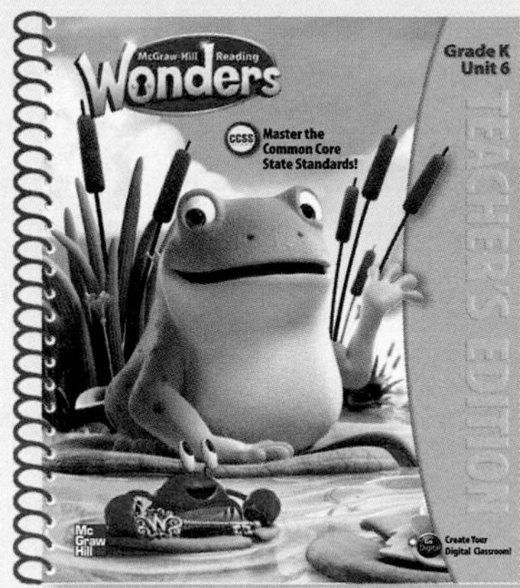

Teacher's Edition

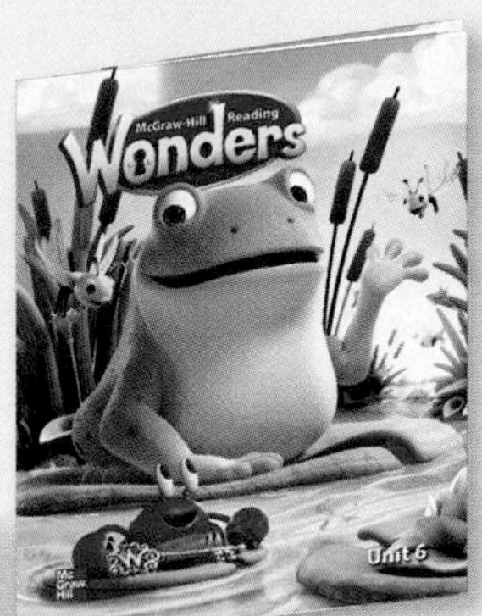

Voice, p. 32

Nouns, p. 33

Reading/Writing Workshop

Interactive Whiteboard

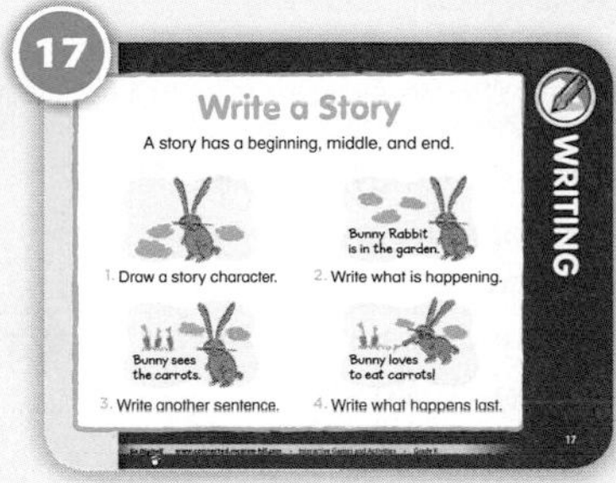

Leveled Workstation Card
Write a Story, Card 17

Grammar and Spelling/Dictation

Grammar
Naming Words (Nouns), T101

Spelling/Dictation
Words with *k, ck* and *m, p, s, t, a, e, i, o*, T129, T139

Interactive Whiteboard

Teacher's Edition

Online Grammar Games

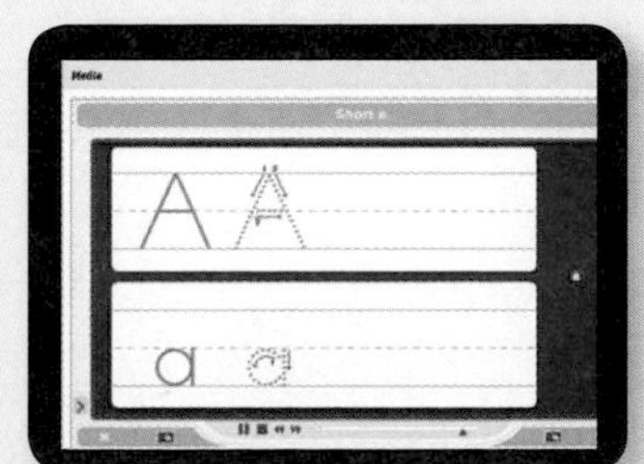

Handwriting

SUGGESTED LESSON PLAN

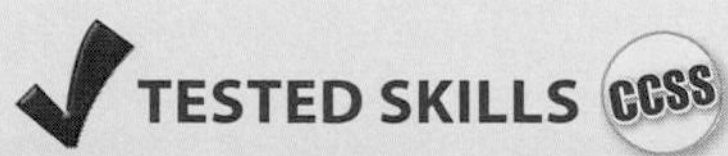

		DAY 1	DAY 2
Whole Group	**READING**		
	Teach and Model Literature Big Book Reading/Writing Workshop	**Build Background** What's the Weather? T92 **Oral Vocabulary Words** predict, temperature, T92 ✓ **Listening Comprehension** • Genre: Fantasy • Strategy: Visualize, T95 **Big Book** *Rain* ✓ **Word Work** **Phonemic Awareness** • Phoneme Isolation, T96 **Phonics** • Introduce /k/*k*, T97 **Handwriting** Kk, T98 **High-Frequency Words** she, was, T99 **Practice** *Your Turn* 163–166	**Oral Language** What's the Weather? T102 ✓ **Category Words** Weather Words, T103 ✓ **Listening Comprehension** • Genre: Fantasy • Strategy: Visualize, T104 • Skill: Key Details: Sequence • Guided Retelling, T109 • Model Fluency, T109 **Big Book** *Rain* ✓ **Word Work** **Phonemic Awareness** • Phoneme Blending, T110 **Phonics** • Review /k/*k*, T110 **High-Frequency Words** she, was, T111 **Shared Reading** "Kim and Nan," T112–T113 **Practice** *Your Turn* 167
Small Group	**DIFFERENTIATED INSTRUCTION** Choose across the week to meet your student's needs.		
	Approaching Level 	**Leveled Reader** *The Rain,* T142–T143 **Phonological Awareness** Recognize Rhyme, T144 TIER 2 **Phonics** Sound-Spelling Review, T146 TIER 2 **High-Frequency Words** Reteach Words, T148 TIER 2	**Leveled Reader** *The Rain,* T142–T143 **Phonemic Awareness** Phoneme Isolation, T144 TIER 2 **Phonics** Connect *k* and *ck* to /k/, T146 TIER 2 **High-Frequency Words** Cumulative Review, T148
	On Level 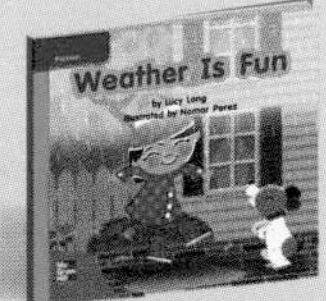	**Leveled Reader** *Weather Is Fun,* T150–T151 **Phonemic Awareness** Phoneme Isolation, T152	**Leveled Reader** *Weather Is Fun,* T150–T151 **Phoneme Awareness** Phoneme Blending, T152 **Phonics** Review Phonics, T153 Picture Sort, T153 **High-Frequency Words** Review Words, T155
	Beyond Level 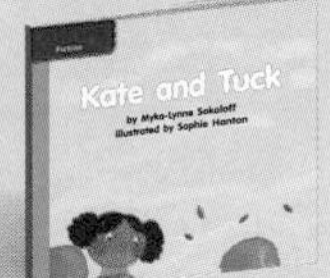	**Leveled Reader** *Kate and Tuck,* T156–T157 **Phonics** Review, T158	**Leveled Reader** *Kate and Tuck,* T156–T157 **High-Frequency Words** Review, T158
	English Language Learners 	**Leveled Reader** *Weather Is Fun,* T160–T161 **Phonological Awareness** Recognize Rhyme, T144 TIER 2 **Phonics** Sound-Spelling Review, T146 TIER 2 **Vocabulary** Preteach Oral Vocabulary, T162 **Writing** Shared Writing, T164	**Leveled Reader** *Weather Is Fun,* T160–T161 **Phonemic Awareness** Phoneme Isolation, T144 TIER 2 **Phonics** Connect *k* and *ck* to /k/, T146 TIER 2 **High-Frequency Words** Cumulative Review, T148 **Vocabulary** Preteach ELL Vocabulary, T162
Whole Group	**LANGUAGE ARTS**		
	Writing and Grammar	**Shared Writing** Writing Trait: Voice, T100 Write a Personal Narrative, T100 **Grammar** Naming Words (Nouns), T101	**Interactive Writing** Writing Trait: Voice, T114 Write a Personal Narrative, T114 **Grammar** Naming Words (Nouns), T115

Nathan Love

Go Digital

CUSTOMIZE YOUR OWN LESSON PLAN

www.connected.mcgraw-hill.com

WEEK 2

DAY 3	DAY 4	DAY 5 Review and Assess
READING		
Oral Language What's the Weather? T116 **Oral Vocabulary** drought, clever, storm, T116 ✓**Listening Comprehension** • Genre: Folktale • Strategy: Visualize, T117 • Make Connections, T117 **Interactive Read Aloud** "The Frog and the Locust," T117 ✓**Word Work** **Phonemic Awareness** • Phoneme Blending, T118 **Phonics** • Blend Words with *k*, *ck* and *i*, *l*, *o*, *r*, T119 • Picture Sort, T120 **High-Frequency Words** she, was, T121 **Practice** *Your Turn* 168–170	**Oral Language** What's the Weather? T124 ✓**Category Words** Weather Words, T125 ✓**Listening Comprehension** • Genre: Informational Text • Strategy: Visualize, T126 • Text Feature: Speech Bubbles, T126 • Make Connections, T127 **Big Book** Paired Read: "Cloud Watch," T126 ✓**Word Work** **Phonemic Awareness** • Phoneme Segmentation, T128 **Phonics** • Blend Words with *k*, *ck* and *a*, *i*, *m*, *p*, *s*, *t*, T128 **High-Frequency Words** she, was T129 **Shared Reading** "Kim and Nan," T130–T131 **Integrate Idea** Research and Inquiry, T134–T135 **Practice** *Your Turn* 171	**Integrate Ideas** • Text Connections, T136 • Talk About Reading, T137 • Research and Inquiry, T137 ✓**Word Work** **Phonemic Awareness** Phoneme Segmentation, T138 **Phonics** • Read Words with *k*, *ck* and *a*, *e*, *i*, *o*, T138 **High-Frequency Words** she, was T139 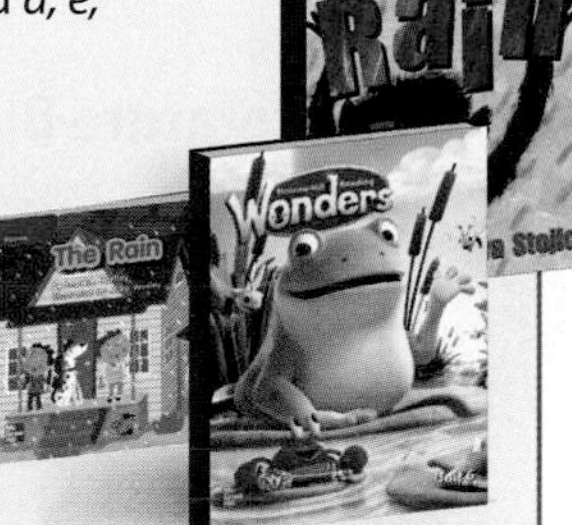 **Practice** *Your Turn* 172
DIFFERENTIATED INSTRUCTION		
Leveled Reader *The Rain*, T142–T143 **Phonemic Awareness** Phoneme Blending, T145 **Phonics** Reteach /k/*k*, T146 **High-Frequency Words** Reteach Words, T148	**Leveled Reader** *The Rain*, T142–T143 **Phonemic Awareness** Phoneme Segmentation, T145 **Phonics** Blend Words with /k/*k*, T147 **Oral Vocabulary** Review Words, T149	**Leveled Reader** Literacy Activities, T143 **Phonemic Awareness** Phoneme Segmentation, T145 **Phonics** Reread for Fluency, T147 Build Fluency with Phonics, T147 **Comprehension** Self-Selected Reading, T149
Leveled Reader *Weather Is Fun*, T150–T151 **Phonemic Awareness** Phoneme Segmentation, T152 **Phonics** Blend Words with /k/*k*, T154	**Leveled Reader** *Weather Is Fun*, T150–T151 **Phonics** Blend Words with /k/*k*, T154 Reread for Fluency, T154	**Leveled Reader** Literacy Activities, T151 **Comprehension** Self-Selected Reading, T155
Leveled Reader *Kate and Tuck*, T156–T157 **Vocabulary** Oral Vocabulary: Synonyms, T159  Gifted and Talented	**Leveled Reader** *Kate and Tuck*, T156–T157 **Phonics** Innovate, T158	**Leveled Reader** Literacy Activities, T157 **Comprehension** Self-Selected Reading, T159 Gifted and Talented
Leveled Reader *Weather Is Fun*, T160–T161 **Phonemic Awareness** Phoneme Blending, T145 **Phonics** Reteach /k/*k*, T146 **High-Frequency Words** Review Words, T163 **Writing** Writing Trait: Voice, T164	**Leveled Reader** *Weather Is Fun*, T160–T161 **Phonemic Awareness** Phoneme Segmentation, T145 **Phonics** Blend Words with /k/*k*, T147 **Vocabulary** Review Category Words, T163 **Grammar** Nouns, T165	**Leveled Reader** Literacy Activities, T161 **Phonemic Awareness** Phoneme Segmentation, T145 **Phonics** Reread for Fluency, T147 Build Fluency with Phonics, T147
LANGUAGE ARTS		
Independent Writing Writing Trait: Voice, T122 Write a Personal Narrative Prewrite/Draft, T123 **Grammar** Naming Words (Nouns), T123	**Independent Writing** Writing Trait: Voice, T132 Write a Personal Narrative Revise/Final Draft, T132 **Grammar** Naming Words (Nouns), T133	**Independent Writing** Write a Personal Narrative Prepare/Present/Evaluate/Publish, T140 **Grammar** Naming Words (Nouns), T141

DIFFERENTIATE TO ACCELERATE

ACT Scaffold to Access Complex Text

TEXT COMPLEXITY

IF the text complexity of a particular section is too difficult for children

THEN see the references noted in the chart below for scaffolded instruction to help children Access Complex Text.

	Literature Big Book	Reading/Writing Workshop	Leveled Readers

Quantitative	*Rain* **Lexile** 400 Paired Selection: "Cloud Watch" **Lexile** 270	"Kim and Nan" **Lexile** 120	**Approaching Level** **Lexile** BR **On Level** **Lexile** BR **Beyond Level** **Lexile** 280 **ELL** **Lexile** BR
Qualitative	What Makes the Text Complex? • **Lack of Prior Knowledge** Unfamiliar Setting, T104 ACT *See Scaffolded Instruction in Teacher's Edition, T104.*	What Makes the Text Complex? **Foundational Skills** • Decoding with *k*, T110–T111 • Identifying high-frequency words, T111	What Makes the Text Complex? **Foundational Skills** • Decoding with *k* • Identifying high-frequency words *she, was* *See Level Up lessons online for Leveled Readers.*
Reader and Task	The Introduce the Concept lesson on pages T92–T93 will help determine the reader's knowledge and engagement in the weekly concept. See pages T94–T95, T105–T109, T126–T127 and T134–T137 for questions and tasks for this text.	The Introduce the Concept lesson on pages T92–T93 will help determine the reader's knowledge and engagement in the weekly concept. See pages T112–T113, T130–T131 and T134–T137 for questions and tasks for this text.	The Introduce the Concept lesson on pages T92–T93 will help determine the reader's knowledge and engagement in the weekly concept. See pages T142–T143, T150–T151, T156–T157, T160–T161 and T134–T137 for questions and tasks for this text.

BR = Epitome of a beginning reader

WEEK 2

Monitor and *Differentiate*

IF you need to differentiate instruction

THEN use the Quick Checks to assess children's needs and select the appropriate small group instruction focus.

Comprehension Strategy Visualize, T117

Phonemic Awareness/Phonics /k/*k* (initial), /k/*ck* (final), T99, T111, T121, T129, T139

High-Frequency Words *she, was,* T99, T111, T121, T129, T139

If No → **Approaching** **Reteach,** pp. T142–T149

ELL **Develop,** pp. T160–T165

If Yes → **On Level** **Review,** pp. T150–T155

Beyond Level **Extend,** pp. T156–T159

Level Up with Leveled Readers

IF children can read their leveled text fluently and answer comprehension questions

THEN work with the next level up to accelerate children's reading with more complex text.

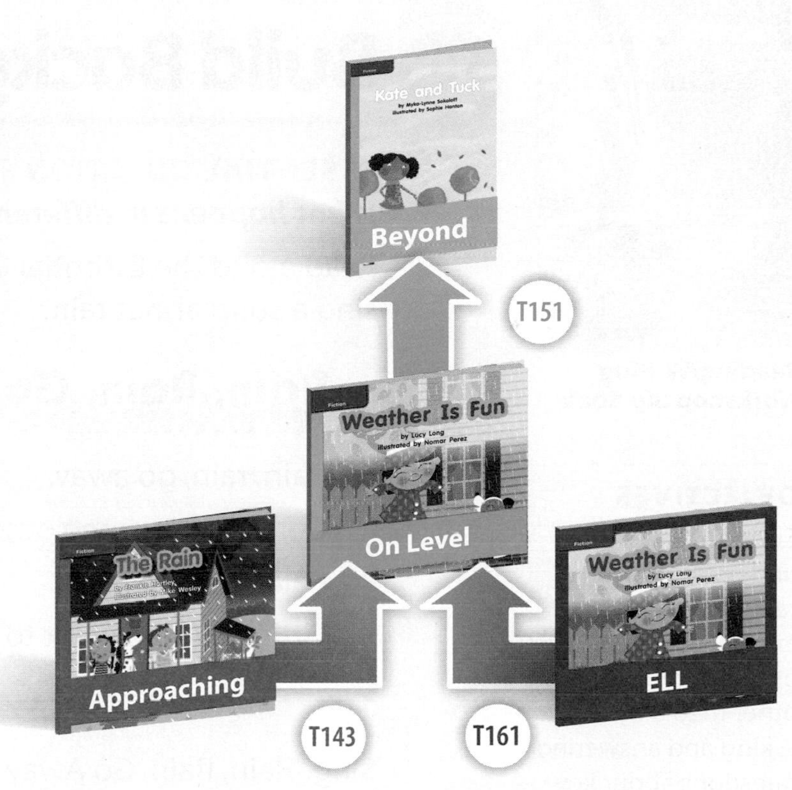

ENGLISH LANGUAGE LEARNERS SCAFFOLD

IF ELL students need additional support **THEN** scaffold instruction using the small group suggestions.

Reading-Writing Workshop	Leveled Reader	Phonological Awareness	Phonics	Oral Vocabulary	Writing	Grammar
Reading-Writing Workshop T93 "It's Raining Cats and Dogs!" **Integrate Ideas** T135	**Leveled Reader** T160–T161 *Weather Is Fun*	**Phonological Awareness** Recognize Rhyme, T144 Phoneme Isolation, T144 Phoneme Blending, T145 Phoneme Segmentation, T145	**Phonics,** /k/*k*, (initial) /k/ *ck*, (final), T146–T147	**Oral Vocabulary,** T162 predict, temperature, storm, clever, drought **High-Frequency Words,** T163 *she, was*	**Writing** Shared Writing, T164 Writing Trait: Voice, T164	**Grammar** T165 Nouns

Note: Include ELL Students in all small groups based on their needs.

WHOLE GROUP
DAY 1

Materials

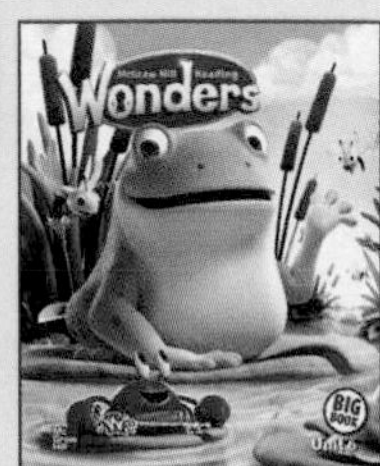
Reading/Writing Workshop Big Book
UNIT 6

Literature Big Book
Rain

Visual Vocabulary Cards
predict
temperature

"Rain, Rain, Go Away"
"Koala"

Response Board

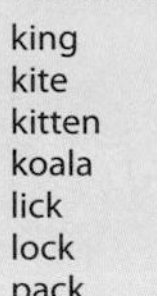
Photo Cards
king
kite
kitten
koala
lick
lock
pack
rock
sock

Sound-Spelling Card
Koala

High-Frequency Word Cards
she
was

Think Aloud Cloud

Introduce the Concept

MINILESSON 10 Mins

Build Background

Reading/Writing Workshop Big Book

OBJECTIVES

CCSS Confirm understanding of a text read aloud or information presented orally or through other media by asking and answering questions about key details and requesting clarification if something is not understood. **SL.K.2**

CCSS Identify real-life connections between words and their use. **L.K.5c**

ESSENTIAL QUESTION

What happens in different kinds of weather?

Read aloud the Essential Question. Tell children that you are going to sing a song about rain.

Rain, Rain, Go Away

Rain, rain, go away.
Come again some other day.
Rain, rain, go away.
Little children want to play.

Sing "Rain, Rain, Go Away" with children.

Ask children which type of weather the song is telling about. (rain) Tell children that this week they will read to learn about weather and how it affects people and places.

Oral Vocabulary Words

Use the **Define/Example/Ask** routine to introduce the oral vocabulary words **predict** and **temperature**.

To introduce the theme "What's the Weather?" explain that weather changes each day and throughout the year. Ask children what they wear to school in different kinds of weather.

Go Digital

"What's the Weather?"

Video

Visual Glossary

Visual Vocabulary Cards

Oral Vocabulary Routine

Define: To **predict** is to guess what will happen in the future.

Example: I predict that you will enjoy that book.

Ask: Who do you predict will win the race?

Define: The **temperature** tells how hot or cold something is.

Example: The outside temperature today is around 70 degrees.

Ask: Do you like warmer or colder temperatures? Why?

Talk About It: What's the Weather?

COLLABORATE

Discuss how different kinds of weather. Ask children what activities you can do in different weather. List their responses. Display pages 20–21 of the **Reading/Writing Workshop** and have children do the **Talk About It** activity with a partner.

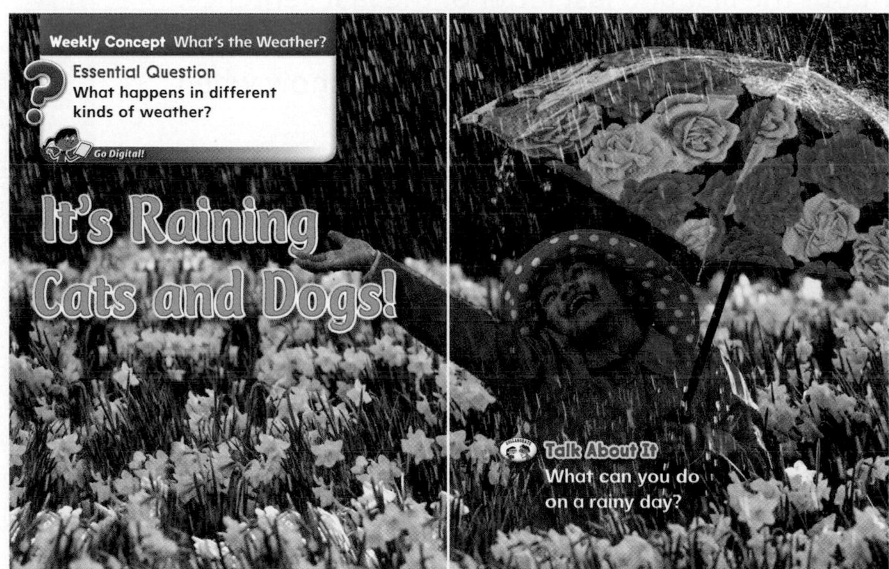

READING/WRITING WORKSHOP BIG BOOK, pp. 20–21

Collaborative Conversations

Be Open to All Ideas As children engage in partner, small group, and whole group discussions, tell them

- That all ideas, questions, or comments are important.
- To ask questions if something is unclear.
- To respect the opinions of others.
- To give their opinions, even if they are different from others'.

ENGLISH LANGUAGE LEARNERS SCAFFOLD

Beginning

Comprehend Point to the umbrella in the picture. Say *umbrella* and have children echo. Explain that people can use umbrellas to stay dry in the rain. Ask: *Does this picture show nice weather?* (no) Allow children ample time to respond.

Intermediate

Describe Explain what is happening in the picture. Ask: *How would being out in the rain make you feel?* Restate children's responses in order to develop their oral language proficiency.

Advanced/Advanced High

Expand Have children describe the picture. Ask them how the girl feels to be in the rain. *Why is rain important?* (water helps plants to grow) Model correct pronunciation as needed.

Listening Comprehension

Literature Big Book

OBJECTIVES

CCSS With prompting and support, name the author and illustrator of a story and define the role of each in telling the story. **RL.K.6**

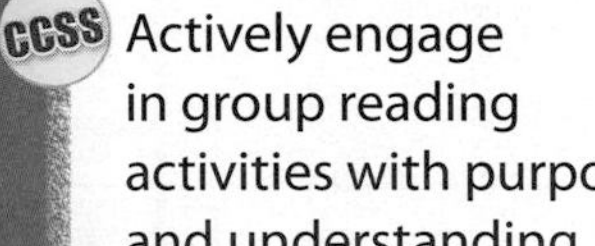

CCSS Actively engage in group reading activities with purpose and understanding. **RL.K.10**

ACADEMIC LANGUAGE

sentences, letters

Read the Literature Big Book

Connect to Concept: What's the Weather?

Tell children that you will now read about the rainy season in a part of Africa. *What is the weather like today?*

Concepts of Print

Sentences and Quotation Marks Display page 6 of the **Big Book**. Tell children that sentences are complete thoughts. Read aloud the sentences. Then point out the first and last letter of the first sentence. Explain to children that the next sentences tell what the porcupine says. Point out the quotation marks and explain that they show when a character is talking.

Genre: Fantasy

Model *Rain* is fantasy. Remind children that fantasy stories are made up. Share these characteristics of fantasy:

- Fantasy stories have characters, people, or animals who aren't real.
- Some events in fantasy, such as animals talking, could never happen in real life.

Story Words Preview these words before reading:
cracked: broken
water hole: a pond where animals drink water

Set a Purpose for Reading

- Identify and read aloud the title and the name of the author.
- Remind children that the author writes the words of the story. Point out that for this story, the author also drew the pictures.
- Ask children to listen as you read aloud the Big Book so they can find out how the weather changes in the story.

Go Digital

Rain

Think Aloud Cloud

Strategy: Visualize

Model Tell children that they can use the words and pictures in a story to make pictures in their minds of what is happening.

Think Aloud As I read this book, I will pause every so often to imagine what is happening. I will picture the characters and events in my mind. This will help me to better understand what I'm reading.

Apply As you read, use the **Think Aloud Cloud** to model the strategy.

Think Aloud On pages 4–5, I read that the red soil is hot and dry. I can see the red soil and a bright, hot sun. I close my eyes and imagine this scene. The air feels hot. The ground feels dry, and I can see cracks in it. This helps me to better understand the setting of the story.

Respond to Reading

After reading, prompt children to share what they learned about the rainy season in parts of Africa. Discuss what pictures they made in their minds as they listened to the story. Then have children draw a picture of their favorite kind of weather. Help them to label their pictures.

Make Connections

Use *Rain* to discuss the ways animals and people are affected by the weather. Revisit the concept behind the Essential Question *What happens in different kinds of weather?* by paging through the **Big Book**.

Write About It Have children write about ways the rain affects the animals in the story.

ENGLISH LANGUAGE LEARNERS SCAFFOLD

Beginning

Comprehend Read aloud pages 4–5. Then say: *Close your eyes. Make a picture in your mind of an old loaf of bread. Is the bread dry?* (yes) *Is the bread hot?* (no) Clarify children's responses as needed and add details. For example, say: *Old bread gets dry but not hot. In this picture, everything is dry* ***and*** *hot.*

Intermediate

Describe Read aloud pages 4–5. Ask children to make a picture in their minds of this scene. Ask: *How would this weather make you feel?* (thirsty, tired) Model correct pronunciation as needed.

Advanced/Advanced High

Expand Read aloud pages 4–5. Have children tell you about a time when the weather around them was dry and hot. Ask them to picture in their minds what they did to cool off and tell the class. (Possible responses: I went swimming; I drank a cool drink.) Clarify children's responses by providing needed vocabulary.

Word Work

Quick Review

Review /b/, /l/: Ask children to tell the initial sound of the *ball* and *ladder* Photo Cards, and the ending sound of the *web* Photo Card.

Build Fluency: Sound-Spellings: Display the following **Word-Building Cards:** *b, e, f, h, l, r*. Have children say each sound. Repeat and vary the pace.

MINILESSON 5 Mins

Phonemic Awareness

OBJECTIVES

CCSS Isolate and pronounce the initial, medial vowel, and final sounds (phonemes) in words. **RF.K.2d**

CCSS Demonstrate basic knowledge of one-to-one letter-sound correspondences by producing the primary or many of the most frequent sounds for each consonant. **RF.K.3a**

Phoneme Isolation

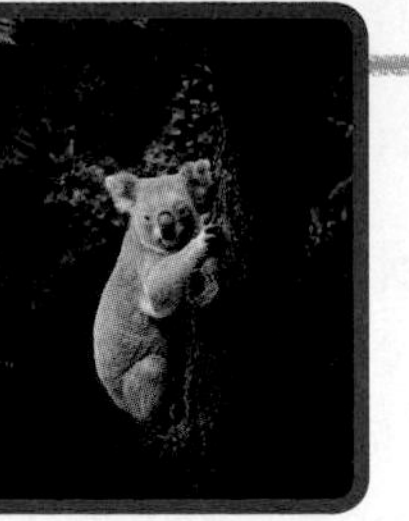

Photo Card

1 Model Display the **Photo Card** for *koala. Listen for the sound at the beginning of* koala. Koala *has the /k/ sound at the beginning. Say the sound with me: /k/.* Say *key, king, kite* and have children repeat. Emphasize initial /k/.

Repeat the instruction with final /k/. Use the *lock* Photo Card and the words *lick, pack*, and *rock*. Emphasize final /k/.

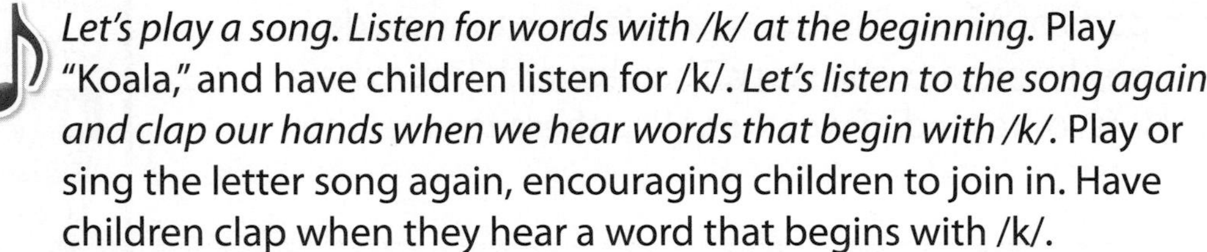

Let's play a song. Listen for words with /k/ at the beginning. Play "Koala," and have children listen for /k/. *Let's listen to the song again and clap our hands when we hear words that begin with /k/.* Play or sing the letter song again, encouraging children to join in. Have children clap when they hear a word that begins with /k/.

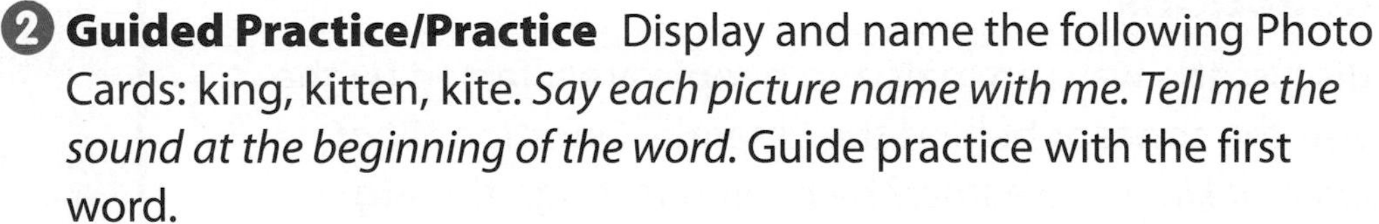

2 Guided Practice/Practice Display and name the following Photo Cards: king, kitten, kite. *Say each picture name with me. Tell me the sound at the beginning of the word.* Guide practice with the first word.

Repeat with words that end with the /k/ sound spelled *ck* and the *lock, sock, rock* Photo Cards.

ARTICULATION SUPPORT

Demonstrate the way to say /k/. Open your mouth. Put your tongue on the top of your mouth, toward the back. Let a puff of air out as you lower your tongue. Hold your hand up to your mouth. Do you feel the puff of air? Then have children say these words: *kangaroo, kid, key*. Emphasize initial /k/ when you say the word, then have them repeat.

Go Digital

Phonemic Awareness

Phonics

ENGLISH LANGUAGE LEARNERS

Pronunciation Display and have children name Photo Cards from this lesson to reinforce phonemic awareness and word meanings. Point to the *koala* Photo Card and ask: *What do you see? What is the sound at the beginning of the word* koala*? Repeat* using the *kitten, kite,* and *king* Photo Cards.

Phonics

Introduce /k/*k*

Sound-Spelling Card

1 Model Display the *Koala* **Sound-Spelling Card**. *This is the* Koala *card. The sound is /k/. The /k/ sound can be spelled with the letter* k. *Say it with me: /k/. This is the sound at the beginning of the word* koala. *Listen: /k/, /k/, /k/,* koala. *What is the name of this letter?* (k) *What sound does this letter stand for?* (/k/)

Repeat this instruction with the ending sound /k/ spelled *ck* using the *lock* **Photo Card**.

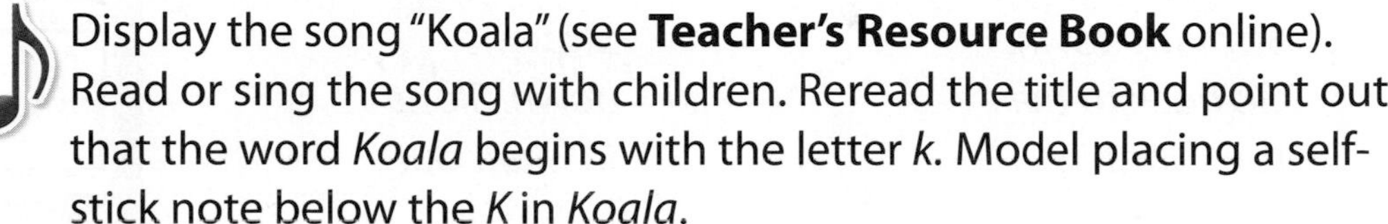

Display the song "Koala" (see **Teacher's Resource Book** online). Read or sing the song with children. Reread the title and point out that the word *Koala* begins with the letter *k*. Model placing a self-stick note below the *K* in *Koala*.

2 Guided Practice/Practice Read each line of the song. Stop after each line and ask children to place self-stick notes below words that begin with *K* or *k* and say the letter name.

Koala

Koala, koala, as happy as can be.
Koala, koala, won't you come and dance with me?
Koala, koala, sitting high up in the tree,
Koala, koala, munching eucalyptus leaves.

Corrective Feedback

Sound Error Model the sound /k/ in the initial position, then have children repeat the sound. *My turn. Key /k/ /k/ /k/. Now it's your turn.* Have children say the words *kit* and *kiss* and isolate the initial sound. Repeat for words that end with /k/ spelled *ck,* such as *back* and *sick*.

ENGLISH LANGUAGE LEARNERS

Phonemic Awareness: Variations in Languages Speakers of Hmong may have difficulty perceiving and pronouncing /k/. Focus on articulation. Make the /k/ sound and point out your mouth position. Have children repeat. Use the articulation photos.

Quick Check: Can children identify initial and final sound /k/?

YOUR TURN PRACTICE BOOK pp. 163–166

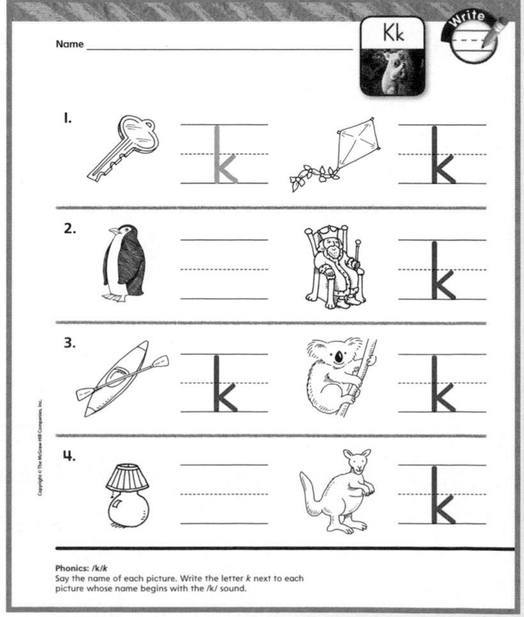
Name

Kk

Write

1. k k
2. k
3. k k
4. k

Phonics: /k/k
Say the name of each picture. Write the letter *k* next to each picture whose name begins with the /k/ sound.

Word Work

MINILESSON 5 Mins

Handwriting: Write *Kk*

OBJECTIVES

CCSS Write a letter or letters for most consonant and short-vowel sounds. **L.K.2c**

CCSS Demonstrate basic knowledge of one-to-one letter-sound correspondences by producing the primary or many of the most frequent sounds for each consonant. **RF.K.3a**

CCSS Read common high-frequency words by sight. **RF.K.3c**

ACADEMIC LANGUAGE
uppercase, lowercase

1 Model Say the handwriting cues below as you write and then identify the uppercase and lowercase forms of *Kk*. Then trace the letters on the board and in the air as you say /k/.

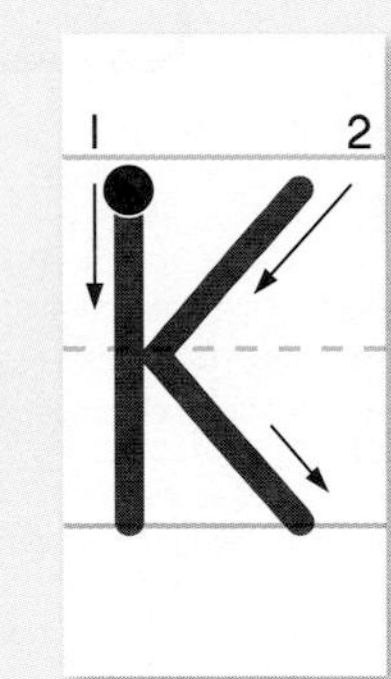

Straight down. Go back to the top. Slant in, slant out.

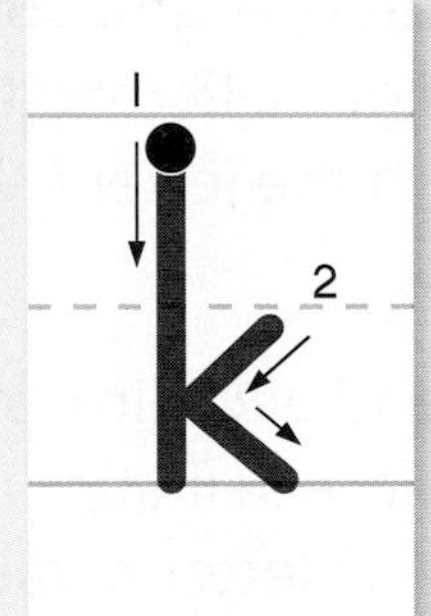

Straight down. Slant in, slant out.

2 Guided Practice/Practice

- Say the cues together as children trace the letter with their index finger. Have them identify the uppercase and lowercase forms of the letter.
- Have children write *K* and *k* in the air as they say /k/ multiple times.
- Distribute **Response Boards** or paper. Observe children's pencil grip and paper position, and correct as necessary. Have children say /k/ every time they write the letter *Kk*.

Repeat steps 1–2 to review writing *c*. Then have children spell and write *ck*.

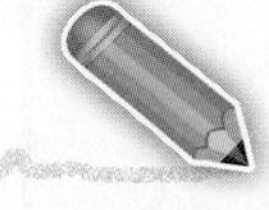

Daily Handwriting

Throughout the week teach uppercase and lowercase letters *Kk* using the Handwriting models. At the end of the week, have children use **Your Turn Practice Book** page 172 to practice handwriting.

Go Digital

Handwriting

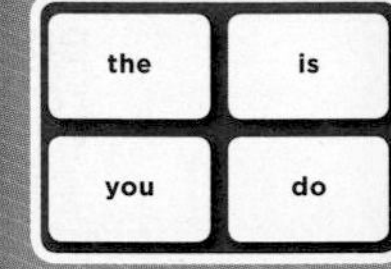

High-Frequency Word Routine

High-Frequency Words

she, was

High-Frequency Word Cards

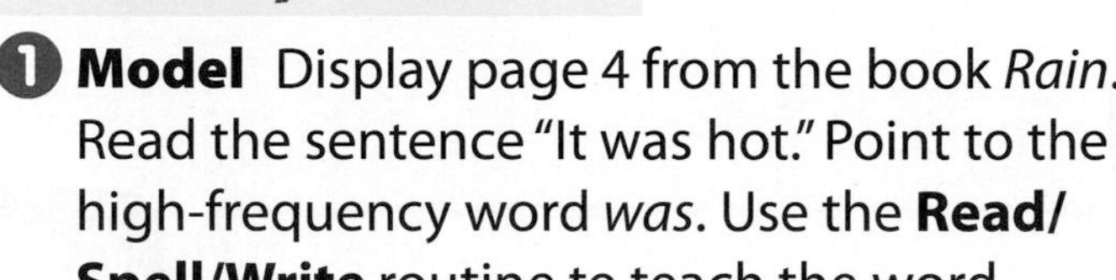

❶ **Model** Display page 4 from the book *Rain*. Read the sentence "It was hot." Point to the high-frequency word *was*. Use the **Read/Spell/Write** routine to teach the word.

→ **Read** Point to the word *was* and say the word. *This is the word* was. *Say it with me:* was. I was happy.

→ **Spell** *The word* was *is spelled* w-a-s. *Spell it with me.*

→ **Write** *Let's write the word in the air as we say each letter:* w-a-s.

→ Point out that the letter *a* in *was* has a different sound from the /a/ sound in *nap*. Let children know that the letter *s* has a /z/ sound as in *is*.

→ Have partners create sentences using the word.

Display page 6 from *Rain* and read aloud the sentence "'It's time,' she whispered." Point to the high-frequency word *she*. Use the **Read/Spell/Write** routine to teach the word. Point out that the letter *e* has a different sound from the /e/ sound in *pet*.

❷ **Guided Practice/Practice** Build sentences using **High-Frequency Word Cards**, **Photo Cards**, and teacher-made punctuation cards. Have children point to the high-frequency words *she* and *was*. Use these sentences.

She can go to the farm.

Was she with the baby?

She was the little girl.

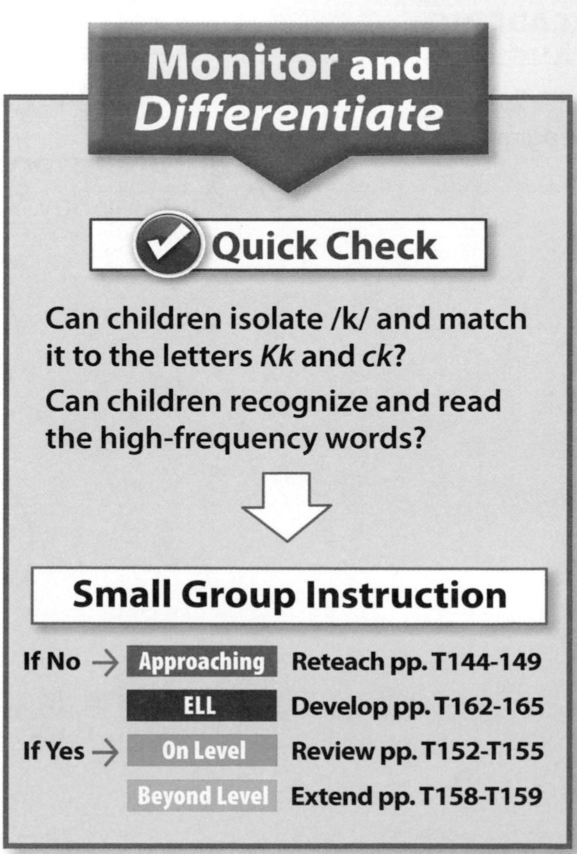

Monitor and *Differentiate*

Quick Check

Can children isolate /k/ and match it to the letters *Kk* and *ck*?

Can children recognize and read the high-frequency words?

Small Group Instruction

If No →	Approaching	Reteach pp. T144-149
	ELL	Develop pp. T162-165
If Yes →	On Level	Review pp. T152-T155
	Beyond Level	Extend pp. T158-T159

Language Arts

Shared Writing

OBJECTIVES

 With guidance and support from adults, recall information from experiences or gather information from provided sources to answer a question. **W.K.8**

 Form regular plural nouns orally by adding /s/ or /es/ (e.g., *dog, dogs; wish, wishes*). **L.K.1c**

Write narrative sentences

ACADEMIC LANGUAGE

- *noun, plural*
- Cognates: *plural*

Writing Trait: Voice

1 Model Tell children that authors can show how they feel about a topic with the words they choose. Readers can understand an author's feelings by reading their writing and listening to the tone of their words. Writers use their voice to show their feelings about a topic. This gets readers involved and excited.

2 Guided Practice/Practice Reread the **Big Book** to children and ask: *How does the author feel about the rain? Does the author think the rain is a good thing or a bad thing? How do you know?* (Possible response: The author feels the rain is a good thing. It is important to the animals and the land. I know this because the author writes that land is very dry and uses dialogue to show that the animals are very excited about the coming rain.)

Write a Personal Narrative

Focus and Plan Tell children that this week they will write about what they like to do on a rainy day.

Brainstorm Ask children to tell each other what they can do on a rainy day. Write children's responses in a word web.

Write Model making sentences, using responses from the Web. Read aloud the sentences with children.

Go Digital

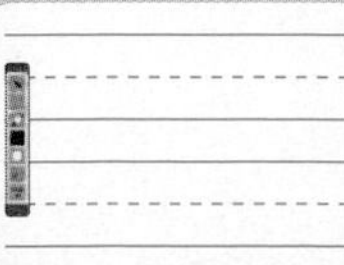
Writing

Grammar

Grammar

Naming Words (Nouns)

1 Model Remind children that nouns are naming words that tell the names of people, places, animals, and things. Read aloud sentences from the **Big Book**:

→ *The rain is coming! I must tell the zebras.*

Point out that *rain* and *zebras* are naming words. Also point out that *zebras* names more than one thing. It is a plural noun. Point to the letter *-s* at the end of *zebras*. Remind children that an *-s* at the end of many naming words means more than one thing.

2 Guided Practice/Practice Read the following sentences from the Big Book to practice identifying naming words.

→ *Lightning flashed.*

→ *We must tell the baboons.*

→ *Thunder boomed.*

→ *A raindrop splashed.*

Have children work with a partner. Ask them to find the naming words in each sentence. (lightning, baboons, thunder, raindrop) Then have them tell which naming word names more than one thing. (baboons) Tell children to point to the letter that shows that it names more than one baboon. (s) Have children track the print as they say *baboons*.

Talk About It

Distribute several **Photo Cards** to each pair of students. Have partners practice naming plural nouns by saying the word shown on the card, then making the word plural.

ENGLISH LANGUAGE LEARNERS SCAFFOLD

Beginning

Explain Review several of the Big Book pages with children. Work with them to identify pictures that show plural nouns. For each picture, locate the corresponding words on the page and read aloud with children. Restate children's responses to develop their oral language proficiency.

Intermediate

Practice Have children work in pairs to identify pictures of single and plural nouns in the Big Book. Guide them to locate the corresponding words on the page, pointing out the letter that indicates a plural noun. Allow children ample time to respond.

Advanced/Advanced High

Practice Have children work in pairs to identify pictures of single and plural nouns in the Big Book. Have them locate the corresponding words on the page and point out the letter that indicates a plural noun. Allow children ample time to respond.

Daily Wrap Up

- Review the Essential Question and encourage children to discuss it, using the new oral vocabulary words. *What happens in different kinds of weather?*
- Prompt children to share the skills they learned. How might they use those skills?

WHOLE GROUP
DAY 2

Materials

Reading/Writing Workshop Big Book
UNIT 6

Literature Big Book
Rain

Visual Vocabulary Cards
predict
temperature

Puppet

Sound-Spelling Card
Koala

Photo Card
cloud
koala
lightning
snow
sock
sun
umbrella

Response Board

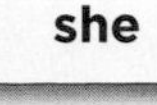

High-Frequency Word Cards
she
was

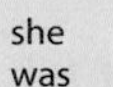

Word-Building Cards

"Rain, Rain, Go Away"

Retelling Cards

Build the Concept

MINILESSON 10 Mins

Oral Language

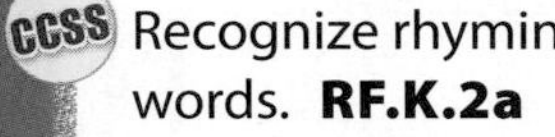

OBJECTIVES

CCSS Use words and phrases acquired through conversation. **L.K.6**

CCSS Recognize rhyming words. **RF.K.2a**

CCSS Identify real-life connections between words and their use (e.g., note places at school that are *colorful*). **L.K.5c**

Develop oral vocabulary

ACADEMIC LANGUAGE

- *rhyme*
- Cognates: *rima*

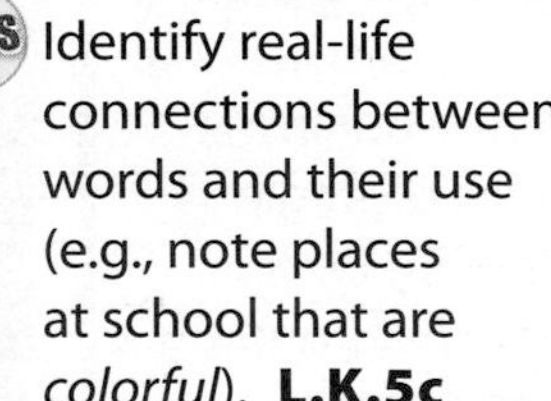

ESSENTIAL QUESTION

What happens in different kinds of weather?

Remind children that this week they are learning about weather and how it can affect people and places. Point out that some types of weather repeat year after year, such as the rainy season in parts of Africa. Ask children to describe the weather outside today.

Sing with children "Rain, Rain, Go Away."

Phonological Awareness

Recognize Rhyme

Tell children that the words *away* and *day* in this song rhyme. Remind them that words that rhyme have the same ending sounds. Say the following word pairs and have children tell if the words rhyme: *car, far; joy, toy; rain, pan; go, slow; want, sing; day, door; up, cup.*

Review Oral Vocabulary

Use the **Define/Example/Ask** routine to review the oral vocabulary words **predict** and **temperature.** Prompt children to use the words in sentences.

Visual Vocabulary Cards

Go Digital

Visual Glossary

Category Words

Category Words: Weather Words

1 Model Use the **Big Book** *Rain* to point out weather words: *hot,* page 4; *rain,* page 6; *lightning,* page 8; *thunder,* page 10; and *cool,* page 22. Explain that these words describe the weather. *Which word tells about the weather?* (rainy) *What is it like outside when it rains?* (wet) Repeat using other weather words from the book.

Recite the nursery rhyme "Rain, Rain, Go Away." Then ask children to identify the weather word.

Rain, rain, go away.
Come again some other day.
Little children want to play.

→ Discuss other kinds of weather that might make it hard to play outside, such as *windy, snowy,* and *gloomy.*

2 Guided Practice/Practice Write the weather words *rainy, cloudy, windy, snowy, gloomy,* and *sunny*. Say each word. Have children draw a picture to illustrate a weather word. Help children label their pictures with appropriate weather words.

Vocabulary Strategy: Shades of Meaning

1 Model Explain to children that similar words and phrases that show action can have small differences in meaning. Use *Rain* to model how to identify the shades of meaning between verbs.

Think Aloud In *Rain,* the word *whispered* is in this sentence: *"It's time," she whispered.* The word *whispered* is one way to say something. The word *said* is another way: *"The rain is coming!" said the zebras.* Both *whispered* and *said* are words that describe ways to communicate.

2 Guided Practice Work with children to find more examples of words that show how to say something.

"The rain is coming!" ***cried*** *the baboons.*
"We can't hear the rain now," ***shouted*** *the baboons, "but we can eat fresh, juicy fruit from the trees."*

3 Practice Have children find more examples of action words that tell how to say something. (sighed, purred) Ask them to act out the words *whispered, said, cried, shouted, sighed, purred.* Discuss how similar words can describe the same action.

ENGLISH LANGUAGE LEARNERS

Discuss Display **Photo Cards** for *cloud, lightning, snow, sun,* and *umbrella.* Help children identify the weather that is associated with each photograph. Then ask: *What different kinds of clouds have you seen? What is the weather like on a cloudy day?*

LET'S MOVE!

Demonstrate actions to go with different weather words, such as opening an umbrella for *rainy,* shoveling snow for *snowy,* and putting on sunglasses for *sunny*. Call out different weather words and have children act out the appropriate action.

Listening Comprehension

Literature Big Book

OBJECTIVES

CCSS With prompting and support, ask and answer questions about key details in a text. **RL.K.1**

CCSS With prompting and support, retell familiar stories, including key details. **RL.K.2**

- Strategy: Visualize
- Skill: Key Details: Sequence

ACADEMIC LANGUAGE

- *sequence*
- Cognates: *secuencia*

MINILESSON 15 Mins

Reread Literature Big Book

Genre: Fantasy

Display *Rain*. Remind children that fantasy stories are made up by the authors. They also contain events that could never happen in real life, such as animals talking. *What makes* Rain *fantasy?* (The animals talk.) Have children point to evidence in the text and the pictures to show that the story is fantasy.

Strategy: Visualize

Remind children that good readers use the words and pictures in a story to make pictures in their minds. *As we reread, you can make pictures in your mind of how the weather is changing in the story.*

Skill: Key Details: Sequence

Remind children that the events in fiction and fantasy are usually told in a certain order, or sequence. *We can talk about the order of events by using words such as first, then, next, and last.* Model using these words with pages 18–19 of *Rain. First, it rained. Next, the rain stopped. Then, the grasses and leaves grew.* Have children listen for evidence in the text that tells about the sequence of the story. Use the prompts to fill out the graphic organizer.

Access Complex Text

Lack of Prior Knowledge This book tells about the rainy season in a part of Africa.

→ Explain that in some parts of the world, the land has a rainy season and a dry season. These periods can last a long time, and they can be difficult for humans and animals alike. Guide children to understand that this book tells how the animals live before, during, and after the rainy cycle.

Go Digital

Rain

Retelling Cards

PAGES 4–5

KEY DETAILS: SEQUENCE

Think Aloud On this page I read that it is hot and dry. This is the beginning of the story, so I will add this to my chart under "first."

PAGES 6–7

HIGH-FREQUENCY WORDS

Have children identify and read the high-frequency word *she*.

pp. 6–7

sniffed: When I sniffed the flowers, I smelled the flowers. Pantomime sniffing a flower. Ask children to pretend they are sniffing the air like the porcupine.

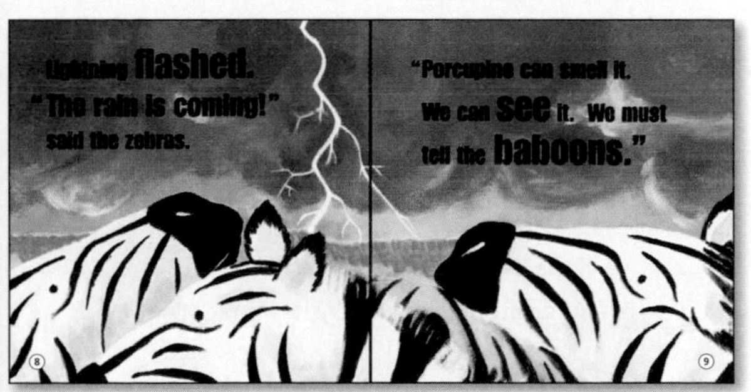

PAGES 8–9

VISUALIZE

Think Aloud I read that there is lightning and see a drawing of it. I can make a picture in my mind of lightning flashing brightly in the sky. This helps me to understand what is happening near the zebras.

pp. 8–9

baboons: Explain that baboons are a type of monkey. Ask children to share what they know about monkeys. (Possible answers: They have tails, have hands like humans, and live in jungles.)

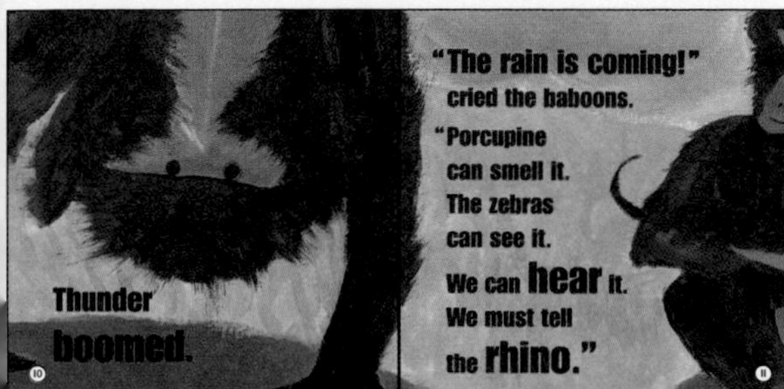

PAGES 10–11

KEY DETAILS: SEQUENCE

We just read that lightning flashed. What happened next in the weather? (Thunder boomed.)

pp. 10–11

boomed: When something booms, it makes a loud noise. Say *boomed,* emphasizing the sound. Have children echo.

Listening Comprehension

PAGES 12–13

CONCEPTS OF PRINT

Remind children that quotation marks begin and end the words a character says. Have children point out the quotation marks on these pages. Ask: *Who is speaking?* (the rhino)

pp. 12–13

splashed: When the raindrop hit the ground, it splashed. Make a fist and drop it toward the ground. When you reach the ground, spread out your fingers to mimic a raindrop splashing. Have children repeat the gesture with you as you chorally read the first sentence again.

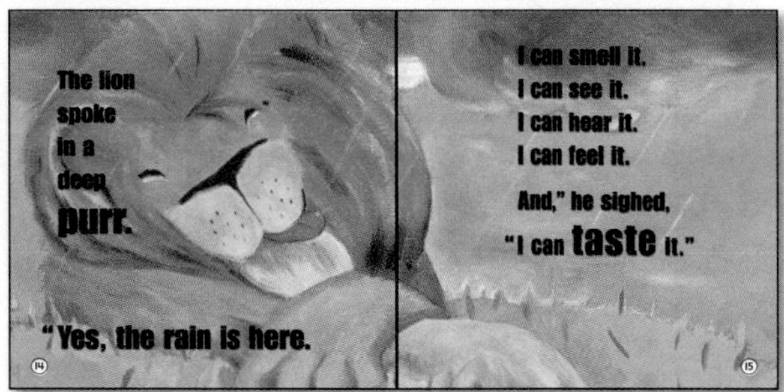

PAGES 14–15

KEY DETAILS: SEQUENCE

What is happening in the story now? (Possible answers: It is raining. The lion says he can taste the rain.) Add children's answers to the organizer.

pp. 14–15

purr: Tell children that cats purr, but *purr* can also mean speaking softly. Read aloud the lion's dialogue on pages 14–15 in a gentle way to show purring.

PAGES 16–17

VISUALIZE

Think Aloud I read before that the rain was just starting. Now I read that it rained and rained. I make a picture in my mind of a strong rainstorm. I see puddles filling. Rain is everywhere. This helps me to understand how the weather in the story changed.

pp. 16–17

gushed and gurgled: Tell children to picture a river that is flowing very fast. Explain that *gushed* and *gurgled* describe fast-moving water.

PAGES 18–19

KEY DETAILS: SEQUENCE

What happened after it stopped raining? (Grass grew; trees sprouted leaves.) *Let's add this to our sequence organizer.*

pp. 18–19

feathery: Show children a feather, or a picture of a feather. Explain that birds have feathers. *If something is feathery, it looks or feels like a feather.*

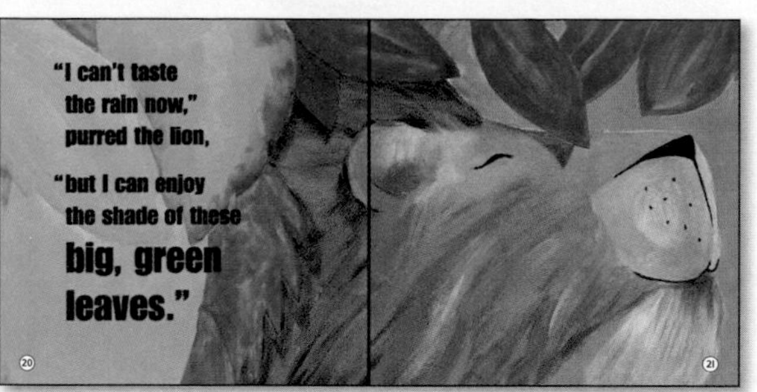

PAGES 20–21

CHARACTER

How does the lion feel after the rain stops? How do you know? (Possible answer: He is happy. He says that he enjoys the shade. He looks happy in the picture.)

pp. 20–21

shade: If the day is sunny, make a shadow by holding your hand over a table. Say: *The dark place under my hand is the shade. Trees make shade outside.*

PAGES 22–23

VISUALIZE

Think Aloud I read that the rhino is in the mud. The text says the mud is cool and soft. I make a picture in my mind of the rhino splashing in the cool mud. I know it used to be hot. This helps me understand that the rain made the rhino feel happy.

PAGES 24–25

KEY DETAILS: SEQUENCE

What do the baboons do after the rain stops? (They eat fruit from the trees.)

PAGES 26–27

CONCEPTS OF PRINT

Reread page 27. Have children identify and read the first and last words of the sentence. (We, hole) Help them recognize that a comma is not end punctuation, but a period is.

pp. 26–27

refreshing: Tell children that something refreshing makes you feel better. Say: *I think spending time with friends is refreshing.* Ask children what they think is refreshing.

Listening Comprehension

PAGES 28–29

SHADES OF MEANING

Help children understand differences between words. Point to *whispered* and whisper "I can't smell the rain now." Have children mimic. Then say the same sentence in a normal voice. Have children mimic. Have them tell how *whispered* and *said* are different.

PAGES 30–31

HIGH-FREQUENCY WORDS

Have children identify and read the high-frequency word *was*.

pp. 30–31

plain: Tell children that one meaning of *plain* is "flat land." Have them tell you a word that describes the opposite of a plain. (mountain, hill)

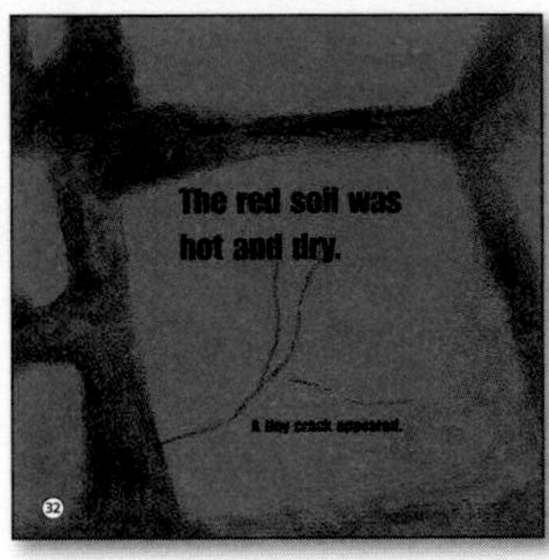

PAGE 32

KEY DETAILS: SEQUENCE

What happens at the end of the story? (It is dry and hot again.) *Let's add this to our organizer under "last."*

Text Evidence

Explain Remind children that when they answer a question they need to show where in the story (both words and pictures) they found the answer.

Discuss *How do you know that the weather has changed again at the end of the book?* (On page 32, the words say it got hot and dry again. The picture shows cracks in the soil.)

Key Details: Sequence

Review Skill Remind children that when they read fantasy stories, they can look for a sequence of events, or the order in which things happen. Discuss the order of events in *Rain* using the completed graphic organizer. Model using *first, next, then,* and *last.*

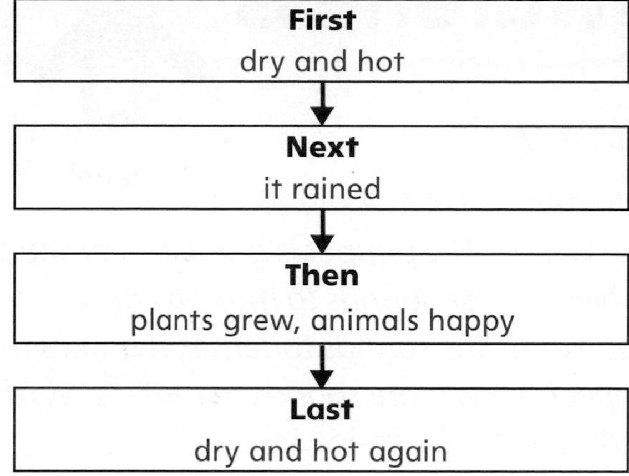

Guided Retelling

Tell children that they will use the **Retelling Cards** to retell the story.

→ Show Retelling Card 1. Based on children's needs, use the Modeled, Guided or ELL retelling prompts. The ELL prompts contain support for English language learners based on levels of language acquisition. Repeat with cards 2–4, using the prompts as a guide.

Model Fluency

Read page 29 of *Rain*. Explain that when you read what characters say, you try to speak as the character would. Point out the word *whispered*. Tell children this is a clue to how the porcupine sounds. Read the page, whispering, and have children repeat and mimic.

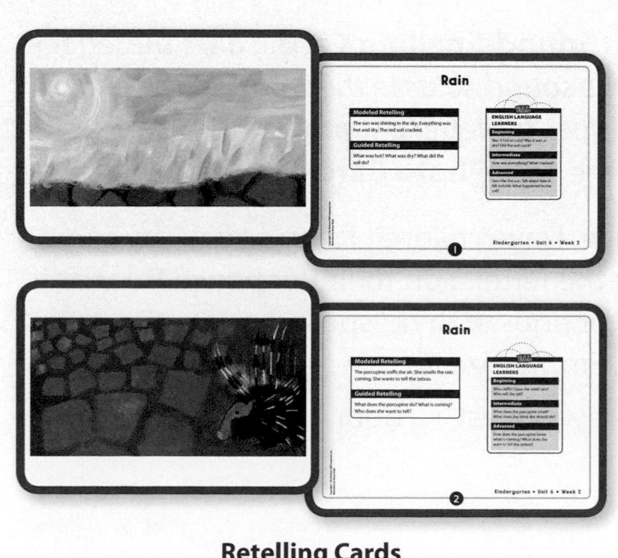

Retelling Cards

YOUR TURN PRACTICE BOOK p. 167

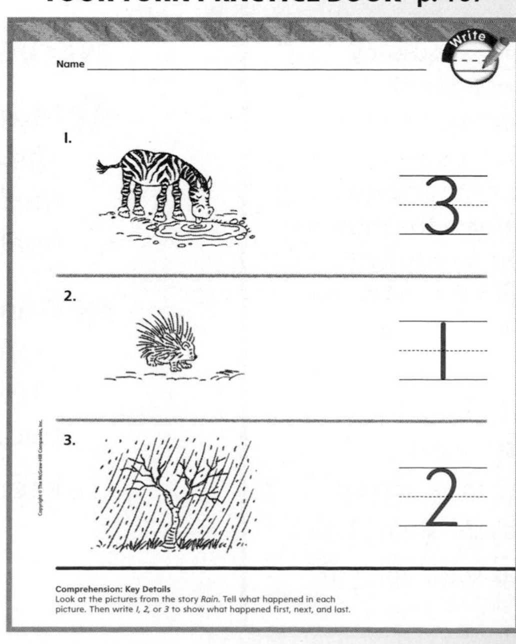

Word Work

Quick Review

Build Fluency: Sound-Spellings: Display the following **Word-Building Cards:** *b, e, f, g, k, l, r.* Have children say each sound. Repeat and vary the pace.

MINILESSON 5 Mins

Phonemic Awareness

Puppet

Phoneme Blending

1 Model Use the puppet to demonstrate how to blend phonemes to make words. *The puppet is going to say sounds in a word, /k/ /i/ /t/. It can blend those sounds to make a word: /kiiit/* kit. *When the puppet blends the sounds together, it makes the word* kit. *Listen as the puppet blends more sounds to make a word.* Continue modeling blending with the following:

/k/ /i/ /s/ /k/ /i/ /d/ /k/ /ē/ /p/

2 Guided Practice/Practice Tell children that the puppet is going to say the sounds in a word. *Listen to the puppet as it says each sound. You will repeat the sounds, then blend them to say the word.* Guide practice with the first word.

/k/ /i/ /k/ kick /k/ /ē/ key /k/ /e/ /n/ Ken /k/ /ī/ /t/ kite

Repeat instruction with words ending with /k/ spelled *ck,* such as *lock, sick,* and *pack.*

OBJECTIVES

CCSS Demonstrate basic knowledge of one-to-one letter-sound correspondences by producing the primary or many of the most frequent sounds for each consonant. **RF.K.3a**

CCSS Read common high-frequency words by sight. **RF.K.3c**

Blend phonemes to make words

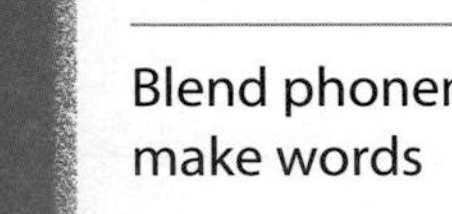

MINILESSON 5 Mins

Phonics

Review /k/*k*

1 Model Display the *Koala* **Sound-Spelling Card**. *This is the letter* k. *The letter* k *can stand for the sound /k/ as in the word* koala. *What is the letter?* (k) *What sound does the letter* k *stand for?* (/k/) Repeat for final /k/ spelled *ck* using the sock **Photo Card**.

2 Guided Practice/Practice Have children listen as you say some words. Ask them to write the letter *k* on their **Response Boards** if the word begins with /k/ or ends with /k/ spelled *ck.* Do the first two words with children. Emphasize /k/.

keep lock king key nest door kite sick

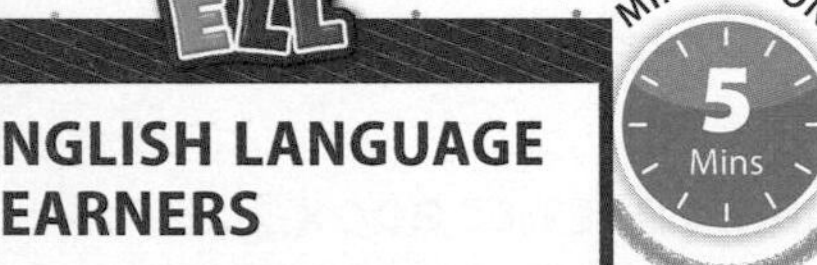

ELL

ENGLISH LANGUAGE LEARNERS

High-Frequency Words: Build Meaning Display the High-Frequency Word Cards *she* and *was.* Reinforce the meaning of the words by asking the following questions, pointing to a child, and having children respond.

- Is *she* a girl?
- Can *she* stand up?
- Was *she* sitting?
- Was *she* laughing?

Go Digital

Phonemic Awareness

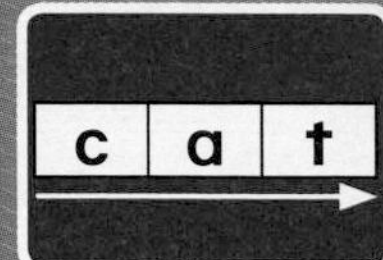

Phonics

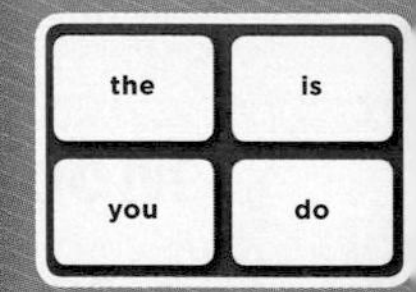

High-Frequency Word Routine

Handwriting

Blend Words with /k/*k* and /k/*ck*

1 Model Place **Word-Building Cards** *k, i, t* in a pocket chart. Point to the letter *k*. *This is the letter* k. *The letter* k *stands for /k/. Say /k/. This is the letter* i. *The letter* i *stands for /i/. Say /i/. This is the letter* t. *The letter* t *stands for /t/. Listen as I blend the sounds together: /kiiit/. Now blend the sounds with me to read the word.*

2 Guided Practice/Practice Change the Word-Building Cards to *kid*. Point to the letter *k* and have children say /k/. Point to the letter *i* and have children say /i/. Point to the letter *d* and have children say /d/. Then move your hand from left to right under the word and have children blend and read the word, *kid*. Repeat Steps 1–2 with these words from the *-ock* word family: *rock, sock, lock.*

High-Frequency Words

she, was

she

High-Frequency Word Cards

1 Guided Practice Display the **High-Frequency Word Cards** *she* and was. Use the **Read/Spell/Write** routine to teach the words. Ask children to close their eyes, picture the word in their minds, and then write it the way they see it. Have children self-correct by checking the High-Frequency Word Cards.

2 Practice Add the high-frequency words *she* and *was* to the cumulative word bank.

- Have partners create sentences using the words.
- Have children count the number of letters in each word and then write *she* and *was* again.

Cumulative Review Review *little, is, with, he, are, my, to, and, go, you, do.*

- Repeat the **Read/Spell/Write** routine. Mix the words and have children chorally say each one.

Monitor and *Differentiate*

Quick Check

Can children isolate /k/ and match it to the letters *Kk* and *ck*?

Can children read and recognize the high-frequency words?

Small Group Instruction

If No →	Approaching	Reteach pp. T144-149
	ELL	Develop pp. T162-165
If Yes →	On Level	Review pp. T152-155
	Beyond Level	Extend pp. T158-159

Shared Read

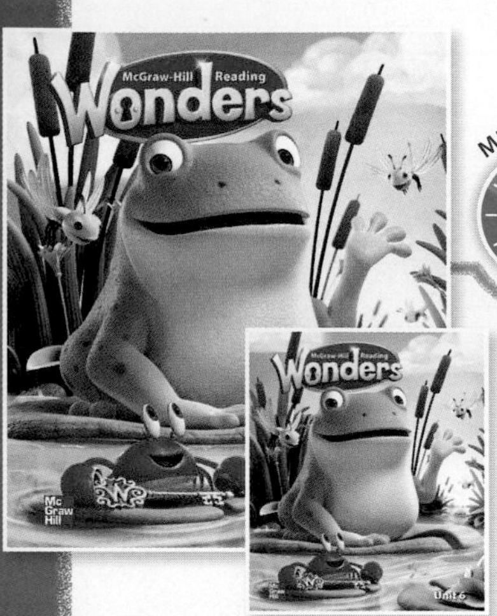

Reading/Writing Workshop Big Book and Reading/Writing Workshop

OBJECTIVES

CCSS Read common high-frequency words by sight. **RF.K.3c**

CCSS Read emergent-reader texts with purpose and understanding. **RF.K.4**

CCSS Recognize and name end punctuation. **L.K.2b**

ACADEMIC LANGUAGE

- *predict*
- Cognates: *predecir*

MINILESSON 10 Mins

Read "Kim and Nan"

Model Skills and Strategies

Model Concepts About Print Point out the punctuation in each sentence of the story. *As I read, I look for different kinds of punctuation, such as periods and exclamation points. For example, the second sentence on page 27 ends with an exclamation point. The exclamation point tells us to read the sentence with expression, or feeling.* Invite volunteers to take turns coming up to the **Big Book** and pointing to the punctuation in each sentence.

Predict Read the title together. Encourage children to describe the first illustration. Invite them to tell what the weather is like and what the little girl might do on this day.

Read Have children chorally read the story with you. Point to each word as you read it together. Help children sound out the decodable words and say the sight words. If children have difficulty, provide corrective feedback and guide them page by page using the student **Reading/Writing Workshop**.

Ask the following:

→ *Look at page 23. How might the weather change today? How can you tell?* (Possible answers: Although it is sunny, there are dark clouds starting to form. The grandmother has an umbrella. Kim has an umbrella in her backpack.)

→ *Look at page 27. How has the weather changed?* (It has become very windy.)

→ *Look at page 28. Why are Kim and her grandmother running home?* (It has started to rain.)

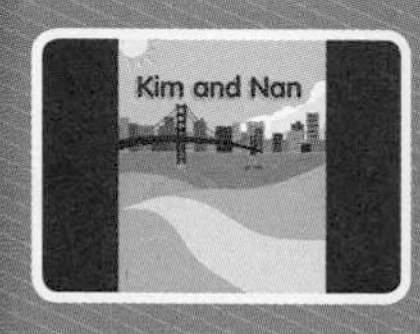

"Kim and Nan"

"Kim and Nan"

READING/WRITING WORKSHOP, pp. 22–29

Rereading

Have small groups use the **Reading/Writing Workshop** to reread "Kim and Nan." Then review the skills and strategies using the *Phonics* and *Words to Know* pages that come before the selection.

→ As they reread, have children visualize and describe what sunny, cloudy, and rainy days might be like. Then invite them to retell the story, providing key details and describing the sequence of events and the changing weather.

→ Have children use page 21 to review the high-frequency words *she* and *was*.

→ Have children use page 20 to review that the letters *k* and *ck* can stand for the sound /k/. Encourage them to identify and name each picture that includes the sound /k/ in the initial or final position. Guide them to blend the sounds to read the words.

ENGLISH LANGUAGE LEARNERS

Reinforce Vocabulary Display the **High-Frequency Word Cards** *she, was, see, like*. Point to classroom objects and different children as you use the high-frequency word in sentences, such as the following: *Is she standing by the clock?* (Yes, she is standing by the clock.) *Was yesterday Tuesday?* (Yes, yesterday was Tuesday.) *Do you see the flag?* (Yes, we see the flag.) *Do you like math or recess?* (We like recess!)

WHOLE GROUP
DAY 2

Language Arts

Interactive Writing

OBJECTIVES

Use a combination of drawing, dictating, and writing to narrate a single event or several loosely linked events, tell about the events in the order in which they occurred, and provide a reaction to what happened. **W.K.3**

Form regular plural nouns orally by adding /s/ or /es/ (e.g., *dog, dogs; wish, wishes*). **L.K.1c**

- Write narrative sentences
- Recognize nouns

ACADEMIC LANGUAGE

- *observations, noun, plural, narrative*
- Cognates: *observaciónes, narrativa, plural*

Writing Trait: Voice

Review Remind children that writers can show how they feel about things with the words they choose. This gets readers involved and excited. Write and read: *I read books on a rainy day. My favorite books make me feel like I am in the story. Sometimes I forget that I am at home!* Point out how your words help the reader understand how you feel about reading a book.

Write a Personal Narrative

Discuss Display the Word Web from Day 1. Read aloud each rainy-day activity. Guide children to pick details from the web to write a personal narrative.

Model/Apply Grammar Tell children that you will work together to write a personal narrative about what they do on rainy days. Write: *I ______ on a rainy day.*

Read the sentence together, tracking the print. *What do you like to do on a rainy day? What should we write about?* Model how to choose an activity to complete the sentence, such as *I do puzzles on a rainy day.*

Write Have children help you create more sentences for a narrative that tells what they do on a rainy day. Remind them to use *I* whenever they are talking about their personal experience. Guide them in forming sentences using other activities from the web or additional activities. Encourage children to include details that help readers know how they feel or what they observe. For example:

→ *I do puzzles inside. My dad makes hot chocolate. It is yummy!*

Point out that *It is yummy!* gives the reader more details about the way the writer feels about hot chocolate.

Write and read aloud each sentence that children create. Share the pen with children and have them write the letters they know.

Go Digital

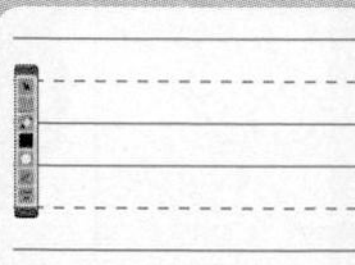
Writing

Grammar

Grammar

Naming Words (Nouns)

1 Review Remind children that we can add the ending *-s* or *-es* to the end of many naming words, or nouns, when we talk about more than one thing.

→ Write and read aloud: *Baboons eat fruit from the trees.*

Ask children which words are naming words. (baboons, fruit, trees) *Which word names an animal?* (Baboons) *Which words name things?* (fruit, trees) *How do we know that there is more than one baboon and more than one tree?* (Those words end in *-s*.)

2 Guided Practice Write and read aloud: *Long grasses grew.* Have children identify the naming word. (grasses) Have children tell if it names one thing or more than one thing. *How do you know that* grasses *names more than one thing?* (It had the ending *-es*.) Explain that *grasses* means there are different kinds that are growing. Ask children how to write the naming word if it named just one kind. (grass)

Write and read aloud:

→ *The buds grew on the branches.*

Have children pick out the naming words. (buds, branches) Write the naming words. Have children underline the *-s* or *-es* that tells them the naming words are plural. *How would you say the naming words if they named just one thing?* (bud, branch)

3 Practice Have children work in pairs. Write and read aloud:

→ *Marshes are wet lands where tall grasses grow.*

Have partners work together to decide on the naming words in the sentence. (marshes, lands, grasses) Then have them say the naming words if they named only one thing. Circulate and offer corrective feedback as needed.

Talk About It

Have partners think about the things they do on a rainy day. Ask them to say the plural form of the word, such as *game, games; puzzle, puzzles;* and *puddle/puddles.*

ENGLISH LANGUAGE LEARNERS

Use Visuals Look at pages in the **Big Book** that support plural words with the illustrations—the pages with baboons, zebras, and leaves. Point to *baboons, zebras,* and *leaves* and then to multiple items in the picture. Provide a sentence frame for children to orally complete using plural words: *I see many* ____. Allow children ample time to respond.

Daily Wrap Up

- Discuss the Essential Question and encourage children to use the oral vocabulary words. *What happens in different kinds of weather?*
- Prompt children to review and discuss the skills they used today. How do those skills help them?

WHOLE GROUP
DAY 3

Materials

Reading/Writing Workshop Big Book
UNIT 6

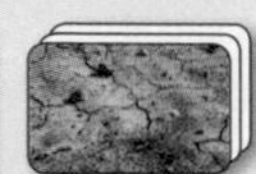
Visual Vocabulary Cards
drought
clever
storm

Word-Building Cards

Puppet

Interactive Read-Aloud Cards

Photo Cards
kangaroo
king
kite
kitten
koala
lock
rock
sock

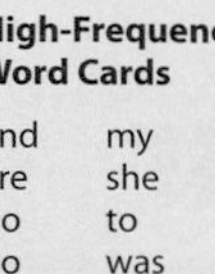
High-Frequency Word Cards
and, are, do, go, he, is, little, my, she, to, was, with, you

I was able to picture in my mind...
Think Aloud Cloud

"Koala"

Build the Concept

MINILESSON 10 Mins

Oral Language

OBJECTIVES

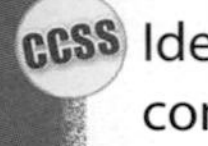
CCSS Actively engage in group reading activities with purpose and understanding. **RL.K.10**

CCSS Identify real-life connections between words and their use. **L.K.5c**

Develop oral vocabulary

ACADEMIC LANGUAGE
folktale

ESSENTIAL QUESTION

COLLABORATE

Remind children that this week they are talking and learning about what happens in different kinds of weather. Guide children to discuss the Essential Question using information from the **Big Book** and the weekly song. Ask children why the rain should go away in "Rain, Rain, Go Away." Then sing the song together.

Oral Vocabulary

Review last week's oral vocabulary words, as well as *predict* and *temperature*. Then use the **Define/Example/Ask** routine to introduce *storm, clever,* and *drought*.

Oral Vocabulary Routine

Define: A **drought** is a long period of time with no rain.

Example: The drought caused the dirt to dry up and crack.

Ask: Why do people wish for rain during a drought?

Define: If you have a **clever** idea, you have a smart idea.

Example: The clever bird played with the ball.

Ask: What clever idea have you had recently? Explain.

Define: During a **storm**, there are strong winds, heavy rain, or snow.

Example: After the rain storm, there were large puddles in the street.

Ask: What would a town look like after a snow storm?

Visual Vocabulary Cards

Go Digital

Visual Glossary

"The Frog and the Locust"

Think Aloud Cloud

Listening Comprehension

Read the Interactive Read Aloud

Genre: Folktale

Tell children you will be reading a folktale. Explain that a *folktale* is a made-up story from long ago that often teaches a lesson. Display the **Interactive Read-Aloud Cards**.

Interactive Read-Aloud Cards

Read the title. Explain that a locust is a type of grasshopper that can fly.

Strategy: Visualize

Remind children that good readers visualize as they read. They make pictures in their minds to help them see and feel what is happening. *You can use information from the words and the illustrations to help you make a picture in your mind.* Model the strategy of visualizing using the **Think Aloud Cloud**.

Think Aloud I read that everything was dusty and dry. Then Paqua sang. I can picture in my mind the cracking ground and the hot frog. And I can see the frog's bulging throat. I imagine that I feel the hot, dry air. Making a picture in my mind helps me understand the characters' feelings and actions. And I can better understand what the setting is like as I read the story.

Read "The Frog and the Locust," pausing occasionally to model the strategy of visualizing.

Make Connections

Guide partners to connect "The Frog and the Locust" with *Rain*. Discuss the ways both stories tell what happens in different kinds of weather. *What kind of weather do the animals in both stories want?* (They want rain.)

ELL

ENGLISH LANGUAGE LEARNERS

Reinforce Meaning As you read "The Frog and the Locust," make meaning clear by pointing to specific characters, places, or objects in the illustrations, demonstrating word meanings, paraphrasing text, and asking children questions. For example, on Card 1, point to the puddles and say: *These are puddles. They used to be a creek or stream, but without rain, there are only muddy puddles left.*

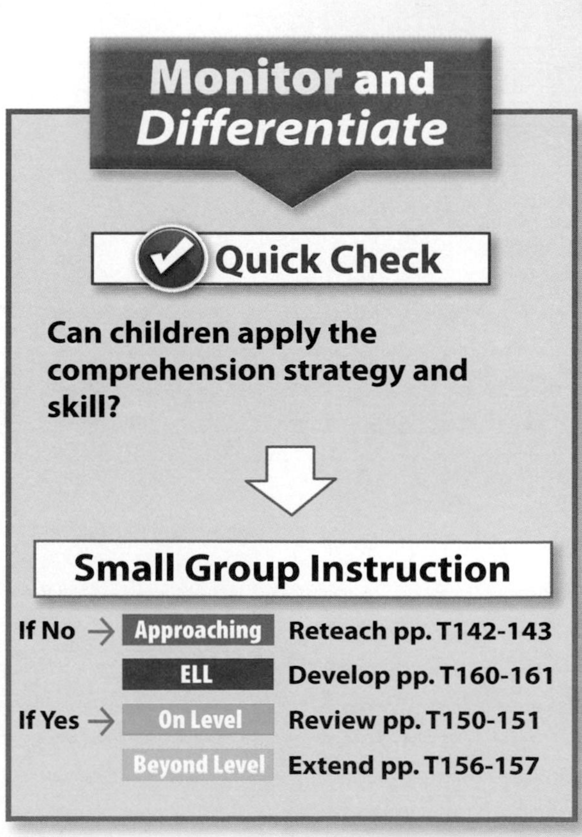

Word Work

Quick Review

Build Fluency: Sound-Spellings: Display the following **Word-Building Cards:** *b, e, f, h, k, l, r.* Have children say each sound. Repeat and vary the pace.

MINILESSON 5 Mins

Phonemic Awareness

Puppet

OBJECTIVES

CCSS Demonstrate basic knowledge of one-to-one letter-sound correspondences by producing the primary or many of the most frequent sounds for each consonant. **RF.K.3a**

CCSS Read common high-frequency words by sight. **RF.K.3c**

Read and blend words with *k, ck*

Phoneme Blending

1 **Model** *The puppet is going to say sounds in a word. Listen: /l/ /o/ /k/. It can blend those sounds together: /llloook/,* lock. *Say the word with the puppet:* lock. Repeat with *kid.*

2 **Guided Practice/Practice** Have children blend sounds to form words. *The puppet is going to say the sounds in a word. Listen to the puppet as it says each sound. Repeat the sounds. Then blend them to say the word.* Guide practice with the first word.

/k/ /i/ /i/ kit /k/ /i/ /k/ kick /b/ /a/ /k/ back
/l/ /o/ /k/ lock /k/ /i/ /d/ kid /k/ /ē/ /p/ keep

Review initial /k/. Play and sing "Koala." Have children clap when they hear initial /k/. Demonstrate as you sing with children.

Go Digital

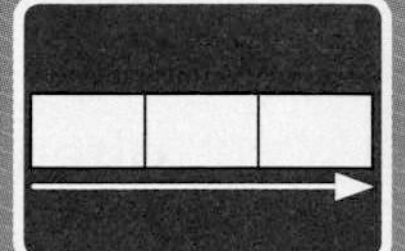

Phonemic Awareness

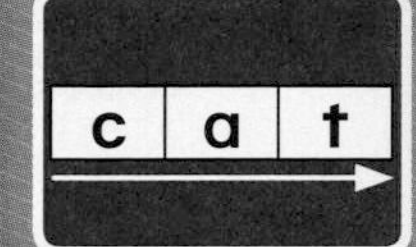

Phonics

Handwriting

Phonics

ck k

Word-Building Cards

Review /k/k and /k/ck

1 Model Display **Word-Building Card** *kick.* Point to letters *ck. The names of these letters are* c *and* k. *When these letters are together, they stand for one sound: /k/. When we hear /k/ at the end of a word, we use the letters* ck *to spell it, as in the word* kick. *Say the sound with me: /k/. Listen as I say the word* kick. *I will write the letters* c *and* k *because* kick *has the /k/ sound at the end.* Review initial /k/k using the same word.

2 Guided Practice/Practice Tell children that you will say words with /k/ either at the beginning or at the end. Have children say /k/ and write the letter *k* on their **Response Boards** when they hear /k/ at the beginning of the word, and say /k/ and write *ck* when they hear /k/ at the end. Guide practice with the first two words.

pick kid truck Rick koala

kitten track pack kiss kite

Blend Words with *k, ck* and *i, l, o, r*

1 Model Display Word-Building Cards *s, i, c, k. This is the letter* s. *It stands for /s/. This is the letter* i. *It stands for /i/. These are the letters* ck. *When these letters are at the end of a word, they stand for /k/. Let's blend the three sounds together: /sssiiik/. The word is* sick. Continue with the following words: *lick, kick, kit.*

2 Guided Practice/Practice Write the following words. Have children read each word, blending the sounds. Guide practice with the first word.

sick tack kin kid

Write these sentences and prompt children to read the connected text, sounding out the decodable words: *I am sick in bed. Did Ken pack the map? I see the red rock.*

Corrective Feedback

Blending: Sound Error Model the sound that children missed, then have them repeat. For example, for the word *lick*, tap under the letters *ck* and ask: *What's the sound?* Return to the beginning of the word. *Let's start over.* Blend the word with children again. Repeat with words that have /k/ at the beginning of the word.

Extend the Lesson

S-Blends

Display Word-Building Cards *s, t. S and* t *together stand for the /st/ sounds as in* stack. *What sounds do the letters* st *stand for together?* Hold up the Word-Building Cards *s, n.* S *and* n *together stand for the /sn/ sounds as in* snack. Repeat with *sp* and the word *speck.*

Using Word-Building Cards, assist children in blending the word *stick*. Continue with *snap* and *spot*.

YOUR TURN PRACTICE BOOK p. 168

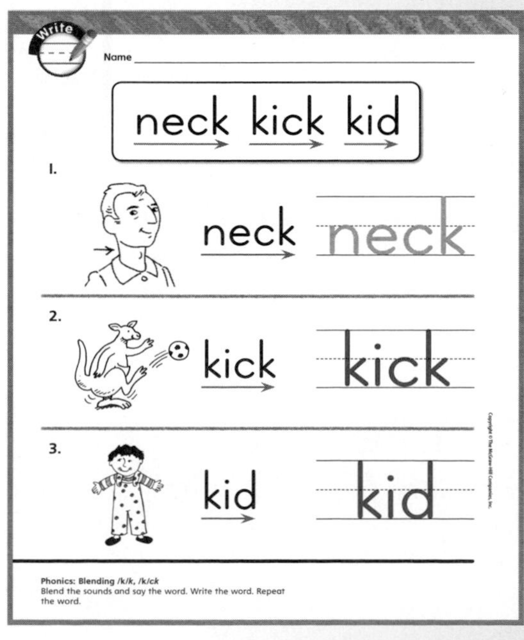

Word Work

Phonics

OBJECTIVES

CCSS Read common high-frequency words by sight. **RF.K.3c**

Sort words by initial sound/letter

ACADEMIC LANGUAGE
sort

Picture Sort

Photo Cards

1 Model Remind children that the letter *k* can stand for /k/. Place the **Word-Building Card** *k* on the left side of a pocket chart. *What is the letter?* (k) *What sound does it stand for?* (/k/)

Hold up the **Photo Card** for *koala. Here is the picture for* koala. Koala *has the /k/ sound at the beginning. I will place* koala *under the letter* k *because the letter* k *stands for /k/.*

Use the same routine for final /k/ spelled *ck*. Place Word-Building Cards *ck* on the right side of the pocket chart. Use the Photo Card for *lock*.

2 Guided Practice/Practice Have children sort the Photo Cards *kangaroo, king, kite, kitten, rock, sock*. Have them tell if /k/ is at the beginning or at the end of the word and tell if the photo card should be placed under the letter *k* or *ck*.

Photo Cards

Go Digital

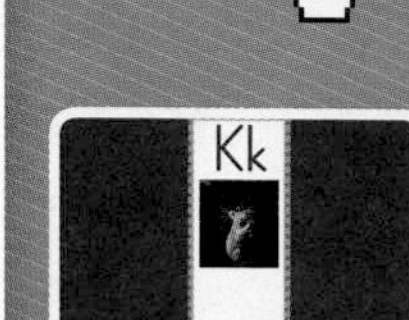

Phonics

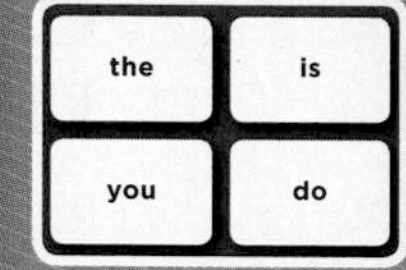

High-Frequency Word Routine

High-Frequency Words

she, was

1 Guided Practice Display the **High-Frequency Word Cards** *she* and *was*. Review the words using the **Read/Spell/Write** routine.

2 Practice Point to the High-Frequency Word Cards *she* and *was* and have children read them. Repeat with previous weeks' words *little, is, with, he, are, my, to, and, go, you, do.*

Build Fluency

Word Automaticity Write the following sentences and have children chorally read aloud as you track the print. Repeat several times.

She was sad.
Was the cat on the bed?
Was Bill on the cot?
She can go with you and Kim.

Read for Fluency Distribute pages 169–170 of **Your Turn Practice Book** and help children assemble their Take-Home Books. Chorally read the Take-Home Book with children. Then have children reread the book to review high-frequency words and build fluency.

YOUR TURN PRACTICE BOOK pp. 169–170

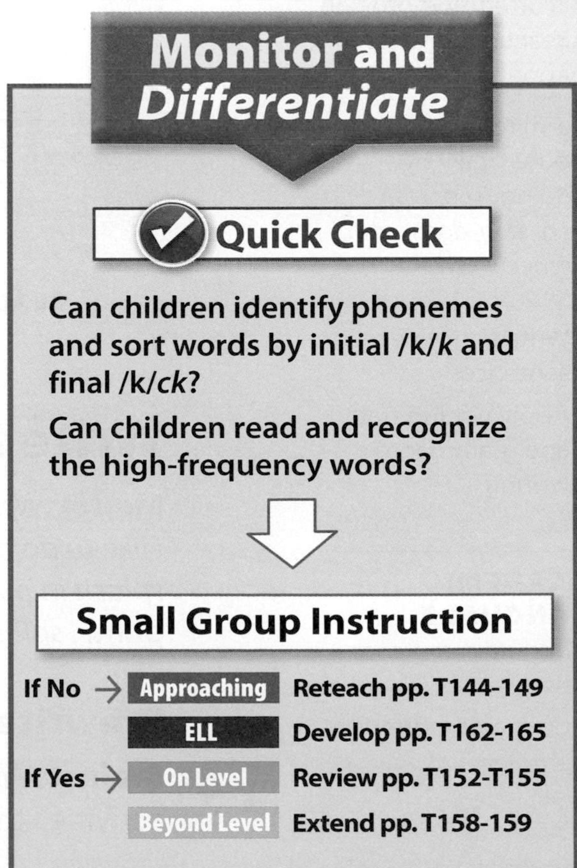

Language Arts

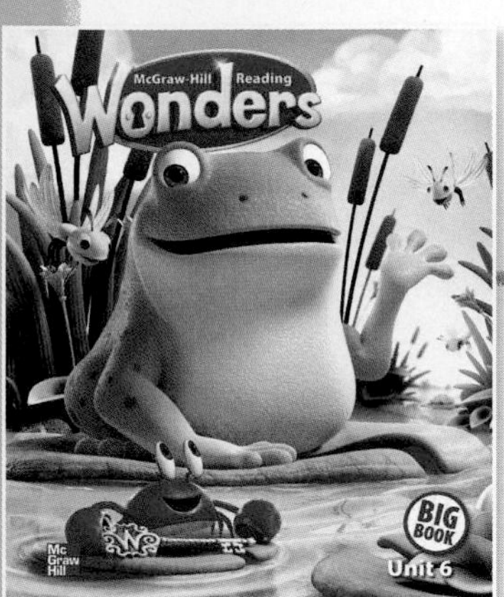

Reading/Writing Workshop Big Book

OBJECTIVES

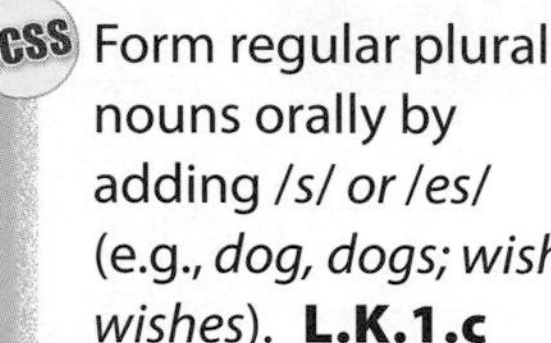

Use a combination of drawing, dictating, and writing to narrate a single event or several loosely linked events, tell about the events in the order in which they occurred, and provide a reaction to what happened. **W.K.3**

Form regular plural nouns orally by adding /s/ or /es/ (e.g., *dog, dogs; wish, wishes*). **L.K.1.c**

- Write narrative sentences
- Apply writing trait and grammar to writing

ACADEMIC LANGUAGE

- *narrative, sentence, noun*
- Cognates: *narrativa*

Independent Writing

Writing Trait: Voice

1 Practice Tell children that today they will draw and write sentences about things they like to do on rainy days. They will include words that show how they feel.

2 Guided Practice Share the Readers to Writers page in the **Reading/Writing Workshop**. Read the model sentences aloud.

READING/WRITING WORKSHOP BIG BOOK, pp. 32–33

Write a Personal Narrative

Model Write: *I _____ on a rainy day.* Say: *I will write about something I like to do on a rainy day.* Display the Word Web from Day 1. Write: *splash in puddles* on the line. Read the sentence aloud, tracking the print: *I splash in puddles on a rainy day.*

Prewrite

Brainstorm Have children work with a partner. Ask them to think of activities they like to do on a rainy day.

Draft

Ask children to draw pictures of what they like to do on a rainy day. Have them write: *I ______ on a rainy day.* Help children write an activity in the blank. Guide children in writing or dictating another sentence that gives more details about the activity they chose.

Apply Writing Trait As children write and draw, have them describe how they feel when they do the rainy day activity. For example: *I smile as I splash in the puddles. It makes me happy.*

Apply Grammar Tell children to point to and name nouns in their sentences and tell whether they are singular or plural. Tell them to make sure their plural nouns end with an *-s* or *-es*.

ENGLISH LANGUAGE LEARNERS

Explain Point out the clues in the sentence frames that tell whether the noun should be singular or plural. In *My two ______ are a dog and a cat,* the *two* tells that *pet* should be plural. Write and read: *My dog is a ______. Should I use* pet *or* pets *to finish the sentence?*

Grammar

Naming Words (Nouns)

1 Review Review with children that plural nouns often end in *-s* or *-es,* and name more than one thing. Have children tell the plural form of *root* and *plant* to complete the sentence: *The ______ of the ______ are under ground.* (roots, plants)

2 Guided Practice/Practice Write and read: *My two ______ are a dog and a cat.* Write *pet* on a self-stick note. Ask children if you can put *pet* in the sentence or if it needs an *-s*. (needs an *-s*) Add the *-s* to *pet* on the self-stick note and place it in the sentence.

Have children work in pairs. Provide children with sentence frames and self-stick notes with singular nouns written on them, such as *glass.*

→ *These are my favorite ______.* (glasses)

→ *I poured her a ______ of milk.* (glass)

Help children read the sentence frames and words. Have children work together to decide whether the nouns need the ending *-s* or *-es*. Have children put the self-stick note with the correct form of the noun in the sentence frame and share their sentences with the class.

Talk About It

Have partners work together to orally generate sentences with plural nouns. Challenge them to create sentences with more than one plural noun.

Daily Wrap Up

- Review the Essential Question and encourage children to discuss it, using the oral vocabulary words. *What activities do you do in different kinds of weather?*
- Prompt children to review and discuss the skills they used today. Guide them to give examples of how they used each skill.

Materials

Reading/Writing Workshop Big Book
UNIT 6

Literature Big Book
Rain

Visual Vocabulary Cards
she
was

Response Board

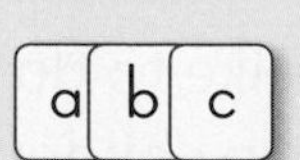

Word-Building Cards

Interactive Read-Aloud Cards

Photo Cards
bus
car
fan
inch
kite
lightning
nut
October
quilt

High-Frequency Word Cards
she
was

Extend the Concept

MINILESSON 10 Mins

Oral Language

OBJECTIVES

CCSS Use words and phrases acquired through conversations, reading and being read to, and responding to texts. **L.K.6**

CCSS Recognize and produce rhyming words. **RF.K.2a**

Develop oral vocabulary

ESSENTIAL QUESTION

Remind children that this week they have been talking and reading about what happens in different kinds of weather. Have them sing "Rain, Rain, Go Away" and think what the weather is like. Then ask how the animals knew the rain was coming in *Rain*. (Lightning flashed and thunder boomed. They could sense the rain.)

Phonological Awareness

Recognize Rhyme

Point out the rhyming words *away* and *day* in the song "Rain, Rain, Go Away." Say: *Words that rhyme have the same end sound. Listen:* away, day. *I can say more words with the same end sound:* play, say, may, ray. Ask children to listen as you say different word pairs and raise their hands if those words rhyme. Pause between word pairs: *rake/rip; late/wait; seat/some; tip/hip; pan/man.*

Review Oral Vocabulary

Reread the Interactive Read Aloud Use the **Define/Example/Ask** routine to review the oral vocabulary words *predict, temperature, storm, clever,* and *drought*. Then have children listen as you reread "The Frog and the Locust."

→ *What did Paqua want after the drought had lasted many weeks?* (rain)

→ *What was the temperature like near the creek?* (very hot)

Go Digital

Visual Glossary

"The Frog and the Locust"

Category Words

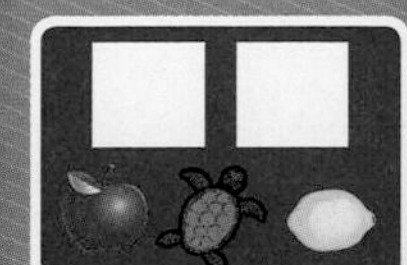

Category Words: Weather Words

1 Explain/Model Write the following sentence frames. Have children provide a weather word to complete each sentence.

When it rains, we say it is ______. (rainy)
When the sun shines, we say it is ______. (sunny)
When the sky is full of clouds, we say it is ______. (cloudy)
When the wind blows, we say it is ______. (windy)

→ Discuss each weather word. *What do you do when it is rainy? What does a tree look like on a windy day?* Encourage children to use weather words in their responses.

2 Guided Practice Display **Photo Cards** for *October, lightning, quilt, fan,* and *kite*. Work with children to make up sentences using Photo Cards and weather words. (Possible answer: I lie under a quilt when it is snowy outside.)

→ Ask children why *rainy, snowy, windy, sunny,* and *gloomy* are weather words. (Possible answer: They tell what it is like outside.)

Vocabulary Strategy: Shades of Meaning

1 Model Remind children that similar words that show action can tell about the action in different ways. Use *Rain* to identify the shades of meaning between verbs.

Think Aloud In *Rain,* we read the sentence: *It rained until every river gushed and gurgled.* The words *gushed* and *gurgled* are two ways to describe how the river sounded after it rained and rained. Both action words mean almost the same thing.

2 Guided Practice/Practice Help children find similar word pairs in *Rain*, such as *sniffed* and *smell, grew* and *sprout*. Have children take turns inserting the pairs of words into the same sentence. Then have them act out the words. Discuss how each word describes the same action in a little different way.

ENGLISH LANGUAGE LEARNERS

Understand Discuss the local weather with children. Talk about today's weather and the weather during the past week. Provide magazines or newspapers to help children find pictures of similar weather. Have children name the different kinds of weather they find.

LET'S MOVE!

Play "Simon Says," giving directions that include weather words. For example: *Simon says, open an umbrella in the rain. Simon says, put on sunscreen to block the sun. Fly a kite on a windy day.*

YOUR TURN PRACTICE BOOK p. 171

Name ______

1.

2.

3.

Category Words: Weather Words
Put a marker on pictures that show different kinds of weather. Talk to a partner about the kinds of weather that are shown. Then talk about your favorite kind of weather.

Listening Comprehension

Read "Cloud Watch"

Genre: Informational Text

Display "Cloud Watch" on pages 33–36 of the **Big Book** and read aloud the title. Explain to children that informational text can have made-up characters, but the information is true.

Set a Purpose for Reading

Read aloud the speech bubbles on page 33. Tell children to listen as you continue reading aloud the selection about clouds.

Strategy: Visualize

Remind children that good readers sometimes use the text and illustrations to make pictures in their minds of what is happening in a story. Have children visualize the weather on page 33. *What things would you be doing outside when the sky looks like the one in the picture?* (Possible answers: ride a bike, play in the park, and so on.)

Text Feature: Speech Bubbles

Explain Point out the speech bubbles on page 33. Explain that speech bubbles contain the words, or dialogue, that the characters are saying. *We should read dialogue with expression, the way that the characters would be speaking.* Explain to children that the top left speech bubble should be read first. Point to the indicators on the bubbles that show who is speaking. Have children point from each bubble to its character. Read aloud the speech bubbles and have children echo read.

Apply Turn to page 34. Have children point to the speech bubble that should be read first. Ask children to point from each bubble to the character who is speaking. Read aloud the speech bubbles and have children echo read.

Literature Big Book

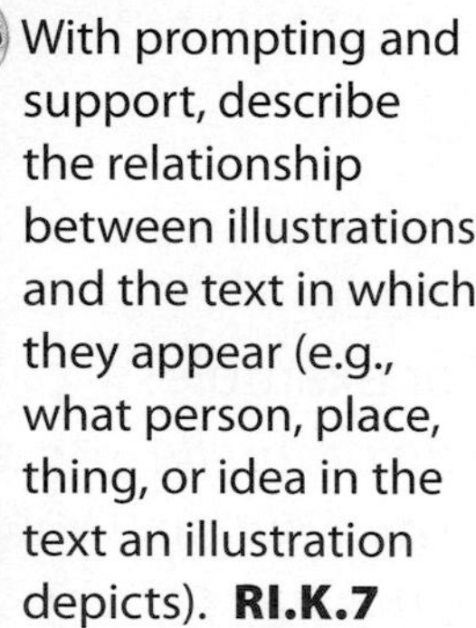

OBJECTIVES

CCSS With prompting and support, describe the relationship between illustrations and the text in which they appear (e.g., what person, place, thing, or idea in the text an illustration depicts). **RI.K.7**

- Use the text feature speech bubbles to gather information
- Apply the comprehension strategy: Visualize
- Make connections across texts

ACADEMIC LANGUAGE

- *speech bubbles, dialogue*
- Cognates: *diálogo*

Go Digital

"Cloud Watch"

LITERATURE BIG BOOK PAGE 33

VISUALIZE

The text says the clouds look like feathers. Close your eyes and think about feathers. What do feathers look like? (a line with other thin lines coming from the sides) *How do feathers feel?* (soft and light)

LITERATURE BIG BOOK PAGES 34–35

KEY DETAILS: SEQUENCE

What happens at the end of the story? (The cat runs inside because dark clouds appear and it begins to rain.)

LITERATURE BIG BOOK PAGE 36

ASK AND ANSWER QUESTIONS

The text asks: Can you predict the weather by looking at each cloud? What is your answer? (Yes, the clouds' shapes tell about the kinds of weather to expect.)

ENGLISH LANGUAGE LEARNERS

Reinforce Meaning As you read aloud the text, make the meaning clear by pointing to the details in the illustrations. Ask children questions and elicit language.

Retell and Respond

Have children discuss the selection by asking the following questions:

→ *What can children do when there are few clouds in the sky?* (Possible responses: play basketball; fly a kite.)

→ *What will happen if you see dark clouds?* (It's going to rain or storm.)

Make Connections

Have children recall the selections they read this week.

→ *How did the animals in Africa know it was going to rain?* (They smelled, saw, heard, and felt when it was going to rain.)

Write About It Write about why it finally rained for Paqua and her friends.

CONNECT TO CONTENT

Weather Report Review with children the different kinds of clouds that can tell you what the weather is like (cirrus, feathery; cumulus, puffy; cumulonimbus, dark). Have partners look out the window and discuss the kind of clouds they see and what the weather is like outside. Have them discuss whether they would do indoor or outdoor activities, and ask them to describe some of the activities.

STEM

WHOLE GROUP
DAY 4

Word Work

Quick Review

Build Fluency: Sound-Spellings: Show the following **Word-Building Cards:** *a, b, c, d, e, f, h, i, l, m, n, o, p, r, s, t.* Have children say each sound. Repeat and vary the pace.

MINILESSON 5 Mins

Phonemic Awareness

OBJECTIVES

CCSS Distinguish between similarly spelled words by identifying the sounds of letters that differ. **RF.K.3d**

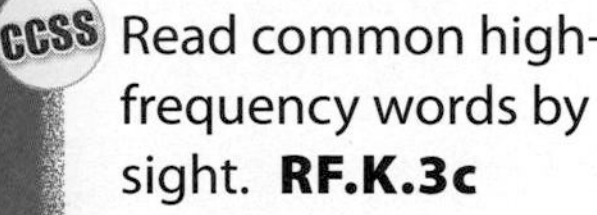

CCSS Read common high-frequency words by sight. **RF.K.3c**

Segment words into phonemes

Phoneme Segmentation

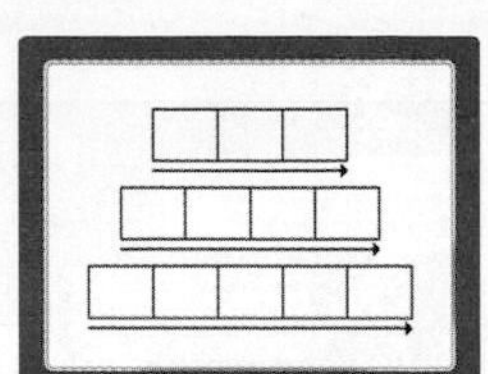

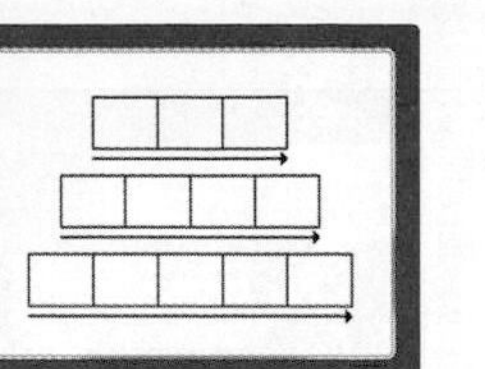

Sound Box

1 **Model** Use the **Sound Boxes** and markers. *Listen as I say a word:* kiss. *Say the word with me:* kiss. *There are three sounds in* kiss. *Say the sounds in* kiss *with me: /k/ /i/ /s/. Let's place a marker in a box for each sound: /k/ /i/ /s/.* Repeat for *luck.*

2 **Guided Practice/Practice** Distribute Sound Boxes and markers. Have children say each sound in the word as they place a marker in a box. Then have them say the word and tell the number of sounds in the word. Guide children with the first word.

keep, /k/ /ē/ /p/	dock, /d/ /o/ /k/	Kim, /k/ /i/ /m/
key, /k/ /ē/	kit, /k/ /i/ /t/	sick, /s/ /i/ /k/

MINILESSON 5 Mins

Phonics

Blend Words with *k, ck* and *a, i, m, p, s, t*

1 **Guided Practice** Display **Word-Building Cards** *k, i, t.* Point to the letter *k. This is the letter* k. *The letter* k *stands for /k/. Say /k/. This is the letter* i. *The letter* i *stands for /i/. Listen as I blend the two sounds together /kiii/. Say /kiii/. This is the letter* t. *The letter* t *stands for /t/. Listen as I blend the three sounds /kiiit/,* kit. *Now you say it. Let's change* t *to* ck. Use the same routine to blend *kick.*

2 **Practice** Write *sack, sick, sock.* Have children blend and read the words. Ask children which letters are the same. (s, ck) Ask children to tell which letters are different. (a, i, o) Discuss the sounds each letter stands for and how it changes the word.

Go Digital

Phonemic Awareness

Phonics

Handwriting

Visual Glossary

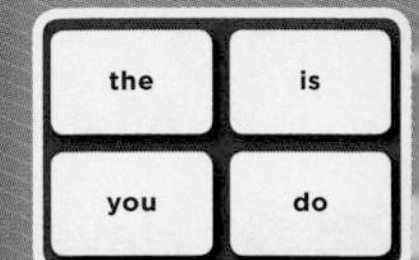

High-Frequency Word Routine

Dictation

Review Dictate each of the sounds for children to spell. Have them repeat the sound and then write the letter that stands for the sound.

/b/ /l/ /f/ /r/ /i/ /t/ /k/

Dictate the following words for children to spell: *kit, kid, sick, back.* Model for children how to segment each word to scaffold the spelling.

When I say the word kit, *I hear three sounds: /k/ /i/ /t/. I know the letter* k *stands for /k/, the letter* i *stands for /i/, and the letter* t *stands for /t/. I will write the letters* k, i, t *to spell* kit.

When children finish, write the letters and words for them to self-correct.

Extend the Lesson

S-Blends

Write the word *stack*. Circle *st*. Point out that *s* and *t* together stand for the /st/ sounds as in *stack*. Blend and read the word and have children repeat. Continue with the words *stop, spill, sped, snap, snack.*

High-Frequency Words

Practice Say the words *she* and *was* and have children write them. Then display the **Visual Vocabulary Cards** for *she* and *was*. Follow the Teacher Talk routine on the back.

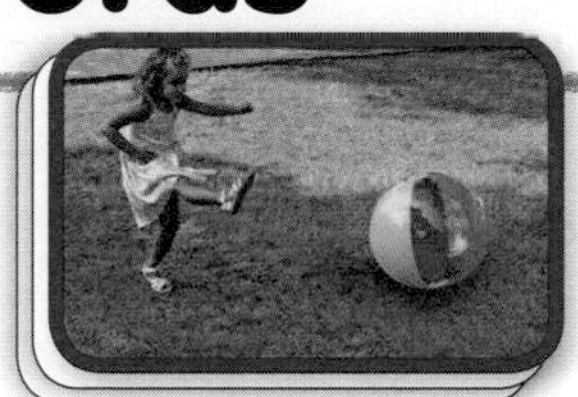

Visual Vocabulary Cards

Build Fluency Build sentences in a pocket chart using **High-Frequency Word Cards** and **Photo Cards**. Use index cards to create punctuation cards for a period and a question mark. Have children chorally read the sentences as you track the print. Then have them identify the words *she* and *was.*

She can see the balloon.
Was she with you?
The kitten **was** with me.

Also online

High-Frequency Words Practice

Have partners create sentences using the words *she* and *was.*

Monitor and *Differentiate*

Can children blend words with /k/ and match it to the letters *Kk* and *ck*?

Can children read and recognize high-frequency words?

Small Group Instruction

If No →	Approaching	Reteach pp. T144-149
	ELL	Develop pp. T162-165
If Yes →	On Level	Review pp. T152-155
	Beyond Level	Extend pp. T158-159

Shared Read

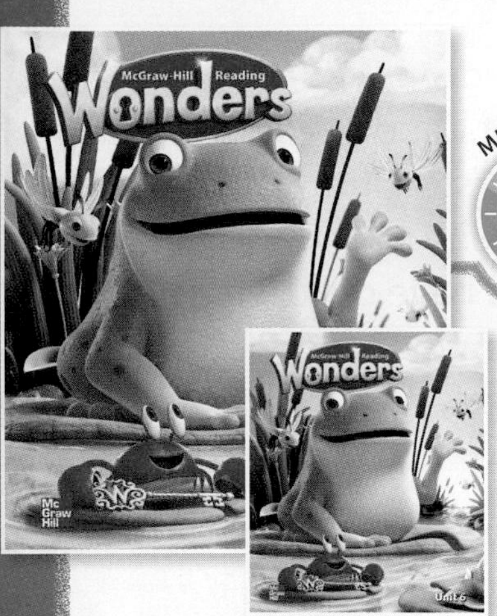

Reading/Writing Workshop Big Book and Reading/Writing Workshop

OBJECTIVES

CCSS Read common high-frequency words by sight. **RF.K.3c**

CCSS Read emergent-reader texts with purpose and understanding. **RF.K.4**

CCSS Recognize and name end punctuation. **L.K.2b**

MINILESSON 10 Mins

Read "Kim and Nan"

Model Skills and Strategies

Model Concepts About Print Begin reading the story. Point out the first and last words in each sentence and the punctuation at the end of each sentence. *When I read, I notice that the first word in each sentence always begins with a capital letter. At the end of each sentence, I notice that after the last word, there is a punctuation mark that ends the sentence. It can be a period, a question mark, or an exclamation point.* Then invite volunteers to come up to the **Big Book**. Have them point to and read the first and last words in each sentence and then identify the punctuation at the end of each sentence.

Reread Have children chorally read the story. Children should sound out the decodable words and say the sight words. Offer support as needed using the student **Reading/Writing Workshop**.

Ask the following:

- *Look at page 25. What is the weather like? How do you know?* (It is sunny and hot. It's probably hot because Kim is wearing her hat and sipping a drink.)
- *Look at page 26. What has Kim taken out of the bag?* (birdseed)
- *Look at page 29. How would you describe the expression on Kim's face?* (Possible answer: thoughtful; Kim is figuring out her next adventure.)

Go Digital

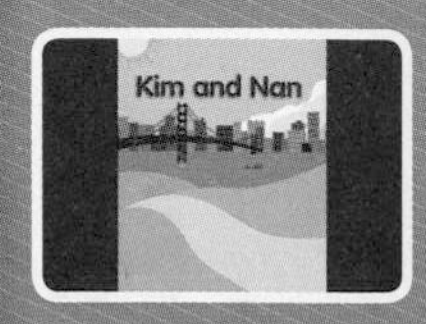

"Kim and Nan"

"Kim and Nan"

READING/WRITING WORKSHOP, pp. 22–29

Fluency: Intonation

1 Explain Tell children that as you read the story, you will change the tone of your voice when reading sentences that end with a period or an exclamation point. Point out different kinds of punctuation in the story.

2 Model Model reading page 27 of "Kim and Nan." Read each sentence with the proper intonation and expression. Then point to the punctuation mark at the end of each sentence. *When I read each sentence, the tone of my voice sounds different. When there is a period at the end of the sentence, I am making a statement. When there is an exclamation point at the end of the sentence, I read it with more emotion, like this.* Read each sentence with appropriate intonation. Then point out differences in intonation by reading other sentences in the story that end with a period or an exclamation point.

3 Guided Practice Read each sentence in the story and have children echo you. Encourage them to repeat the sentence, using proper intonation. Afterward, invite the class to choral read the story as you listen for proper intonation.

Language Arts

Independent Writing

OBJECTIVES

CCSS With guidance and support from adults, respond to questions and suggestions from peers and add details to strengthen writing as needed. **W.K.5**

CCSS Form regular plural nouns orally by adding /s/ or /es/ (e.g., *dog, dogs; wish, wishes*). **L.K.1c**

Revise a personal narrative

ACADEMIC LANGUAGE
- *revise, draft, noun*
- Cognates: *revisar*

Write a Personal Narrative

Revise

Distribute the children's draft sentences and drawings from Day 3.

Apply Writing Trait: Voice Explain that as writers revise, they add words that show how they feel. Write and read aloud: "*I do a puzzle.*" *I can use words that describe how I feel about doing a puzzle.* Write and read aloud: "*I love doing a puzzle with different colors and shapes.*" *This sentence gives the reader a better picture of what I like.*

Help children think of how they can add such details. Then have children read the sentences they wrote and check for the following:

- → Did I write about things that happen on a rainy day?
- → Did I use words that show how I feel and what I like to do on a rainy day?
- → Do my naming words end with *-s* or *-es* when they tell about more than one thing?

Apply Grammar Ask children to identify the naming word that names more than one in the following sentence: *I go outside in my bright, green rain boots.* (boots) Have children tell how they know *boots* names more than one. (It is a naming word that ends in *-s*.)

Peer Edit Have children work in pairs to do a peer edit, in which they read their partner's draft. Partners can read the sentences aloud to see if they can imagine the story from the details or if they need more description. Have children check that any plural nouns end in *-s* or *-es*. Provide time for children to make revisions to their sentences.

Final Draft

After children have edited their own papers and finished their peer edits, have them write their final draft. Remind them to space out their words well so that readers can read their writing. As children work, conference with them to provide guidance.

Go Digital

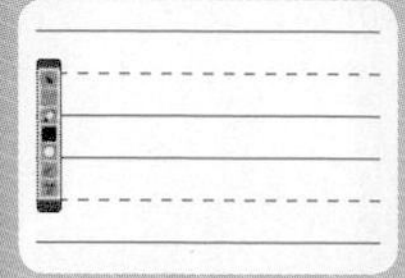

Writing

Grammar

Grammar

Naming Words (Nouns)

1 Review Remind children that nouns are naming words. Review that plural nouns name more than one thing and often end in the ending *-s* or *-es*. Write and read aloud: *class* and *glass*.

Underline the letters *ss* at the end of the words. Tell children that we usually add *-es* to the naming words that end with these letters to make them plural.

→ Ask children to tell you the plural forms as you write them: *classes, glasses*.

2 Guided Practice Show the **Photo Cards** for *bus* and *car*. *How can we make each naming word plural?* Point to the ending letter of each word. Have children tell whether to add *-s* or *-es*. (buses, cars)

Ask children to draw more than one bus on a sheet of paper and to label it *buses*. Have them do the same for *cars*.

3 Practice Show the Photo Cards for *inch* and *nut*. Ask children to work together to make each naming word plural. Have them underline the ending letter or letters of each word. Have children tell whether to add *-s* or *-es*. (inches, nuts)

Ask one partner to draw a ruler showing more than one inch on a sheet of paper while the other partner labels it *inches*. Have children do the same for *nuts*. Provide help as you have children label their drawings with the plural nouns.

Talk About It

Have partners think of things they like to do when it is sunny. Ask them to orally generate sentences. Have them identify the nouns in the sentence and identify if they are singular or plural nouns.

ENGLISH LANGUAGE LEARNERS SCAFFOLD

Photo Cards and Sentences
Provide plural forms that go with images on the Photo Cards and drawings you sketch to show the plural. Hold up a Photo Card or a drawing as you have children say the plural form *buses,* for example. Repeat correct answers slowly and clearly to the class.

Daily Wrap Up

- Review the Essential Question and encourage children to discuss, using the oral vocabulary words.
- Prompt children to discuss the skills they practiced and learned today. Guide them to share examples of each skill.

www.connected.mcgraw-hill.com
RESOURCES
Research and Inquiry

Wrap Up the Week
Integrate Ideas

RESEARCH AND INQUIRY

What's the Weather?

OBJECTIVES

 Participate in shared research and writing projects (e.g., explore a number of books by a favorite author and express opinions about them). **W.K.7**

 With guidance and support from adults, recall information from experiences or gather information from provided sources to answer a question. **W.K.8**

ACADEMIC LANGUAGE
research, inquiry, chart

Wind Chart

Make a simple windsock in advance and place it so that it can be seen from the classroom windows. Tell children that they will do a research project with a partner to observe how strong the wind is for one day or a couple of days. Review the steps in the research process.

STEP 1 Choose a Topic

Encourage children to talk about the wind. Show them the windsock and explain what it is used for. If possible bring in a compass and show children how to use it to figure out which direction the wind is blowing.

STEP 2 Find Resources

Talk about locating and using resources to find out more about the wind. Direct children to use the selections from the week. Have children use the Research Process Checklist online.

STEP 3 Keep Track of Ideas

Have children note their observations of the wind by drawing pictures or writing words.

Collaborative Conversations

Provide Details As children engage in partner, small-group, and whole-class discussions, encourage them to:

- give details to express their thoughts, feelings, and ideas clearly.
- use details to describe people, places, things, and events.
- give details when asking about something they do not understand.

STEM

STEP 4 Create the Project: Wind Chart

Explain the characteristics of the project:

- **Information** This chart will show how strong the wind is during one day.
- **Text** Each drawing of the windsock will have a sentence that tells about the wind. Provide this sentence frame:

  Now the wind is ______.
- **Illustration** The two drawings will show how the windsock looks in the morning and in the afternoon.

Have partners work together to create a chart by drawing a line through the middle of a piece of paper. One box should be labeled *Morning* and the other box should be labeled *Afternoon.*

- Guide children to observe the windsock two times during the day and complete the sentence frame in each box.
- Encourage children to include details in their illustrations that they may have seen during their observation of the windsock.

ENGLISH LANGUAGE LEARNERS SCAFFOLD

Beginning	Intermediate	Advanced/Advanced High
Actively Engage Pair children with more fluent speakers. Prompt the more fluent speaker to name details in the partners' illustration and to have the partner repeat the words. Make sure that both children play an equal role in creating the illustration.	**Demonstrate Understanding** Encourage partners to talk about the details in their illustrations, both as they work and when they present to the class. Have them answer questions such as these: *What does the windsock look like? What does that mean?*	**Expand** Encourage the use of longer sentences by providing this sentence frame: *Now the wind is* ____ *because* ____. As children talk about their chosen weather and activity, elicit fuller responses by asking additional questions. Restate students' responses in complete sentences, as needed.

WHOLE GROUP
DAY 5

Materials

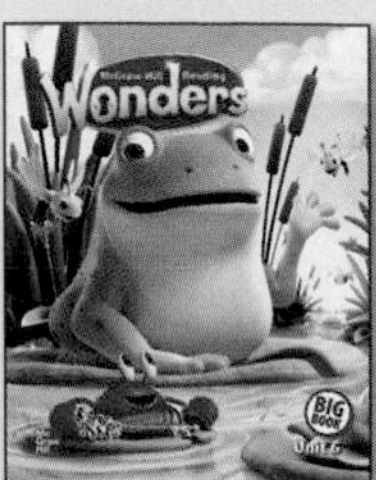
Reading/Writing Workshop Big Book
UNIT 6

Literature Big Book
Rain

Visual Vocabulary Cards
she
was

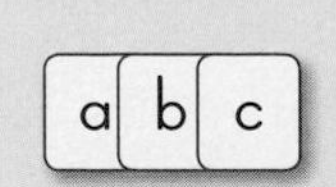
Response Board

Word-Building Cards

Interactive Read-Aloud Cards

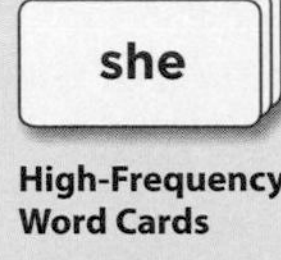

High-Frequency Word Cards
are
he
is
little
my
she
was
with

Integrate Ideas

TEXT CONNECTIONS

Connect to Essential Question

OBJECTIVES

With prompting and support, compare and contrast the adventures and experiences of characters in familiar stories. **RL.K.9**

Participate in collaborative conversations with diverse partners about *kindergarten topics and texts* with peers and adults in small and larger groups. **SL.K.1**

- Make connections among texts
- Make connections to the world

Text to Text

Remind children that all week they have been reading selections about the weather. Tell them that now they will connect the texts, or think about how the selections are alike. Model comparing *Rain* with another selection from the week.

Think Aloud In *Rain,* I read about how all the animals sensed that rain was coming. In "Cloud Watch," I read about how some children planned their activities depending on the kinds of clouds they saw in the sky. In both stories, the illustrations showed me details about the weather.

Guide children to compare the weather conditions in *Rain* and "The Frog and the Locust."

Text to Self

Have children talk about their favorite kinds of weather. Prompt each child to give a reason for his or her choice.

Text to World

Talk about how different kinds of weather might affect people. *What would it be like to live in a place that's very warm all year long? What would it be like to live in a place that is snowy and cold most of the year?*

TALK ABOUT READING

Analyze and Explain

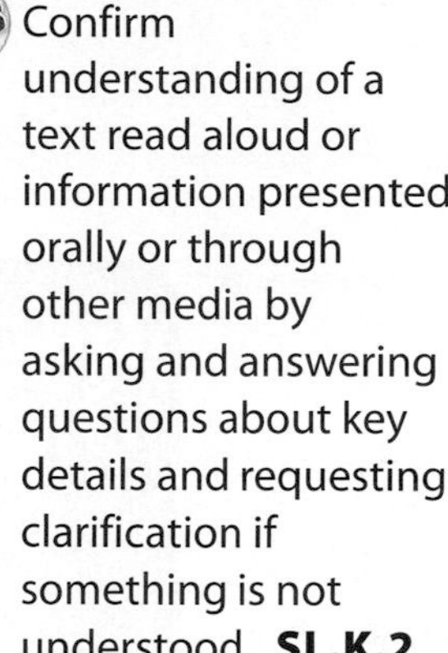

OBJECTIVES

CCSS Confirm understanding of a text read aloud or information presented orally or through other media by asking and answering questions about key details and requesting clarification if something is not understood. **SL.K.2**

Becoming Readers

Talk with children about the genres, strategy, and skill they have learned about this week. Prompt them to discuss how this knowledge helps them to read and understand selections.

→ Remind children that one genre they learned about is fantasy. Recall with them some characteristics of fantasy.

→ Discuss with children the strategy of visualizing. *How did picturing the weather in your mind help you to understand* Rain?

→ Talk about how the children learned to notice details about sequence, or the order of events. *What sequence did you notice in this week's selections? How did understanding the sequence help you understand what you were reading?*

RESEARCH AND INQUIRY

What's the Weather?

OBJECTIVES

CCSS Participate in shared research and writing projects (e.g. explore a number of books by a favorite author and express opinions about them). **W.K.7**

Wrap Up the Project

COLLABORATE

Guide partners to share information from their wind charts and to point out details in their pictures. Encourage children to use words and phrases they learned this week. Have children use the Presenting and Listening checklists online.

Word Work

Quick Review

Build Fluency: Sound-Spellings: Display the following **Word-Building Cards:** *b, e, f, h, k, l, r.* Have children chorally say each sound. Repeat and vary the pace.

Phonemic Awareness

OBJECTIVES

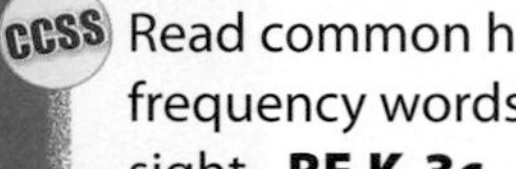

CCSS Spell simple words phonetically, drawing on knowledge of sound-letter relationships. **L.K.2d**

CCSS Read common high-frequency words by sight. **RF.K.3c**

Segment words into phonemes

Phoneme Segmentation

1. **Model** Use the **Sound Boxes** and markers. *Listen to this word:* kit. *There are three sounds in* kit. *Say the sounds in* kit *with me: /k/ /i/ /t/. Let's place one marker for each sound in the Sound Box: /k/ /i/ /t/.* Repeat for *pick*.

2. **Guided Practice/Practice** Distribute Sound Boxes and markers. Have children say each sound in the word as they place a marker in a box. Then have them say the word and tell the number of sounds in the word. Guide children with the first word.

Ken, /k/ /e/ /n/	sock, /s/ /o/ /k/	Dan, /d/ /a/ /n/
key, /k/ /ē/	keep, /k/ /ē/ /p/	kick, /k/ /i/ /k/

Phonics

Read Words with *k, ck* and *a, e, i, o*

1. **Guided Practice** Remind children that the letter *k* and the letters *ck* together stand for /k/. Display **Word-Building Cards** *p, a, c, k.* Point to the letter *p. The letter* p *stands for /p/. Say /p/. The letter* a *stands for /a/. Say /aaa/. The letters* ck *together stand for /k/. Say /k/. Let's blend the letters to make the word: /paaak/* pack. *Now let's change* p *to* b. Blend *back* with children. Repeat with *kid*.

2. **Practice** Write these words and sentences for children to read:

pick peck kid Ken

Mack is at the dock.
Can you sit on the deck?
Ken is sick in bed.
Dot will pack to go.

Remove words from view before dictation.

♪ Review initial /k/*k*. Have children write *k* on their **Response Boards**. Play and sing "Koala." Have children hold up and show the letter *k* on their boards when they hear initial /k/. Demonstrate as you sing with children.

Go Digital

Phonemic Awareness

Phonics

Handwriting

High-Frequency Word Routine

Dictation

1 Review Dictate the following sounds for children to spell. As you say each sound, have children repeat it and then write the letter that stands for the sound.

/b/ /l/ /f/ /r/ /e/ /h/ /k/

2 Dictate the following words for children to spell. Model for children how to use sound boxes to segment each word to scaffold the spelling. *I will say a word. You will repeat the word, then think about how many sounds are in the word. Use your Sound Boxes to count the sounds. Then write one letter for each sound you hear.*

sack kit dock Kim pick back

Then write the letters and words for children to self-correct.

MINILESSON 5 Mins

High-Frequency Words

she, was

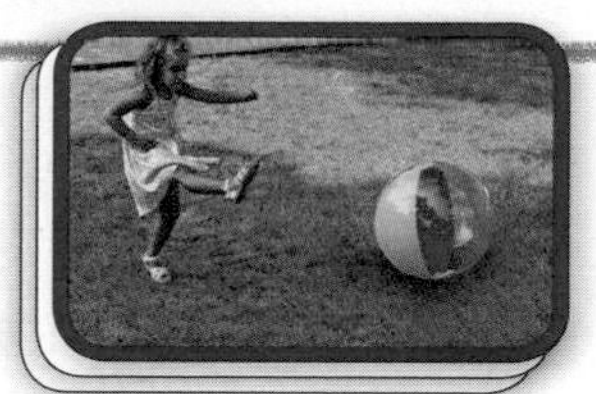
Visual Vocabulary Cards

1 Review Display the **Visual Vocabulary Cards** *she* and *was*. Read the sentences and have children point to the words *she* and *was*. Have children **Read/Spell/Write** the words. Then choose a Partner Talk Activity.

Distribute one of the following **High-Frequency Word Cards** to children: *she, was, little, is, he, are, my*. Tell children that you will say some sentences. *When you hear a word that is on your card, stand and hold up your word card.*

My umbrella *is* blue.
He has big yellow rain boots.
The dog is *with* me.
She was afraid of the storm.
A *little* ray of sun shone.
I *was* late for school.

2 Build Fluency: Word Automaticity Display High-Frequency Word Cards *little, is, with, he, she, was.* Point to each card, at random, and have children read the word as quickly as they can.

Monitor and *Differentiate*

Quick Check

Can children read and decode words with /k/*k, ck*?

Can children read and recognize high-frequency words?

Small Group Instruction

If No →	Approaching	Reteach pp. T144-149
	ELL	Develop pp. T162-165
If Yes →	On Level	Review pp. T152-155
	Beyond Level	Extend pp. T158-159

Language Arts

Independent Writing

OBJECTIVES

 Speak audibly and express thoughts, feelings, and ideas clearly. **SL.K.6**

 Form regular plural nouns orally by adding /s/ or /es/ (e.g., *dog, dogs; wish, wishes*). **L.K.1c**

- Make a presentation
- Listen to others

ACADEMIC LANGUAGE

- *present, publish, noun*
- Cognates: *presente*

Write a Personal Narrative

Prepare

Tell children that they will present their finished sentences and drawings from Day 4 to the class. Hold up an example from Day 4 and read it aloud, tracking the print. *I read my sentences at a medium pace—not too slow and not too fast. I read my sentences loudly enough so everyone can hear me.*

Present

Have children take turns standing up and reading their sentences aloud. Remind children to read their sentences at a medium pace and to read their sentences loudly enough so everyone can hear them. Encourage the rest of the class to listen quietly and to wait until the presenter has finished before asking any questions.

Evaluate

Have children discuss their own presentations and evaluate their performances, using the presentation rubric. Use the teacher's rubric to evaluate children's writing.

Publish

After children have finished presenting, post their work on a bulletin board titled *What to Do on a Rainy Day,* with raindrops and clouds around them. Discuss the activities that more than one child chose and review how each child's interests are different.

Have children add their writing to their Writer's Portfolio. Then have them look back at their previous writing and discuss how they have changed as writers throughout the year.

Go Digital

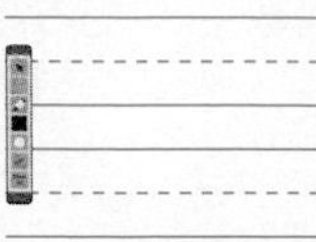

Writing

Grammar

Grammar

Naming Words (Nouns)

1 Review Have children tell what we call words that name people, places, animals, and things. (nouns) Remind children that plural nouns name more than one thing and can end in -*s* or -*es*.

→ Write and read aloud nouns, such as *sandwich, bag, spoon.*

What letters do we have to add to make these nouns plural? Have children tell you what to add to make each word plural. (-*es* for *sandwich* and -*s* for *bag* and *spoon*)

2 Review Practice Have children work in groups. Provide groups with nouns that have various endings, such as *apple, barn,* and *bench*, written on index cards. Have children work together to determine whether to add -*s* or -*es* to make each word plural. Circulate to help children with their spelling and to offer corrective feedback as needed.

Have children draw pictures on index cards to match each word in their singular and plural forms. Then have groups mix up all the index cards and work together to match drawings with their labels.

Wrap Up the Week

- Review blending words with initial /k/ *k* and final /k/ *ck*. Remind children that nouns tell the names of people, places, animals, and things, and that plural nouns are often formed by adding -*s* or -*es* at the end of nouns.
- Use the **High-Frequency Word Cards** to review the Words to Know.
- Remind children that they can share their experiences through words.

Approaching Level

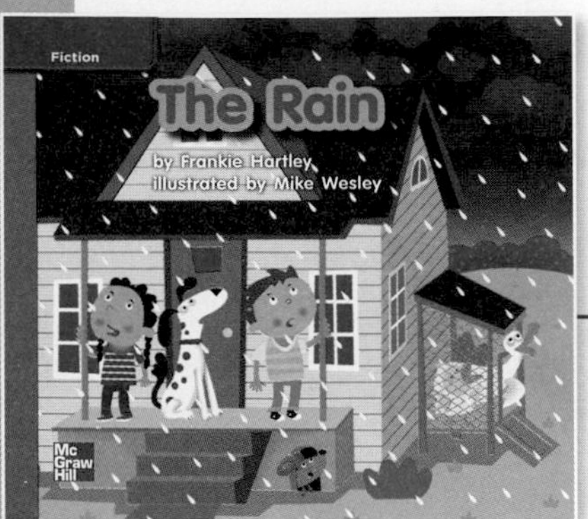

Leveled Reader

OBJECTIVES

 With prompting and support, ask and answer questions about key details in a text. **RL.K.1**

 With prompting and support, retell familiar stories, including key details. **RL.K.2**

 Demonstrate understanding of the organization and basic features of print. **RF.K.1**

 Read emergent-reader texts with purpose and understanding. **RF.K.4**

Leveled Reader: *The Rain*

Leveled Reader

Before Reading

Preview and Predict

Read the title and the names of the author and illustrator as children follow along in their copies of the book. Ask children to tell what they see on the cover and what they think the story will be about. Preview the illustrations throughout the book with children and ask them to describe what they see. Ask: *Who is fast in this picture?*

Review Genre: Fiction

Explain to children that they have read a fantasy this week and now will read fiction. Remind them that in fiction the characters and events are made-up. Unlike fantasy, events in fiction could happen in real life.

Model Concepts of Print

Have children point to the first and last words in the sentence on page 2. Have them follow along as you read the sentence.

Review High-Frequency Words

Point to the high-frequency word *was* on each page of the story. Ask children to say the word aloud each time they point to it on a new page.

Essential Question

Set a purpose for reading: *Let's find out what happens when it rains.* Remind children to use the rebuses and illustrations as they read.

During Reading

Guided Comprehension

As children read *The Rain*, monitor and provide guidance by correcting blending and modeling the strategy and skill.

Strategy: Visualize

Remind children that as they read they can make pictures in their mind of what is happening in the story.

Skill: Key Details

Tell children that the key details in a story help them understand what's happening. Explain that they can find details in the illustrations and in the words.

Think Aloud As I read pages 2 and 3, I see that the rain starts out as a few drops on page 2. On page 3, there are more drops. The text tells me that the dog and the chick are fast. I will keep reading to see what happens next.

Point out to children that the rain keeps getting harder, and that is a key detail that is shown in the illustrations. Guide children to talk about which animals run from the rain first. Explain to children that each page shows another key detail about the rainstorm.

After Reading

Respond to Reading

- *What happens as the rain comes closer and gets heavier?* (The dog, chick, mouse, girl, boy, and duck run to get away from the rain.)
- *Which animal runs from the rain first? Next?* (the dog; the chick)
- *What happens at the end of the story?* (It is raining hard.)

Retell

Have children take turns retelling the story. Help them make a personal connection by asking: *Have you ever been caught in the rain? What happened?*

Model Fluency

Read the story aloud, using expression in your voice as you read.

Apply Have children practice reading aloud with expression. Then have children work in pairs and read the story to each other, displaying expression in their voices.

LITERACY ACTIVITIES

Have children complete the activities on the inside back cover of the reader.

Level Up

IF Children read *The Rain* **Approaching Level** with fluency and correctly answer the Respond to Reading questions,

THEN Tell children that they will read another story about what happens in different kinds of weather.

- Have children page through *Weather Is Fun* **On Level** and make connections to what they know about the things we do in different weather.
- Have children read the story, monitoring their comprehension and providing assistance as necessary.

Approaching Level

Phonological Awareness

RECOGNIZE RHYME

TIER 2

OBJECTIVES

Recognize and produce rhyming words. **RF.K.2a**

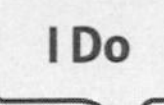
I Do

Remind children that words that rhyme have the same ending sounds. Tell them that in "Rain, Rain, Go Away," the words *away* and *day* rhyme. Say the words and have children repeat them with you. *The word* say *also rhymes with* away *and* day. *Say the words with me:* away, day, say.

We Do

Say the following word pairs and guide children to say if the words rhyme: *bake, lake; sand, Sam; jump, thump; vest, pest; skin, skip.*

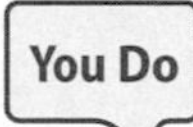
You Do

I'll say some word pairs. Give a thumbs up if the words rhyme: fish, dish; Tim, tip; tug, ton; hall, fall; patch, scratch; wrong, strong.

PHONEME ISOLATION

TIER 2

OBJECTIVES

Isolate and pronounce the initial, medial vowel, and final sounds (phonemes) in three-phoneme words. **RF.K.2d**

I Do

Display the *Koala* **Photo Card**. *This is a koala. The first sound in koala is /k/. Say the word and the beginning sound with me:* koala, /k/.

We Do

Display the *Kitten* Photo Card. *This is a kitten.* Have children say the name. *What is the first sound in* kitten? Say /k/ together. Repeat with the *Key* Photo Card.

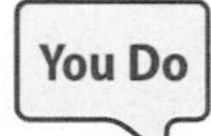
You Do

Display and name the *King* Photo Card. Have children name it and say the initial sound. Repeat with the *Kite* and *Key* Photo Cards.

Repeat the routine for final /k/ spelled *ck* using the *Rock* Photo Card in *I Do* and the Photo Cards for *Lock* and *Sock* in the rest of the lesson.

You may wish to review Phonological Awareness and Phonemic Awareness with ELL using this section.

PHONEME BLENDING

OBJECTIVES

CCSS Isolate and pronounce the initial, medial vowel, and final sounds (phonemes) in three-phoneme words. **RF.K.2d**

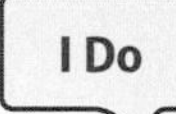

Listen as the puppet says the sounds in a word: /k/ /ī/ /t/. The puppet will blend the sounds to make a word: /kīīīt/, kite. *The puppet has blended the sounds /k/ /ī/ /t/ to make the word* kite. Repeat with *kit*.

Listen to the puppet say the sounds in a word. Have the puppet say /k/ /i/ /m/. Have children repeat. *Now let's blend the sounds and say the word with the puppet:* /kiiimmm/, Kim. Repeat with *kid*.

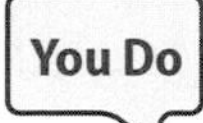

Have the puppet say the following sounds. Ask children to blend the sounds and say the words: /k/ /ē/ /p/, /kēēēp/, *keep*; /k/ /i/ /s/, /kiiisss/, *kiss*.

Repeat the routine for final /k/ spelled *ck* using these words: *tack*, /t/ /a/ /k/; *sick*, /s/ /i/ /k/; *deck*, /d/ /e/ /k/.

PHONEME SEGMENTATION

OBJECTIVES

CCSS Isolate and pronounce the initial, medial vowel, and final sounds (phonemes) in three-phoneme words. **RF.K.2d**

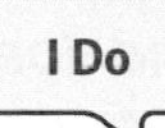

Use **Sound Boxes** and markers. *Listen as I say a word:* kit. *There are three sounds in* kit: /k/ /i/ /t/. *I'll place a marker in one box for each sound*. Repeat for the word *keep*.

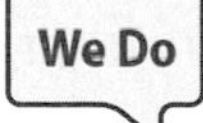

Distribute Sound Boxes and markers. *Let's listen for the number of sounds in more words. Listen as I say a word:* key. *Say the word with me:* key. *Say the sounds with me: /k/ /ē/. Let's place a marker in one box for each sound. There are two sounds in* key. Repeat with *kin*.

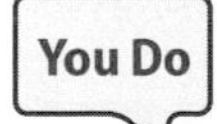

Repeat the practice with the following words: *kiss*, /k/ /i/ /s/; *kite*, /k/ /ī/ /t/; *Ken*, /k/ /e/ /n/.

Repeat the routine for final /k/ spelled *ck* using the sounds in these words: *lick*, /l/ /i/ /k/; *sack*, /s/ /a/ /k/; *peck*, /p/ /e/ /k/; *tuck*, /t/ /u/ /k/.

ELL ENGLISH LANGUAGE LEARNERS

For the **ELLs** who need **phonics, decoding,** and **fluency** practice, use scaffolding methods as necessary to ensure children understand the meaning of the words. Refer to the Language Transfer Handbook for phonics elements that may not transfer in children's native languages.

Approaching Level

Phonics

SOUND-SPELLING REVIEW

TIER 2

OBJECTIVES

CCSS Demonstrate basic knowledge of one-to-one letter-sound correspondences by producing the sounds for each consonant. **RF.K.3a**

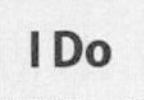
Display **Word-Building Card** *l*. Say the letter name and the sound it stands for: *l*, /l/. Repeat for *b, f, r, e, h*.

Display Word-Building Cards one at a time and together say the letter name and the sound that each letter stands for.

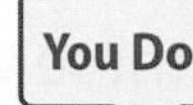
Display Word-Building Cards one at a time and have children say the letter name and the sound that each letter stands for.

CONNECT *k* AND *ck* TO /k/

TIER 2

OBJECTIVES

CCSS Demonstrate basic knowledge of one-to-one letter-sound correspondences by producing the primary or many of the most frequent sounds for each consonant. **RF.K.3a**

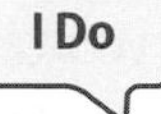
Display the *Koala* **Sound-Spelling Card**. *The letter* k *can stand for /k/ at the beginning of* koala. *What is this letter? What sound does it stand for? I will write* k *when I hear /k/ in these words:* kangaroo, lion, Ken, flash, kazoo.

The word keep *begins with /k/. Let's write* k. Guide children to write *k* when they hear a word that begins with */k/*: *leaf, kept, kitten, fudge, Kansas.*

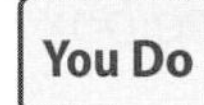
Have children write *k* if a word begins with /k/: *fish, kettle, kind, rope, king.*

Repeat the routine for final /k/ spelled *ck*. Use the *Lock* Sound-Spelling Card and the words *hack, ham, base, black, pack, page, stack, stove, brick, band.*

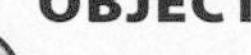

RETEACH

OBJECTIVES

CCSS Know and apply grade-level phonics and word analysis skills in decoding words. **RF.K.3**

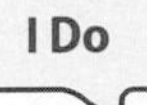
Display **Reading/Writing Workshop**, p. 20. *The letter* k *stands for the /k/ sound you hear at the beginning of* koala. Say *koala*, emphasizing /k/. Repeat for final /k/ spelled *ck* by using the *Sock* **Photo Card**.

Have children name each picture in row 1. Repeat the name, emphasizing initial /k/. Repeat for row 2, emphasizing final /k/ spelled *ck*.

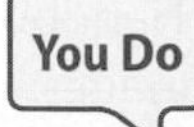
Guide children in reading the words in row 3. Then have them read the words in row 4, offering assistance as needed.

BLEND WORDS WITH /k/ *k*

OBJECTIVES

CCSS Isolate and pronounce the initial, medial vowel, and final sounds (phonemes) in three-phoneme words. **RF.K.2d**

Display **Word-Building Cards** *k, i, n. This is the letter* k. *It stands for /k/. This is the letter* i. *It stands for /i/. This is the letter* n. *It stands for /n/. Listen as I blend all three sounds: /kiiinnn/, kin. The word is* kin.

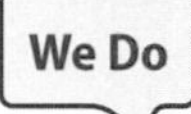

Now let's blend more sounds to make words. Make the word *Kim*. *Let's blend:* /kiiimmm/, Kim. Have children blend to read the word. Repeat with the word *kit*. *Let's blend:* /kiiit/, kit.

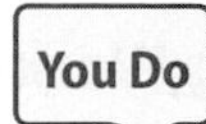

Distribute sets of Word-Building Cards with *k, c, e, i, d, n,* and *t*. Write: *Ken, kid, kit*. Have children form the words and then blend and read the words.

Repeat the routine for final /k/ spelled *ck*, reminding children to use two letters, *c* and *k* to make words. Use the words *back, sack, deck, lick*.

REREAD FOR FLUENCY

OBJECTIVES

CCSS Read emergent-reader texts with purpose and understanding. **RF.K.4**

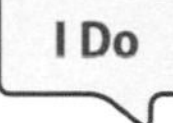

Turn to p. 22 of **Reading/Writing Workshop**, and read aloud the title. *Let's read the title together*. Page through the book. Ask children what they see in each picture. Ask children to find the words *she* and *was* on p. 23.

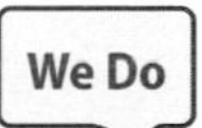

Have children open their books and chorally read the story. Have children point to each word as they read. Provide corrective feedback as needed. After reading, ask children to tell about what Kim and her grandmother do on the dock.

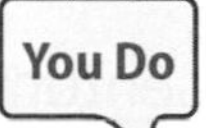

Have children reread "Kim and Nan" with a partner for fluency.

BUILD FLUENCY WITH PHONICS

Sound/Spelling Fluency

Display the following Word-Building Cards: *k, b, l, f, r, e,* and *h*. Have children chorally say each sound. Repeat and vary the pace.

Fluency in Connected Text

Write the following sentences. *Kim was not sick. Nick and Ken like to sit on the dock. Did Rick see my red sock?* Have children read the sentences and identify the words with initial /k/ and final /k/ spelled *ck*.

Approaching Level

High-Frequency Words

TIER 2

RETEACH WORDS

OBJECTIVES

Read common high-frequency words by sight. **RF.K.3c**

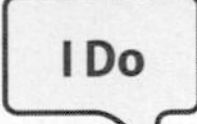
Display **High-Frequency Word Card** *she* and use the **Read/Spell/Write** routine to reteach the word. Repeat for *was.*

Have children turn to p. 21 of **Reading/Writing Workshop** and discuss the first photograph. Then read aloud the first sentence. Reread the sentence with children. Have children point to the word *she* in the sentence. Use the same routine for *was* and the other sentence on the page.

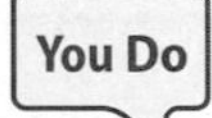
Write the sentence frame *She was at the* ______. Have children copy the sentence frame on their **Response Boards**. Then have partners work together to read and orally complete the frame by talking about places where someone might be. Reteach previously introduced high-frequency words using the **Read/Spell/Write** routine.

CUMULATIVE REVIEW

OBJECTIVES

Read common high-frequency words by sight. **RF.K.3c**

Display the **High-Frequency Word Cards** *I, can, the, we, see, a, like, to, and, go, you, do, my, are, he, with, is, little*. Use the **Read/Spell/Write** routine to review words.

Use the High-Frequency Word Cards to create sentences such as *Do you see my little cap? Ben and Ron are with Pop*. Have children identify the high-frequency words that are used in each sentence.

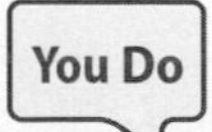
Have partners use the High-Frequency Word Cards and **Word-Building Cards** to create short sentences.

Oral Vocabulary

REVIEW WORDS

OBJECTIVES

CCSS Identify real-life connections between words and their use. **L.K.5c**

Develop oral vocabulary: *predict, temperature, storm, clever, drought*

Use the **Define/Example/Ask** routine to review words. Use the following definitions and provide examples:

predict	To **predict** is to guess what will happen in the future.
temperature	The **temperature** tells how hot or cold something is.
storm	During a **storm**, there are strong winds, heavy rain, or snow.
clever	If you have a **clever** idea, you have a smart idea.
drought	A **drought** is a long period of time with no rain.

We Do

Ask questions to build understanding. *What do you predict will happen during a storm? What is the temperature of an ice cube? What kinds of noises do you hear during a storm? What is a clever idea you once had? Why don't farmers like a drought?*

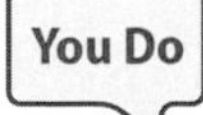

Have children complete these sentence frames: *In winter, I predict the weather will ______. The temperature in the summer feels ______. During a rain storm, I ______. It's hard to have a clever idea when ______. A drought is bad for plants because ______.*

Comprehension

SELF-SELECTED READING

OBJECTIVES

CCSS With prompting and support, ask and answer questions about key details in a text. **RL.K.1**

Apply the strategy and skill to reread text.

Read Independently

Help children select an illustrated story for sustained silent reading. Tell children that they will better understand a story when they know what happens first, next, and last. Remind them to make pictures in their minds as they read to help them understand the order of story events.

Read Purposefully

Before reading, help children draw three boxes in a row. Guide them through the process of writing or drawing a picture to tell what happens first, next, and last in the story. Remind children to make pictures in their minds as they read. After reading, have them share their boxes with the group. *What happened first in the story? What happened next? What happened last?*

On Level

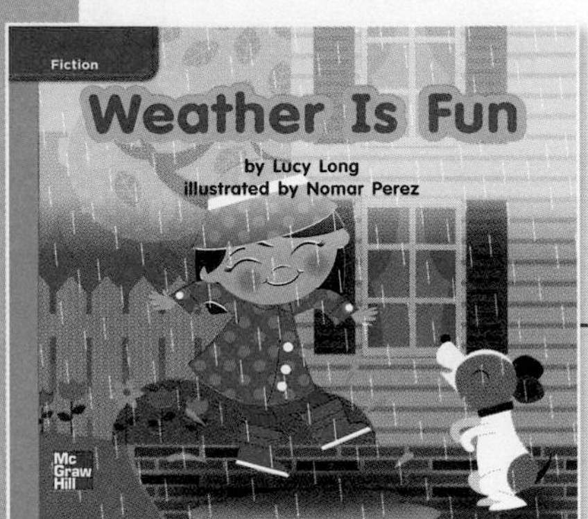

Leveled Reader

OBJECTIVES

CCSS With prompting and support, ask and answer questions about key details in a text. **RL.K.1**

CCSS With prompting and support, retell familiar stories, including key details. **RL.K.2**

CCSS Demonstrate understanding of the organization and basic features of print. **RF.K.1**

CCSS Read emergent-reader texts with purpose and understanding. **RF.K.4**

Leveled Reader: *Weather is Fun*

Leveled Reader

Before Reading

Preview and Predict

Read the title and the names of the author and illustrator as children follow along in their copies of the book. Discuss the cover illustration and ask children to predict what the book might be about. Preview each illustration and allow children to confirm or revise their predictions about the book.

Review Genre: Fiction

Remind children that like fantasy, fiction tells stories about made-up characters and events. Explain that the difference is that the events in a fantasy story could not happen in real life. Say: *Look at the pictures in this story. Do the things that happen in this story look like they could happen in real life?*

Model Concepts of Print

Ask children to point to the first and last word in each sentence. Review that the first word in a sentence starts with a capital letter and the last word is followed by a punctuation mark.

Review High-Frequency Words

Point out the word *was* on page 2. Have children point to the word *was* on each page and read the word.

Essential Question

Set a purpose for reading: *Let's find out what people can do in different kinds of weather.*

During Reading

Guided Comprehension

As children whisper-read, monitor and provide guidance by correcting blending and modeling the strategy and skill.

Strategy: Visualize

Remind children that as they read they can make pictures in their mind of what is happening in the story.

Skill: Key Details (Sequence)

Remind children that they should look for key details in the text and in the illustrations to help them understand the story. Explain that details are usually given in the order that events happen in the story.

Think Aloud On page 2, I learn from the details in the text and the illustration that it is winter and the girl is throwing snowballs. On page 3, I don't see any snow and the girl is not wearing a coat. I think it is now spring. I will keep reading to see what happens next.

As children read, guide them to pay attention to what the girl does in each season.

After Reading

Respond to Reading

- In what weather do we throw snowballs? (snowy winter weather)
- What does the girl do in the rain? (She jumps in puddles.)
- What happened after the girl swings? (She slept in a tent.)
- Why happens at the end of the story? (The girl kicks leaves.)

Retell

Have partners take turns retelling and acting out the story for each other. Help them make personal connections by asking: *What kind of weather do you think is fun? Why?*

Model Fluency

Read the sentences one at a time and demonstrate how to use expression in your voice, especially to emphasize an action word.

Apply Have children practice reading with partners. Encourage them to read with expression.

LITERACY ACTIVITIES

Have children complete the activities on the inside back cover of the reader.

Level Up

IF Children read *Weather is Fun* **On Level** with fluency and correctly answer the Respond to Reading questions,

THEN Tell children that they will read another story about what happens in different kinds of weather.

- Have children page through *Kate and Tuck* **Beyond Level** as you talk about what we wear in different kinds of weather.
- Have children read the story, monitoring their comprehension and providing assistance as necessary.

On Level

Phonemic Awareness

PHONEME ISOLATION

OBJECTIVES

CCSS Isolate and pronounce the initial, medial vowel, and final sounds (phonemes) in three-phoneme words. **RF.K.2d**

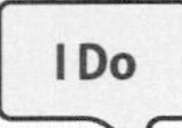

Display the *Koala* **Photo Card**. *This is a koala. The first sound is /k/. Say it with me.* Repeat for final /k/ using the *Lock* Photo Card.

Say *kite* and have children repeat it. *What is the first sound in* kite? Say the sound together. Continue with *keen, fin,* and *lab*. Repeat for final /k/ using the words *flock, frown, far,* and *stick.*

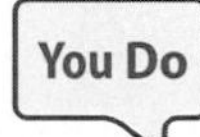

Say *led, kin, rat, bet, lit, Ken, kiss* and have children tell the initial sound in each word. Repeat for final /k/ using the words *train, trick, wick, miss, ran.*

PHONEME BLENDING

OBJECTIVES

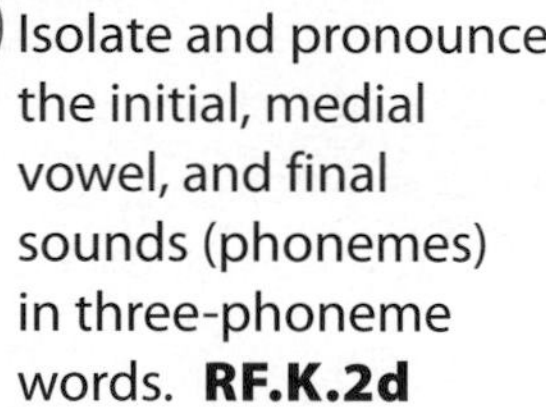

CCSS Isolate and pronounce the initial, medial vowel, and final sounds (phonemes) in three-phoneme words. **RF.K.2d**

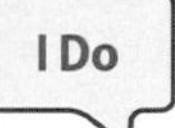

Listen as the puppet says the sounds in a word: /k/ /i/ /t/. *Now the puppet will blend the sounds to make a word:* /kiiit/, kit. Repeat for final /k/ with *pick.*

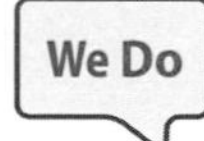

The puppet is going to say the sounds in a word. Listen: /k/ /i/ /m/. Have children repeat. *Now let's blend the sounds with the puppet and say the word:* /k/ /iii/ /mmm/, /kiiimmm/, Kim. Repeat with *kin, kiss, tack, sick.*

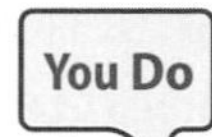

Say the following sounds. Ask children to blend the sounds and say the words: /k/ /i/ /n/, kin; /k/ /i/ /d/, kid; /p/ /a/ /k/, pack; /d/ /o/ /k/, dock.

PHONEME SEGMENTATION

OBJECTIVES

CCSS Isolate and pronounce the initial, medial vowel, and final sounds (phonemes) in three-phoneme words. **RF.K.2d**

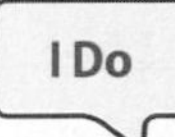

Use **Sound Boxes** and markers. *Listen to the sounds in* kick. *There are three sounds*: /k/ /i/ /k/. *I'll place a marker in one box for each sound*. Repeat for *keep.*

Distribute Sound Boxes and markers. *Listen as I say:* key, /k/ /ē/. *Let's place a marker in one box for each sound. There are two sounds in* key. Repeat for *rock.*

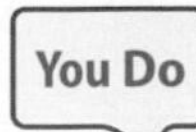

Repeat the practice with the words *lick, back, kit, mock, Kim.*

Phonics

REVIEW PHONICS

OBJECTIVES

CCSS Know and apply grade-level phonics and word analysis skills in decoding words. **RF.K.3**

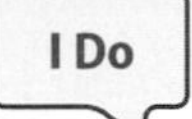

Display **Reading/Writing Workshop**, p. 20. Point to the *Koala* **Sound-Spelling Card**. *What letter stands for the /k/ sound you hear at the beginning of* koala? *The letter is* k. Repeat for final /k/ using the *Sock* **Photo Card**.

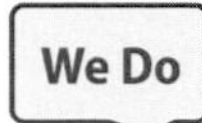

Have children say the name of each picture in rows 1 and 2. Then have them identify words with /k/ in the beginning. Repeat for words with /k/ at the end.

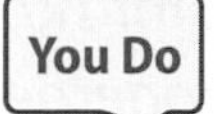

Have children read each word in rows 3 and 4. Have children raise their hands when they hear /k/ at the beginning of a word. Repeat, having them raise their hands when they hear /k/ at the end of a word.

PICTURE SORT

OBJECTIVES

Isolate and pronounce the initial, medial vowel, and final sounds (phonemes) in three-phoneme words. **RF.K.2d**

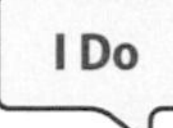

Display **Word-Building Cards** *k* and *b* in a pocket chart. Then show the *Kite* **Photo Card**. Say /k/ /ī/ /t/, *kite*. *The sound at the beginning is /k/. The letter* k *stands for /k/. I will put the kite under the letter* k. Show the *Bus* Photo Card. Say /b/ /u/ /s/, *bus*. *The sound at the beginning is /b/. The letter* b *stands for /b/. I will put the bus under the* b.

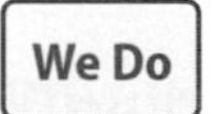

Show the *Bat* Photo Card and say *bat*, /b/ /a/ /t/. Have children repeat and tell the sound they hear at the beginning of *bat*. Ask them if they should place the photo under the *k* or the *b*. (b)

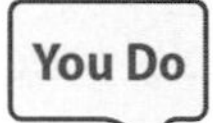

Continue the activity using *Box, Key, Boat,* and *King* Photo Cards. Have children say the picture name and the sounds in the name. Then have them place the card under the *k* or *b*.

Change the Word-Building Cards to *ck* and *n*. Repeat the routine for final /k/ spelled *ck* and final /n/ *n*. Use the Photo Cards *Lock, Sock, Rock, Pen, Fan, Man*.

On Level

Phonics

BLEND WORDS WITH /k/ *k*

OBJECTIVES

CCSS Isolate and pronounce the initial, medial vowel, and final sounds (phonemes) in three-phoneme words. **RF.K.2d**

Use **Word-Building Cards** or write *l, i, c, k. This is the letter* l. *It stands for /l/. Say it with me: /lll/. This is the letter* i. *It stands for /i/. Say it with me: /iii/. These are the letters c* and *k. Together they stand for /k/ at the end of a word. Say the sound with me: /k/. I'll blend the sounds together to read the word:* /llliiik/, lick. Repeat the routine using the word *kid*.

Write *pick* and *kit*. Guide children to blend the words sound by sound to read each word.

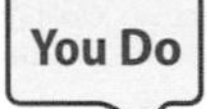

Write the following words and have children blend the words sound by sound to read each word.

Kim deck kick tack

REREAD FOR FLUENCY

OBJECTIVES

CCSS Read emergent-reader texts with purpose and understanding. **RF.K.4**

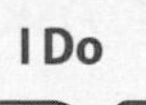

Point to the title "Kim and Nan" on p. 22 of **Reading/Writing Workshop 6**. Tell children that these words should be read with expression because it will be exciting and fun to read about what Kim and Nan are doing. Model reading p. 23: *When I read,* "Kim had a lot to pack," *I read all the way to the end of the sentence before pausing. This makes my reading sound natural, as if I were talking.*

Reread p. 23. Then have children chorally read the page with you. Continue choral reading the remainder of the pages.

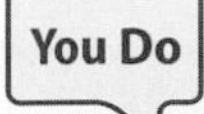

Have children reread "Kim and Nan." Provide time to listen as children read the pages. Comment on their accuracy and expression and provide corrective feedback by modeling proper fluency.

High-Frequency Words

REVIEW WORDS

OBJECTIVES

Read common high-frequency words by sight. **RF.K.3c**

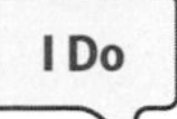

Use the **High-Frequency Word Card** *she* with the **Read/Spell/Write** routine to review the word. Repeat with *was*.

Have children turn to p. 21 of **Reading/Writing Workshop**. Discuss the photographs and read aloud the first sentence. Point to the word *she* and have children read it. Then chorally read the sentence. Have children frame and read the word *she* in the sentence. Repeat with the second sentence and *was*.

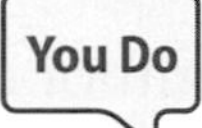

Say the word *she*. Ask children to close their eyes, picture the word, and write it as they see it. Have children self-correct. Repeat the routine for *was*.

Reteach previously introduced high-frequency words using the **Read/Spell/Write** routine.

Fluency Point to the High-Frequency Word Cards *little, is, go, my, he, you, are, do,* and *with* in random order. Have children chorally read. Repeat at a faster pace.

Comprehension

SELF-SELECTED READING

OBJECTIVES

CCSS With prompting and support, ask and answer questions about key details in a text. **RL.K.1**

Apply the strategy and skill to reread the text.

Read Independently

Have children select an illustrated story for sustained silent reading. Remind them that knowing what happens first, next, and last in a story will help them better understand it. Explain that visualizing as they read can help them figure out what happens first, next, and last.

Read Purposefully

Before reading, ask children to draw three boxes in a row. Tell them to write *first, next,* and *last* above each box. Then have children write a few words in each box to tell what happens first, next, and last as they read. After reading, ask them to share their boxes with the class. Encourage them to share how they made pictures in their minds to help them understand events in the story.

Beyond Level

Leveled Reader

OBJECTIVES

 With prompting and support, ask and answer questions about key details in a text. **RL.K.1**

 With prompting and support, retell familiar stories, including key details. **RL.K.2**

 Recognize common types of texts (e.g., storybooks, poems). **RL.K.5**

Leveled Reader: *Kate and Tuck*

Before Reading

Preview and Predict

Ask children to point to the title and the name of the author on the covers of their books as you read them aloud. Ask children to use the cover illustration to try to identify the characters of Kate and Tuck. Ask: *Who do you think is Kate? Which one do you think is Tuck?* Invite children to look through the illustrations and predict what they think the story will be about.

Review Genre: Fiction

Remind children that fiction books are made-up stories with characters and events. Explain that unlike a fantasy story, the events in some fiction stories could happen in real life. Ask: *Do you think the things that happen in this story could happen in real life?*

Essential Question

Remind children of the Essential Question: *What happens in different kinds of weather?* Have children set a purpose for reading. Say: *Let's read to find out what Kate and Tuck do in different kinds of weather.*

During Reading

Guided Comprehension

As children read, monitor and provide guidance by correcting blending and modeling the strategy and skill. Point out quotation marks to children. Ask: *How can you tell when a character is talking in a fiction story?*

Strategy: Visualize

Remind children that they will understand a story better if they try to picture in their mind what the characters are doing.

Go Digital

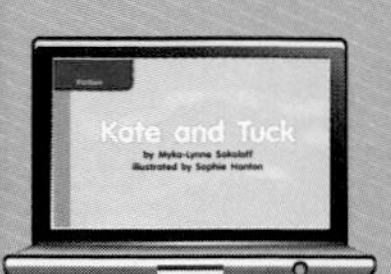

Leveled Reader

Skill: Key Details (Sequence)

Remind children that finding key details in the text and the illustrations will help them to understand the story. Explain that in this book, the illustrations provide key details about the weather.

Think Aloud On page 2, the story says that it was a cool fall day. I learn from the text and the illustration that Kate and Tuck are wearing sweaters to keep warm. On page 3, there is a new character, Mack. So, first Kate and Tuck put on sweaters and then they play in the leaves with Mack. I will keep reading to see what happens next.

Guide children to look for key details about what Kate and Tuck do and wear next. Discuss how the weather changes when the seasons change.

After Reading

Respond to Reading

- → *What does Kate wear on a cold winter day?* (mittens, boots, and a scarf)
- → *What do Kate and Tuck do after they are dressed warmly for winter?* (they play with Mack)
- → *Why must we dress differently in different kinds of weather?* (We have to keep our bodies warm or cool or protected from the weather.)

Retell

Have children take turns retelling the story. Help them make a personal connection by asking: *What do you wear in different types of weather?*

Gifted and Talented

EVALUATING Have children think about what they wear in different weather. First have them name different weather and then decide what clothing would be best for that type of weather.

HAVE children make a poster and draw what people should wear in each type of weather.

LITERACY ACTIVITIES

Have children complete the activities on the inside back cover of the reader.

Beyond Level

Phonics

REVIEW

OBJECTIVES

CCSS Know and apply grade-level phonics and word analysis skills in decoding words. **RF.K.3**

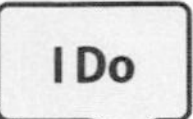

Display **Reading/Writing Workshop**, p. 20. Point to the *Koala* **Sound-Spelling Card**. *What is the sound at the beginning of* koala? *What letter can stand for /k/? The letter is* k. Repeat for final /k/ spelled *ck* using the *Lock* Photo Card.

Have children say the name of each picture. Then ask children to share other words they know that begin with /k/ spelled *k*. Repeat for words that end with /k/ spelled *ck*.

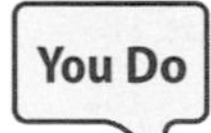

Have partners read each decodable word. Ask them to write the words on their **Response Boards**, underlining the letters in each word that stand for initial and final /k/.

Fluency Have children turn to p. 22 in **Reading/Writing Workshop** and reread "Kim and Nan" for fluency.

Innovate Have children create a new page for "Kim and Nan" by completing the sentence frame *Kim and Nan go to the* ______. and naming places that Kim and Nan can go.

High-Frequency Words

REVIEW

OBJECTIVES

CCSS Read common high-frequency words by sight. **RF.K.3c**

Create **High-Frequency Word Cards** for *old* and *new*. Introduce the words using the **Read/Spell/Write** routine.

We Do

Display the High-Frequency Word Cards for *see, and, a, little, I, like, the,* and *my*. Have children help you complete the following sentence frames using the High-Frequency Word Cards: *Rick and Bob like the old* ______. *I see a new* ______.

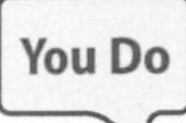

Have partners write sentences using the High-Frequency Words *old* and *new* on their Response Boards. Have them read their sentences.

Vocabulary

ORAL VOCABULARY: SYNONYMS

OBJECTIVES

CCSS With guidance and support from adults, explore word relationships and nuances in word meanings. **L.K.5**

Develop oral vocabulary: Synonyms

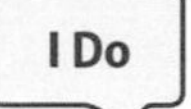

Review meanings of the oral vocabulary words *predict* and *temperature*. Explain that a synonym is a word that means almost the same thing as another word.

A synonym for predict *is* guess. *We guess when we decide what will probably happen*. I can guess what will happen next by looking at the pictures.

A synonym for drought *is* dryness. *Dryness happens when there is no water for a long time*. The dryness caused the plants to droop.

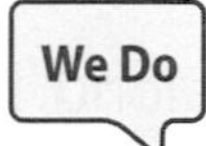

Write a few sentences together using the new words *guess* and *dryness*. Read the sentences aloud.

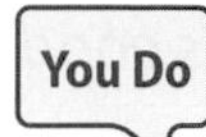

Have partners write a weather report. Have them include the words *guess* and *dryness* in their report. Ask them to report the weather to the group.

Extend Have children choose which type of weather is their favorite. Then have partners take turns interviewing each other. Encourage children to guess why the type of weather they named is their favorite.

Comprehension

SELF-SELECTED READING

OBJECTIVES

With prompting and support, ask and answer questions about key details in a text. **RL.K.1**

Apply the strategy and skill to reread the text.

Read Independently

Have children select an illustrated story for sustained silent reading. Tell them that visualizing while reading can help them better understand the order of story details in the beginning, middle, and end of the story.

Read Purposefully

Before reading, have children draw four boxes in a row. Tell them to fill in the boxes with story events in time order. Remind them to visualize as they write in each box. After reading, have them read what they wrote. Have them explain how writing down events in order helps them better understand the story. Ask what would happen if the story events were written out of order.

Independent Study Have children write a few sentences giving an opinion about a text they read this week. Tell them to remember to give reasons to support their opinion. Ask them to create a book cover illustrating what they wrote about.

English Language Learners

Leveled Reader

OBJECTIVES

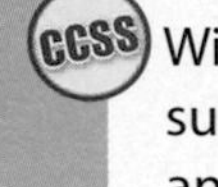
With prompting and support, ask and answer questions about key details in a text. **RL.K.1**

With prompting and support, retell familiar stories, including key details. **RL.K.2**

Read emergent-reader texts with purpose and understanding. **RF.K.4**

Shared Read: *Weather Is Fun*

Go Digital

Leveled Reader

Before Reading

Preview and Predict

Point to and read aloud the title while children follow along. Ask children to name what they see in the cover illustration. Make sure that they understand the English word *weather*. Ask: *What is good weather? What is bad weather?*

Walk children through the book, discussing each illustration and reading the labels on the pictures. Use simple language to describe each picture.

Essential Question

Remind children of the Essential Question: *What happens in different kinds of weather?* Set a purpose for reading: *Let's find out what the girl does in different weather*. Encourage children to ask questions and seek clarification when necessary.

During Reading

Interactive Question Response

Pages 2–3 Point to the illustration on page 2. Ask questions and encourage children to use full sentences to respond. Ask: *Where is the girl?* (The girl is in the snow.) *What can the girl throw?* (The girl can throw a snowball.) *Let's read the sentence together*. Point to the illustration on page 3. Ask: *Where is the girl?* (The girl is in her backyard.) *What can she do?* (The girl can run.) *What kind of weather is this?* (spring/warm weather) *Let's read the sentence together*.

Pages 4–5 Point to the illustration and label on page 4. Say: *This is a puddle. It is water from the rain. What does the girl do in this picture?* (The girl jumps in the puddle.) *It can be fun to play in the rain*. Point to the text on page 5. Ask: *Where is the girl?* (The girl is under the tree.) *What can the girl do under the tree?* (She can read.)

Pages 6–7 Point to the illustration and label on page 6. Ask: *Where is the girl?* (The girl is on the swing.) *What can the girl do?* (She can swing.) Point to the illustration on page 7 and the label pointing to the tent. Ask: *What is this?* (tent) *What can the girl do here?* (She can sleep.) *Let's read the sentences on these pages.*

Page 8 Point to the illustration. Ask: *What is the girl doing?* (The girl is kicking.) *What can the girl kick?* (She can kick leaves.) *In what kind of weather can we kick leaves?* (We can kick leaves on a fall day.)

After Reading

Respond to Reading

- *What is something people can do in the snow?* (throw snowballs)
- *On what kind of day does the girl read outside?* (on a warm summer day)
- *Why is it fun to play in puddles?* (You can get wet.)

Retell

Say: *Let's retell the book together. What does the girl do in the different seasons?* (play) Ask children to act out the story as they retell it.

Model Fluency

As you read each sentence, demonstrate how to read fluently and with expression.

Apply Ask partners to read together. Encourage them to take turns reading a page aloud, using expression in their voices.

LITERACY ACTIVITIES

Have children complete the activities on the inside back cover of the reader.

Level Up

IF Children read *Weather Is Fun* **ELL Level** with fluency and correctly answer the Respond to Reading questions,

THEN Tell children that they will read a more detailed version of the story.

- Have children page through *Weather Is Fun* **On Level** and conduct a picture walk to describe what is happening in each picture.
- Have children read the story, monitoring their comprehension and providing assistance as necessary.

English Language Learners

Vocabulary

PRETEACH ORAL VOCABULARY

OBJECTIVES

CCSS Speak audibly and express thoughts, feelings, and ideas clearly. **SL.K.6**

LANGUAGE OBJECTIVE

Preview vocabulary

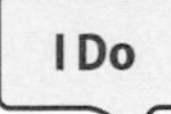

Display the images from the **Visual Vocabulary Cards** and follow the routine to preteach the oral vocabulary words.

Display each image again and explain how they can relate to your own world. Model using sentences to describe the image.

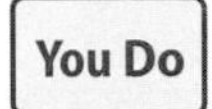

Display the word *temperature* again and explain that temperatures can be warm or cold and can be given in numbers called *degrees*. Tell children today's temperature and talk about whether it is warm or cold.

Beginning	Intermediate	Advanced/High
Prompt children to talk about today's temperature.	Ask children to predict what the weather will be like tomorrow.	Ask children to use the words in a sentence of their own.

PRETEACH ELL VOCABULARY

OBJECTIVES

Speak audibly and express thoughts, feelings, and ideas clearly. **SL.K.6**

LANGUAGE OBJECTIVE

Preview ELL vocabulary

Display the images from the **Visual Vocabulary Cards** one at a time to preteach the ELL vocabulary words *activity* and *change*. Follow the routine. Say each word and have children repeat it. Define each word in English.

Display each image again and incorporate the words in a short discussion about the images. Model using sentences to describe the image.

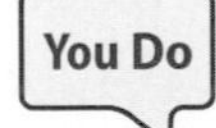

Display the word *activity* again and have children talk to a partner about their favorite activity in sunny weather. List their ideas as they say them.

Beginning	Intermediate	Advanced/High
Say each word in a sentence and ask children to chorally repeat the sentence after you.	Ask children to work in pairs to complete the sentence frame *My favorite rainy day activity is* ____.	Ask children to work with a partner and talk about what happens when the weather changes from sunny to rainy.

High-Frequency Words

REVIEW WORDS

OBJECTIVES

 Read common high-frequency words by sight (e.g., *the, of, to, you, she, my, is, are, do, does*). **RF.K.3c**

LANGUAGE OBJECTIVE

Review high-frequency words

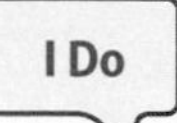 Display the **High-Frequency Word Cards** for *she* and *was*. Read the words. Use the **Read/Spell/Write** routine to teach the words. Have children write the words on their **Response Boards**.

 Write a sentence frame that uses the week's high-frequency words: *She was* ______. Track print as children read and complete the sentence. Explain to children that the word *was* is used when talking about something that already happened.

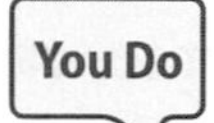 Display a sentence that uses the high-frequency words *she* and *was*. Ask children to point to the words and say them aloud. Then work with children to read and say the entire sentence aloud.

Beginning	Intermediate	Advanced/High
Help children complete the sentence frame: *She was* ____.	Ask partners to find the words in any classroom book. Have them take turns reading the sentences.	Ask children to name more things to complete the sentence starter *She was* ____.

REVIEW CATEGORY WORDS

OBJECTIVES

 Identify real-life connections between words and their use (e.g., note places at school that are colorful). **L.K.5c**

LANGUAGE OBJECTIVE

Use category words

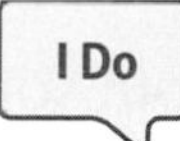 Display the **Visual Vocabulary Card** and say the words aloud. Define the words in English and then in Spanish, if appropriate, identifying any cognates.

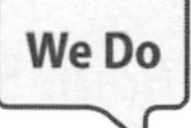 Write the words *rainy, cloudy, windy, snowy, gloomy,* and *sunny* and say the words aloud. Ask children to repeat each word after you. Tell children that these words have to do with weather. Ask children to choose the word that describes today's weather.

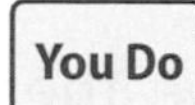 Have children work with partners. Ask them to choose one of the category words together and draw a picture of themselves in that type of weather.

Beginning	Intermediate	Advanced/High
Prompt children to describe the weather in their drawings.	Guide children to work together to use one or two of the category words in a sentence.	Have children choose one of the category words and describe what that kind of weather is like.

English Language Learners

Writing

SHARED WRITING

OBJECTIVES

Use a combination of drawing, dictating, and writing to narrate a single event or several loosely linked events, tell about the events in the order in which they occurred, and provide a reaction to what happened. **W.K.3**

LANGUAGE OBJECTIVE

Contribute to a shared writing project

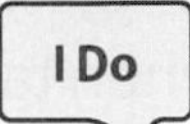

Review the chart in the Whole Group Shared Writing project for possible ideas of rainy day activities. Then model using one of the items on the list to write a sentence: *I like to splash in puddles on a rainy day.*

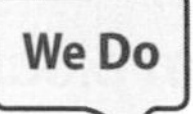

With children, choose an activity from the chart to write a shared sentence. Use a sentence starter such as *we like to* ______ *on rainy days*.

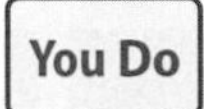

Help partners complete the sentence frame that tells about their favorite activity to do on a rainy day.

Beginning	Intermediate	Advanced/High
Provide pictures of rainy day activities so children can talk about their favorite activities.	Ask partners to draw and share a picture to go with their sentence.	Ask children to write a sentence about more than one activity.

WRITING TRAIT: VOICE

OBJECTIVES

With guidance and support from adults, respond to questions and suggestions from peers and add details to strengthen writing as needed. **W.K.5**

LANGUAGE OBJECTIVE

Organize ideas for writing

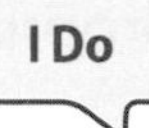

Explain that writers can show how they feel about something with the words they choose. These words are the writer's voice, and they help readers understand how a writer feels about a topic.

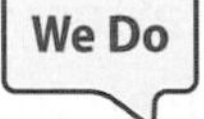

Reread pages 12–13 of the **Big Book** selection *Rain*. Say: *The writer shows excitement about the coming rain on these pages. Which words help us feel excitement about the rain?* (The rhino's lines, "The rain is here!" and "I must tell the lion" show excitement about the rain)

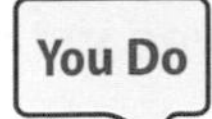

Have children write a sentence about today's weather. Have them use the sentence frames: *It is* ______ *outside. It makes me want to* ______.

Beginning	Intermediate	Advanced/High
Prompt children to talk about the weather.	Guide children to complete the sentence frames in pairs and read it aloud.	Ask children to write their own sentences without using the sentence frame.

Grammar

NAMING WORDS (NOUNS)

OBJECTIVES

CCSS Use frequently occurring nouns and verbs. **L.K.1b**

LANGUAGE OBJECTIVE

Recognize and use nouns correctly

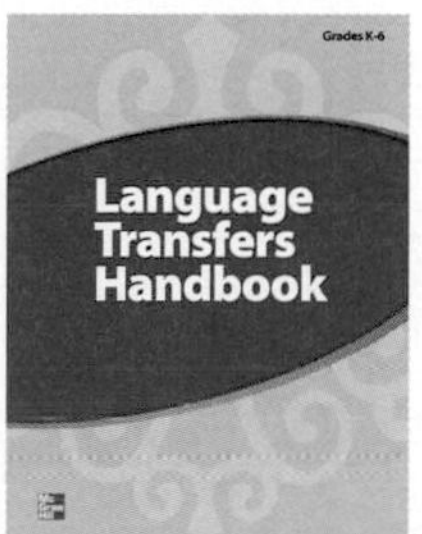

Language Transfers Handbook

In Cantonese, Haitian Creole, Hmong, Korean, and Vietnamese, there is no article before nouns in the native language or no difference between *the* and *a*. Remind children to use articles before nouns correctly.

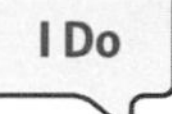

Review that a noun is a word that describes a person, place, or thing. Say the sentence: *Jack has an umbrella.* Repeat the sentence and explain that both *Jack* and *umbrella* are nouns. Jack *is a person.* Umbrella *is a thing.*

Say the following sentences. Ask children to identify the nouns in each sentence.

Sarah goes to the park.

Rain falls from the sky.

There is snow on the ground.

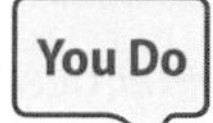

Say the following sentence: *I like to play in the* ______.

Pair children and have them orally complete the sentence frame by providing details from this week's readings. Circulate, listen in, and take note of each child's language use and proficiency.

Beginning	Intermediate	Advanced/High
Before guiding children to complete the sentence frame, remind them that a noun is a person, place, or thing.	Help children use the selections to identify their favorite weather.	Have children use the selections to help them complete the sentence frame on their own.

PROGRESS MONITORING

Weekly Assessment

Use your Quick Check observations and the assessment opportunities identified below to evaluate children's progress in key skill areas.

✓ TESTED SKILLS CCSS	Quick Check Observations	Pencil and Paper Assessment
PHONEMIC AWARENESS/ PHONICS k /k/, /ck/ (initial k, final ck) **RF.K.3a**	Can children isolate /k/ and match the sound to the letters *Kk* and *ck*?	Practice Book, pp. 163–164, 165–166, 168
HIGH-FREQUENCY WORDS she *she, was* **RF.K.3c**	Can children recognize and read the high-frequency words?	Practice Book, pp. 169–170
COMPREHENSION Key Details: Sequence **RL.K.1**	As you read *Rain* with children, can they identify key details and discuss their sequence in the text?	Practice Book, p. 167

Quick Check Rubric

Skills	1	2	3
PHONEMIC AWARENESS/ PHONICS	Does not connect the sound /k/ with the letters *Kk* or *ck*.	Usually connects the sound /k/ with the letters *Kk* and *ck*.	Consistently connects the sound /k/ with the letters *KK* and *ck*.
HIGH-FREQUENCY WORDS	Does not identify the high-frequency words.	Usually recognizes the high-frequency words with accuracy, but not speed.	Consistently recognizes the high-frequency words with speed and accuracy.
COMPREHENSION	Does not identify key details and their sequence in the text.	Usually identifies key details and their sequence in the text.	Consistently identifies key details and their sequence in the text.

Go Digital! www.connected.mcgraw-hill.com

Using Assessment Results

TESTED SKILLS	If ...	Then ...
PHONEMIC AWARENESS/ PHONICS	**Quick Check Rubric:** Children consistently score 1 or **Pencil and Paper Assessment:** Children get 0–2 items correct	... reteach tested Phonemic Awareness and Phonics skills using Lessons 16–17 and 27–29 in the ***Tier 2 Phonemic Awareness Intervention Online PDFs*** and Lesson 29 in the ***Tier 2 Phonics/Word Study Intervention Online PDFs.***
HIGH-FREQUENCY WORDS	**Quick Check Rubric:** Children consistently score 1	... reteach tested skills by using the High-Frequency Word Cards and asking children to read and spell the word. Point out any irregularities in sound-spellings.
COMPREHENSION	**Quick Check Rubric:** Children consistently score 1 or **Pencil and Paper Assessment:** Children get 0–1 items correct	... reteach tested skill using Lessons 10–12 in the ***Tier 2 Comprehension Intervention Online PDFs.***

Response to Intervention

Use the children's assessment results to assist you in identifying children who will benefit from focused intervention.

Use the appropriate sections of the ***Placement and Diagnostic Assessment*** to designate children requiring:

TIER 2 **Tier 2 Intervention Online PDFs**

TIER 3 **WonderWorks Intervention Program**

- → Phonemic Awareness
- → Phonics
- → Vocabulary
- → Comprehension
- → Fluency

WEEKLY OVERVIEW

Literature Big Book

Listening Comprehension

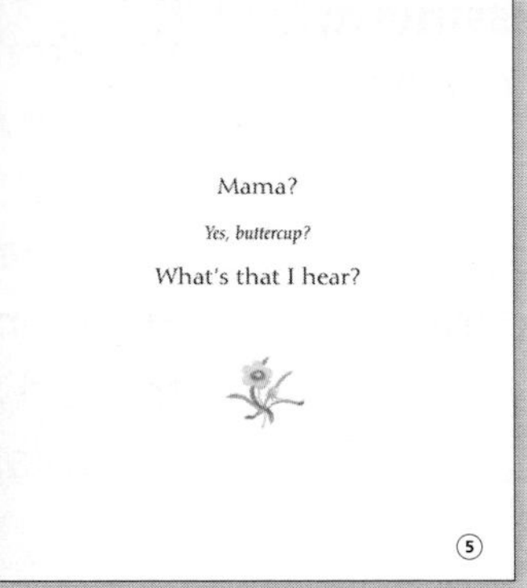

Waiting Out the Storm, 4–27
Genre Fiction

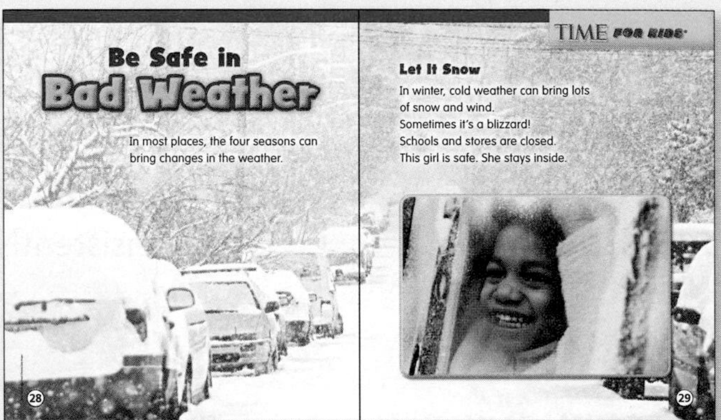

"Be Safe in Bad Weather" 28–32
Genre Informational Text

Interactive Read-Aloud Cards

"Rainbow Crow"
Genre Myth

Oral Vocabulary

celebration	prepare
enough	safe
notice	

Minilessons

✓ TESTED SKILLS CCSS

✓ **Comprehension Strategy** .... Visualize, T177

✓ **Comprehension Skill** .... Key Details, T191

Go Digital

www.connected.mcgraw-hill.com

STORMY WEATHER

Essential Question

How can you stay safe in bad weather?

WEEK 3

Big Book and Little Book Reading/Writing Workshop

Shared Reading

"Mack and Ben," 36–43

Genre Fiction

High-Frequency Words

are, he, is, little, my, she, was, with, T181

Minilessons

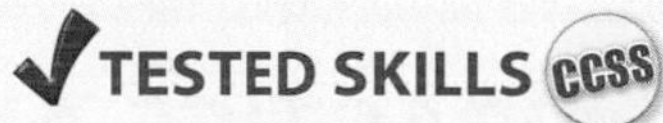

✓ TESTED SKILLS CCSS

✓ **Phonics** .... /e/e, /h/h, /f/f, T179

Writing Trait........................ Voice, T182

Grammar .... Nouns, T183

Differentiated Text

Approaching

On Level

Beyond

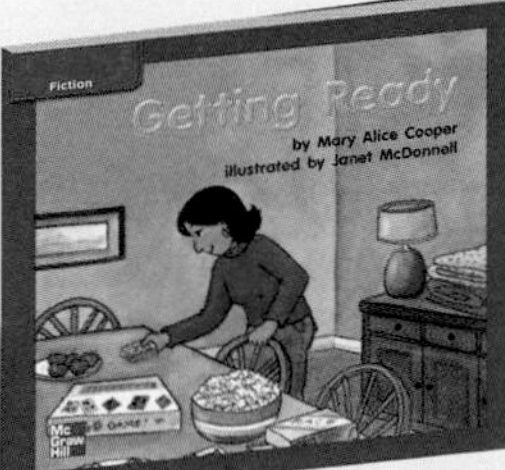

ELL

TEACH AND MANAGE

What You Do

INTRODUCE

Weekly Concept
Stormy Weather

Reading/Writing Workshop Big Book, 34–35

TEACH AND APPLY

Listening Comprehension
Big Book
Waiting Out the Storm
Genre Fiction
Paired Read "Be Safe in Bad Weather"
Genre Informational Text

Minilessons
Strategy: Visualize
Skill: Key Details

Shared Reading
Reading/Writing Workshop
"Mack and Ben"

Minilessons
/e/e, /h/h, /f/f, High-Frequency Words: are, he, is, little, my, she, was, with Writing, Grammar

Go Digital

Interactive Whiteboard

Interactive Whiteboard

Mobile

What Your Students Do

WEEKLY CONTRACT

PDF Online

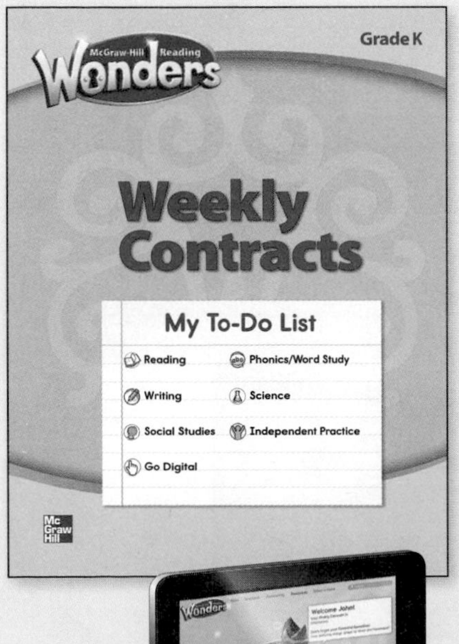

PRACTICE AND ONLINE ACTIVITIES

Your Turn Practice Book, pp. 173–184

Leveled Readers

Go Digital

Online To-Do List

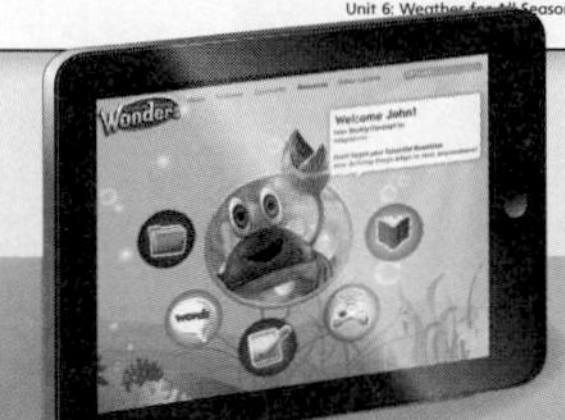
Online Activities

Mobile

WEEK 3

DIFFERENTIATE

Small Group Instruction

Leveled Readers

Mobile

INTEGRATE

Research and Inquiry

Safety Book, pp. T216–T217

Text Connections

Compare Storms, p. T218

Talk About Reading

Becoming Readers, p. T219

Online Research

WORKSTATION CARDS

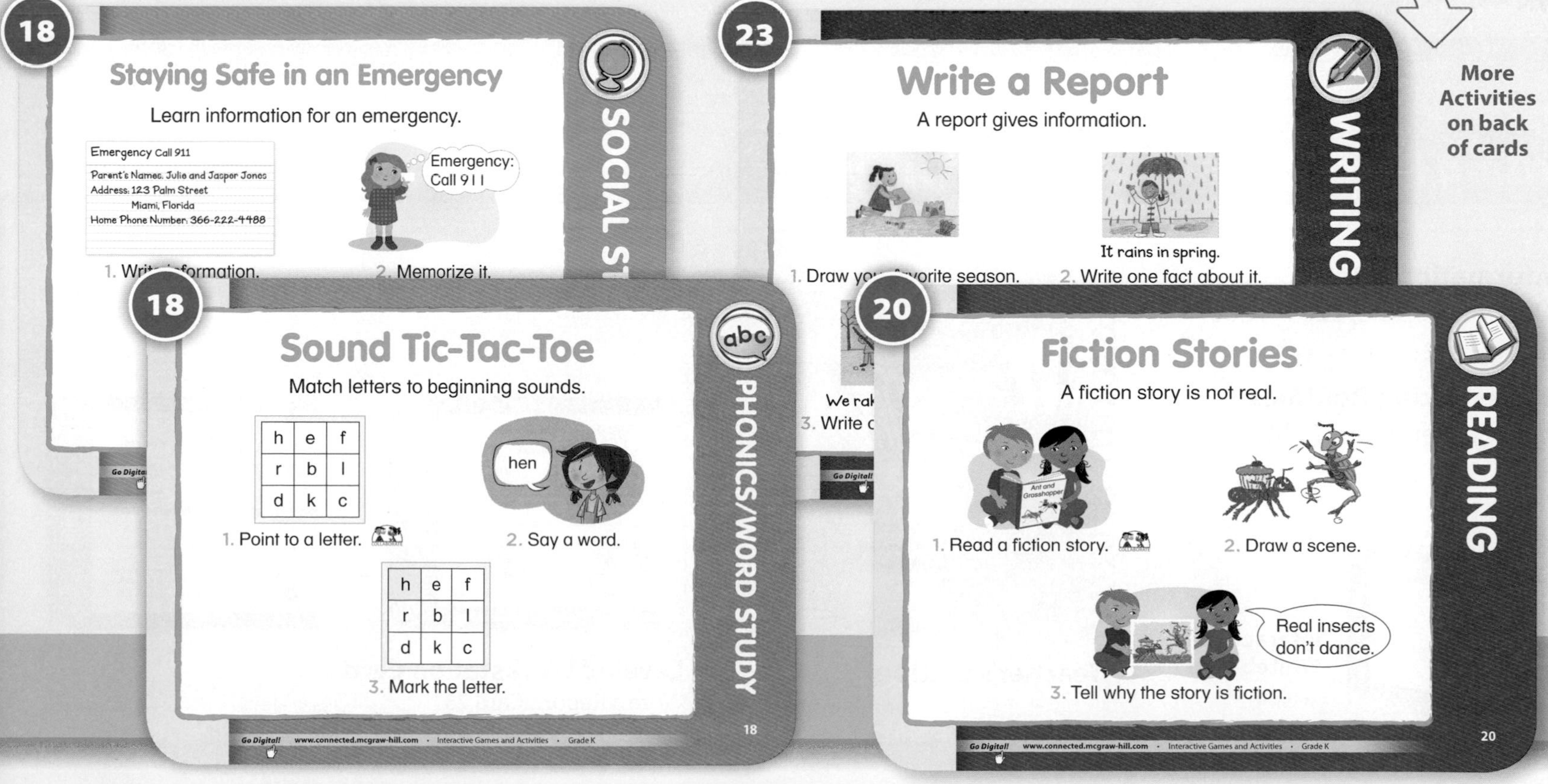

More Activities on back of cards

18 Staying Safe in an Emergency
Learn information for an emergency.
Emergency Call 911
Parent's Names: Julie and Jasper Jones
Address: 123 Palm Street
Miami, Florida
Home Phone Number: 366-222-4488
Emergency: Call 911
1. Write information.
2. Memorize it.
SOCIAL ST

23 Write a Report
A report gives information.
1. Draw your favorite season.
It rains in spring.
2. Write one fact about it.
We rak
3. Write c
WRITING

18 Sound Tic-Tac-Toe
Match letters to beginning sounds.

h	e	f
r	b	l
d	k	c

1. Point to a letter.
hen
2. Say a word.

h	e	f
r	b	l
d	k	c

3. Mark the letter.
PHONICS/WORD STUDY
Go Digital! www.connected.mcgraw-hill.com • Interactive Games and Activities • Grade K
18

20 Fiction Stories
A fiction story is not real.
1. Read a fiction story.
2. Draw a scene.
Real insects don't dance.
3. Tell why the story is fiction.
READING
Go Digital! www.connected.mcgraw-hill.com • Interactive Games and Activities • Grade K
20

DEVELOPING READERS AND WRITERS

Write About Reading • Analytical Writing

Write to Sources and Research

Respond to Reading, T177, T225, T233, T239, T243

Connect to Essential Question, T177, T209

Key Details, T191

Research and Inquiry, T216

Teacher's Edition

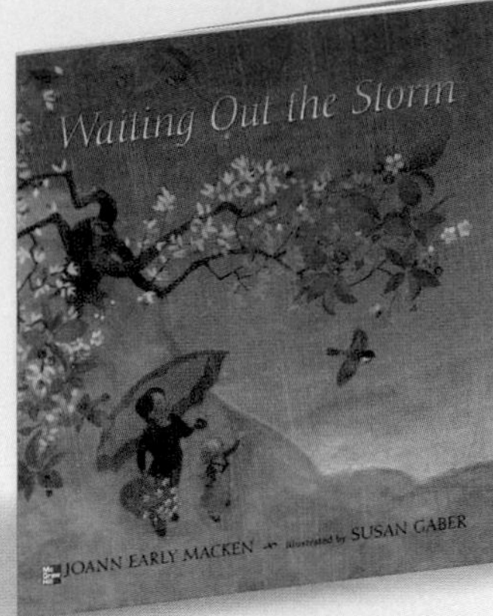

Literature Big Book
Waiting Out the Storm
Paired Read: *Be Safe in Bad Weather*

Interactive Whiteboard

Leveled Readers
Responding to Texts

Writing Process • Independent Writing

Informational Text
Weather Report, T204–T205, T214, T222

Conferencing Routines
Peer Conferences, T214

Interactive Whiteboard

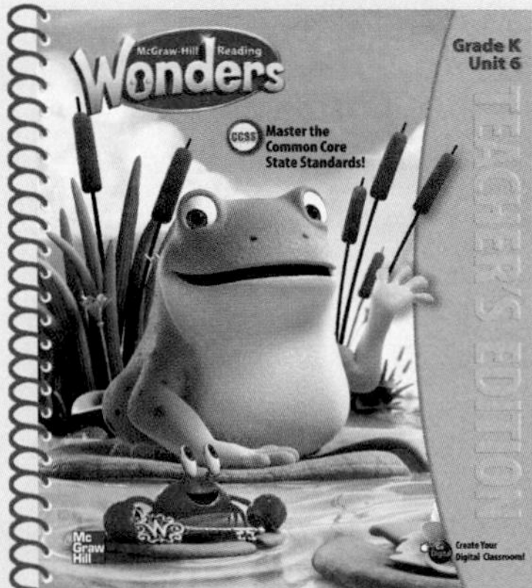

Teacher's Edition

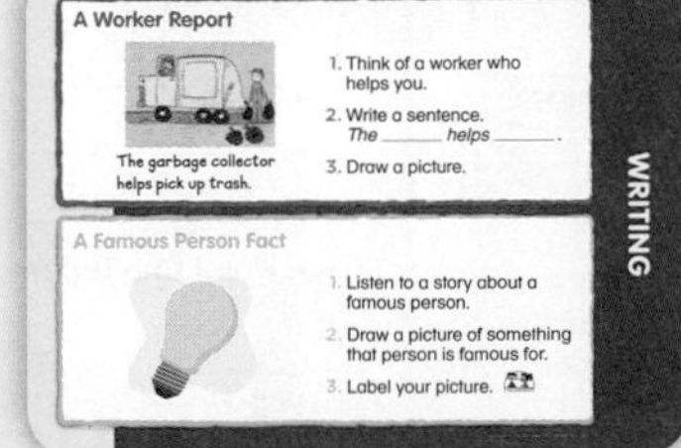

Leveled Workstation Card
Write a Report, Card 23

WEEK 3

Writing Traits • Shared and Interactive Writing

Writing Trait:
Voice
Weather Report, T182, T196

Teacher's Edition

Voice, p. 46
Nouns, p. 47

Reading/Writing Workshop

Interactive Whiteboard

Leveled Workstation Card
Write a Report, Card 23

Grammar and Spelling/Dictation

Grammar
Naming Words (Nouns), T183

Spelling/Dictation
Words with Short *e*, *o*, and *d*, *f*, *r*, *b*, *l*, *k*, *t*, *ck*, T211, T221

Interactive Whiteboard

Teacher's Edition

Online Grammar Games

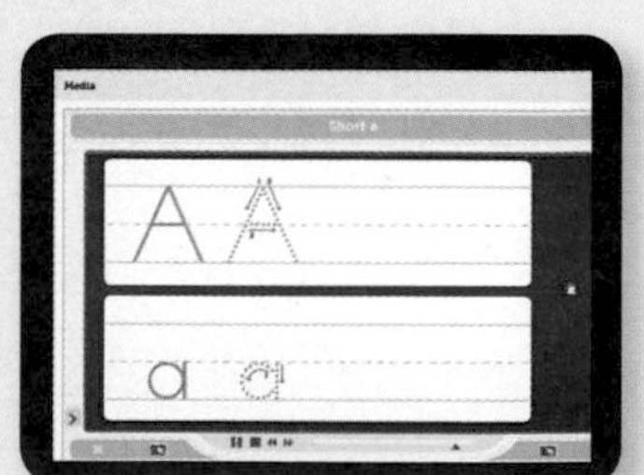
Handwriting

SUGGESTED LESSON PLAN

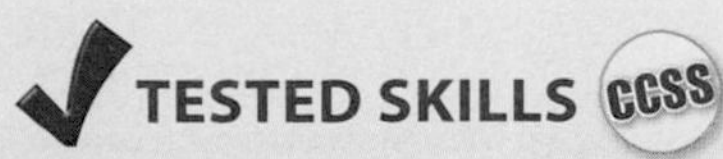

✓ TESTED SKILLS CCSS

		DAY 1	DAY 2
Whole Group	**READING**		
	Teach and Model Literature Big Book Reading/Writing Workshop	**Build Background** Stormy Weather, T174 **Oral Vocabulary** safe, prepare, T174 ✓**Listening Comprehension** • Genre: Fiction • Strategy: Visualize, T177 • Make Connections, T177 **Big Book** *Waiting Out the Storm* ✓**Word Work** **Phonemic Awareness** • Phoneme Identity, T178 **Phonics** • Review /e/e, /h/h, /f/f, T179 **Handwriting** h, e, f, r, b, l, k, ck, T180 **High-Frequency Words** are, he, is, little, my, she, was, with, 181 **Practice** *Your Turn* 173	**Oral Language** Stormy Weather, T184 ✓**Category Words** Question Words, T185 ✓**Listening Comprehension** • Genre: Fiction • Strategy: Visualize, T186 • Skill: Key Details • Guided Retelling, T191 • Model Fluency, T191 **Big Book** *Waiting Out the Storm* ✓**Word Work** **Phonemic Awareness** • Phoneme Blending, 192 **Phonics** • Review /r/r, /b/b, /l/l, /k/k, T192 **High-Frequency Words** are, he, is, little, my, she, was, with, T193 **Shared Reading** "Mack and Ben," T194–T195 **Practice** *Your Turn* 174
Small Group	**DIFFERENTIATED INSTRUCTION** Choose across the week to meet your student's needs.		
	Approaching Level 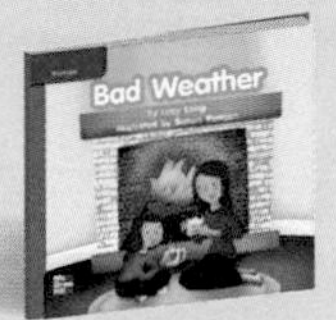	**Leveled Reader** *Bad Weather,* T224–T225 **Phonological Awareness** Recognize Alliteration, T226 TIER 2 **Phonics** Sound-Spelling Review, T228 TIER 2 **High-Frequency Words** Reteach Words, T230 TIER 2	**Leveled Reader** *Bad Weather,* T224–T225 **Phonemic Awarenesss** Phoneme Identity, T226 TIER 2 **Phonics** Connect Sounds to Spelling, T228 TIER 2 **High-Frequency Words** Cumulative Review, T230
	On Level 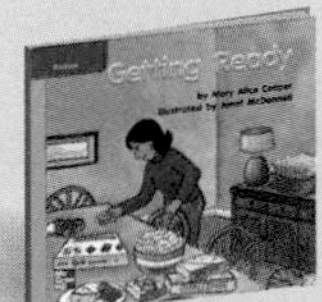	**Leveled Reader** *Getting Ready,* T232–T233 **Phonemic Awareness** Phoneme Identity, T234	**Leveled Reader** *Getting Ready,* T232–T233 **Phoneme Awareness** Phoneme Blending, T234 **Phonics** Review Phonics, T235 Picture Sort, T235 **High-Frequency Words** Review Words, T237
	Beyond Level 	**Leveled Reader** *The Storm,* T238–T239 **Phonics** Review, T240	**Leveled Reader** *The Storm,* T238–T239 **High-Frequency Words** Review, T240
	English Language Learners 	**Leveled Reader** *Getting Ready,* T242–T243 **Phonological Awareness** Recognize Alliteration, T226 TIER 2 **Phonics** Sound-Spelling Review, T228 TIER 2 **Vocabulary** Preteach Oral Vocabulary, T244 **Writing** Shared Writing, T246	**Leveled Reader** *Getting Ready,* T242–T243 **Phonemic Awareness** Phoneme Identity, T226 TIER 2 **Phonics** Connect Sounds to Spelling, T228 TIER 2 **High-Frequency Words** Cumulative Review, T230 **Vocabulary** Preteach ELL Vocabulary, T244
Whole Group	**LANGUAGE ARTS**		
	Writing and Grammar	**Shared Writing** Writing Trait: Voice, T182 Write a Weather Report, T182 **Grammar** Naming Words (Nouns), T183	**Interactive Writing** Writing Trait: Voice, T196 Write a Weather Report, T196 **Grammar** Naming Words (Nouns), T97

Go Digital

CUSTOMIZE YOUR OWN LESSON PLAN

www.connected.mcgraw-hill.com

WEEK 3

DAY 3	DAY 4	DAY 5 Review and Assess
READING		
Oral Language Stormy Weather, T198 **Oral Vocabulary** notice, celebration, enough, T198 ✓**Listening Comprehension** • Genre: Myth • Strategy: Visualize, T199 • Make Connections, T199 **Interactive Read Aloud** "Rainbow Crow," T199 ✓**Word Work** **Phonemic Awareness** • Phoneme Blending, T200 **Phonics** • Review Short *e* and /h/*h*, /f/*f*, /r/*r*, /b/*b*, /l/*l*, /k/*k*, T201 • Picture Sort, T202 **High-Frequency Words** are, he, is, little, my, she, was, with, T203 **Practice** *Your Turn* 175–180	**Oral Language** Stormy Weather, T206 ✓**Category Words** Question Words, T207 ✓**Listening Comprehension** • Genre: Informational Text • Strategy: Visualize, T208 • Text Feature: Directions, T208 • Make Connections, T209 **Big Book** Paired Read: "Be Safe in Bad Weather," T208 ✓**Word Work** **Phonemic Awareness** • Phoneme Addition, T210 **Phonics** • Blend Words with Short *e, o* and *d, l, ck,* T210 **High-Frequency Words** are, he, is, little, my, she, was, with, T211 **Shared Reading** "Mack and Ben," T212–T213 **Integrate Ideas** Research and Inquiry, T216–T217 **Practice** *Your Turn* 181–183	**Integrate Ideas** • Text Connections, T218 • Talk About Reading, T219 • Research and Inquiry, T219 ✓**Word Work** **Phonemic Awareness** • Phoneme Addition, T220 **Phonics** • Read Words with *f, r, b, l, k, t, ck,* T220 **High-Frequency Words** are, he, is, little, my, she, was, with, T221 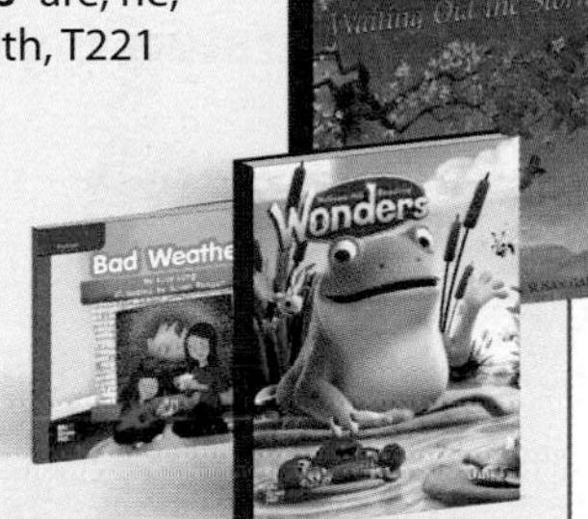 **Practice** *Your Turn* 184
DIFFERENTIATED INSTRUCTION		
Leveled Reader *Bad Weather,* T224–T225 **Phonemic Awareness** Phoneme Blending, T227 **Phonics** Reteach, T228 **High-Frequency Words** Cumulative Review, T230	**Leveled Reader** *Bad Weather,* T224–T225 **Phonemic Awareness** Phoneme Addition, T227 **Phonics** Blend Words with *h, e, f, r, b, l, k,* T229 **Oral Vocabulary** Review Words, T231	**Leveled Reader** Literacy Activities, T225 **Phonemic Awareness** Phoneme Addition, T227 **Phonics** Reread for Fluency, T229 Build Fluency with Phonics, T229 **Comprehension** Self-Selected Reading, T231
Leveled Reader *Getting Ready,* T232–T233 **Phonemic Awareness** Phoneme Addition, T234 **Phonics** Blend Words with *h, e, f, r, b, l, k,* T236	**Leveled Reader** *Getting Ready,* T232–T233 **Phonics** Blend Words with *h, e, f, r, b, l, k,* T236 Reread for Fluency, T236	**Leveled Reader** Literacy Activities, T233 **Comprehension** Self-Selected Reading, T237
Leveled Reader *The Storm,* T238–T239 **Vocabulary** Oral Vocabulary: Synonyms, T241	**Leveled Reader** *The Storm,* T238–T239 **Phonics** Innovate, T240	**Leveled Reader** Literacy Activities, T239 **Comprehension** Self-Selected Reading, T241 
Leveled Reader *Getting Ready,* T242–T243 **Phonemic Awareness** Phoneme Blending, T227 **Phonics** Reteach, T228 **High-Frequency Words** Review Words, T245 **Writing** Writing Trait: Voice, T246	**Leveled Reader** *Getting Ready,* T242–T243 **Phonemic Awareness** Phoneme Addition, T227 **Phonics** Blend Words with *h, e, f, r, b, l, k,* T229 **Vocabulary** Review Category Words, T245 **Grammar** Nouns, T247	**Leveled Reader** Literacy Activities, T243 **Phonemic Awareness** Phoneme Addition, T227 **Phonics** Reread for Fluency, T229 Build Fluency with Phonics, T229
LANGUAGE ARTS		
Independent Writing Writing Trait: Voice, T204 Write a Weather Report Prewrite/Draft, T204–T205 **Grammar** Naming Words (Nouns), T205	**Independent Writing** Writing Trait: Voice, T214 Write a Weather Report Revise/Final Draft, T214 **Grammar** Naming Words (Nouns), T215	**Independent Writing** Write a Weather Report Prepare/Present/Evaluate/Publish, T222 **Grammar** Naming Words (Nouns), T223

DIFFERENTIATE TO ACCELERATE

ACT Scaffold to Access Complex Text

IF the text complexity of a particular section is too difficult for children

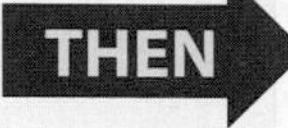
THEN see the references noted in the chart below for scaffolded instruction to help children Access Complex Text.

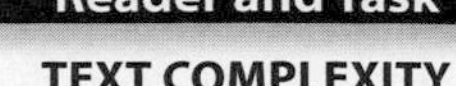

TEXT COMPLEXITY

	Literature Big Book	Reading/Writing Workshop	Leveled Readers

Quantitative	*Waiting Out the Storm* **Lexile** 350 Paired Selection: "Be Safe in Bad Weather" **Lexile** 480	"Mack and Ben" **Lexile** 250	**Approaching Level** **Lexile** BR **On Level** **Lexile** 30 **Beyond Level** **Lexile** 170 **ELL** **Lexile** BR
Qualitative	**What Makes the Text Complex?** • **Sentence Structure** Complex Sentences and Italics, T186 ACT *See Scaffolded Instruction in Teacher's Edition, T186.*	**What Makes the Text Complex?** **Foundational Skills** • Decoding with *r, b, l, k*, T192–T193 • Identifying high-frequency words, T193	**What Makes the Text Complex?** **Foundational Skills** • Decoding with *r, b, l, k* • Identifying high-frequency words *are, he, is, little, my, she, was, with* *See Level Up lessons online for Leveled Readers.*
Reader and Task	The Introduce the Concept lesson on pages T174–T175 will help determine the reader's knowledge and engagement in the weekly concept. See pages T176–T177, T187–T191, T208–T209 and T216–T219 for questions and tasks for this text.	The Introduce the Concept lesson on pages T174–T175 will help determine the reader's knowledge and engagement in the weekly concept. See pages T194–T195, T212–T213 and T216–T219 for questions and tasks for this text.	The Introduce the Concept lesson on pages T174–T175 will help determine the reader's knowledge and engagement in the weekly concept. See pages T224–T225, T232–T233, T238–T239, T242–T243 and T216–T219 for questions and tasks for this text.

BR = Epitome of a beginning reader

Go Digital! www.connected.mcgraw-hill.com

WEEK 3

Monitor and *Differentiate*

IF you need to differentiate instruction

THEN use the Quick Checks to assess children's needs and select the appropriate small group instruction focus.

Quick Check

Comprehension Strategy Visualize, T199

Phonemic Awareness/Phonics /h/h, /e/e, /f/f, /r/r, /b/b, /l/l, /k/k, *ck*, T181, T193, T203, T211, T221

High-Frequency Words *my, are, he, with, is, little, she, was,* T181, T193, T203, T211, T221

If No → **Approaching** **Reteach,** pp. T224–T231

ELL **Develop,** pp. T242–T247

If Yes → **On Level** **Review,** pp. T232–T237

Beyond Level **Extend,** pp. T238–T241

Level Up with Leveled Readers

IF children can read their leveled text fluently and answer comprehension questions

THEN work with the next level up to accelerate children's reading with more complex text.

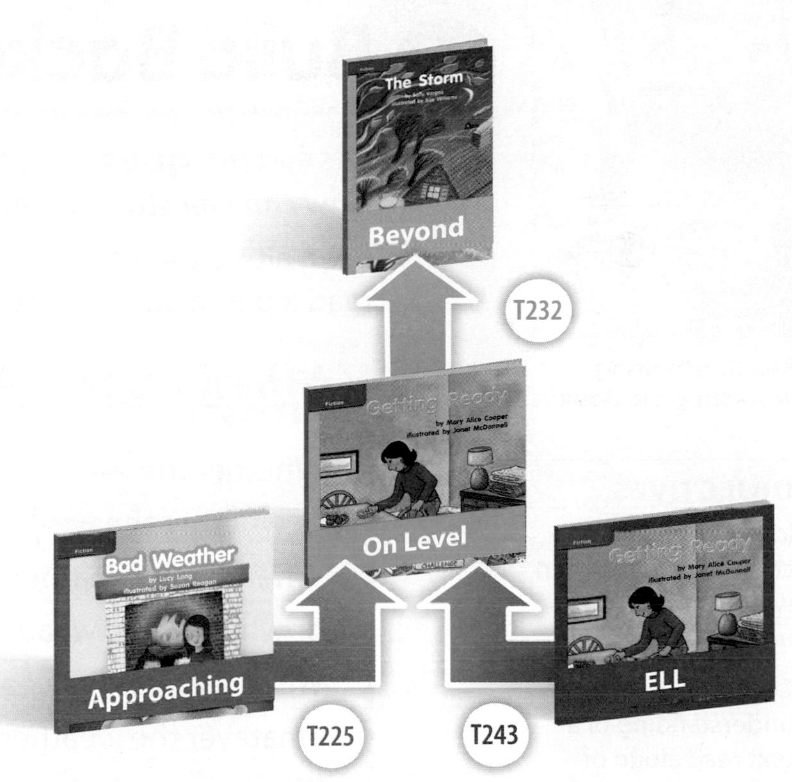

ENGLISH LANGUAGE LEARNERS SCAFFOLD

IF ELL students need additional support **THEN** scaffold instruction using the small group suggestions.

Reading-Writing Workshop	Leveled Reader	Phonological Awareness	Phonics,	Oral Vocabulary, T244	Writing	Grammar
Reading-Writing Workshop T175 "Lightning Strikes!" **Integrate Ideas** T217	**Leveled Reader** T242–T243 *Getting Ready*	**Phonological Awareness** Recognize Alliteration, T226 Phoneme Identity, T226 Phoneme Blending, T227 Phoneme Addition, T227	**Phonics,** /h/h, /e/e, /f/f, /r/r, /b/b, /l/l, /k/k, *ck,* T228–T229	**Oral Vocabulary,** T244 safe, prepare, notice, celebration, enough **High-Frequency Words,** T245 my, are, he, with, is, little, she, was	**Writing** Shared Writing, T246 Writing Trait: Voice, T246	**Grammar** T247 Nouns

Note: Include ELL Students in all small groups based on their needs.

WHOLE GROUP
DAY 1

Materials

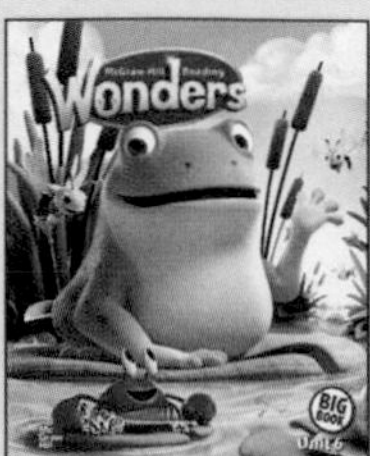

Reading/Writing Workshop Big Book
UNIT 6

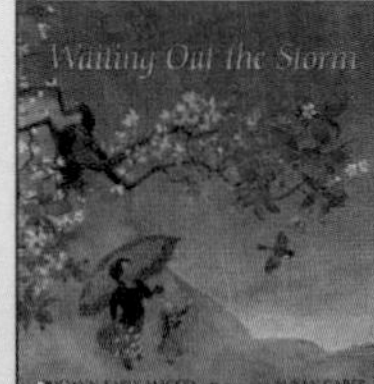

Literature Big Book
Waiting Out the Storm

Visual Vocabulary Cards
safe
prepare

Photo Cards
barn, deer, dog, door, egg, elbow, elevator, envelope, exit, fan, farm, fire, fish, five, football, fork, fox, hair, hand, hat, hay, helicopter, hippo, nest, nose, nut

Sound-Spelling Cards
egg
hippo
fire

High-Frequency Word Cards
are, he, is, little, my, she, was, with

Think Aloud Cloud

"Scrambled Egg, Fried Egg"

Introduce the Concept

MINILESSON 10 Mins

Build Background

Reading/Writing Workshop Big Book

OBJECTIVES

CCSS Identify real-life connections between words and their use. **L.K.5c**

CCSS Confirm understanding of a text read aloud or information presented orally or through other media by asking and answering questions about key details and requesting clarification if something is not understood. **SL.K.2**

ESSENTIAL QUESTION

How can you stay safe in bad weather?

Read aloud the Essential Question. Tell children that you are going to read a poem about weather.

Whether the Weather

Whether the weather be fine,
or whether the weather be not,
Whether the weather be cold,
or whether the weather be hot,
We'll weather the weather,
whatever the weather
Whether we like it or not.

Say "Whether the Weather" with children. Read each line and have children echo. Ask children which types of weather the poem is telling about. (fine; not fine; hot; cold) Tell children that this week they will read to learn about weather and how it affects people and places.

Oral Vocabulary Words

Use the **Define/Example/Ask** routine to introduce the oral vocabulary words **safe** and **prepare**.

To introduce the theme "Stormy Weather," explain that weather can change every day and throughout the year. Sometimes the weather is stormy, or bad. Ask children how they stay safe in bad weather.

Go Digital

"Stormy Weather"

Video

Visual Glossary

Visual Vocabulary Cards

Oral Vocabulary Routine

Define: When you are **safe**, you are not in danger.

Example: I feel safe when I am with my family.

Ask: What helps you feel safe? Why?

Define: When you **prepare**, you get ready for something.

Example: A runner can prepare for a race by stretching.

Ask: How do you prepare for school?

Talk About It: Stormy Weather

COLLABORATE

Discuss how stormy weather can be dangerous. Ask children to tell what they know about tornadoes or hurricanes, and list their responses. Display pages 34–35 of the **Reading/Writing Workshop Big Book** and have children do the **Talk About It** activity with a partner.

READING/WRITING WORKSHOP BIG BOOK, pp. 34–35

Collaborative Conversations

Provide Details As children engage in partner, small group, and whole group discussions, encourage them to:

- Give details to express their thoughts, feelings and ideas clearly.
- Use details to describe people, places, things, and events.
- Give details when asking about things they do not understand.

ENGLISH LANGUAGE LEARNERS SCAFFOLD

Beginning

Use Visuals Point to the lightning in the picture. Ask: *Is this lightning?* (yes) *Is this good weather?* (no) *Should you be outside in this weather?* (no) Explain that it is important to stay inside when there is thunder and lightning. Restate children's responses in order to develop their oral language proficiency.

Intermediate

Describe Ask children to describe the different things in the picture. Have them identify the clouds, lightning, grass, and fence. Encourage them to use the sentence frames:

- That is ______.
- This is a ______.

Advanced/Advanced High

Discuss Have children discuss what you should do when there is lightning. Ask: *Where should you go?* (It is important to go inside.) Correct the meaning of children's responses as needed.

WHOLE GROUP
DAY 1

Listening Comprehension

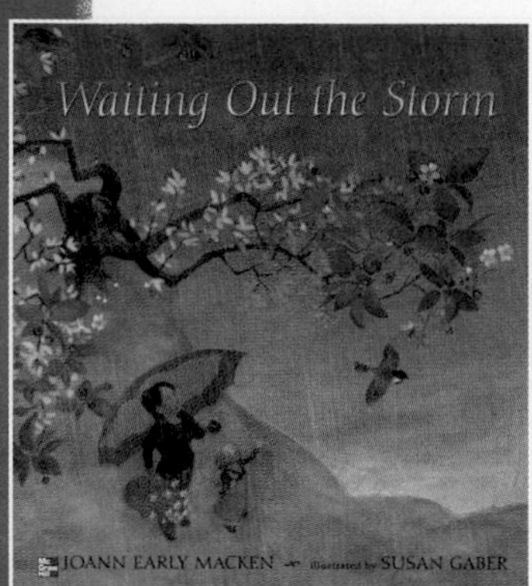

Literature Big Book

OBJECTIVES

CCSS With prompting and support, name the author and illustrator of a story and define the role of each in telling the story. **RL.K.6**

CCSS Actively engage in group reading activities with purpose and understanding. **RL.K.10**

- Recognize characteristics of fiction
- Connect Big Book to Weekly Concept

ACADEMIC LANGUAGE
sentences, purpose

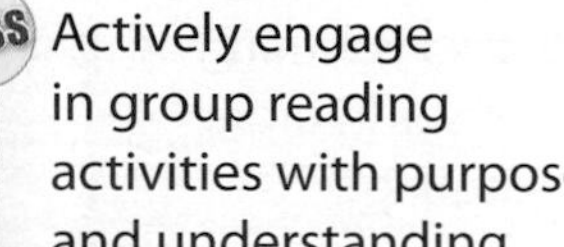

Read the Literature Big Book

Connect to Concept: Stormy Weather

Tell children that you will now read about what happens during a storm. *What kind of stormy weather have you been in?*

Concepts of Print

Boundaries and Punctuation Display page 7 of the **Big Book**. Remind children that sentences are complete thoughts. Read aloud the sentences. Then point out the beginning and ending of each sentence. Explain the purpose of the question mark.

Genre: Fiction

Model Explain that *Waiting Out the Storm* is fiction. Remind children that fiction stories are made up. Share these characteristics of fiction:

- Fiction stories have made-up characters. The stories tell what happens to the characters.
- Many fiction stories have illustrations.

Story Words Preview these words before reading:
tumble: to fall or roll
dashes: moves quickly
snuggle: hug or cuddle

Set a Purpose for Reading

- Read aloud the title and the names of the author and the illustrator.
- Remind children that the author wrote the words in the story. *Who drew the pictures?* (the illustrator)
- Ask children to listen as you read aloud the Big Book to find out about stormy weather.

Go Digital

Waiting Out the Storm

Think Aloud Cloud

Strategy: Visualize

Explain Remind children that they can use the words and pictures in a story to make pictures in their minds of what is happening.

Think Aloud As I read this book, I will pause to imagine what is happening. I will picture the characters, events, and weather in my mind. This will help me to better understand what I'm reading.

Model As you read, use the **Think Aloud Cloud** to model the strategy.

Think Aloud On pages 6–7, I read that the wind is whistling in the treetops. I close my eyes and make a picture in my mind. I can see leaves waving in the wind. I can hear the wind whistling and moving the leaves. This helps me understand what it is like before a storm comes.

AUTHOR'S CRAFT

Descriptive Language Point out that the author of this book uses a lot of creative and interesting words to tell about the things happening in the story. Explain that authors do this to help make stories more fun and interesting to read. *The author writes that the raindrops "burst from the cloud, skipping and leaping and laughing out loud." This makes the raindrops seem like children playing and having fun. The storm does not seem scary.* Point out other descriptive language throughout the story. Encourage children that when they write, it can be fun to try to use descriptive language.

ENGLISH LANGUAGE LEARNERS SCAFFOLD

Beginning

Listen Say: *Close your eyes. Make a picture in your mind of a windy day. Listen to this sound.* Make a whistling sound. Ask: *Does this sound like wind?* (yes) Restate their responses, adding details. For example: *Yes, that sounds like the wind I heard last night.* Ask children to make a whistling sound.

Intermediate

Express Ask children to make pictures in their minds of a windy day. Use the following prompts to help them express their feelings about wind. Elicit more details to support their answers.

- I like wind because ______.
- I do not like wind because ______.

Advanced/Advanced High

Discuss Have children visualize a windy day. Ask them to tell you what sounds they hear. (Possible responses: leaves shaking; windows rattling; trees creaking) Model correct pronunciation as needed.

Respond to Reading

After reading, prompt children to share what they learned about the weather and how it affects animals. Discuss what pictures they made in their minds as they listened to the story. Have children draw a picture of one of the animals from the book waiting out the storm.

Make Connections

Use *Waiting Out the Storm* to discuss the ways animals and people are affected by stormy weather. Discuss the Essential Question *How can you stay safe in bad weather?* by paging through the **Big Book**.

Write About It Write about how one animal stays safe.

WHOLE GROUP
DAY 1

Word Work

Quick Review

Review /e/, /f/, /h/: Ask children to tell the initial sound of the *egg, fan,* and *hammer* Photo Cards.
Build Fluency: Sound-Spellings: Display the following **Word-Building Cards:** *e, f, h.* Have children say each sound. Repeat and vary the pace.

MINILESSON 5 Mins

Phonemic Awareness

OBJECTIVES

CCSS Isolate and pronounce the initial sounds in words. **RF.K.2d**

CCSS Associate the long and short sounds with common spellings (graphemes) for the five major vowels. **RF.K.3b**

Phoneme Identity

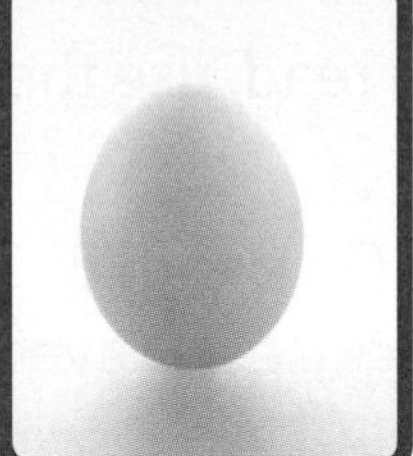

Photo Card

1 Model Display the **Photo Cards** for egg, elevator, and exit. *I will say three picture names:* egg, elevator, exit. *Say the names with me:* egg, elevator, exit. *What sound is the same in* egg, elevator, exit? *Yes, the first sound, /e/, is the same.* Repeat the instruction with Photo Cards *football, five, farm* (to review initial /f/); *hand, helicopter, hippo* (to review initial /h/); and *jet, gem, net* (to review /e/ in the medial position).

2 Guided Practice/Practice Show children sets of the Photo Cards. Name the pictures with children and have them say the first sound of the words in each set. Guide practice with the first set.

fire, fish, fork	hat, hair, hippo
envelope, egg, elevator	football, fox, fan
hay, hook, horse	exit, elbow, egg
deer, dog, door	nest, nut, nose

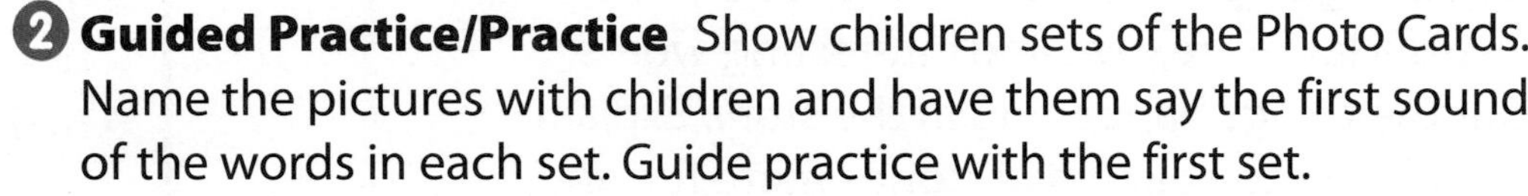

ARTICULATION SUPPORT

If children need additional support, refer to Articulation Support in Unit 5: page T14 for /h/; T96 for /e/; 178 for /f/ and /r/. Refer to Unit 6: page T14 for /b/ and /l/, and T96 for /k/.

Go Digital

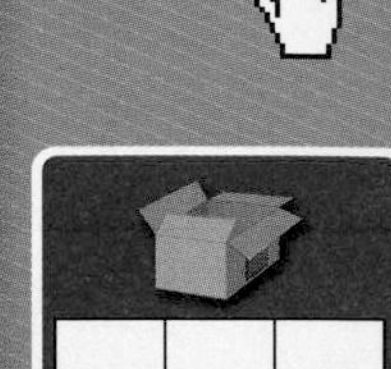

Phonemic Awareness

Phonics

ENGLISH LANGUAGE LEARNERS

Pronunciation Display and have children name Photo Cards from this lesson to reinforce phonemic awareness and word meanings. Point to the *hat* Photo Card and ask: *What do you see? What is the sound at the beginning of the word* hat? Repeat using the *box, egg, feet, hay, lightning, web, kite,* and *sock* Photo Cards.

Phonics

Sound-Spelling Card

Review /e/e, /h/h, /f/f

1 Model Display the *Egg* **Sound-Spelling Card**. *This is the letter* e. *The letter* e *can stand for the sound /e/ as at the beginning of the word* egg *or in the middle of the word* gem. *What is the letter?* (e) *What sound does the letter* e *stand for?* (/e/) Repeat for /h/*h* with the *Hippo* Sound-Spelling Card and /f/*f* with the *Fire* Sound-Spelling Card.

2 Guided Practice/Practice Have children listen as you say some words. Ask them to write the letter *e* on their **Response Boards** if the word begins with /e/. Do the first two words with children.

exit dig end road ever echo tip empty

Repeat for /h/*h* and /f/*f*.

help pack hit home nose hill hand

face fox make five fish cow foot

Review /e/*e*. Have children write the letter *e* on their Response Boards. Play "Scrambled Egg, Fried Egg." Have children show their Response Boards with the letter *e* when they hear /e/.

Corrective Feedback

Sound Error Model the sound /h/ in the initial position, then have children repeat the sound. Say: *My turn. Hit. /h/ /h/ /h/. Now it's your turn.* Have children say the words *hot* and *hat* and isolate the initial sound. Repeat for /f/ with the words *fan, foot, fed;* initial /e/ with the words *egg, elf*; and medial /e/ with *pen, bed*.

ENGLISH LANGUAGE LEARNERS

Phoneme Variations in Languages Speakers of Spanish, Hmong, Cantonese, Haitian, Creole, and Korean may have difficulty perceiving and pronouncing /e/. Some children, particularly those whose first language is Spanish, may need extra practice identifying the /h/ sound, as the *h* in Spanish is silent. Speakers of Korean may have difficulty perceiving and pronouncing /f/. Emphasize the /e/, /h/, or /f/ sound and demonstrate the correct mouth positions.

YOUR TURN PRACTICE BOOK p. 173

Word Work

Handwriting: Write Sentences with *h, e, f, r, b, l, k, ck*

OBJECTIVES

CCSS Write a letter or letters for most consonant and short-vowel sounds. **L.K.2c**

CCSS Demonstrate basic knowledge of one-to-one letter-sound correspondences by producing the primary or many of the most frequent sounds for each consonant. **RF.K.3a**

CCSS Read common high-frequency words by sight. **RF.K.3c**

ACADEMIC LANGUAGE
uppercase, lowercase

1 Model Review handwriting and letter sound correspondence with the letters *h, e, f, r, b, l, k, ck*.

→ Write the following sentence. *Rick and Kim had fed the cat.* Read the sentence with children and track the print.

→ *I hear the /r/ sound in the word* Rick. *I know that the letter* r *stands for /r/. I will underline the letter* r *because it stands for /r/. Which words have the sound /k/?* (Rick, Kim) *Which letter(s) stands for /k/?* Underline the letter *k* at the beginning of *Kim* and *ck* at the end of *Rick*. Continue asking children which word has the sound /h/ and which letter stands for the sound (had, *h*); /f/ (fed, *f*) and /e/ (fed, *e*). Underline the letters that stand for the sounds and read the words with children.

2 Guided Practice/Practice

→ Write the following sentence for children to copy: *Ben let Rob pack the hat.* Give them ample time to write the sentence. Chorally read the sentence.

→ Ask children to identify which words have the sound /b/. (Ben, Rob) Have them underline the letter that stands for the sound (*b*) and read the words. Ask children to identify words with the following sounds and to underline the letter that stands for the sound: /l/ (let, *l*); /e/ (Ben, let *e*); /r/ (Rob, *r*); /k/ (pack, *ck*); and /h/ (hat, *h*).

→ Have children check that the words in their sentences are separated by spaces. Remind them that all sentences begin with a capital letter and have end punctuation. Have them correct as needed.

Daily Handwriting

Throughout the week review writing words and sentences with *h, e, k, f, r, b, l, ck*. At the end of the week, have children use **Your Turn Practice Book** page 184 to practice writing words.

Go Digital

Handwriting

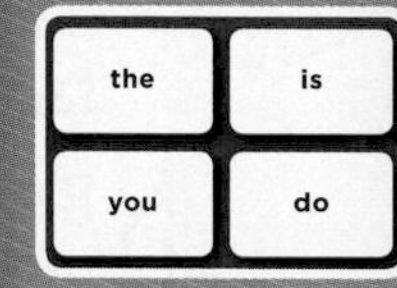

High-Frequency Word Routine

High-Frequency Words

are, he, is, little, my, she, was, with

1 Model Display the **Big Book** *Waiting Out the Storm*. Read the following sentence from the book: "It's only the wind in the treetops, my dear." Point to the high-frequency word *my*. Display the **High-Frequency Word Card** *my* to review the word using the **Read/Spell/Write** routine.

- → **Read** Point to the word *my* and say the word. *This is the word* my. *Say it with me:* my. *I like to ride my bicycle.*
- → **Spell** *The word* my *is spelled* m-y. *Spell it with me.*
- → **Write** *Let's write the word in the air as we say each letter:* m-y.

Repeat the routine with *are, he, is, little, she, was,* and *with.*

2 Guided Practice/Practice Build sentences using High-Frequency Word Cards, **Photo Cards**, and teacher-prepared punctuation cards. Have children point to the high-frequency words *are, he, is, little, my, she, was, with.* Use these sentences.

She was with the queen.

Are you little?

He can see a little barn.

Also online

High-Frequency Words Practice

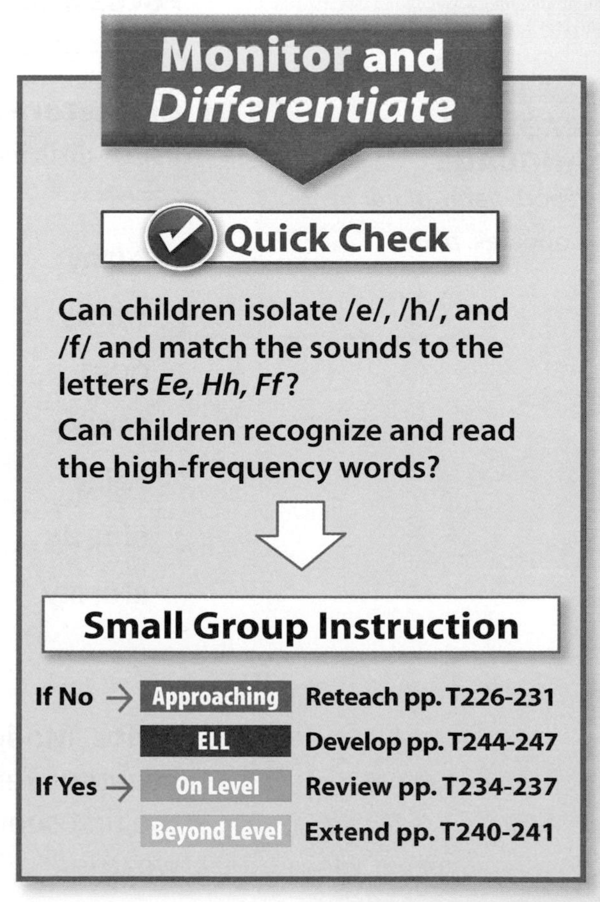

Language Arts

Shared Writing

OBJECTIVES

 Use a combination of drawing, dictating, and writing to compose informative/explanatory texts in which they name what they are writing about and supply some information about the topic. **W.K.2**

 Form regular plural nouns orally by adding /s/ or /es/ (e.g., *dog, dogs; wish, wishes*). **L.K.1c**

Write a list

ACADEMIC LANGUAGE

- *report, noun, plural*
- Cognates: *plural*

Writing Trait: Voice

1. **Model** Tell children that writers use their voice to show their feelings and ideas about something. Display p. 7 of the **Big Book**. Read: *The wind calls the raindrops to come out and play.* The author writes about the wind as if it is something that the rain plays with. Through the character of the mother, the author's voice tells us not to be afraid of the wind.
2. **Guided Practice/Practice** Display p. 13. Read: *Thunder stomps. Thunder stumbles and bumbles around.* Ask children how the author feels about the thunder. (Possible answer: The author says it is loud.)

Write a Weather Report

Focus and Plan Tell children that this week they will write a weather report and draw a picture to go with it.

Brainstorm Ask children to name different kinds of weather. Make a list of children's responses.

sunny
windy
cold
snowy
rainy
cloudy
stormy

Write Model making a sentence, using the list. *It is snowy and very beautiful.* Tell children that by adding the words "and very beautiful" to the first sentence, the writer tells how he or she feels about the snowy weather.

Go Digital

Grammar

Naming Words (Nouns)

1 Model Remind children that naming words tell the names of people, places, animals, and things. Remind children that plural nouns ending in *-s* or *-es* name more than one thing.

→ Write: *wish, lock, lash.*

What endings do we need to add to make these words tell about more than one thing? (*-es* for *wish* and *lash* and *-s* for *lock*)

2 Guided Practice/Practice Have children work with partners. Provide each pair with a list of the following naming words:

pot
dress
stick

Have children work together to determine whether to add *-s* or *-es* to the noun to make it plural. Ask children to check the ending of each word and to look at the endings you listed in the model. Circulate around the classroom to offer guidance.

Talk About It

Distribute several **Photo Cards** to each pair of students. Have partners practice naming plural nouns by saying the word shown on the card, then making the word plural. Have them decide if the plural ending is *-s* or *-es*.

ENGLISH LANGUAGE LEARNERS SCAFFOLD

Beginning

Recognize Plural Forms Say a naming word in its singular or plural form. Ask children to raise their hands if the word names more than one. Encourage children to repeat the word after you say each word. Repeat correct answers slowly and clearly to the class.

Intermediate

Recognize and Name Plural Forms Say a naming word in its singular and plural forms. Ask children to tell which form of the word names more than one. Repeat the words. Ask children to tell how they know that the word names more than one. Allow children ample time to respond.

Advanced/Advanced High

Speak and Write Plural Nouns Write and say a naming word in its singular form. Ask children to tell you the plural form of the word. Guide children in writing the correct plural form. Model correct pronunciation as needed.

Daily Wrap Up

- Review the Essential Question and encourage children to discuss it, using the new oral vocabulary words. *How can you stay safe in bad weather?*
- Prompt children to share the skills they learned. How might they use those skills?

WHOLE GROUP
DAY 2

Materials

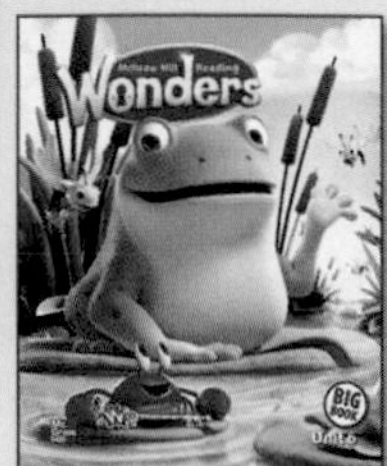
Reading/Writing Workshop Big Book
UNIT 6

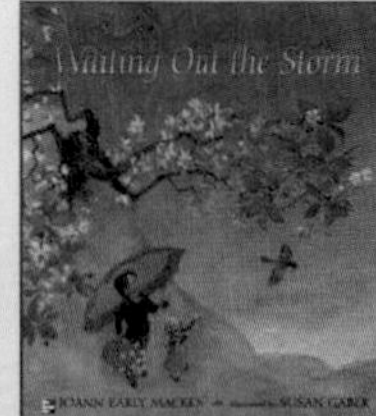
Literature Big Book
Waiting Out the Storm

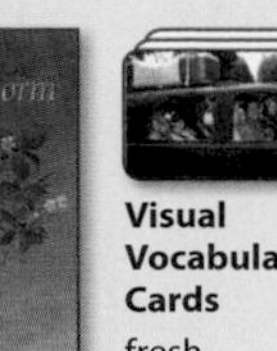
Visual Vocabulary Cards
fresh
safe
prepare

Response Board

Retelling Cards

"There's a Hippo in the House"
"Let's Build a Fire"

Puppet

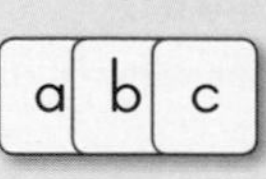

Word-Building Cards

Sound-Spelling Card
Bat
Lemon
Koala
Rose

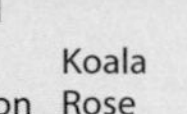

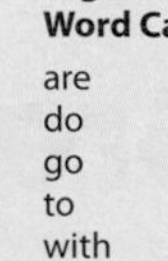
High-Frequency Word Cards
are
do
go
to
with
you

Build the Concept

Oral Language

OBJECTIVES

CCSS Isolate and pronounce the initial, medial vowel, and final sounds (phonemes) in three-phoneme (consonant-vowel-consonant, or CVC) words. **RF.K.2d**

CCSS Identify real-life connections between words and their use (e.g., note places at school that are *colorful*). **L.K.5c**

Develop oral vocabulary

ACADEMIC LANGUAGE

- *poem*
- Cognates: *poema*

ESSENTIAL QUESTION

How can you stay safe in bad weather?

Remind children that this week they are learning about ways to stay safe in a storm or other dangerous weather. Point out that stormy weather can hurt people, animals, trees, and buildings.

Read "Whether the Weather." Say each line and have children repeat.

Phonological Awareness

Recognize Alliteration

Tell children that some words begin with the same sounds. Say *whatever* and *weather* from the poem and point out that both start with the /w/ sound. Then say the following word sets, have children repeat, and then raise their hands if the words in the set begin with the same sound: *happy hairy hippo; big book; wet floor; lost little lamb.*

Review Visual Vocabulary

Use the **Define/Example/Ask** routine to review the oral vocabulary words **safe** and **prepare**. Prompt children to use the words in sentences.

Visual Vocabulary Cards

Go Digital

Visual Glossary

Category Words

Category Words: Question Words

1 Model Use the **Big Book** *Waiting Out the Storm* to point out question words: *what*, page 5; *why*, page 7; *when*, page 8; *where*, page 20. Explain that we use these words to find out information about something.

Sing the following verses from "Mary Had a Little Lamb."

Mary had a little lamb whose fleece was white as snow.
And everywhere that Mary went, the lamb was sure to go.
It followed her to school one day, which was against the rules.
It made the children laugh and play, to see a lamb at school.

→ Use question words to ask children about the nursery rhyme. *Who is the song about?* (Mary) *What did she have?* (a lamb)

2 Guided Practice/Practice Say the following words. If the word is a question word, children should raise their hands.

who	word	talk	where
what	teacher	why	time

Vocabulary Strategy: Word Categories/Question Words

1 Model Explain that words that have something in common can be grouped into categories. Use *Waiting Out the Storm* to model how words can be grouped into categories.

Think Aloud In the story *Waiting Out the Storm,* the little girl asks many questions. We can group all of the question words together because they are similar. The words *why, what, how, where,* and *who* are words that fit into a category called question words.

2 Guided Practice Help children locate words in the book that fall into different kinds of categories, such as *question words* and *weather words.* Make a list of the words in each category.

3 Practice Work with children to ask questions about preparing for storms, using each of the question words. Discuss and answer the questions.

ENGLISH LANGUAGE LEARNERS

Understand Help children understand how question words are used. Explain that when we want to find out about a person, we ask *who,* as in *Who is going to the store?* When we want to find out where a place is, we ask *where,* as in *Where is the store?* Have children repeat the question words in English and in their native language.

LET'S MOVE!

Have children stand side by side. Children should take one step forward if you say a sentence with a question word. Have them take one step backward if the sentence does not have a question word.

Listening Comprehension

Literature Big Book

OBJECTIVES

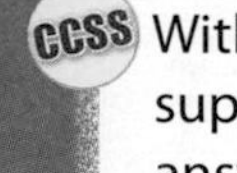

With prompting and support, ask and answer questions about key details in a text. **RL.K.1**

Ask and answer questions about unknown words in a text. **RL.K.4**

- Strategy: Visualize
- Skill: Key Details

ACADEMIC LANGUAGE

- *illustrations*
- Cognates: *ilustraciones*

Reread Literature Big Book

Genre: Fiction

Display *Waiting Out the Storm.* Remind children that fiction stories are made-up events about made-up characters but the events could happen in real life. Have children name other stories that are fiction.

Strategy: Visualize

Remind children that good readers use the words and pictures in a story to make new pictures in their minds. *As we reread, you can make pictures in your mind of what is happening during the storm.*

Skill: Key Details

Remind children that they can find important details in the text and illustrations. Illustrations sometimes give information that is not in the author's words. *Details from the illustrations can help you make a picture in your mind of what is happening.* As you read, have children look for evidence in the text and illustrations that tell more details about the story. Use the prompts to fill in the graphic organizer.

Access Complex Text

Sentence Structure Complex sentence structures throughout a text may impede understanding of the text as a whole. *Waiting Out the Storm* includes dialogue printed in italics and regular font. The story does not include quotation marks or other dialogue indicators.

→ Guide children to understand that the words printed in ordinary letters are what the girl says. The words printed in italics, or slanted letters, are what the mother says.

Go Digital

Waiting Out the Storm

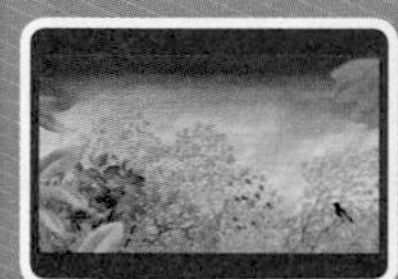

Retelling Cards

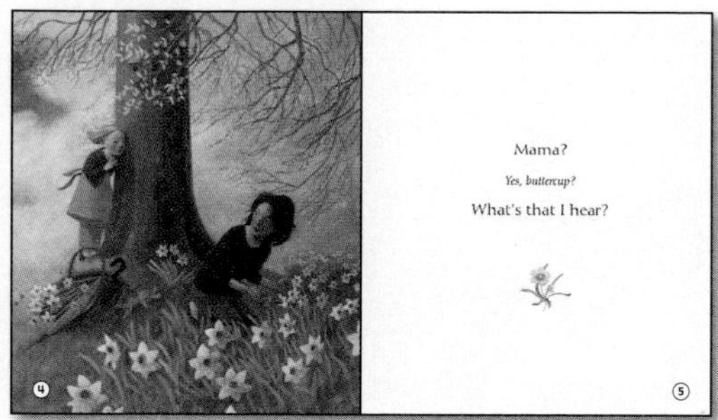

PAGES 4–5

VISUALIZE

Think Aloud The girl asks her mother what she is hearing. I see in the photo that they are outside. In my mind I can picture the grass and trees. I imagine that birds might be chirping and the wind might be blowing. I will keep reading to find out what the girl hears.

pp. 4–5

buttercup: Tell children that *buttercup* is a special name the mother calls her daughter. Discuss other special names that show affection, such as *sweetheart, love,* and *dear*. Say each word and have children echo.

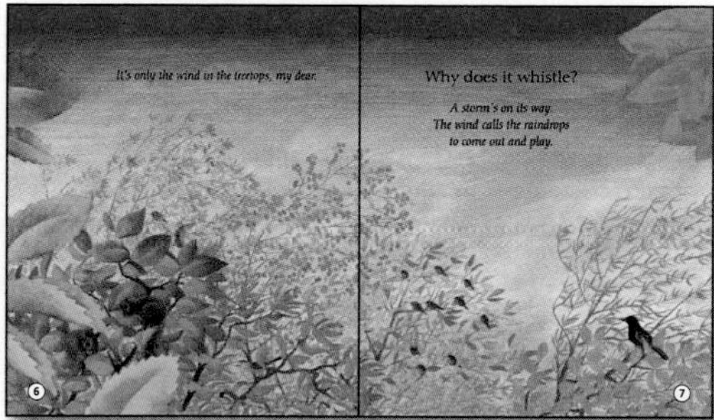

PAGES 6–7

KEY DETAILS

Think Aloud I read that the the wind is whistling in the trees. Mama says that this means a storm is coming. I will add "wind" to my details organizer.

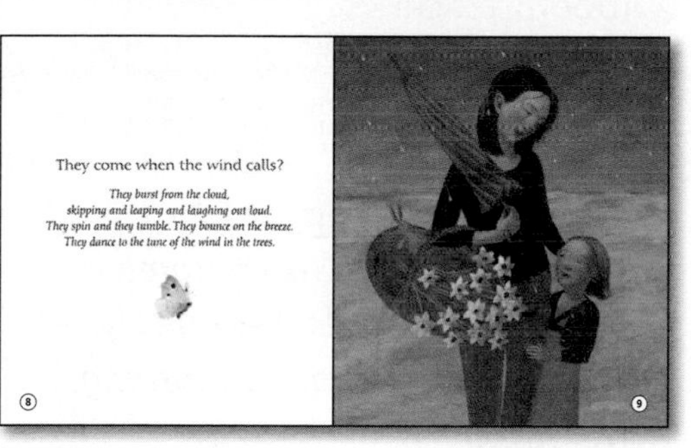

PAGES 8–9

KEY DETAILS

What is happening now? What detail can we learn about the storm that is coming? (It is raining. I can see the raindrops in the illustration.) *Let's add "raindrops" to our details organizer.*

pp. 8–9

burst: Tell children to imagine a balloon filled with too much air. Say: *When the balloon pops, it bursts.* Have children make the sound of a balloon bursting.

Listening Comprehension

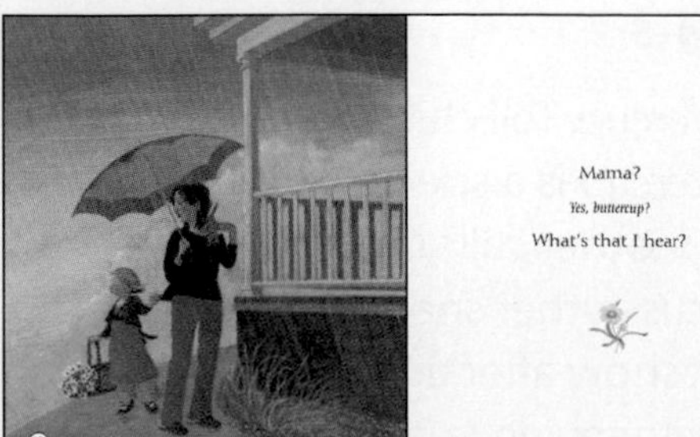

PAGES 10–11

CONCEPTS OF PRINT

These sentences all have the same end punctuation. What kind do they have? What does that mean? (Question marks. These sentences are all questions.)

PAGES 12–13

KEY DETAILS

What details about the storm can we learn on these pages? (Possible Answer: There is thunder. In the picture I see it raining very hard.) Add "thunder" to the details organizer.

pp. 12–13

rumble, stomps: Tell children that rumbles and stomps are sounds. Have children tap their hands on their desks to make a rumble. Then have them stomp their feet to make stomping sounds. Ask: *What is another sound that thunder can make?* (boom, crack)

PAGES 14–15

KEY DETAILS

I read that the lightning flashes and dashes. Look at the illustration. What does the illustration tell you about the lightning? (Possible response: It is bright and it makes crooked lines.) *Let's add "lightning" to our details chart.*

pp. 14–15

tricky: If something is tricky, it is sneaky or clever. The lightning is tricky because it flashes quickly. You never know where lightning will strike.

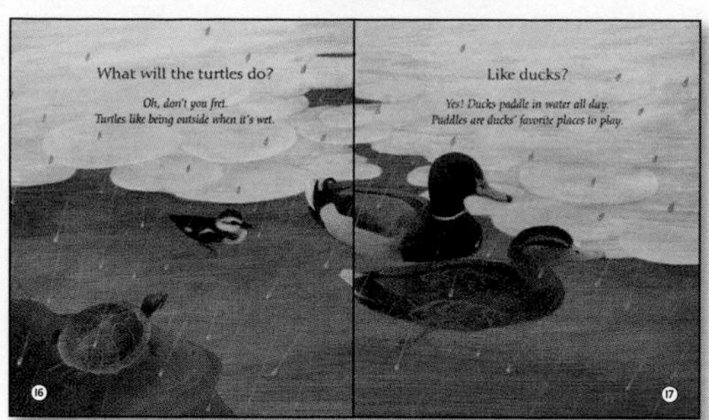
PAGES 16–17

VISUALIZE

Think Aloud I read that the ducks like to paddle all day. I can see their feet in the pictures. I close my eyes and make a picture in my mind of the ducks' feet moving quickly under the water. They are swimming and happy. This helps me to better understand what ducks do in the rain.

pp. 16–17

fret: fret *is another way to say "worry."* Ask children why the girl in the story might be worried.

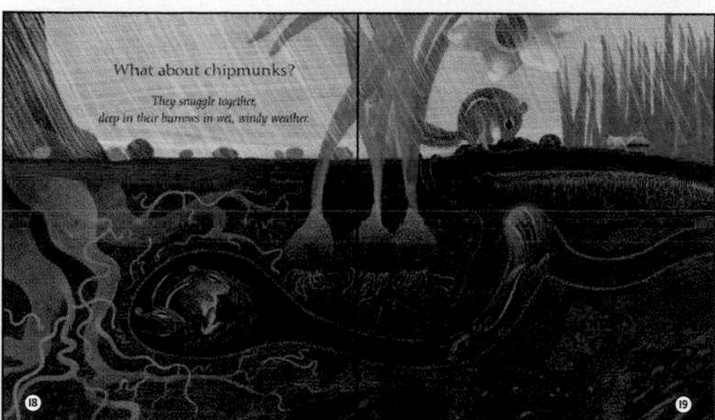
PAGES 18–19

VOCABULARY

Reread the second sentence. *What do you think a* burrow *is? Use the illustration and other clues to help you.* (a hole dug deep in the ground) Remind children to ask and answer questions about other unfamiliar words in the story.

pp. 18–19

burrows: Explain that a burrow is a chipmunk's home in the ground.

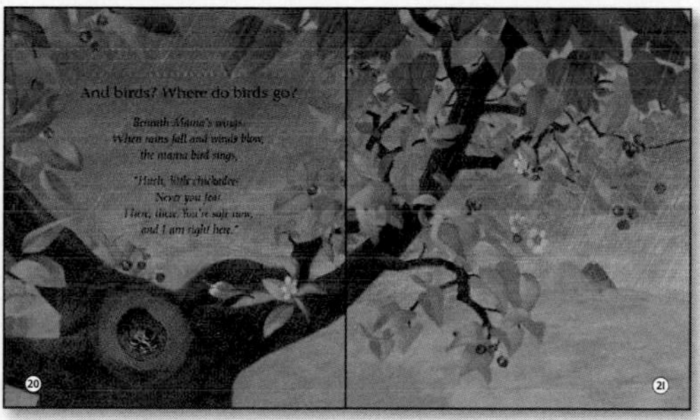
PAGES 20–21

PHONICS

Reread page 20 and have children identify the words with the initial /b/ and initial /l/ sounds. (birds, beneath, blow, little)

pp. 20–21

There, there: Tell children that *there, there* is another way to say "don't worry." *The mother bird is telling her little chicks not to worry about the storm.*

Listening Comprehension

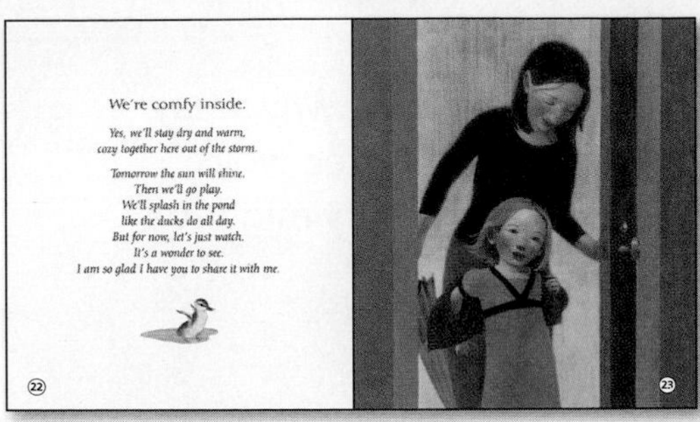
We're comfy inside.

Yes, we'll stay dry and warm,
cozy together here out of the storm.

Tomorrow the sun will shine.
Then we'll go play.
We'll splash in the pond
like the ducks do all day.
But for now, let's just watch.
It's a wonder to see.
I am so glad I have you to share it with me.

22 23

PAGES 22–23

HIGH-FREQUENCY WORDS

Have children identify the high-frequency word *with.*

So come, darling buttercup,
here where it's warm.
Like chickadee babies,
we're safe from the storm.
While winds blow and rains fall,
we'll wait out the weather.

24 25

PAGES 24–25

VISUALIZE

Can you picture in your mind being inside during a storm? What does it feel like? What do you hear outside? Is it warm?

pp. 24–25

wait out: Explain that when you wait out something, you wait until it is finished. Say: *The mother and daughter will wait until the storm is finished. Then, they will go outside.*

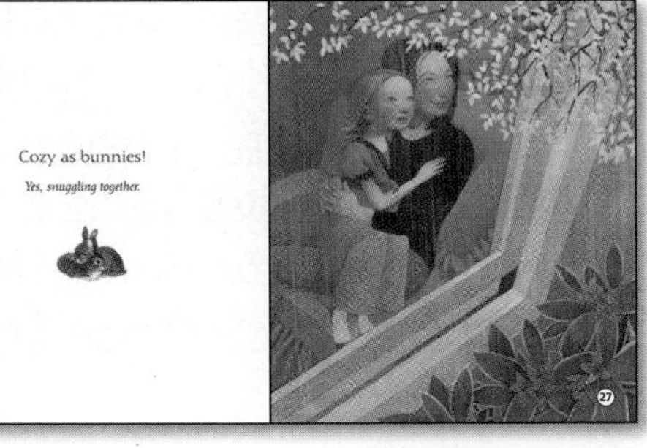
Cozy as bunnies!

Yes, snuggling together.

26 27

PAGES 26–27

KEY DETAILS

How do the girl and her mother feel? How do you know? (Possible answer: They are happy. I can see them smiling in picture.)

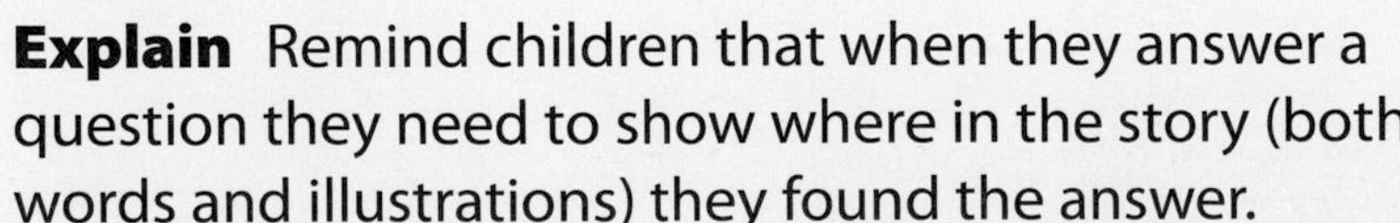

Text Evidence

Explain Remind children that when they answer a question they need to show where in the story (both words and illustrations) they found the answer.

Discuss *How do you know the little chickadees are safe in the storm?* (On page 20, the words say, "There, there. You are safe now." The mama bird is taking care of her babies.)

Key Details

Review Skill Remind children that when they read stories they can find important details in the text and illustrations. Discuss details the children learned about storms from *Waiting Out the Storm* using the completed graphic organizer. Encourage children to give more examples.

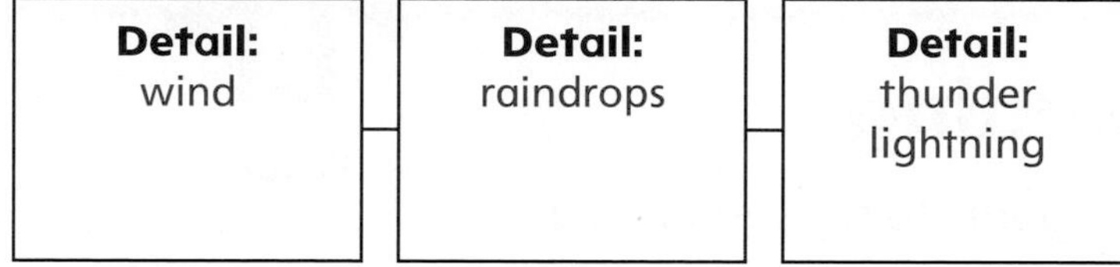

Guided Retelling

Tell children that they will use the **Retelling Cards** to retell the story.

→ Show Retelling Card 1. Based on children's needs, use the Modeled, Guided or ELL retelling prompts. The ELL prompts contain support for English language learners based on levels of language acquisition. Repeat with cards 2–4, using the prompts as a guide.

→ Discuss the story. Have children tell which animal they think has the most fun in the storm, and why.

Model Fluency

Reread page 16 of *Waiting Out the Storm* to model expression. Remind children that the different styles of letters show that two people are speaking. Change your voice as you reread the dialogue. Then have partners each take a role and repeat what the girl and the mother say to each other. Continue with other pages in the book, if time allows.

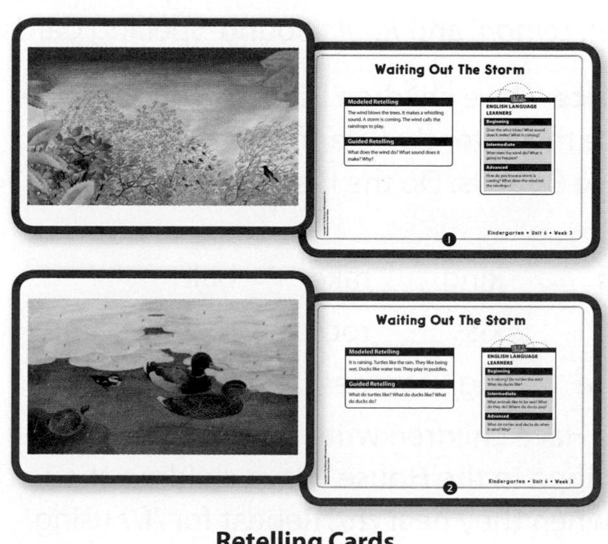

Retelling Cards

YOUR TURN PRACTICE BOOK p. 174

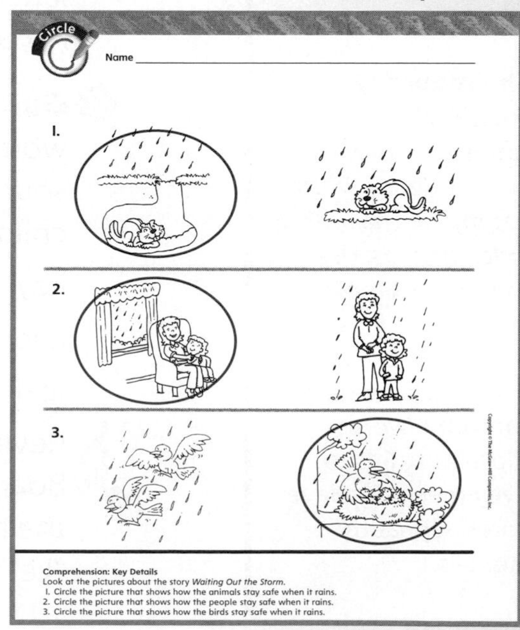

Circle

Name ________________

1.

2.

3.

Comprehension: Key Details
Look at the pictures about the story *Waiting Out the Storm.*
1. Circle the picture that shows how the animals stay safe when it rains.
2. Circle the picture that shows how the people stay safe when it rains.
3. Circle the picture that shows how the birds stay safe when it rains.

Word Work

Quick Review

Build Fluency: Sound-Spellings: Display the following **Word-Building Cards:** *b, k, l, r.* Have children say each sound. Repeat and vary the pace.

Phonemic Awareness

Puppet

Phoneme Blending

OBJECTIVES

CCSS Demonstrate basic knowledge of one-to-one letter-sound correspondences by producing the primary or many of the most frequent sounds for each consonant. **RF.K.3a**

CCSS Read common high-frequency words by sight. **RF.K.3c**

Blend phonemes to make words

1 Model *The puppet is going to say sounds in a word, /b/ /e/ /t/. It can blend those sounds to make a word: /beeet/,* bet. *Listen as the puppet blends more sounds to make a word.* Model phoneme blending with the following: /k/ /i/ /k/, /h/ /o/ /p/, /n/ /e/ /t/.

2 Guided Practice/Practice Tell children that the puppet is going to say the sounds in words. Have them repeat the sounds and then blend them to say the word.

/l/ /e/ /s/, less	/k/ /i/ /t/, kit	/f/ /a/ /n/, fan
/r/ /e/ /d/, red	/s/ /n/ /a/ /k/, snack	/s/ /p/ /e/ /k/, speck

Phonics

Review /r/r, /b/b, /l/l, /k/k

1 Model Display the *Rose* **Sound-Spelling Card**. *This is the letter* r. *The letter* r *can stand for the sound /r/ as in the word* rose. *What is the letter?* (r) *What sound does the letter* r *stand for?* (/r/) Repeat for /b/*b*, /l/*l*, and /k/*k* with the *Bat*, *Lemon*, and *Koala* Sound-Spelling Cards.

2 Guided Practice/Practice Have children listen as you say some words. Ask them to write the letter that stands for the beginning sound on their **Response Boards**. Do the first two words with children.

key	light	big	king	rake	ball
keep	lamp	bus	kiss	rock	road
leaf	bite	rope	log	best	kind

Review /h/*h* from Day 1. Have children write *h* on their Response Boards. Play "There's a Hippo in the House." Have children show their Response Boards when they hear /h/. Repeat for /f/*f* using "Let's Build a Fire."

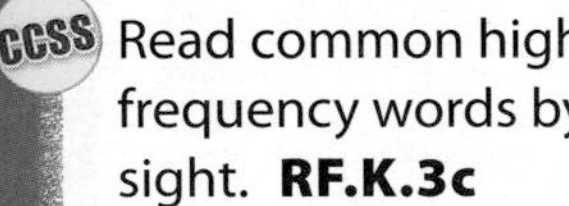

ENGLISH LANGUAGE LEARNERS

High-Frequency Words: Build Meaning Display the High-Frequency Word Cards *my, are, he, with, is, little, she, was.* Use the words in simple sentences, such as *She was with my sister*. As you say each sentence, point to the words and use gestures to convey meaning. Have children repeat the sentences.

Go Digital

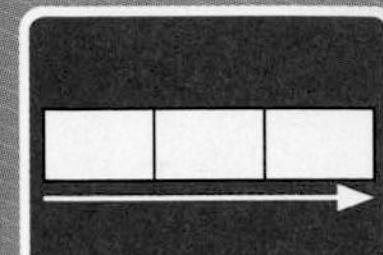
Phonemic Awareness

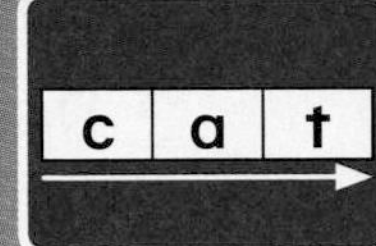

Phonics

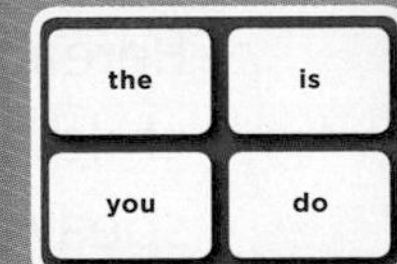

High-Frequency Word Routine

Handwriting

Blend Words with Short *e* and *b, d, l, r*

1. **Model** Place **Word-Building Cards** *b, e,* and *d* in a pocket chart. Point to the letter *b. This is the letter* b. *The letter* b *stands for /b/. Say /b/. This is the letter* e. *The letter* e *stands for /e/. Say /eee/. This is the letter* d. *The letter* d *stands for /d/. Say /d/. Listen as I blend the sounds together: /beeed/. Now blend the sounds with me to read the word.*

2. **Guided Practice/Practice** Place Word-Building Cards *l, e,* and *d* in the pocket chart. Point to the letter *l* and have children say /l/. Point to the letter *e* and have children say /e/. Point to the letter *d* and have children say /d/. Then move your hand from left to right under the word and have children blend and read the word, *led*. Repeat with the word *red.*

High-Frequency Words

are, he, is, little, my, she, was, with

1. **Guided Practice** Display the **High-Frequency Word Card** *are*. Use the **Read/Spell/Write** routine to review the words. Ask children to close their eyes, picture the word in their minds, and then write it the way they see it. Have children self-correct by checking the High-Frequency Word Card.

2. **Practice** Review the current words in the word bank.

→ Have partners create sentences using the word.

→ Have children count the number of letters in the word and then write the word again.

Repeat with the other high-frequency words.

Cumulative Review Review *to, and, go, you, do* and *with.*

Repeat the **Read/Spell/Write** routine. Mix the words and have children chorally say each one.

Monitor and *Differentiate*

Can children isolate /r/, /b/, /l/, and /k/ and match the sounds to *Rr, Bb, Ll, Kk,* and *ck*?

Can children read and recognize the high-frequency words?

Small Group Instruction

If No →	Approaching	Reteach pp. T226-231
	ELL	Develop pp. T244-247
If Yes →	On Level	Review pp. T234-237
	Beyond Level	Extend pp. T240-241

WHOLE GROUP
DAY 2

Shared Read

Reading/Writing Workshop Big Book and Reading/Writing Workshop

OBJECTIVES

CCSS Read common high-frequency words by sight. **RF.K.3c**

CCSS Read emergent-reader texts with purpose and understanding. **RF.K.4**

CCSS Recognize and name end punctuation. **L.K.2b**

ACADEMIC LANGUAGE

- *predict*
- Cognates: *predecir*

MINILESSON 10 Mins

Read "Mack and Ben"

Model Skills and Strategies

Model Concepts About Print Turn to page 40 and read each sentence. Explain that the first word in each sentence begins with a capital letter, and a punctuation mark comes at the end of a sentence. Read the sentences again with the appropriate intonation and expression. *The first sentence should be read with emotion, or feeling, because it ends with an exclamation point. The second sentence ends with a period so it is a statement.* Invite volunteers to come up to the **Big Book**. Encourage them to point to and identify the punctuation marks that end each sentence.

Predict Read the title together. Invite children to look closely at the illustration on pages 36 and 37. Encourage them to describe what they see and tell what the story might be about.

Read Have children chorally read the story with you. Point to each word as you read it together. Help children sound out decodable words and say the sight words. If children have difficulty, provide corrective feedback and guide them page by page using the student **Reading/Writing Workshop**.

Ask the following:

→ *Look at page 37. Why do you think Mack and Ben want to come into the house?* (Possible answer: It has started to rain, and they do not want to get wet.)

→ *Look at page 38. Why is Mack hiding under the covers?* (Possible answer: He doesn't like the storm. The thunder and lightning frighten him.)

→ *Look at page 42. Why did Mack and Ben pack a bag?* (It is sunny and they can go outside.)

Go Digital

"Mack and Ben"

"Mack and Ben"

READING/WRITING WORKSHOP, pp. 36–43

Rereading

Have small groups use the **Reading/Writing Workshop** to reread "Mack and Ben." Then review the skills and strategies using the *Phonics* and *Words to Know* pages that come before the selection.

- Invite children to reread the story. Have them visualize what it would be like to be at home during a bad storm. What might they see and hear? Then encourage children to use the illustrations in the story to describe the key details. Finally, invite them to discuss who tells the story.
- Have children use page 35 to review high-frequency words *my, are, he, was, is, little, she,* and *with*.
- Have children use page 34 to review the letters *h, e, f, r, b, l, k,* and *ck* and their corresponding sounds. Guide children to blend the sounds to read the words.

ENGLISH LANGUAGE LEARNERS

Reinforce Vocabulary Display the **High-Frequency Word Cards** *my, are, he, with, is, little, she, was.* Point to pictures in the classroom and groups of children as you use the high-frequency words in sentences, such as the following: *Do you see my little paper clips?* (Yes, we see your little paper clips.) *Is the fish in the fish tank?* (Yes, the fish is in the fish tank.) *Are these my keys?* (Yes, those are your keys.) *Does Dad drive when he goes to the store?* (Yes, Dad drives when he goes to the store.) *Can I cut with these scissors?* (Yes, you can cut with those scissors.) *Was she talking to me?* (Yes, she was talking to you.)

Language Arts

Interactive Writing

OBJECTIVES

Use a combination of drawing, dictating, and writing to compose informative/explanatory texts in which they name what they are writing about and supply some information about the topic. **W.K.2**

Form regular plural nouns orally by adding /s/ or /es/ (e.g., *dog, dogs*; *wish, wishes*). **L.K.1c**

Write an explanatory sentence

ACADEMIC LANGUAGE

- *report, sentence, plural, noun*
- Cognates: *plural*

Writing Trait: Voice

Review Remind children that writers can show how they feel about things with the words they choose. This gets readers involved in the story. Say these two sentences: *I listen to the raindrops tapping on my window. I hear the rain pounding against my window.* Point out that both sentences are about rain. Ask how the writer feels about the rain in each sentence.

Write a Weather Report

Discuss Display the list from Day 1. Read aloud each weather-related word. Ask children for other weather words they know, such as *hot, warm, cool, lightning, thunder.*

Model/Apply Grammar Tell children that you will work together to write sentences for a weather report.

Write the following: *Today it is* ______. *The wind is warm and wonderful.*

Read the sentences together, tracking the print. Model how to choose a weather-related word to complete the first sentence. *What can we say about the weather in the first sentence?* (It is windy.) Complete the sentence frame and read aloud: Today it is windy. The wind is warm.

Point out that *wind* is a naming word. *What do we need to add to the word* wind *to make it plural, or more than one?* (winds)

Write Have children help you create explanatory sentences that report on the weather. Provide possible sentence frames, such as these: *Today it is* ______. *There is* ______. Then guide them in completing the sentence frames. Write the words that children dictate. Share the pen with children and have them write the letters they know. Encourage children to choose words that show how they feel about the weather.

Go Digital

Writing
Grammar

Grammar

Naming Words (Nouns)

1 Review Review that plural nouns ending in *-s* or *-es* name more than one thing.

→ Write and read aloud: *dishes, sink, nights.* Ask children which naming words are plural. (dishes, nights) *What do we have to add to the word* sink *to make it name more than one thing?* (add -s)

2 Guided Practice Point to things in the **Big Book**, such as flowers, trees, umbrella, basket, and squirrels. Have children name the things. Write the things on the board. Read aloud the words with children. Ask children if there is more than one of each thing. Have a volunteer underline the letters under each word that tell them that there is more than one thing.

Have children make sentences using the things in the Big Book pages. For example: *The squirrels play in the trees.* Write children's dictated sentences.

3 Practice Have children work with partners. Ask them to draw a picture for one of the sentences. Then have them write the sentence under their drawings. Have children share their pictures and sentences with the class.

Talk About It

Have partners work together to orally generate sentences with plural nouns, such as *dishes, sinks,* and *nights.* Challenge them to create sentences with more than one plural noun.

ENGLISH LANGUAGE LEARNERS

Use Visuals Look at pages in the Big Book that support plural words with these pictures: *leaves, flowers, clouds, birds, ducks, chipmunks, bunnies.* Point to the objects in the picture as you name what they are. Provide a sentence frame for children to complete using plural words: *Look at all the ____.* Repeat correct answers slowly and clearly to the class.

Daily Wrap Up

- Discuss the Essential Question and encourage children to use the oral vocabulary words. *How do you prepare for bad weather?*
- Prompt children to review and discuss the skills they used today. How do those skills help them?

WHOLE GROUP
DAY 3

Materials

Reading/Writing Workshop Big Book
UNIT 6

Visual Vocabulary Cards
notice
celebration
enough

Puppet

Word-Building Cards

Interactive Read-Aloud Cards

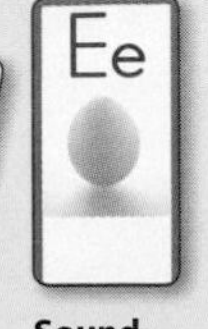

Sound-Spelling Cards
Bat, Egg, Fire, Hippo, Koala, Lemon, Rose

Photo Cards
ant, banana, boat, boot, bowl, bus, feet, fish, five, fork, hair, hand, hat, hook, inch, kangaroo, key, kite, ladder, ladybug, lamp, leaf, rabbit, rake, ring, rope

High-Frequency Word Cards
are, he, is, little, my, she, was, with

Think Aloud Cloud

"A Rose"
"Play Ball"

Build the Concept

Oral Language

MINILESSON 10 Mins

OBJECTIVES

CCSS With prompting and support, compare and contrast the adventures and experiences of characters in familiar stories. **RL.K.9**

CCSS Identify real-life connections between words and their use. **L.K.5c**

Develop oral vocabulary

ACADEMIC LANGUAGE
myth

ESSENTIAL QUESTION

COLLABORATE

Remind children that this week they are talking and learning about how they can stay safe in bad weather. Guide children to discuss the Essential Question using information from the **Big Book** and the weekly rhyme. Remind children that "Whether the Weather" explains that people can be fine no matter what the weather is like. Say the rhyme and have children join in.

Oral Vocabulary

Review last week's oral vocabulary words, as well as *safe* and *prepare* from Day 1. Use the **Define/Example/Ask** routine to introduce *notice, celebration,* and *enough.*

Oral Vocabulary Routine

Define: When you **notice** something, you see it clearly.

Example: I notice the stripes on a zebra.

Ask: What do you notice when a storm is coming?

Define: A **celebration** is a special activity in honor of a person or an event.

Example: We had a big celebration for 100 days in school.

Ask: If you could have a celebration, what would it be for? Why?

Define: When something is **enough**, it is all that is needed.

Example: We brought enough snacks for everyone to share.

Ask: How many pencils would be enough for everyone in our class to have one?

Visual Vocabulary Cards

Go Digital

Visual Glossary

"Rainbow Crow"

Think Aloud Cloud

Listening Comprehension

Read the Interactive Read Aloud

Genre: Myth

Tell children you will be reading a myth, which is like a fable. Remind them that a *fable* is a story that teaches a lesson. Display the **Interactive Read-Aloud Cards**.

Interactive Read-Aloud Cards

Read the title. Explain that the Lenape are a group of Native American people who live in North America.

Strategy: Visualize

Remind children that as they read it can be helpful to make a picture in their mind of what is happening in the story. This is called visualizing. They can use information from the words and illustrations to help them visualize. Model the strategy of visualizing using the **Think Aloud Cloud**.

Think Aloud I read that the sun was shining, but then snow fell and covered all the plants. The animals were shivering and shaking. In my mind I picture the sun being covered by clouds. I picture flakes of snow falling and the crow trembling and shaking because of the cold. I imagine the cold wind and hear it whistling through the trees. This helps me understand how hard it will be for the animals to live.

Read "Rainbow Crow," pausing occasionally to model the strategy of visualizing.

Make Connections

Guide partners to connect "Rainbow Crow" with *Waiting Out the Storm*. Discuss the weather in both stories. Have children tell about the different storms. *How did the characters in each story stay safe in bad weather?*

ELL

ENGLISH LANGUAGE LEARNERS

Reinforce Meaning As you read "Rainbow Crow," make meaning clear by pointing to specific characters, places, or objects in the illustrations, demonstrating word meanings, paraphrasing text, and asking children questions. For example, on Card 1, point to the animals and say: *This is a crow. This is an owl and a coyote.*

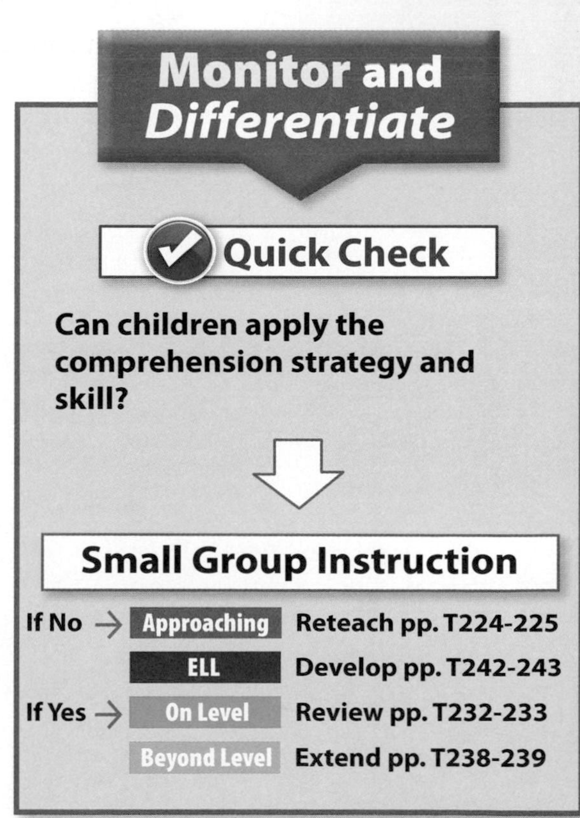

Word Work

Quick Review

Build Fluency: Sound-Spellings: Display the following **Word-Building Cards:** *b, k, l, r.* Have children say each sound. Repeat and vary the pace.

MINILESSON 5 Mins

Phonemic Awareness

Puppet

OBJECTIVES

CCSS Demonstrate basic knowledge of one-to-one letter-sound correspondences by producing the primary or many of the most frequent sounds of each consonant. **RF.K.2b**

CCSS Associate the long and short sounds with common spellings (graphemes) for the five major vowels. **RF.K.3b**

Blend phonemes to make words

Phoneme Blending

1 **Model** *The puppet is going to say the sounds in a word. Listen: /m/ /e/ /t/. It can blend these sounds together: /mmmeeet/,* met. *Now say the word with the puppet:* met. Repeat with *lip.*

2 **Guided Practice/Practice** Have children blend sounds to form words. Guide practice with the first word. *The puppet is going to say the sounds in a word. Listen to the puppet as it says each sound. Then blend the sounds to say the word.*

/r/ /i/ /d/, rid	/s/ /o/ /k/, sock	/k/ /i/ /s/, kiss
/s/ /t/ /a/ /k/, stack	/h/ /i/ /p/, hip	/h/ /e/ /d/, head
/e/ /l/ /k/, elk	/f/ /a/ /s/ /t/, fast	/r/ /ī/ /d/, ride
/b/ /o/ /ks/, box	/l/ /u/ /k/, luck	/k/ /i/ /d/, kid

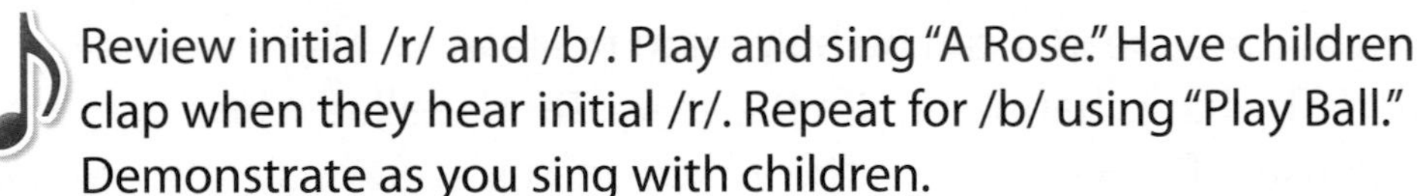

Review initial /r/ and /b/. Play and sing "A Rose." Have children clap when they hear initial /r/. Repeat for /b/ using "Play Ball." Demonstrate as you sing with children.

Go Digital

Phonemic Awareness

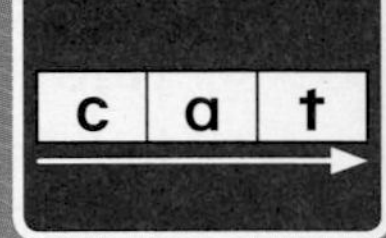

Phonics

Handwriting

Phonics

Sound-Spelling Card

Review Short *e* and /h/*h*, /f/*f*, /r/*r*, /b/*b*, /l/*l*, /k/*k*

1. **Model** Display the *Egg* **Sound-Spelling Card**. Review the sound /e/ spelled *e* using the words *egg* and *den*. Repeat the routine for /h/*h*, /f/*f*, /r/*r*, /b/*b*, /l/*l*, /k/*k* using the *Hippo*, *Fire*, *Rose*, *Bat*, *Lemon* and *Koala* Sound-Spelling Cards. Display **Word-Building Cards** *c* and *k*. Review the sound /k/ spelled *ck* using the word *deck*.

2. **Guided Practice/Practice** Have children practice connecting the letter and sound. Point to the Sound-Spelling Card and the letter *e*. *What is this letter?* (e) *What sound does it stand for?* (/e/) Repeat the routine for /h/*h*, /f/*f*, /r/*r*, /b/*b*, /l/*l*, /k/*k*.

Blend Words with Short *e, a* and *b, f, h, r, ck*

1. **Model** Display Word-Building Cards *b, e, t. This is the letter* b. *It stands for /b/. This is the letter* e. *It stands for /e/. This is the letter* t. *It stands for /t/. Let's blend the three sounds together: /beeet/. The word is* bet. Continue with the following words: *pet, peck, deck.*

2. **Guided Practice/Practice** Write the following words. Have children read each word, blending the sounds. Guide practice with the first word.

   led red fed had back

   Write these sentences and prompt children to read the connected text, sounding out the decodable words: *Tom can nap on the bed. The red hen can peck.*

Corrective Feedback

Blending: Sound Error Model the sound that children missed, then have them repeat. For example, for the word *red,* say: *My turn.* Tap under the letter *r* and ask: *Sound? What's the sound?* Return to the beginning of the word. *Let's start over.* Blend the word with children again.

YOUR TURN PRACTICE BOOK pp. 175–178

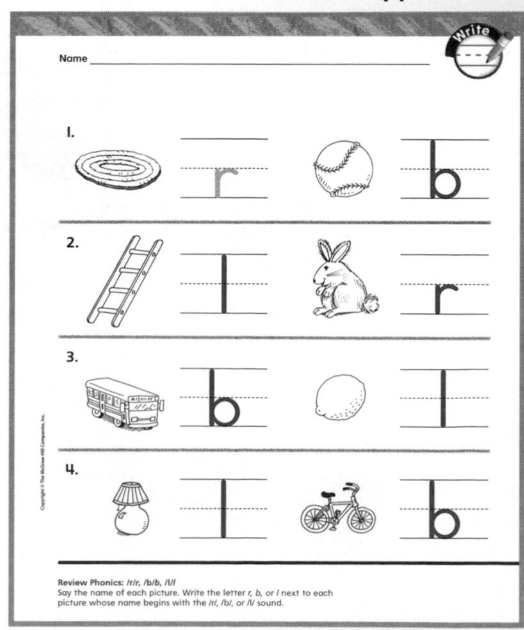
Name

1. r b
2. l r
3. b l
4. l b

Review Phonics: /r/r, /b/b, /l/l
Say the name of each picture. Write the letter r, b, or l next to each picture whose name begins with the /r/, /b/, or /l/ sound.

Word Work

Phonics

Photo Cards

Picture Sort

OBJECTIVES

CCSS Read common high-frequency words by sight. **RF.K.3c**

Sort words by initial sound/letter

ACADEMIC LANGUAGE
sort

❶ **Model** Remind children that the letter *r* can stand for /r/. Place the **Word-Building Card** *r* on the left side of a pocket chart. *What is the letter?* (r) *What sound does it stand for?* (/r/) Continue the same routine for the letters *k* and *h*.

Hold up the **Photo Card** for *rabbit*. *Here is the picture for* rabbit. Rabbit *has the /r/ sound at the beginning. Listen, /rrrabit/. I will place* rabbit *under the letter* r *because the letter* r *stands for /r/.*

Use the same routine for *hat* and *kite*.

❷ **Guided Practice/Practice** Have children sort the Photo Cards *rope, hair, key, hook, kangaroo, rake, ring, hand.* Have them say the sound at the beginning of the word and tell which letter the Photo Card should be placed under.

Repeat the routine for /b/*b*, /l/*l*, /f/*f* using the following photo cards: *banana, boat, boot, bowl, feet, fish, five, fork, lamp, ladder, ladybug, leaf.*

Photo Cards

Go Digital

Phonics

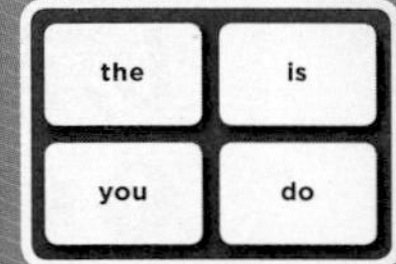

High-Frequency Word Routine

High-Frequency Words

are, he, is, little, my, she, was, with

1. **Guided Practice** Display the **High-Frequency Word Cards** *are, he, is, little, my, she, was,* and *with*. Review each word using the **Read/Spell/Write** routine.

2. **Practice** Point to the High-Frequency Word Card *are* and have children read it. Repeat with words *he, is, little, my, she, was* and *with.*

Build Fluency

Word Automaticity Write the following sentences and have children chorally read aloud as you track the print. Repeat several times.

She can go with Matt.
Dan and Kim are with me.
My cat is little.
Did he see my pet?
Ted was sick.

Read for Fluency Distribute pages 179–180 of the **Your Turn Practice Book** and help children assemble their Take-Home Books. Chorally read the Take-Home Book with children. Then have children reread the book to review high-frequency words and build fluency.

YOUR TURN PRACTICE BOOK pp. 179–180

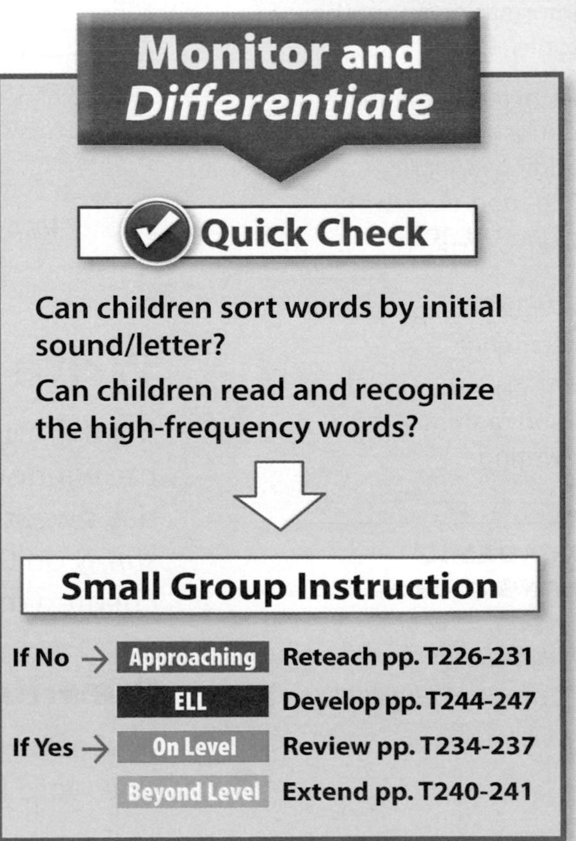

WHOLE GROUP
DAY 3

Language Arts

Reading/Writing Workshop Big Book

OBJECTIVES

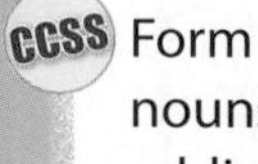

CCSS Use a combination of drawing, dictating, and writing to compose informative/explanatory texts in which they name what they are writing about and supply some information about the topic. **W.K.2**

CCSS Form regular plural nouns orally by adding /s/ or /es/ (e.g., *dog, dogs; wish, wishes*). **L.K.1c**

- Write an explanatory sentence
- Apply writing trait and grammar to writing

ACADEMIC LANGUAGE

- *report, sentence, plural, noun*
- Cognates: *plural*

MINILESSON 10 Mins

Independent Writing

Writing Trait: Voice

1. **Practice** Tell children that today they will draw and write sentences to give a report on the weather.

2. **Guided Practice** Share the **Readers to Writers** page in the **Reading/Writing Workshop**. Read the model sentences aloud.

READING/WRITING WORKSHOP BIG BOOK, pp. 46–47

Write a Weather Report

Model Display the list from Day 1. Write: *Today it is* ______. Look out the window and then look on the chart for a word that matches the day's weather. *I will write about today's weather. Today it is sunny.* Write *sunny* on the line. Read the sentence aloud, tracking the print. Remind children that there are other words that can also tell the day's weather.

Prewrite

Brainstorm Have children work with a partner to choose more than one word from the list that they can use to give a good weather report.

Draft

Ask children to draw pictures that show what the weather is today. Then guide them in writing several sentences that tell about the weather. Provide sentence frames if necessary. Encourage them to use words that show how they feel about the weather.

Apply Writing Trait Remind children to make their sentences and drawings clear, so that others will know what the weather is like.

Apply Grammar Tell children to point to and read the naming words in their sentences. Ask them to name any plural nouns.

ENGLISH LANGUAGE LEARNERS

Express the Meaning of Plurals
Have children draw a picture showing the plural form of the Photo Cards for *ant, apple, banana, bus.* Help them label each drawing with the plural form of the word. Point to the label and have children repeat after you as you say the word. Model correct pronunciation as needed.

Grammar

Naming Words (Nouns)

1. **Review** Remind children that plural nouns usually end in *-s* or *-es.* Write and read the words *fish* and *fishes. Which word names more than one fish?*

2. **Guided Practice/Practice** Write and read the words *apples* and *maps*. Have children repeat each word after you say it. *Do the words name one thing or more than one thing?* Remind them that the *-s* sounds different in each word, but *apples* tells there is more than one *apple* and *maps* tells there is more than one *map*.

   Write and read the words *light* and *dolls*. Have children repeat each word after you say it. *Which word names one thing? Which word names more than one thing?*

   Have children work in pairs. Provide the **Photo Cards** for *ant, banana, bus, inch, key, lamp.* Ask partners to pick a Photo Card and tell what the plural is. Have partners work together to form the plural form of each word and use it in a sentence. Provide help as needed.

Talk About It

Have partners work together to orally generate sentences with plural nouns about the weather, such as *It is raining. We need to take our umbrellas.*

Daily Wrap Up

- Review the Essential Question and encourage children to discuss it, using the oral vocabulary words *safe* and *prepare. How can we stay safe in bad weather?*
- Prompt children to review and discuss the skills they used today. Guide them to give examples of how they used each skill.

WHOLE GROUP
DAY 4

Materials

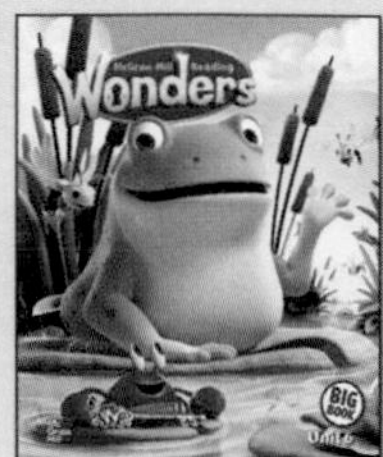
Reading/Writing Workshop Big Book
UNIT 6

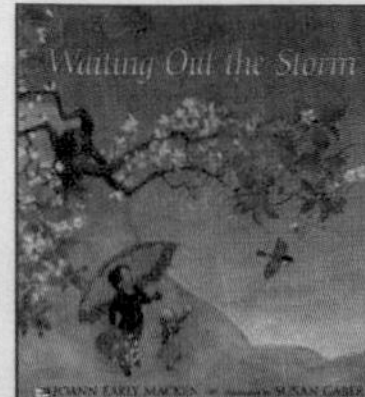
Literature Big Book
Waiting Out the Storm

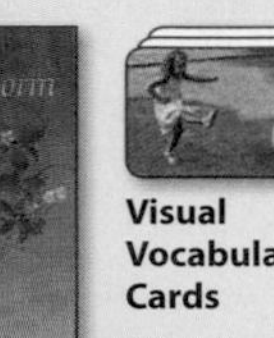
Visual Vocabulary Cards
are
he
is
little
my
she
was
with

Puppet

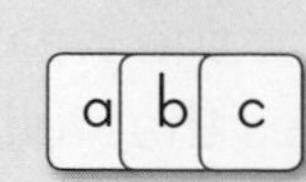

Word-Building Cards

Interactive Read-Aloud Cards

High-Frequency Word Cards
are
he
is
little
my
she
was
with

Photo Cards
bike
door
elbow
envelope
farm
gate
gorilla
helicopter
juggle
lemon
nest
shirt
watermelon
yak

Extend the Concept

MINILESSON 10 Mins

Oral Language

OBJECTIVES

CCSS Use words and phrases acquired through conversations, reading and being read to, and responding to texts. **L.K.6**

CCSS Demonstrate understanding of spoken words, syllables, and sounds (phonemes). **RF.K.2**

Develop vocabulary

ESSENTIAL QUESTION

Remind children that this week they have been talking and reading about ways to stay safe in bad weather. Have them recite "Whether the Weather" and think about how people stay safe when the weather is stormy. *How do the chipmunks stay safe in* Waiting Out the Storm*?*

Phonological Awareness

Recognize Alliteration

Remind children that some words, such as *whatever* and *weather*, begin with the same sounds. Say the following and have children repeat: *Peter piper picked a peck of pickled peppers.* Ask children if most of the words begin with the same sound? Which sound? (/p/) Repeat with the following having children raise their hands if the phrase is alliterative: *goodness gracious; big boy; handy dandy; last laugh, oh no.*

Review Oral Vocabulary

Reread the Interactive Read Aloud Use the **Define/Example/Ask** routine to review the oral vocabulary words *safe, prepare, notice, celebration,* and *enough*. Then have children listen as you reread "Rainbow Crow." Ask:

- *Why did the animals cheer in celebration when Rainbow Crow returned?* (He brought back fire to melt the ice and snow.)
- *What did Rainbow Crow notice about his feathers when he had returned?* (They had turned black.)

Go Digital

Visual Glossary

"Rainbow Crow"

Category Words

Category Words: Question Words

1 Model Remind children that *who, what, why, when, where* and *how* are question words. *Listen to this story. Raise your hands when you hear a question word.* Demonstrate as you recite:

"We are going on a field trip!" Mr. Garcia told the class.
*"**Where** are we going?" Julia asked.*
"We are going to the museum," Mr. Garcia answered.
*"**What** will we see?" Michael asked.*
"We will see fossils," said Mr. Garcia
*"**How** will we get there?" Raven wanted to know.*
"We will take a bus," replied Mr. Garcia.
*"**When** are we going?" Maggie asked.*
"Tomorrow!" Mr. Garcia said.

2 Guided Practice Place the following **Photo Cards** face down: *door, elbow, envelope, farm, gate, gorilla, helicopter, juggle, nest.* Have children choose a Photo Card. Ask them to make up questions about the picture. For example: *What is the gorilla thinking? How do you juggle?*

Vocabulary Strategy: Word Categories/Question Words

1 Model Explain that grouping words into categories helps us notice how they are similar or related.

Think Aloud When we want to find out more about something, we ask questions. To ask good questions, we first need to think of question words. *How, where, why, who, what,* and *when* are all words that fit into the word category of "question words." We can use these words to ask good questions.

2 Guided Practice/Practice Write a list of question words on the board. Ask volunteers to use the question words to ask questions about the illustrations in *Waiting Out the Storm.* Encourage other children to answer the questions.

LET'S MOVE!

Assign groups a question word. Then give simple directions using question words, such as *If you are a what, wave your arms in the air. If you are a why, move to the play area.*

ENGLISH LANGUAGE LEARNERS

Practice Display the Photo Cards from the Guided Practice activity. Then write on the board some of the oral sentences that children made up. Help children identify the question word in each sentence. Underline and repeat the question word in each sentence.

YOUR TURN PRACTICE BOOK p. 181

Listening Comprehension

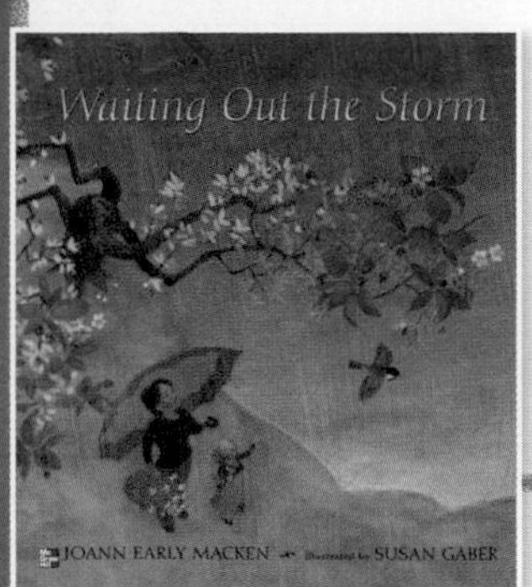

Literature Big Book

OBJECTIVES

CCSS With prompting and support, ask and answer questions about key details in a text. **RI.K.1**

- Understand the characteristics of informational text
- Use the text feature directions to gather information
- Apply the comprehension strategy: Visualize
- Make connections across texts

ACADEMIC LANGUAGE
visualize, directions

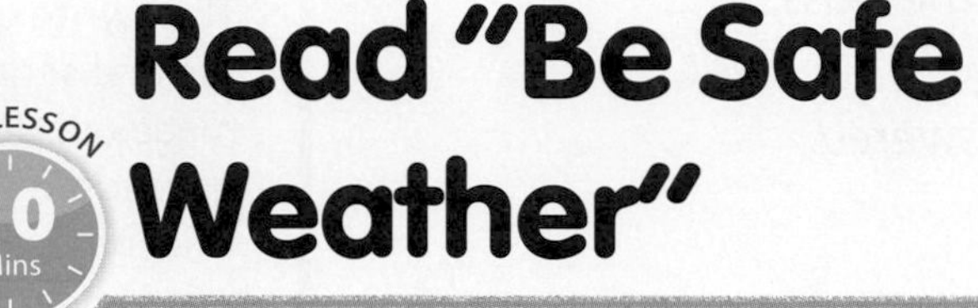

Read "Be Safe in Bad Weather"

"Be Safe in Bad Weather"

Genre: Informational Text

Display "Be Safe in Bad Weather" on pages 28–32 of the **Big Book** and read aloud the title. Review that informational text tells about real people, places, and events.

Set a Purpose for Reading

Read aloud page 28. Tell children to listen as you continue reading the selection so they can learn how to stay safe in bad weather.

Strategy: Visualize

Remind children that good readers use the text and the photographs to picture in their minds what is happening. Have children visualize page 28. *Make a picture in your mind. What is a blizzard like?* (The wind is blowing; the house is creaking; it is very cold and snowy.)

Text Feature: Directions

Explain Read aloud page 31. Point out the sentences that are directions. Explain that directions tell readers what to do. *What should you do if you are outside and hear thunder?* (Stay away from trees; quickly find shelter indoors.)

Apply Turn to page 32. Read aloud the page. *What do the directions tell us to practice saying?* (phone number; street address; the name of your town and state)

LITERATURE BIG BOOK PAGES 28–29

VISUALIZE

Look at the photographs. Picture in your head what people might be doing after it stops snowing. (Possible responses: I see people shoveling snow, clearing their cars of snow, and playing in the snow.)

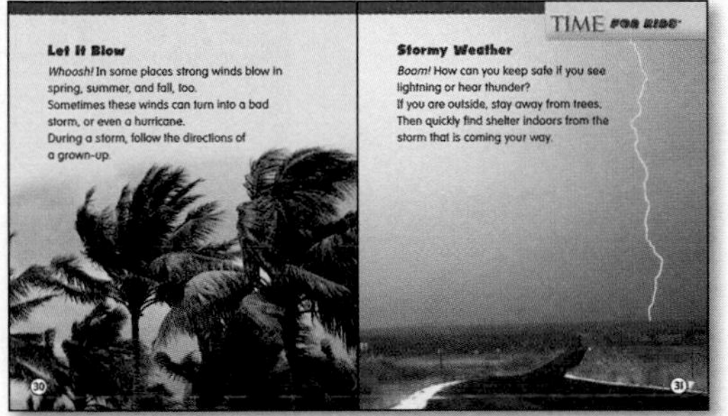

LITERATURE BIG BOOK PAGES 30–31

KEY DETAILS

Look at the photograph on page 31. *What things in the picture tell you that there is a storm coming?* (Possible responses: the dark sky and the lightning)

LITERATURE BIG BOOK PAGE 32

KEY DETAILS

The list tells about things in a safety kit. What other things would you need? (Possible responses: radio, candles, matches)

Retell and Respond

Have children discuss the selection by asking the following questions:

→ *What kinds of storms have strong winds?* (blizzards, hurricanes)

→ *What should you do during a storm?* (follow the directions of a grown-up)

Make Connections

Have children recall the selections they read this week.

→ *What did the mother and the girl do during the storm?* (They were inside, where they stayed safe and warm.)

Write About It Write about how Rainbow Crow saved the other animals.

ENGLISH LANGUAGE LEARNERS

Reinforce Meaning As you read aloud the text, make the meaning clear by pointing to the details in the photographs. Ask children questions and elicit language.

SOCIAL STUDIES

CONNECT TO CONTENT

Stormy Weather Review with children the different kinds of bad weather they learned about (blizzards, wind storms, hurricanes). Have partners tell each other their address, phone number, and the name of the city or town and state in which they live.

Word Work

Quick Review

Build Fluency: Sound-Spellings: Display the following **Word-Building Cards**: *b, e, f, h, k, l, r*. Have children say each sound. Repeat and vary the pace.

Phonemic Awareness

OBJECTIVES

CCSS Add or substitute individual sounds (phonemes) in simple, one-syllable words to make new words. **RF.K.2e**

CCSS Distinguish between similarly spelled words by identifying the sounds of the letters that differ. **RF.K.3d**

CCSS Read common high-frequency words by sight. **RF.K.3c**

Blend letter sounds to read words

Phoneme Addition

1 **Model** *Listen as I say a word:* all. *Repeat the word:* all. *When I add /f/ to the beginning of* all, *I make the word* fall. Fall *is the word I make when I add /f/ to the beginning of* all. Repeat: Add /f/ to *ill* to make *fill.*

2 **Guided Practice/Practice** Have children add initial phonemes to words to make new words. Guide children with the first question.

What word do you have if you add /l/ to the beginning of it? (lit)
What word do you have if you add /f/ to the beginning of Ed? (fed)
What word do you have if you add /h/ to the beginning of am? (ham)
What word do you have if you add /t/ to the beginning of rain? (train)
What word do you have if you add /b/ to the beginning of in? (bin)

MINILESSON 5 Mins

Phonics

Blend Words with Short *e, o* and *d, l, ck*

1 **Guided Practice** Display **Word-Building Cards** *d, e, c, k*. Point to the letter *d. This is the letter* d. *The letter* d *stands for /d/. Say /d/. This is the letter* e. *The letter* e *stands for /e/. Listen as I blend the two sounds together: /deee/. Say /deee/. These are the letters* ck. *The letters together stand for /k/. Listen as I blend the three sounds: /deeek/,* deck. *Now you say it. Let's change* e *to* o. Use the same routine to blend the word *dock*.

2 **Practice** Write *deck, dock* and *let, lit, lot*. Have children blend the words. Point to *deck* and *dock*. *Which letters are the same?* (*d, ck*). *Which letters are different?* (*e* and *o*) Discuss the sound each letter stands for and how it changes the word. Repeat with *let, lit,* and *lot*.

Go Digital

Phonemic Awareness

Phonics

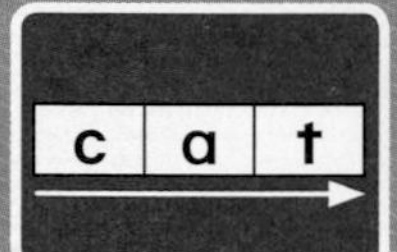

Visual Glossary

Handwriting

High-Frequency Word Routine

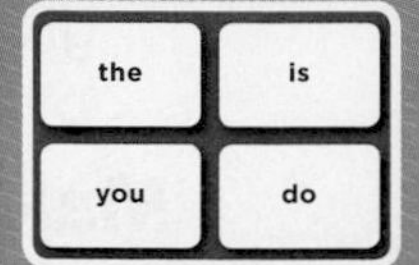

Dictation

Review Dictate each of the sounds for children to spell. Have them repeat the sound and then write the letter that stands for the sound.

/h/ /e/ /f/ /r/ /b/ /l/

Dictate the following words for children to spell: *fed, hit, rock, bet.* Model for children how to segment each word to scaffold the spelling.

When I say the word fed, *I hear three sounds: /f/ /e/ /d/. I know the letter* f *stands for /f/, the letter* e *stands for /e/, and the letter* d *stands for /d/. I will write the letters* f, e, d *to spell* fed.

When children finish, write the letters and words for them to self-correct.

High-Frequency Words

Practice Say the word *are* and have children write it. Then display the **Visual Vocabulary Card** *are.* Follow the Teacher Talk routine on the back. Repeat with *he, is, little, my, she, was,* and *with.*

Build Fluency Build sentences in a pocket chart using **High-Frequency Word Cards** and **Photo Cards**. Use index cards to create punctuation cards for a period and a question mark. Have children chorally read the sentences as you track the print. Then have them identify the words *are, he, is, little, my, she, was, with.*

He can go to my farm.

Is she with you?

The pillow and the plate are blue.

She was with the little dog.

Have partners create sentences using the words *are, he, is, little, my, she, was, with.*

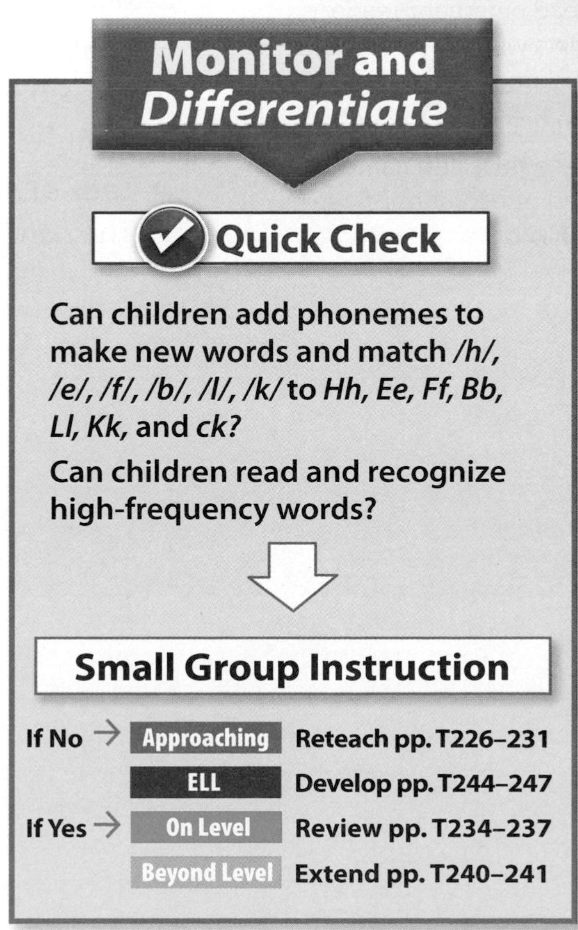

Monitor and *Differentiate*

Quick Check

Can children add phonemes to make new words and match */h/, /e/, /f/, /b/, /l/, /k/* to *Hh, Ee, Ff, Bb, Ll, Kk,* and *ck?*

Can children read and recognize high-frequency words?

Small Group Instruction

If No →	Approaching	Reteach pp. T226–231
	ELL	Develop pp. T244–247
If Yes →	On Level	Review pp. T234–237
	Beyond Level	Extend pp. T240–241

Shared Read

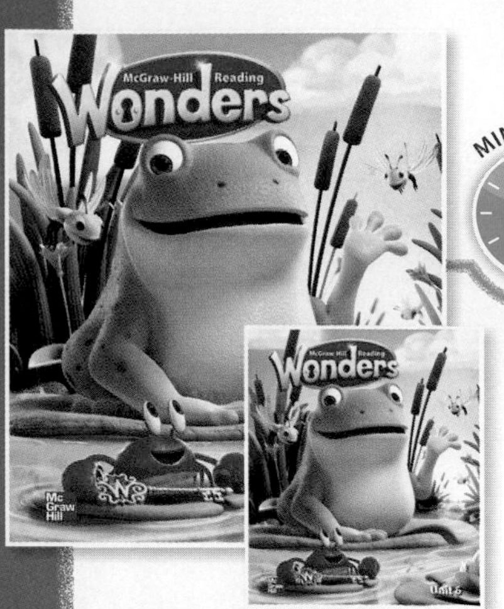

Reading/Writing Workshop Big Book and Reading/Writing Workshop

OBJECTIVES

CCSS Read common high-frequency words by sight. **RF.K.3c**

CCSS Read emergent-reader texts with purpose and understanding. **RF.K.4**

CCSS Recognize and name end punctuation. **L.K.2b**

MINILESSON 10 Mins

Read "Mack and Ben"

Model Skills and Strategies

Model Concepts About Print As you read the story, point out sentence boundaries. Review how the first word in each sentence begins with a capital letter and ends with a punctuation mark. Invite volunteers to come up to the **Big Book** and point to the capital letter that begins the first word in each sentence. Then have them identify the punctuation mark that completes each sentence.

Reread Have children chorally read the story. Children should sound out the decodable words and say the sight words. Offer support as needed using the student **Reading/Writing Workshop**.

Ask the following:

- *Look at page 38. What is it like outside?* (Possible answers: It is raining hard. There are dark clouds and lightning in the sky.)
- *Look at page 41. How do you know that the storm is almost over?* (Possible answer: The Sun is out and it looks like the weather is clearing.)
- *Look at page 42. Why are Mack and Ben packing?* (Possible answer: They are planning to go out and play now that the Sun is out.)

Go Digital

"Mack and Ben"

"Mack and Ben"

READING/WRITING WORKSHOP, pp. 36–43

Fluency: Expression

1. **Explain** Tell children that as you read the story, you will read with expression, or feeling. Mention that you will stress different words and change your voice when reading sentences that end with a period or an exclamation point. You will also pause after a word or group of words for effect.

2. **Model** Model reading "Mack and Ben" with expression. *When I read the story, I change my tone when I read sentences with different kinds of end punctuation. I also pause after sentences, words, or groups of words for effect, like this.* Read each sentence with appropriate emotion, or feeling.

3. **Guided Practice** Invite children to choral read the story with feeling. If necessary, have them listen to you first, then echo each sentence. Encourage them to match your intonation and expression.

Language Arts

Independent Writing

OBJECTIVES

CCSS With guidance and support from adults, respond to questions and suggestions from peers and add details to strengthen writing as needed. **W.K.5**

CCSS Form regular plural nouns orally by adding /s/ or /es/ (e.g., *dog, dogs; wish, wishes*). **L.K.1c**

Revise a weather report

ACADEMIC LANGUAGE
revise, draft, noun

Write a Weather Report

Revise

Distribute the children's draft sentences and drawings from Day 3.

Apply Writing Trait: Voice Explain that as writers revise reports, they may add sentences to be sure that others understand what the weather is like. Write and read: *It is rainy. It is windy. Let's work together to make sure I have made it clear what the weather is like today. What could we add? What else could we write to show how we feel about the weather?* Guide children to add a sentence, such as *The rain helps plants grow.*

Then have children reread the sentences they wrote on Day 3 and check for the following:

- Did I clearly tell what the weather is today?
- Can I add any sentences to tell more?
- Do my sentences tell about everything in my drawing?
- Did I use the correct naming words?

Apply Grammar Ask children to identify the naming words in the sentences: *It is stormy today. The weather is very windy.* (today, weather)

Peer Edit Have children work with a partner to do a peer edit. Partners can read each other's sentences aloud to see if they are clear. Ask partners to suggest a detail they could add to their reports. Provide time for children to make revisions to their reports.

Final Draft

After children have edited their own papers and finished their peer edits, have them write their final draft. Remind them that their drawings and sentences should make it very clear what the weather is like today. As children work, conference with them to provide guidance.

Go Digital

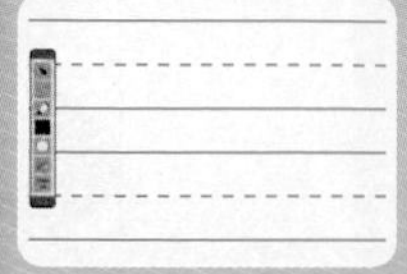

Writing

Grammar

Grammar

Naming Words (Nouns)

1 Review Remind children that plural nouns name more than one thing and can end in *-s* or *-es*.

→ Write and read aloud: *The blocks are red.*

Ask children to draw a picture that matches the sentence. (Drawings should have more than one red block.)

2 Guided Practice Show the **Photo Card** for *lemon*.

→ Write and read aloud the following sentences on the board:

I put two lemons on the dish.
I put a lemon on the dish.

Ask children to draw a picture for each sentence. Have children write a label for each drawing with the words *One lemon* and *Two lemons*.

3 Practice Show the Photo Card for *shirt*. Have children work in pairs to create sentences with *shirt* in both singular and plural forms. Then have children draw a picture for each sentence.

Talk About It

Have partners work together to orally generate sentences with plural nouns about the things they do at home when the weather is bad, such as *I play games.*

ENGLISH LANGUAGE LEARNERS SCAFFOLD

Photo Cards and Sentences
Display the Photo Cards for *bike, yak,* and *watermelon.* Write sentences with plural nouns that go with images on the Photo Cards, such as *The yak has two horns. The bike has two wheels. There are two slices of watermelon.* As you read each sentence aloud, point to the noun to show that it is plural.

Daily Wrap Up

- Review the Essential Question and encourage children to discuss it, using the oral vocabulary words.
- Prompt children to discuss the skills they practiced and learned today. Guide them to share examples of each skill.

WHOLE GROUP
DAY 4

www.connected.mcgraw-hill.com
RESOURCES
Research and Inquiry

Wrap Up the Week
Integrate Ideas

RESEARCH AND INQUIRY

SOCIAL STUDIES

Stormy Weather

OBJECTIVES

Participate in shared research and writing projects (e.g., explore a number of books by a favorite author and express opinions about them). **W.K.7**

With guidance and support from adults, recall information from experiences or gather information from provided sources to answer a question. **W.K.8**

ACADEMIC LANGUAGE
research, inquiry

Make a Book

Review the steps in the research process. Tell children that today partners will do research to make a class book about safety during bad weather.

STEP 1 Choose a Topic

Prompt children to discuss weather that occurs in different seasons, such as hurricanes, tornadoes, and blizzards. Guide partners to think of weather-related safety rules, such as what to do during a storm.

STEP 2 Find Resources

Talk about locating and using resources. Direct children to use the selections from the week. You may wish to print out resources from http://www.ready.gov/kids. Have children use the Research Process Checklist online.

STEP 3 Keep Track of Ideas

Have children list ideas for safety tips by drawing pictures or writing words in a two-column chart. Guide them to print out safety tips from the Internet.

Collaborative Conversations

Listen Carefully As children engage in partner, small-group, and whole-class discussions, encourage them to:

- → look at the person who is speaking.
- → listen to the words the speaker is saying.
- → respect others by not interrupting them.
- → repeat classmates' ideas to check understanding.

It is windy. We put toys away.

STEP 4 Create the Project: Safety Book

Explain the characteristics of the project:

→ **Information** This book will give information about how to stay safe in different kinds of weather.

→ **Text** Explain that each page of the book will have sentences that explain the safety tip. Provide these sentence frames:

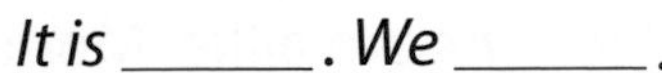

It is ______. We ______.

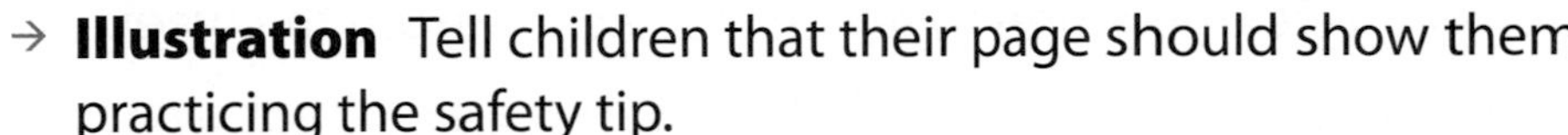

→ **Illustration** Tell children that their page should show them practicing the safety tip.

Explain that each pair will create one page of a book. The page will tell about the weather and give a safety tip. Guide children to use the computer to write and publish the sentences for their safety tip.

→ Tell children that their sentences should name the type of stormy weather and tell what they do to stay safe.

→ Encourage children who can generate more writing to do so.

ELL ENGLISH LANGUAGE LEARNERS SCAFFOLD

Beginning

Practice Have more fluent partners help children practice talking about their illustration. Partners should help each other name details in the illustration as well as talk about what is happening.

Intermediate

Demonstrate Understanding Prompt children to tell not just what the safety tip is but why it's important to follow that safety tip. These children might benefit from a sentence frame such as this: *In bad weather, we ____. This is important because ____.*

Advanced/Advanced High

Demonstrate Command Encourage children to include details in their illustration and to elaborate on those details when they present their page of the book. Encourage the use of concrete nouns that help other children understand the safety tip fully.

WHOLE GROUP
DAY 5

Materials

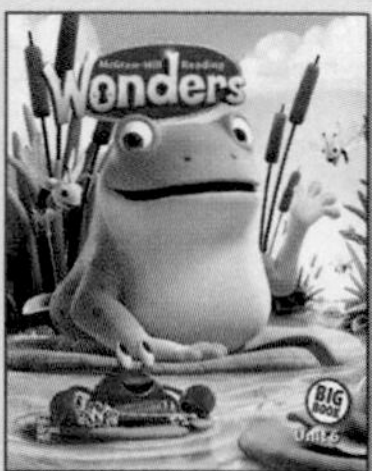

Reading/Writing Workshop Big Book
UNIT 6

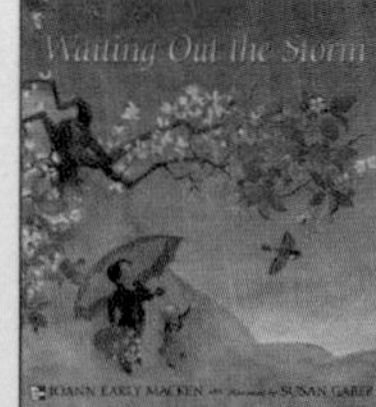

Literature Big Book
Waiting Out the Storm

Response Board

Word-Building Cards

Visual Vocabulary Cards
are
he
is
little
my
she
was
with

High-Frequency Word Cards
are
he
is
little
my
she
was
with

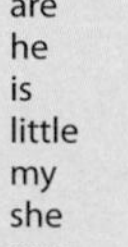
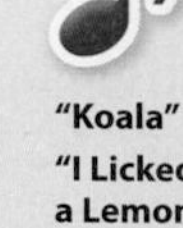
"Koala"
"I Licked a Lemon"

Integrate Ideas

TEXT CONNECTIONS

Connect to the Essential Question

OBJECTIVES

With prompting and support, compare and contrast the adventures and experiences of characters in familiar stories. **RL.K.9**

Participate in collaborative conversations with diverse partners about *kindergarten topics and texts* with peers and adults in small and larger groups. **SL.K.1**

- Make connections among texts
- Make connections to the world

Text to Text

Remind children that all week they have been reading selections about staying safe in stormy weather. Tell them that they will now connect the texts, or think about how the selections are alike. Model comparing *Waiting Out the Storm* to another selection from the week.

COLLABORATE

Think Aloud In *Waiting Out the Storm,* I read about what a girl and her mother did during a storm. In "Be Safe in Bad Weather" I read about ways that people can stay safe in different kinds of storms. In both selections, people go inside to be together during storms.

Guide children to compare the experiences of the characters in *Waiting Out the Storm* and "Rainbow Crow."

Text to Self

Initiate a discussion about stormy weather that children have experienced. Guide comments toward what children did to stay safe.

Text to World

Talk about what happens in the community when there is bad weather. *Does our school ever close for stormy weather? Why?*

TALK ABOUT READING

Analyze and Explain

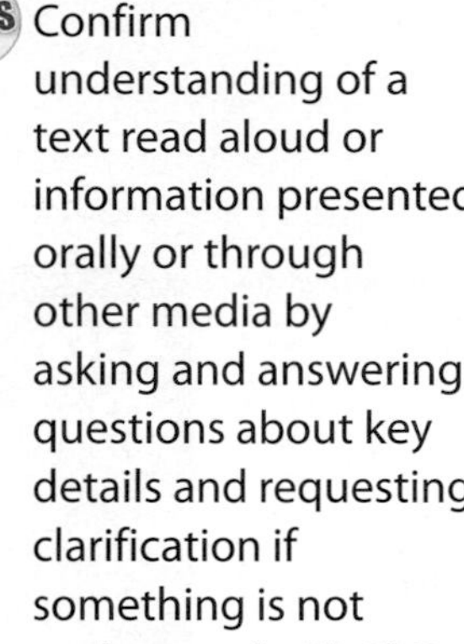

OBJECTIVES

CCSS Confirm understanding of a text read aloud or information presented orally or through other media by asking and answering questions about key details and requesting clarification if something is not understood. **SL.K.2**

Becoming Readers

Talk with children about the genres, strategy, and skill they have learned about this week. Prompt them to discuss how this knowledge helps them to read and understand selections.

- Remind children that one genre they learned about is fiction. Recall with them some characteristics of fiction.
- Discuss with children the strategy of visualizing. *How did picturing details about the weather in your mind help you to understand* Waiting Out the Storm?
- Talk about how the children learned to notice details in the words and illustrations. *The words in* Waiting Out the Storm *don't tell how the girl feels, but the illustrations show how she feels. How did noticing these details help you understand the story?*

RESEARCH AND INQUIRY

Stormy Weather

OBJECTIVES

CCSS Participate in shared research and writing projects (e.g. explore a number of books by a favorite author and express opinions about them). **W.K.7**

Wrap Up the Project

COLLABORATE Guide partners to share their safety tips and to point out details in their illustrated pages. Encourage children to use words and phrases they learned this week. Have children use the Presenting and Listening checklists online.

Word Work

Quick Review

Build Fluency: Sound-Spellings: Display the following **Word-Building Cards:** *b, e, f, h, k, l, r.* Have children say each sound. Repeat and vary the pace.

Phonemic Awareness

OBJECTIVES

CCSS Add or substitute individual sounds (phonemes) in simple, one-syllable words to make new words. **RF.K.2e**

CCSS Spell simple words phonetically, drawing on knowledge of sound-letter relationships. **L.K.2d**

CCSS Read common high-frequency words by sight. **RF.K.3c**

Blend sounds to read words

Phoneme Addition

1 Model *We are going to add sounds to the beginning of words to make new words. Listen to this word:* at. *Say the word:* at. *Let's add /b/ to the beginning of* at. *What is the word when you add /b/ to the beginning of* at? Give children ample time. Bat *is the word when you add /b/ to the beginning of at.* Have children say bat.

2 Guided Practice/Practice Have children add initial sounds to words to form new words. Guide children with the first question.

What word do you have if you add /f/ to the beginning of it? (fit)
What word do you have if you add /r / to the beginning of Ed? (red)
What word do you have if you add /h/ to the beginning of at? (hat)
What word do you have if you add /s/ to the beginning of lip? (slip)

Phonics

Read Words with *f, r, b, l, k, t, ck*

1 Guided Practice Remind children that the letter *e* can stand for the sound /e/. Display **Word-Building Cards** *l, e, t.* Point to the letter *l. The letter* l *stands for the sound /l/. Say /l/. The letter* e *stands for /e/. Say /eee /. The letter* t *stands for /t/. Say /t/. Let's blend the sounds to make the word: /leeet/* let. *Let's change* l *to* b. Blend and read the word *bet* with children.

2 Practice Write these words and sentences for children to read:

deck fed red bed led kit hit

Ed ran with him. Is my pet cat sick?
Rick can nap on a bed. I can fill the sack.

Remove words from view before dictation.

Review initial /k/*k*. Have children write the letter *k* on their **Response Boards**. Play and sing "Koala" Have children show letter *k* on their boards when they hear initial /k/. Demonstrate as you sing with children. Repeat with /l/*l* and "I Licked a Lemon."

Go Digital

Phonemic Awareness

Phonics

Handwriting

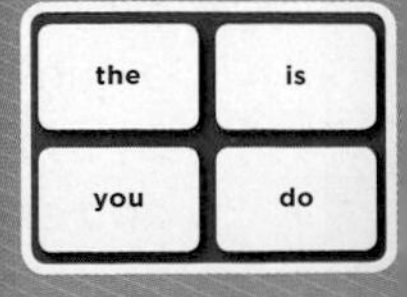

High-Frequency Word Cards

Dictation

Review Dictate the following sounds for children to spell. As you say each sound, have children repeat it and then write the letter that stands for the sound.

/h/ /e/ /f/ /r/ /b/ /l/

Dictate the following words for children to spell. Model for children how to use **sound boxes** to segment each word to scaffold the spelling. *I will say a word. You will repeat the word, then think about how many sounds are in the word. Use your sound boxes to count the sounds. Then write one letter for each sound you hear.*

lap kit fed hop rip deck

Then write the letters and words for children to self-correct.

High-Frequency Words

are, he, is, little, my, she, was, with

1 Review Display **Visual Vocabulary Cards** *are, he, is, little, my, she, was,* and *with*. Have children **Read/Spell/Write** the words. Then choose a Partner Talk activity.

Distribute one of the following **High-Frequency Word Cards** to children: *are, he, is, little, my, she, was, with*. Tell children that you will say some sentences. *When you hear the word that is on your card, stand and hold up your word card.*

There *are* clouds in the sky.
He has a blue umbrella.
She has a yellow one.
What color *is* your umbrella?
My umbrella *is* green with stripes.
It *was* quite a storm.
There *was* a lot of wind *with* the rain.
Your *little* umbrella got wet.

2 Build Fluency: Word Automaticity Display High-Frequency Word Cards *are, he, is, little, my, she, was,* and *with*. Point to each card, at random, and have children read the word as quickly as they can.

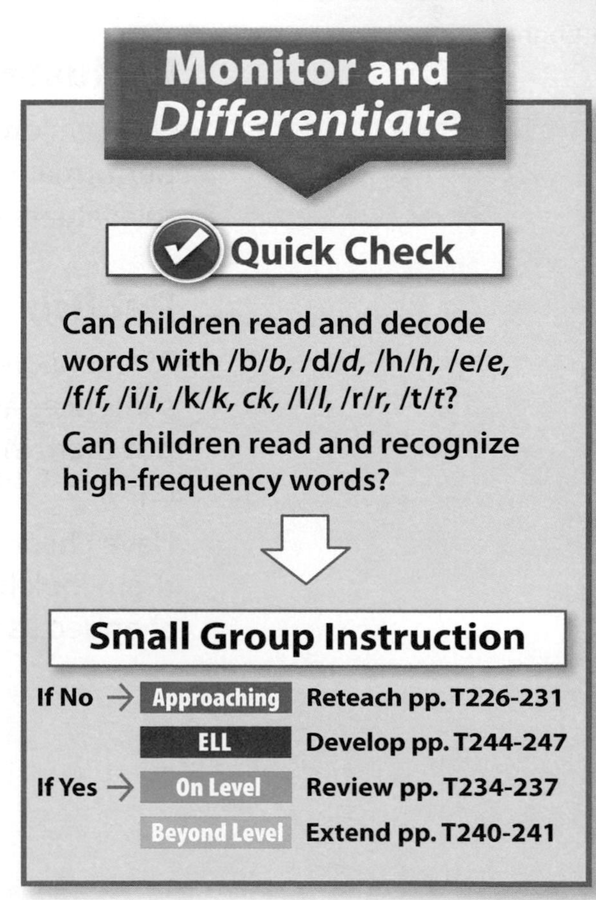

Language Arts

Independent Writing

OBJECTIVES

 Speak audibly and express thoughts, feelings, and ideas clearly. **SL.K.6**

 Form regular plural nouns orally by adding /s/ or /es/ (e.g., *dog, dogs; wish, wishes*). **L.K.1c**

- Make a presentation
- Listen to others

ACADEMIC LANGUAGE
- *present, publish, noun*
- Cognates: *presente*

Write a Weather Report

Prepare

Tell children that they will present their finished sentences and drawings from Day 4 to the class. Hold up an example from Day 4 and read it aloud, tracking the print. *I read my sentence clearly so everyone can understand me. I showed my picture to help everyone see what the weather is like.*

Present

Have children take turns standing up and reading their sentences aloud. Remind children to read their sentences clearly and to show their pictures to the class. Encourage the rest of the class to listen quietly and to wait until the presenter has finished before asking any questions.

Evaluate

Have children discuss their own presentations and evaluate their performances, using the presentation rubric. Use the teacher's rubric to evaluate children's writing.

Publish

After children have finished presenting, hang the pictures with sentences as a banner. Then collect their sentences with drawings and put them in a binder. Discuss how differently they chose to word their reports.

Have children add their writing to their Writer's Portfolio. Then have them look back at their previous writing and discuss how they have changed as writers throughout the year.

Go Digital

Writing

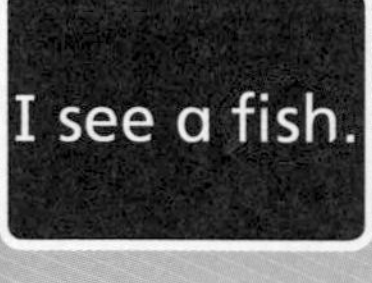

Grammar

Grammar

Naming Words (Nouns)

1 **Review** Remind children that naming words are called nouns and that they tell the names of people, places, animals, and things. Review that plural nouns name more than one thing and can end in *-s* or *-es*.

Draw single and multiple objects on separate index cards, such as chair, tables, pens, pencil. Hold up each card. Have children tell what the thing or things are. Ask children to identify whether the words they say are nouns for one thing or more than one thing.

2 **Review Practice** Have children group the index cards with single nouns in one pile and with plural nouns in the other pile. Have children work in groups to draw single and multiple objects. Circulate among the groups, having children say the names of their objects to you. Then ask children to sort their cards in groups with single and plural nouns. Offer corrective feedback as needed.

Wrap Up the Week

- Review blending words with /h/*h*, /e/*e*, /f/*f*, /r/*r*, /b/*b*, /l/*l*, /k/*k*, *ck*. Remind children that plural nouns are usually formed by adding *-s* or *-es* at the end of nouns.
- Use the **High-Frequency Word Cards** to review the Words to Know.
- Remind children that a weather report tells people how to dress and prepare for the weather.

Approaching Level

Leveled Reader

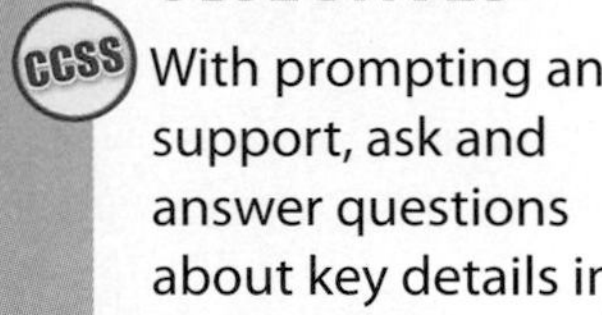

OBJECTIVES

- **CCSS** With prompting and support, ask and answer questions about key details in a text. **RL.K.1**
- **CCSS** With prompting and support, retell familiar stories, including key details. **RL.K.2**
- **CCSS** Demonstrate understanding of the organization and basic features of print. **RF.K.1**
- **CCSS** Read emergent-reader texts with purpose and understanding. **RF.K.4**

Leveled Reader: *Bad Weather*

Before Reading

Preview and Predict

Read aloud the title and the names of the author and illustrator as children follow along in their books. Ask: *What kind of weather is bad weather? What do you think will happen in bad weather?* Preview each illustration and guide children to revise or confirm their predictions. Model the language pattern: *What does the woman get here? Yes, she gets her coat.*

Review Genre: Fiction

Remind children that fiction stories are stories with made-up characters. Ask: *Who are the characters in this story?* (a girl and her mother)

Model Concepts of Print

Remind children that a sentence begins with a capital letter and ends with a punctuation mark.

Review High-Frequency Words

Point to the high-frequency word *she* on each page of the story. Ask children to say the word aloud each time they point to it.

Essential Question

Read the Essential Question: *How can you stay safe in bad weather?* Say: *Let's find out how the characters stay safe in bad weather*. Remind children to use the rebuses and illustrations as they read.

During Reading

Guided Comprehension

As children read *Bad Weather,* monitor and provide guidance by correcting blending and modeling the strategy and skill.

Leveled Reader

Strategy: Visualize

Remind children that as they read, they can use information from the text and illustrations to make pictures in their minds of what is happening.

Skill: Key Details

Remind children that the key details in a story help them understand the story. Explain that they can find the key details by looking at the text and the illustrations.

Think Aloud The pictures in this story tell me what the characters are doing. They tell me the important ideas the author wants me to know. On page 2, I see the woman putting on a coat to go outside in the snow. This shows me how she is getting ready for cold weather.

Guide children to find more key details in the pictures and text. Discuss what details the illustrations add to the text.

After Reading

Respond to Reading

- *What kind of weather are the mother and girl getting ready for?* (snow)
- *What do they do to get ready for the weather?* (They put on coats, hats, boots, and scarves. They get a shovel, hot drink, and flashlight.)
- *Why do the girl and her mother need the flashlight?* (The power has gone out.)

Retell

Have children take turns retelling the story. Then ask: *How do you get ready for different kinds of weather?*

Model Fluency

Read the story aloud with expression. Model how to make the pitch of your voice rise and fall in the same pattern as you read each sentence.

Apply Have children practice reading aloud with proper intonation. Then have children work in pairs and read the story to each other, practicing reading with expression.

LITERACY ACTIVITIES

Have children complete the activities on the inside back cover of the reader.

Level Up

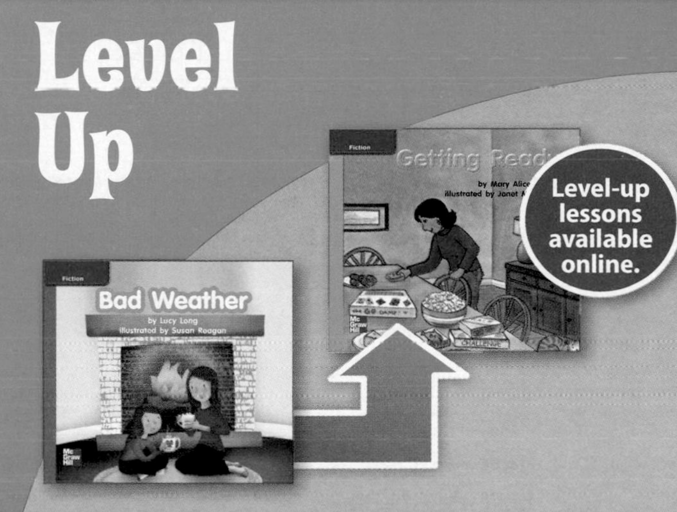

IF Children read *Bad Weather* **Approaching Level** with fluency and correctly answer the Respond to Reading questions,

THEN Tell children that they will read another story about how to stay safe in bad weather.

- Have children page through *Getting Ready* **On Level** and help children make connections to getting ready for a snowstorm.
- Have children read the story, monitoring their comprehension and providing assistance as necessary.

Approaching Level

Phonological Awareness

RECOGNIZE ALLITERATION

TIER 2

OBJECTIVES

Demonstrate an understanding of spoken words, syllables, and sounds. **RF.K.2**

Reread the line *Whether the weather be fine* from the poem "Whether the Weather." Point out that the words *whether* and *weather* sound almost the same at the beginning. Repeat these two words, exaggerating the initial sounds. Have children echo you.

Say "Peter Piper picked a peck of pickled peppers" and have children repeat. Guide them to figure out which sound is the same. (/p/)

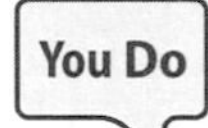

Tell children that you will say some words. Have them repeat the words and tell if the words begin with the same sounds: *huge happy hippo; five fast foxes; big buzzing bee; cute little duck; sing silly songs*.

PHONEME IDENTITY

OBJECTIVES

Isolate and pronounce the initial, medial vowel, and final sounds (phonemes) in three-phoneme words. **RF.K.2d**

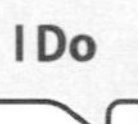

Display the *Rose, Rabbit,* and *Rock* **Photo Cards**. Say the picture names and have children repeat them with you. *What sound is the same in* rose, rabbit, *and* rock? *Yes, the first sound,* /r/, *is the same*. Repeat with the *Pen, Net,* and *Jet* Photo Cards to review the medial /e/ sound.

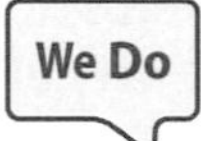

Show and name the following sets of Photo Cards. Have children repeat. Guide them to identify the sound that is the same in each set:

Elbow, Exit, Egg	Five, Fork, Farm	Kitten, Kite, King
Bird, Boat, Boot	Leaf, Lamp, Light	Hair, Hay, House

You Do

Show the sets of Photo Cards again. Have children name each picture in a set and then say the sound that is the same in the set.

You may wish to review Phonological Awareness and Phonemic Awareness with ELL using this section.

PHONEME BLENDING

OBJECTIVES

CCSS Isolate and pronounce the initial, medial vowel, and final sounds (phonemes) in three-phoneme words. **RF.K.2d**

Listen as the puppet says the sounds in a word: /f/ /i/ /b/. Now the puppet will blend the sounds together to make a word: /fffiiib/, fib. *The puppet blended the sounds /f/ /i/ /b/ to make the word* fib. Repeat with *hen, lap*.

Listen to the puppet say the sounds in a word. Have the puppet say /r/ /o/ /k/. Have children repeat. *Now let's blend the sounds and say the word with the puppet:* /r/ /o/ /k/, /rrroook/, rock. Repeat with *kin*.

Have the puppet say the following sounds. Ask children to blend the sounds and say the words:

/l/ /e/ /d/ /r/ /a/ /k/ /h/ /o/ /p/ /f/ /i/ /n/ /b/ /e/ /t/

PHONEME ADDITION

OBJECTIVES

CCSS Add or substitute individual sounds (phonemes) in simple, one-syllable words to make new words. **RF.K.2e**

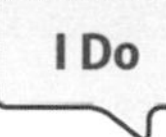

Listen as the puppet says a word: it. Have children repeat the word with the puppet. *Now the puppet will add /l/ to the beginning of* it. Have the puppet say *lit*. *By adding /l/ to* it, *the puppet has made a new word:* lit. *Say the new word with the puppet:* lit. Repeat the routine, adding /f/ and /h/ to *it*.

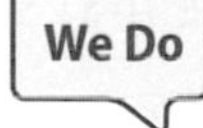

Have the puppet say *Ed*, then add /l/ to make *led*. Have children repeat the new word with the puppet. Then have the puppet guide children to add sounds to *Ed* to make the words *bed, fed,* and *red*.

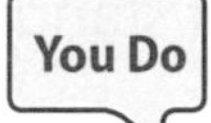

Have the puppet say *in* and the sound /f/. Ask children to add the sound to *in* to make *fin*. Repeat, having them add sounds /b/ and /k/ to *in* to make *bin* and *kin*.

ELL ENGLISH LANGUAGE LEARNERS

For the **ELLs** who need **phonics, decoding,** and **fluency** practice, use scaffolding methods as necessary to ensure children understand the meaning of the words. Refer to the Language Transfer Handbook for phonics elements that may not transfer in children's native languages.

Approaching Level

Phonics

SOUND-SPELLING REVIEW

TIER 2

OBJECTIVES

CCSS Demonstrate basic knowledge of one-to-one letter-sound correspondences by producing the primary or many of the most frequent sounds for each consonant. **RF.K.3a**

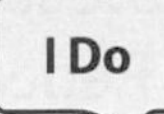

Display **Word-Building Cards** one at a time. Say the letter name and the sound it stands for. For example: Letter *r*, /r/. Repeat for *b, e, f, h, l, c, k*.

Display Word-Building Cards one at a time and together say the letter name and the sound that each letter stands for.

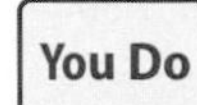

Display Word-Building Cards one at a time and have children say the letter name and the sound that each letter stands for.

CONNECT SOUNDS TO SPELLINGS

TIER 2

OBJECTIVES

Demonstrate basic knowledge of one-to-one letter-sound correspondences by producing the primary or many of the most frequent sounds for each consonant. **RF.K.3a**

Display the *Rose* **Sound-Spelling Card**. *The letter* r *stands for /r/. What is this letter? What sound does it stand for?* Repeat for /h/h, /e/e, /f/f, /b/b, /l/l, and /k/k. *I'll write the letter that stands for the first sound in these words.* Say: *ripe, home, fox, egg, ball, long, kitten.*

Lost *begins with /l/. Let's write* l *on our* ***Response Boards***. Say *help, net, bend, fell, rat, kit.* Guide children to write the letter that stands for the initial sound.

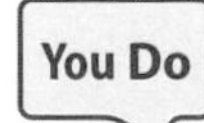

Say the following words and have children write the letter for the initial sound in the word: *egg, hat, fast, band, loop, kitten,* and *race*.

RETEACH

OBJECTIVES

Know and apply grade-level phonics and word analysis skills in decoding words. **RF.K.3**

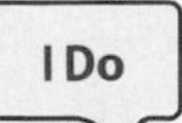

To review letter sounds, display **Reading/Writing Workshop**, p. 34. Point to each picture in rows 1 and 2 and say the picture name.

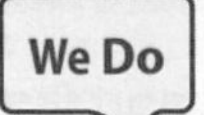

Have children name each picture in rows 1 and 2. Repeat, emphasizing initial sounds for both rows with the exception of final /k/ for *rake* (row 2).

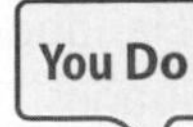

Guide children in reading the words in rows 3 and 4, offering assistance as needed.

BLEND WORDS WITH /h/*h*, /e/*e*, /f/*f*, /r/*r*, /b/*b*, /l/*l*, /k/*k*

OBJECTIVES

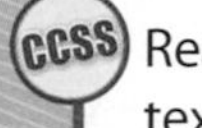

Isolate and pronounce the initial, medial vowel, and final sounds (phonemes) in three-phoneme words. **RF.K.2d**

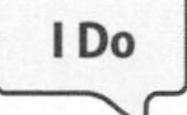

Display **Word-Building Cards** *r, o,* and *b*. *This is the letter* r. *It stands for* /r/. *This is the letter* o. *It stands for* /o/. *This is the letter* b. *It stands for* /b/. *Listen as I blend the sounds: /r/ /o/ /b/, /rrrooob/,* rob. Repeat for *hen*.

Now let's blend more sounds to make words. Make the word *back*. *Let's blend /b/ /a/ /k/: /baaak/,* back. Have children blend to read the word. Repeat with *let*. *Let's blend /l/ /e/ /t/: /llleeet/,* let.

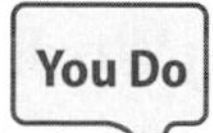

Distribute sets of Word-Building Cards with *e, l, c, k, o, f, h, r, n*. Write: *rib, lock, fed, kin, hen*. Have children form the words and then blend and read them.

REREAD FOR FLUENCY

OBJECTIVES

CCSS Read emergent-reader texts with purpose and understanding. **RF.K.4**

Turn to p. 36 of **Reading/Writing Workshop** and read aloud the title. *Let's read the title together*. Page through the book. Ask children what they see in each picture. Ask children to find the high-frequency words *is, my, was, He*, and *are* on the pages.

Then have children open their books and chorally read the story. Have children point to each word as they read. Provide corrective feedback as needed. After reading, ask children to recall how Mack felt about the rain.

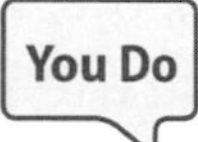

Have children reread "Mack and Ben" with a partner for fluency.

BUILD FLUENCY WITH PHONICS

Sound/Spelling Fluency

Display the following Word-Building Cards: *e, h, f, r, b, l,* and *k*. Have children chorally say each sound. Repeat and vary the pace.

Fluency in Connected Text

Write the following sentences. *My little red fan was on the bed. He is on the hot deck with Bob. Deb led a tan ram to the pen*. Have children read the sentences and identify the words with /e/, /h/, /r/, /k/ spelled *ck*, /f/, and initial and final /b/.

Approaching Level

High-Frequency Words

RETEACH WORDS

TIER 2

OBJECTIVES

Read common high-frequency words by sight. **RF.K.3c**

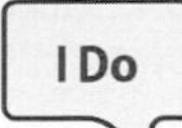
Display **High-Frequency Word Cards** *my, are, he, with, is, little, she,* and *was* and use the **Read/Spell/Write** routine to reteach the high-frequency words.

Have children turn to p. 35 of **Reading/Writing Workshop**. Read aloud the words in rows 1 and 2 with children. Then read aloud the first sentence. Reread the sentence with children. One at a time show the **High-Frequency Word Cards** for *my, are, he, with, is, little, she,* and *was*. Have children say the word on the card. Ask them whether the word is in the sentence. If they say yes, have them touch and say the word in the sentence. Use the same routine for the other sentences on the page.

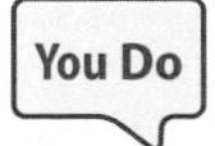
Write the sentence frame *She is on the dock with my little* ______. Have children copy the sentence frame on their **Response Boards**. Then have partners work together to read and orally complete the frame by talking about what or who might be on the dock.

CUMULATIVE REVIEW

OBJECTIVES

Read common high-frequency words by sight. **RF.K.3c**

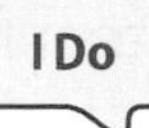
Display the **High-Frequency Word Cards** *I, can, the, we, see, a, like, to, and, go, you, do, my, are, he, with, is, little, she, was*. Use the **Read/Spell/Write** routine to review words.

Use the High-Frequency Word Cards to create sentences, such as *Do you see a rip in the little red sack? He and I are with my mom and pop*. Have children identify the high-frequency words that are used in each sentence.

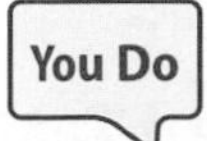
Have children create sentences with a partner. Remind them to refer to the High-Frequency Word Cards as needed. Then have them write the words on their **Response Boards**.

Oral Vocabulary

REVIEW WORDS

OBJECTIVES

CCSS Identify real-life connections between words and their use. **L.K.5c**

Develop oral vocabulary: *safe, prepare, notice, celebration, enough*

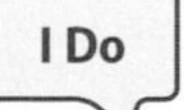

Use the **Define/Example/Ask** routine to review words. Use the following definitions and provide examples:

safe	When you are **safe**, you are not in danger.
prepare	When you **prepare**, you get ready for something.
notice	When you **notice** something, you see it clearly.
celebration	A **celebration** is a special activity in honor of a person or an event.
enough	When something is **enough**, it is all that is needed.

Ask questions to build understanding. *Why do you feel safe inside when it is dark outside? How can you help prepare dinner? Do you notice anything different in our classroom today? What can people do to make a birthday celebration special? How many mittens would be enough for both of your hands?*

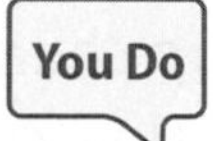

Have children complete these sentence frames: *A cat probably feels safe when ______. I prepare for school by ______. A fish will notice food if you ______. I read about a big celebration in a book about ______. You know you have enough crayons when the box is ______.*

Comprehension

SELF-SELECTED READING

OBJECTIVES

CCSS With prompting and support, ask and answer questions about key details in a text. **RL.K.1**

Apply the strategy and skill to reread the text

Read Independently

Help children select an illustrated story for sustained silent reading. Remind children to use illustrations to form pictures in their minds. This will help them understand what is happening and what the characters see and feel.

Read Purposefully

Before reading, have children take a picture walk through the book. Ask them to point to the character they think is telling the story. After reading, encourage children to identify illustrations and text that helped them figure out who was telling the story. Then ask how making pictures in their minds helped them better understand the story.

On Level

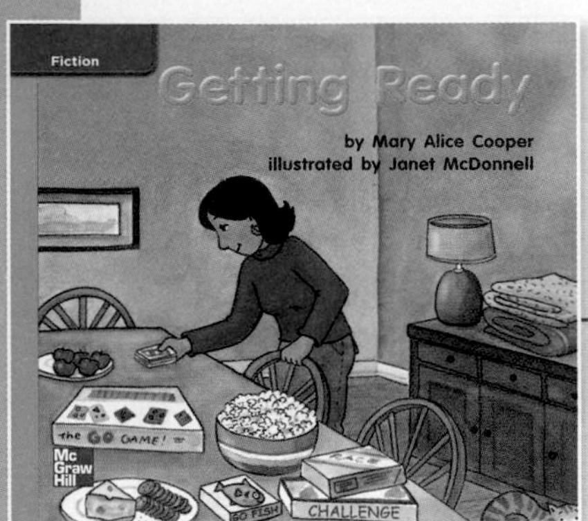

Leveled Reader

OBJECTIVES

- CCSS With prompting and support, ask and answer questions about key details in a text. **RL.K.1**
- CCSS With prompting and support, retell familiar stories, including key details. **RL.K.2**
- CCSS Demonstrate understanding of the organization and basic features of print. **RF.K.1**
- CCSS Read emergent-reader texts with purpose and understanding. **RF.K.4**

Leveled Reader: *Getting Ready*

Go Digital

Leveled Reader

Before Reading

Preview and Predict

Read the title and the names of the author and illustrator. Have children talk about what they see on the cover. Preview the illustrations and allow children to predict what the book is about. Ask: *What kind of weather do you see in the pictures? Why would the woman be getting ready for the snow?*

Review Genre: Fiction

Remind children that fiction tells stories about made-up characters and events. Ask: *Who is the main character in this story? How can you tell?* (the woman; she is in all the pictures)

Model Concepts of Print

Discuss with children what makes up a sentence. Point to the capital letter at the beginning of the first word in a sentence. Then point to the period at the end of the sentence.

Review High-Frequency Words

Point out the word *she* on page 2. Have children find and read the word on each page of the book.

Essential Question

Set a purpose for reading: *Let's find out how people can stay safe in bad weather*. Remind children to use the illustrations to help them understand the story better.

During Reading

Guided Comprehension

As children whisper-read, monitor and provide guidance by correcting blending and modeling the strategy and skill.

Strategy: Visualize

Remind children that as they read, they can use information from the text and illustrations to visualize what is happening.

Skill: Key Details

Remind children that they can find details in a story from the words on the page and from the illustrations. They can find out what a character does and what the story is about.

Think Aloud As I read, I think about what's happening in the story. I use the pictures to see what the woman is doing. She is getting things to help her during a snowstorm that is coming. On page 8, I see that there is snow coming down. All of the things she carries in the pictures show me what she needs to get ready for the storm.

Guide children to choose other pages to analyze for details. Discuss what the woman might need each of the items for during a storm.

After Reading

Respond to Reading

- → *What does the woman need to get ready for the snowstorm?* (water, snacks, wood, blankets, games, candles, and friends)
- → *What does the woman get out of the closet?* (blankets)
- → *Who does the woman spend time with during the storm?* (friends)
- → *Why does she need the flashlights?* (The power may go out.)

Retell

Have children take turns retelling the story. Help them make personal connections. Ask: *What do you think is an important thing to do to get ready for a snowstorm?*

Model Fluency

Read the sentences one at a time with fluency and expression. Emphasize the sentence on page 8 that ends in an exclamation mark.

Apply Have children practice reading with partners. Encourage them to use similar intonation in their voices.

LITERACY ACTIVITIES

Have children complete the activities on the inside back cover of the reader.

Level Up

IF Children read *Getting Ready* **On Level** with fluency and correctly answer the Respond to Reading questions,

THEN Tell children that they will read another story about staying safe in bad weather.

- Have children page through *The Storm* **Beyond Level** as you talk about what people do to get ready for a windy rainstorm.
- Have children read the story, monitoring their comprehension and providing assistance as necessary.

On Level

Phonemic Awareness

PHONEME IDENTITY

OBJECTIVES

Demonstrate understanding of spoken words, syllables, and sounds (phonemes). **RF.K.2**

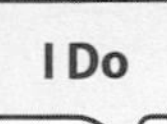
Display and name the *Horse, Hand,* and *Hippo* **Photo Cards**. Have children repeat the names with you. Ask them to identify the sound that is the same in *horse, hand,* and *hippo.*

Show the following sets of Photo Cards. Name the pictures with children and guide them to say the sound that is the same in each set: *Rake, Rope, Ring; Farm, Five, Football; Egg, Exit, Elbow.*

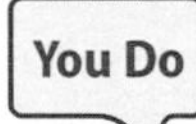
Show these Photo Cards. Have children name each picture and say the sound the words begin with: *Key, King, Koala; Boil, Bear, Bowl; Ladder, Leaf, Lock.*

PHONEME BLENDING

OBJECTIVES

Isolate and pronounce the initial, medial vowel, and final sounds (phonemes) in three-phoneme words. **RF.K.2d**

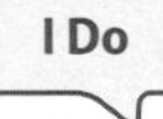
Place *Pen, Hat, Fan, Net, Lock, Rock,* and *Bat* Photo Cards facedown. Choose a card but do not show it to children. *These are the sounds in the word:* /h/ /a/ /t/. *I will blend the sounds:* /haaat/, hat. *The word is* hat. Show the picture.

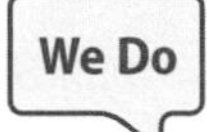
Choose another Photo Card and say the sounds in the name. Together say the sounds and blend them to say the word. Then show the picture.

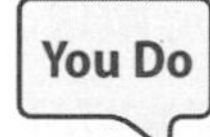
Choose other Photo Cards. For each card, say the sounds of the picture name and have children blend the sounds to say the word.

PHONEME ADDITION

OBJECTIVES

Add or substitute individual sounds (phonemes) in simple, one-syllable words to make new words. **RF.K.2e**

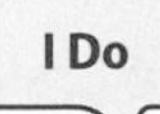
The puppet can add a sound to a word to make a new word. When the puppet adds /h/ to the beginning of am, *it makes* ham. Repeat with *am* and /r/.

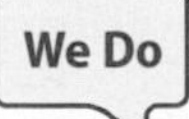
Say the sound /f/ with the puppet: /f/. Let's add /f/ to an: *fan. Say the new word with the puppet:* fan. Repeat with *it* and /l/.

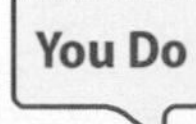
Say *it* and the sound /k/. Have children add the sound to make *kit*. Repeat, having them add the sounds /b/, /l/, /f/, and /h/ to make new words.

Phonics

REVIEW PHONICS

OBJECTIVES

CCSS Know and apply grade-level phonics and word analysis skills in decoding words. **RF.K.3**

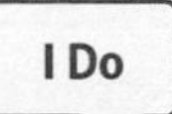

To review letter sounds, display **Reading/Writing Workshop**, p. 34. Point to each picture in rows 1 and 2 and say the picture name.

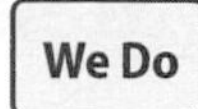

Have children say the name of each picture in rows 1 and 2. Then ask them to identify the words that begin with /f/, /h/, /l/, /r/, /b/, or /e/.

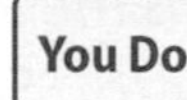

Have children read each word in rows 3 and 4. Repeat, asking them to raise their hands when they hear /e/ in the middle of the word and keep their hands lowered if they do not hear /e/ in the middle. Repeat the routine, asking them to raise their hands when they hear /b/ at the end of a word.

PICTURE SORT

OBJECTIVES

Isolate and pronounce the initial, medial vowel, and final sounds (phonemes) in three-phoneme words. **RF.K.2d**

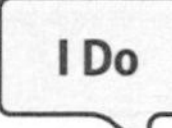

Display **Word-Building Cards** *e* and *o* in a pocket chart. Then show the *Web* **Photo Card**. Say /w/ /e/ /b/, web. *The sound in the middle is /e/. The letter* e *stands for /e/. I will put the* Web *Photo Card under the letter* e. Show the *Fox* Photo Card. Say /f/ /o/ /ks/, fox. *The sound in the middle is /o/.* The letter o stands for /o/. *I will put the* Fox *Photo Card under the* o.

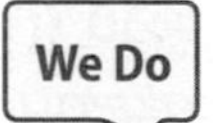

Show the *Mop* Photo Card. *Listen:* mop, /m/ /o/ /p/. *Say it with me:* mop, /m/ /o/ /p/. *What sound is in the middle?* (/o/) *Where do I place this Photo Card?* (under o) Continue with the *Gem* Photo Card.

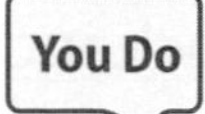

Continue the activity using Photo Cards for *Box, Rock, Lock, Net, Jet,* and *Pen*. Have children say the picture name and the sounds in the name. Then have them place the card under the *e* or *o*.

On Level

Phonics

BLEND WORDS WITH /h/*h*, /e/*e*, /f/*f*, /r/*r*, /b/*b*, /l/*l*, /k/*k*

OBJECTIVES

CCSS Isolate and pronounce the initial, medial vowel, and final sounds (phonemes) in three-phoneme words. **RF.K.2d**

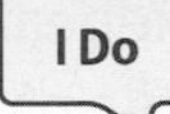

Use **Word-Building Cards** or write *l, o, c, k. This is the letter* l. *It stands for /l/. Say it with me: /lll/. This is the letter* o. *It stands for /o/. Say it with me: /ooo/. These are letters* c *and* k. *At the end of a word, these letters stand for /k/. Say the sound with me: /k/. I'll blend the sounds to read the word: /llloook/,* lock.

Write *bed* and *fan*. Guide children to blend the words sound by sound to read each word.

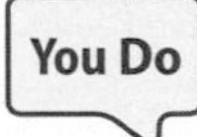

Write the following words and have children blend the words sound by sound to read each word.

rack hen kid fib lab deck back

REREAD FOR FLUENCY

OBJECTIVES

Read emergent-reader texts with purpose and understanding. **RF.K.4**

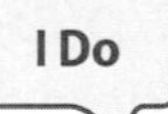

Turn to p. 37 in **Reading/Writing Workshop**. Read the first sentence aloud. *When we see an exclamation point, we make our voice sound excited.* Read the text again and have children repeat, using the same excitement in their voices. Work with children to read for accuracy and expression. Model reading p. 39: *When I read,* "Mom fed Mack and Ben," *I read all the way to the end of the sentence before pausing and reading the next sentence. This makes my reading sound smooth and natural, as if I were talking.*

Reread p. 39. Then have children chorally read the page with you. Continue choral reading the remainder of the pages.

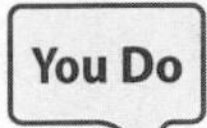

Have children reread "Mack and Ben." Provide time to listen as children read the pages. Comment on their accuracy and expression and provide corrective feedback by modeling proper fluency.

High-Frequency Words

REVIEW WORDS

OBJECTIVES

CCSS Read common high-frequency words by sight. **RF.K.3c**

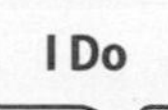

Use the **High-Frequency Word Cards** to review the words *my, are, he, with, is, little, she,* and *was* using the **Read/Spell/Write** routine.

Have children turn to p. 35 of **Reading/Writing Workshop**. Point to *My, was, with, She, are, little, He,* and *is* in the sentences and have children read each word. Then chorally read the sentences. Have children frame and read each high-frequency word in the sentences.

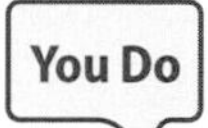

Have children read the words in rows 1 and 2. Say the word *little*. Have children close their eyes, picture the word, and write it as they see it. Have children self-correct. Repeat for *my, are, he, with, is, she,* and *was*.

Fluency Point to the High-Frequency Word Cards *my, are, he, with, is, little, she,* and *was* in random order. Have children chorally read. Repeat at a faster pace.

Comprehension

SELF-SELECTED READING

OBJECTIVES

CCSS With prompting and support, ask and answer questions about key details in a text. **RL.K.1**

Apply the strategy and skill to reread the text.

Read Independently

Have children select an illustrated story for sustained silent reading. Remind them that illustrations can help them understand details in a story. Tell them that illustrations and story details can help them visualize the way things look, as well as the way the characters feel in a story.

Read Purposefully

Before reading, invite children to take a picture walk through the book. Ask them to point out the character they predict will be telling the story. As they read, they should make pictures in their minds to help them figure out who is telling the story. After reading, invite children to explain whether the character they identified prior to reading is the character who told the story. Then have them explain how they visualized to help them understand the story.

Beyond Level

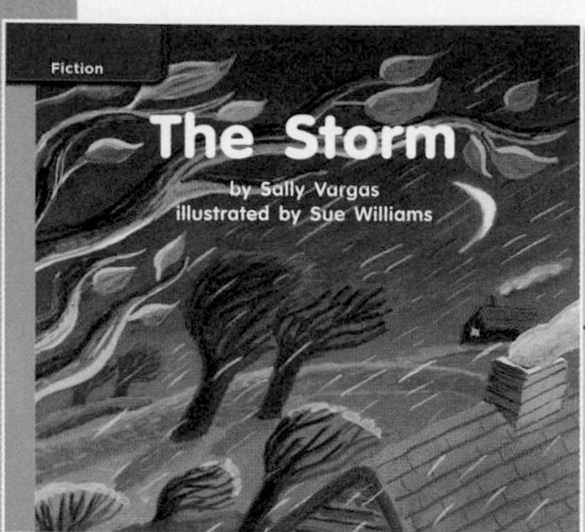

Leveled Reader

OBJECTIVES

CCSS With prompting and support, ask and answer questions about key details in a text. **RL.K.1**

CCSS With prompting and support, retell familiar stories, including key details. **RL.K.2**

CCSS Recognize common types of texts (e.g., storybooks, poems). **RL.K.5**

Leveled Reader: *The Storm*

Before Reading

Preview and Predict

Ask children to point to the title and the names of the author and illustrator as you read them aloud. Ask children to discuss what they see in the cover illustration. Ask: *What kind of weather do you see?* Invite children to look through the illustrations and predict what they think the story will be about.

Review Genre: Fiction

Ask children if they think this book is a fiction or nonfiction book and to tell why. Confirm that nonfiction books give facts and fiction books are stories about made-up characters and events. Explain that we can understand what fiction stories are about by thinking about what the characters say and do. Ask: *How can you tell when a character is talking in a fiction story?* Point out quotation marks to children.

Essential Question

Remind children of the Essential Question: *How can you stay safe in bad weather?* Have children set a purpose for reading: *Let's find out what this family does to get ready for a big rainstorm.*

During Reading

Guided Comprehension

Have children whisper-read *The Storm*. Remind them to pause when they come to words that are unfamiliar. Prompt them to sound out words using what they know about letter-sound relationships and to use picture clues to confirm they understand what they are reading.

Strategy: Visualize

Remind children that as they read, they can use information from the text and illustrations to visualize what is happening.

Go Digital

Leveled Reader

Skill: Key Details

Remind children that they can find details in a story from the words on the page and from the illustrations. Sometimes the illustrations give information that is not in the text.

Think Aloud When I look at the picture on page 3, I see the girl and her mom carrying things from the yard inside the house. I know that they are getting ready for a storm. I can see from this picture that they are doing hard work. Mom says that the things will be safe inside.

Guide children to find key details throughout the story, identifying information in the illustrations and text that tells how the characters are staying safe and preparing for the storm.

After Reading

Respond to Reading

- *What things does the family put away before the storm?* (table, bat, ball, bike)
- *Why would the family need flashlights and candles in a storm?* (to give light if the power goes out)
- *On page 7, it says that the wind bent the trees. What might the wind have done to the toys outside?* (It would have blown them away, and they might have hit something.)
- *Why is it important to get ready for a storm before it comes?* (so we can be safe)

Retell

Have children take turns retelling the story. Help them make a personal connection by asking: *Have you ever gotten ready for a storm? What did you do?*

Gifted and Talented

EVALUATING Have children think about different kinds of weather that people should get ready for ahead of time. Have them work in small groups and help them make a list of their ideas.

HAVE children make a drawing of each type of weather and label it.

LITERACY ACTIVITIES

Have children complete the activities on the inside back cover of the reader.

Beyond Level

Phonics

REVIEW

OBJECTIVES

CCSS Demonstrate basic knowledge of one-to-one letter-sound correspondences by producing the primary or many of the most frequent sounds for each consonant. **RF.K.3a**

To review letter sounds, display **Reading/Writing Workshop**, p. 34. Point to each picture in rows 1 and 2 and say the picture name.

Have children say the name of each picture in rows 1 and 2. Then point to and name the *fish* picture. Ask children to say the beginning sound, /f/, then share other words they know that begin with the same sound. Repeat for *lemon* and *bed*.

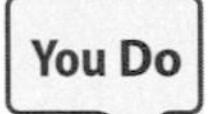

Have partners read each word in rows 3 and 4. Ask them to write the words on their **Response Boards**, underlining the letter in each word that stands for /b/. Repeat, having them underline the letters that stand for /k/.

Fluency Have children reread the story "Mack and Ben" for fluency.

Innovate Have children create a new page for "Mack and Ben" using the sentence frame *Mack hid in my* ______. to name another place that the frightened dog might hide during the bad weather.

High-Frequency Words

REVIEW

OBJECTIVES

CCSS Read common high-frequency words by sight. **RF.K.3c**

Create **High-Frequency Word Cards** for *over* and *under*. Introduce the words using the **Read/Spell/Write** routine.

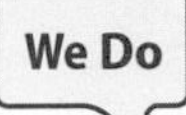

Display the High-Frequency Word Cards for *my, are, he, with, is, little, she,* and *was*. Have children help you complete the following sentence frames using the High-Frequency Word Cards: *She set a little lid over the* ______. *My red sock was under the* ______.

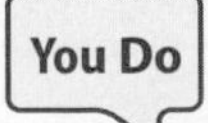

Have partners write sentences using the high-frequency words *over* and *under* on their **Response Boards**. Have them read their sentences.

Vocabulary

ORAL VOCABULARY: SYNONYMS

OBJECTIVES

CCSS With guidance and support from adults, explore word relationships and nuances in word meaning. **L.K.5**

Develop oral vocabulary: Synonyms

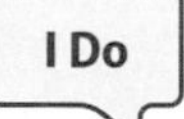

Review the meanings of the oral vocabulary words *safe* and *celebration*. Explain that a synonym is a word that means almost the same thing as another word.

A synonym for safe *is* protect. *To be protected is to be kept away from harm.* Coats and gloves protect us from the cold air.

A synonym for celebration *is* party. *A* party *is a group of people having a good time*. My family went to the celebration for our town's new playground.

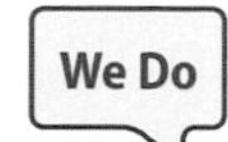

Write a few sentences together using the new words *protected* and *celebration*. Read the sentences aloud.

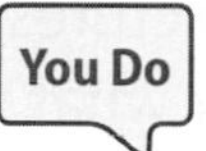

Have partners write a short poem about an animal family. Tell them to include the words *protect* and *celebration*. Explain that the poem doesn't need to rhyme. Have children share their poems with the class.

Extend Have children plan and act out short plays about staying safe in bad weather. Encourage children to use synonyms, *protect* and *party,* in their skits.

Comprehension

SELF-SELECTED READING

OBJECTIVES

With prompting and support, ask and answer questions about key details in a text. **RL.K.1**

Apply the strategy and skill to reread the text.

Read Independently

Have children select an illustrated story for sustained silent reading. Remind them that illustrations often show key story details, and that visualizing can help them understand what is happening in the story.

Read Purposefully

Before reading, have children take a picture walk through the book. Ask them to identify the character they think is telling the story. Remind children to visualize what the character says and does. After reading, invite children to compare and contrast their predictions about the character who told the story. Have children explain how visualizing helped them understand the character's feelings and actions.

Independent Study Have children write a letter to the girl character in *Waiting Out the Storm* instructing her how to stay safe. Have children create an illustration to go with their letter.

English Language Learners

Leveled Reader

OBJECTIVES

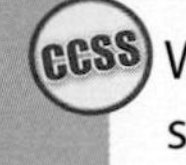
With prompting and support, ask and answer questions about key details in a text. **RL.K.1**

With prompting and support, retell familiar stories, including key details. **RL.K.2**

Read emergent-reader texts with purpose and understanding. **RF.K.4**

Shared Read: *Getting Ready*

Go Digital

Leveled Reader

Before Reading

Preview and Predict

Read aloud the title. Make sure children understand the meaning for the English phrase *getting ready*. Act out or show pictures to demonstrate if necessary. Ask children to tell a partner what they see in the cover illustration. Help them name important items. Walk children through the book, looking at each picture and reading the labels. Reinforce the language pattern in the book. Say: *What does the woman get here? That's right. She gets* ______.

Essential Question

Set a purpose for reading: *Let's find out how people get ready for a snowstorm so they stay safe.* Encourage children to ask questions and seek clarification when necessary. Model asking a question: *I see the label* water *on page 2. Why does the woman need water in a snowstorm?* As you point out each picture, provide clarification for why each item would be needed to stay safe in a storm. These clarifications will help children gain a greater understanding of the Essential Question.

During Reading

Interactive Question Response

Pages 2–3 Point to the illustration on page 2. Ask: *Where is the woman?* (at her car) *What does she get?* (She gets water.) *What can we see on the ground? In the sky?* (We can see snow and clouds.) Read the page aloud with children. Point to the illustration on page 3. Ask: *What does the woman get here?* (She gets food.) *This page shows another thing she does to get ready. She will not have to leave her house in the snow because she has the food she needs. Let's read this page.*

Pages 4–5 Point to the illustration and label on page 4. *What is this?* (wood) *What does this word say?* (wood) Point to the mouse and ask children to find it on the previous pages. *I wonder if the mouse will stay in the woman's house during the storm. Let's read this page.* Point to the text on page 5. *What does the woman get here?* (She gets blankets.) *What will she need blankets for?* (to stay warm) Read the page with children.

Pages 6–7 Point to the illustration and label on page 6. Ask: *What are these?* (games) *What does this word say?* (games) *What do you do with games?* (play) *Why does the woman get games?* (to have something to do during the storm) Point to the illustration on page 7 and the label pointing to the candles. Ask: *What is this?* (candle) *What will the candle do?* (give light) Read the pages with children.

Page 8 Point to the illustration. *Here are her friends. Everyone is together during the storm. They stay warm. They have light. They have food. They are safe in the bad weather. Let's read this sentence.*

After Reading

Respond to Reading

- *What kind of bad weather is the woman getting ready for?* (a snowstorm)
- *What does she buy to get ready?* (water and food)
- *What else does she use inside her house?* (firewood, candles, blankets, and games)

Retell

Say: *Let's retell the book together. What does the woman do in the story?* (get ready for a snowstorm) Begin to name each of the things the woman did to get ready for the storm: get water and food, gather wood for a fire, get blankets ready, and gather games to play and pass the time. She also spent time with friends and stayed together with them.

Model Fluency

As you read each sentence, demonstrate how to read with expression in your voice. Point out the extra rise in your voice as you read the sentence on page 8 that ends with an exclamation mark.

Apply Ask small groups of children to read together. Encourage children to take turns reading a page aloud, using expression in their own voices as they read.

LITERACY ACTIVITIES

Have children complete the activities on the inside back cover of the reader.

Level Up

IF Children read *Getting Ready* **ELL Level** with fluency and correctly answer the Respond to Reading questions,

THEN Tell children that they will read a more detailed version of the story.

- Have children page through *Getting Ready* **On Level** and describe what is happening in each picture.
- Have children read the story, monitoring their comprehension and providing assistance as necessary.

English Language Learners

Vocabulary

PRETEACH ORAL VOCABULARY

OBJECTIVES

Speak audibly and express thoughts, feelings, and ideas clearly. **SL.K.6**

LANGUAGE OBJECTIVE

Preview vocabulary

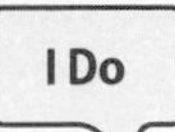

Display the images from the **Visual Vocabulary Cards** and follow the routine to preteach the oral vocabulary words.

Display each image again and explain how it illustrates or demonstrates the word. Model using sentences to describe the image.

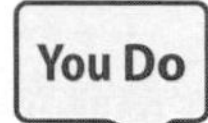

Display the words again and have children talk to a partner about how the pictures demonstrate the words.

Beginning	Intermediate	Advanced/High
Use the words in sentences and have children repeat the sentences chorally.	Ask partners to talk about things that they do to prepare for a rainy day.	Ask partners to ask each other questions and answer using the words.

PRETEACH ELL VOCABULARY

OBJECTIVES

Speak audibly and express thoughts, feelings, and ideas clearly. **SL.K.6**

LANGUAGE OBJECTIVE

Preview ELL vocabulary

Display the images from the **Visual Vocabulary Cards** one at a time to preteach the ELL vocabulary words *hazard* and *security*. Follow the routine. Say each word and have children repeat it. Define the word in English.

Display each image again and incorporate the words in a short discussion about the images. Model using sentences to describe the image.

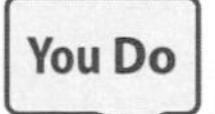

Display the words again and have children say the words. Provide children an opportunity to use the word *hazard* in a sentence by providing this sentence starter: *Ice is a hazard in cold weather because* ______.

Beginning	Intermediate	Advanced/High
Use each word in a sentence and have children chorally repeat the sentence after you.	Have children talk about things that can happen in cold weather before completing the sentence.	Ask children to use the words in a sentence of their own. Provide guidance if necessary.

High-Frequency Words

REVIEW WORDS

OBJECTIVES

CCSS Read common high-frequency words by sight (e.g., *the, of, to, you, she, my, is, are, do, does*). **RF.K.3c**

LANGUAGE OBJECTIVE

Review high-frequency words

I Do Display the **High-Frequency Word Cards** for the words from the last five weeks: *my, are, he, with, is, little, she,* and *was*. Read the words. Use the **Read/Spell/Write** routine to teach the words. Have children write the words on their **Response Boards**.

We Do Provide a sentence frame for each of the high-frequency words and ask children to complete them. **(1)** *My teacher is* ______. **(2)** *We are* ______. **(3)** *He* ______. **(4)** *You are with* ______. **(5)** *The boy is* ______. **(6)** *I see a little* ______. **(7)** *She* ______. **(8)** *He was* ______.

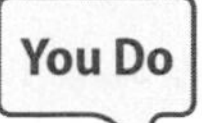

You Do Display one card at a time as children chorally read them. Mix and repeat. Note words children need to review.

Beginning	Intermediate	Advanced/High
Ask children to say each word aloud after you say it.	Ask children to locate the words in reading selections.	Ask children to write three of the five words and use them in sentences.

REVIEW CATEGORY WORDS

OBJECTIVES

Identify real-life connections between words and their use (e.g., note places at school that are *colorful*). **L.K.5c**

LANGUAGE OBJECTIVE

Use category words

I Do Write and say question words such as *what, why, when, where,* and *who*. Define the words in English and then in Spanish, if appropriate, identifying any cognates.

We Do Ask children to repeat the words after you. Ask a question and have children identify which category word you used in your sentence.

You Do Have partners work together to ask a question using any one of the category words. Have one partner ask and the other one answer.

Beginning	Intermediate	Advanced/High
Demonstrate how to ask a question and have children chorally repeat the question after you.	Ask children to use one of the category words to form their own question.	Ask partners to ask and answer questions using all of the words.

English Language Learners

Writing

SHARED WRITING

OBJECTIVES

CCSS Use a combination of drawing, dictating, and writing to narrate a single event or several loosely linked events, tell about the events in the order in which they occurred, and provide a reaction to what happened. **W.K.3**

LANGUAGE OBJECTIVE

Contribute to a shared writing project

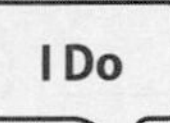

Review the list from the Whole Group Shared Writing project for ideas of possible weather. Then model writing a short weather report using words from the list: *Today it is sunny. Tomorrow will be windy and cold.*

Have children help you write a shared weather report using words from the list. Provide children with a sentence frame, such as: *Yesterday the weather was ______. Today the weather is ______.*

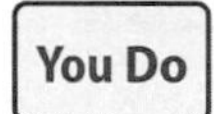

Ask partners to complete these sentence frames: *Today the weather is ______. Tomorrow it will be ______.* Have them draw a picture to go with their report.

Beginning	Intermediate	Advanced/High
Review the weather words on the list before having children complete the sentence frames.	Guide children as they complete the sentence frames. Have them share reports with the class.	Have children write a weather report that covers a few days.

WRITING TRAIT: VOICE

OBJECTIVES

CCSS With guidance and support from adults, respond to questions and suggestions from peers and add details to strengthen writing as needed. **W.K.5**

LANGUAGE OBJECTIVE

Organize ideas for writing

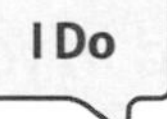

Explain that writers can show how they feel about something with the words they choose. These words are the writer's voice, and they help readers understand how a writer feels about a topic.

Reread page 18 of the **Big Book** *Waiting Out the Storm.* Say: *The writer chose words to tell us that the chipmunks are safe. Which words tell us that?* (snuggle together).

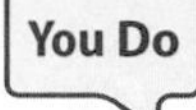

Have children write a sentence about a weather event from the past. Have them use the sentence frames: *The sunny weather made me want to ______.*

Beginning	Intermediate	Advanced/High
Help children use other selections from the week to talk about weather.	Ask children to talk in small groups and write the sentences together.	After children write their sentences, ask them to read them aloud.

Grammar

NAMING WORDS (NOUNS)

OBJECTIVES

CCSS Use frequently occurring nouns and verbs. **L.K.1b**

LANGUAGE OBJECTIVE

Learn to use nouns correctly

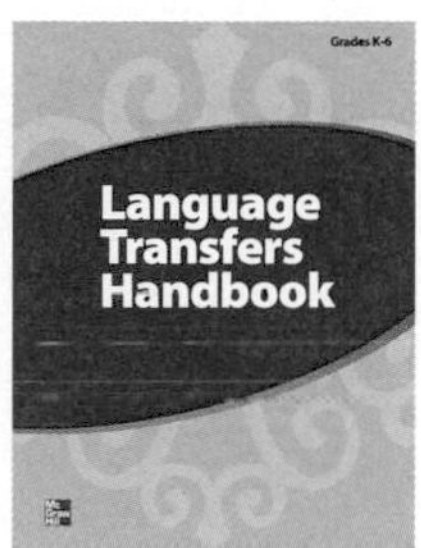

Language Transfers Handbook

Some languages such as Hmong and Spanish use articles that are omitted in English. Children may overuse articles or use them incorrectly because of this. Guide children not to overuse articles in cases such as *The English is difficult. The soccer is popular in the Europe.*

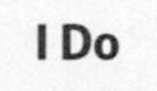

Review that a noun is a word that names a person, place, or thing. Explain that an *-s* or *-es* is added to the end of a word to show more than one. Say the following sentence: *Sue needs boots in the snow. The -s at the end of* boots *means there is more than one boot.*

Say the following sentences. Guide children to listen for the noun in each sentence. Then ask children to tell whether it is a plural noun. Have them use the sentence frame *The plural noun is* ______.

The storms come fast.

The dog is afraid of thunder.

The glasses are covered in snow.

The wind will stop soon.

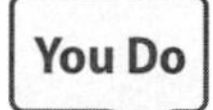

Say the following sentence frame: *The weather is* ______.

Pair children and have them complete the sentence frame by describing the noun using descriptive words from this week's readings. Circulate, listen in, and take note of each child's language use and proficiency.

Beginning	Intermediate	Advanced/High
Guide children to use illustrations from this week's readings to help them choose words to complete the sentence frame.	Review with children how to make a plural noun by adding an *-s* or an *-es* to the end of a noun.	Have children complete the sentence frame. Then have them try to write a sentence with a plural noun.

PROGRESS MONITORING

Weekly Assessment

Use your Quick Check observations and the assessment opportunities identified below to evaluate children's progress in key skill areas.

✓ TESTED SKILLS CCSS	Quick Check Observations	Pencil and Paper Assessment
PHONICS Review **RF.K.3a, RF.K.3b** f	Can children isolate /h/, /e/, /f/, /r/, /b/, /l/, and /k/ and match them to the letters *Hh, Ee, Ff, Rr, Bb, Ll,* and *Kk, ck*?	Practice Book, pp. 173, 175-176
HIGH-FREQUENCY WORDS *my, are, he, with, is, little, she, was* **RF.K.3c** he	Can children recognize and read the high-frequency words?	Practice Book, pp. 179–180
COMPREHENSION Key Details **RL.K.1, RL.K.2**	As you read *Waiting Out the Storm* with children, can they identify and discuss key details using the illustrations and the text?	Practice Book, p. 174

Quick Check Rubric

Skills	1	2	3
PHONICS	Does not connect the sounds /h/, /e/, /f/, /r/, /b/, /l/, and /k/ with the letters *Hh, Ee, Ff, Rr, Bb, Ll,* and *Kk, ck.*	Usually connects the sounds /h/, /e/, /f/, /r/, /b/, /l/, and /k/ with the letters *Hh, Ee,Ff, Rr, Bb, Ll,* and *Kk, ck.*	Consistently connects the sounds /h/, /e/, /f/, /r/, /b/, /l/, and /k/ with the letters *Hh, Ee,Ff, Rr, Bb, Ll,* and *Kk, ck.*
HIGH-FREQUENCY WORDS	Does not identify the high-frequency words.	Usually recognizes the high-frequency words with accuracy, but not speed.	Consistently recognizes the high-frequency words with speed and accuracy.
COMPREHENSION	Does not identify the key details using the illustrations and the text.	Usually identifies the key details using the illustrations and the text.	Consistently identifies the key details using the illustrations and the text.

Go Digital! www.connected.mcgraw-hill.com

Using Assessment Results

TESTED SKILLS	If ...	Then ...
PHONICS	**Quick Check Rubric:** Children consistently score 1 or **Pencil and Paper Assessment:** Children get 0–2 items correct	... reteach tested Phonics skills using Lessons 21, 23 and 25–29 in the ***Tier 2 Phonics/Word Study Intervention Online PDFs.***
HIGH-FREQUENCY WORDS	**Quick Check Rubric:** Children consistently score 1	... reteach tested skills by using the High-Frequency Word Cards and asking children to read and spell the word. Point out any irregularities in sound-spellings.
COMPREHENSION	**Quick Check Rubric:** Children consistently score 1 or **Pencil and Paper Assessment:** Children get 0–1 items correct	... reteach tested skill using Lessons 10–12 in the ***Tier 2 Comprehension Intervention Online PDFs.***

Response to Intervention

Use the children's assessment results to assist you in identifying children who will benefit from focused intervention.

Use the appropriate sections of the ***Placement and Diagnostic Assessment*** to designate children requiring:

TIER 2 **Tier 2 Intervention Online PDFs**

TIER 3 **WonderWorks Intervention Program**

→ Phonemic Awareness

→ Phonics

→ Vocabulary

→ Comprehension

→ Fluency

Reading Digitally

Go Digital!

OBJECTIVES

With prompting and support, identify the main topic and retell key details of a text. **RI.K.2**

With guidance and support from adults, explore a variety of digital tools to produce and publish writing, including in collaboration with peers. **W.K.6**

ACADEMIC LANGUAGE

Internet, Web site, hyperlink, cyber

TIME FOR KIDS®

Changes with the Wind

Before Reading

Preview Explain to children that the Internet connects computers all around the world. Go to the online article "Changes with the Wind" at **http://connected.mcgraw-hill.com**. Explain that the article is on a Web site. Point to the scroll bar and arrows. Model for children how to scroll through the article. Point out interactive features, such as the **hyperlinks**. Then point to the text features, such as the headings and captions. Tell children that you will read the article together first, and then show them how to use the interactive features.

Close Reading Online

Take Notes Scroll back to the top and read the article aloud. Before you read each page, read aloud the headings and captions. Ask what the page will be about. Model taking notes, using a word web (Graphic Organizer 39). Ask children what the main topic of the article is. In the center of the web, write and read aloud: *Winds in Different Seasons.* Then reread each section and have children retell a detail about a wind effect in each season to add to the web. Make sure children understand domain-specific terms, such as *blizzard, hurricane,* and *electricity.*

Access Interactive Elements Model how to access the interactive elements by clicking on each feature. Discuss the information these elements add to the text.

Reread Ask children to tell what type of text this is. Tell children you will reread parts of the informational text article to help them answer a question: *What things can the wind move?*

Navigate Links to Information Point out that online texts may include hyperlinks. Tell children that hyperlinks help you go from the Web page you are on to another screen or video that tells more about the topic. Model how to use a hyperlink to go to another screen or video. Discuss information on the screen related to the question *What things can the wind move?* Before navigating back, demonstrate bookmarking the page, and explain that now the class can return to the page at another time.

Nathan Love

TALK ABOUT READING

Retell Review the information on the word web. Model using the information to retell the section "Spring Breezes Blow," for example: *The wind in spring is not as cold as in winter. The spring winds can carry seeds to new places.*

Ask partners to draw and label pictures of things the wind can do. Invite children to share their pictures to help them retell the article.

Make Connections Have children compare what they learned from the article about the ways weather and seasons affect us with what they learned about weather and seasons in other selections they read in this unit.

CONNECT TO CONTENT

Weather in Different Seasons

Remind children that we can expect different weather during different seasons. Point to photographs of different seasons in the online article. Explain to children that weather changes day by day, but the seasons usually follow a pattern, depending on where you live.

Help children identify information in this article to answer the following questions.

→ *What kind of wind might blow in winter?*

→ *What kind of storm might the winds bring in autumn?*

USING THE INTERNET

Cyber Safety Discuss online safety with children. Explain to children that it is important to be careful when they are online. Explain the following rules:

→ Only go to Web sites that adults have told you are okay to visit.

→ Never give out personal information when you are online. Point out that personal information includes your name, photograph, home address, e-mail address, telephone number, school name, school address, names of family members, and passwords.

RESEARCH ONLINE

Choose a Topic Guide small groups in brainstorming questions about the weather in a specific season to research. For example, they might ask: *What is the weather like in spring?*

Conduct Internet Research Model how to conduct an Internet search. Type in the URL for a child-friendly search engine. Enter key words and click Search. Then, click on the most relevant link to go to a Web site.

Present Ask children to draw pictures or dictate sentences on their research. Help them put the research and writing into a book or use presentation software to share with others.

SUMMATIVE ASSESSMENT

Unit Assessment

CCSS **TESTED SKILLS**

✔ COMPREHENSION:	✔ HIGH-FREQUENCY WORDS:	✔ PHONEMIC AWARENESS:	✔ PHONICS:	✔ CATEGORY WORDS:
• Key Details: Sequence **RL.K.1** • Key Details **RL.K.1**	• *is, little, she, was, my, are, he, with* **RF.K.3c**	• Phoneme Isolation **RF.K.2d** • Phoneme Blending **RF.K.2d** • Phoneme Segmentation **RF.K.2d** • Phoneme Addition **RF.K.2e**	• b (initial/final) **RF.K.3a** • l (initial) **RF.K.3a** • k (initial) **RF.K.3a** • ck (final) **RF.K.3a**	• Weather **L.K.5c** • Questions **L.K.1d**

Use Multiple Assessments for Instructional Planning

To create instructional profiles for your children, look for patterns in the results from the following assessment.

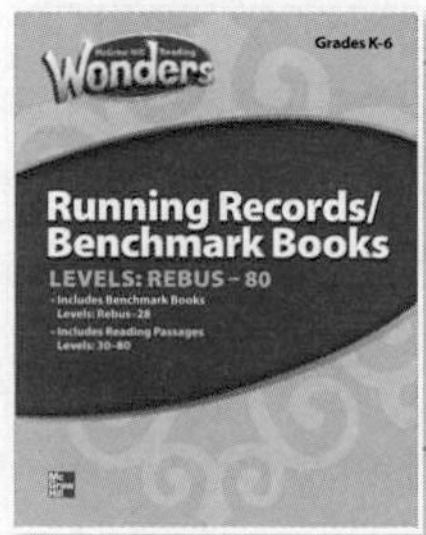

Running Records

Use the instructional reading level determined by the Running Record calculations for regrouping decisions.

Using Assessment Results

TESTED SKILLS	If ...	Then ...
COMPREHENSION	Children answer 0–3 items correctly ...	... reteach tested skills using the ***Tier 2 Comprehension Intervention Online PDFs***
HIGH-FREQUENCY WORDS	Children answer 0–1 items correctly ...	... reteach tested skills using Section 3 of the ***Tier 2 Fluency Intervention Online PDFs***
PHONEMIC AWARENESS	Children answer 0–3 items correctly ...	... reteach tested skills using the ***Tier 2 Phonemic Awareness Intervention Online PDFs***
PHONICS	Children answer 0–3 items correctly ...	...reteach tested skills using the ***Tier 2 Phonics/Word Study Intervention Online PDFs*** and Section 2 of the ***Tier 2 Fluency Intervention Online PDFs***
CATEGORY WORDS	Children answer 0–1 items correctly ...	... reteach tested skills using the ***Tier 2 Vocabulary Intervention Online PDFs***

Response to Intervention

Use the appropriate sections of the ***Placement and Diagnostic Assessment*** and children's assessment results to designate children requiring Tier 2 and Tier 3 intervention.

- → Phonological and Phonemic Awareness
- → Phonics
- → Vocabulary
- → Comprehension
- → Fluency

Program Information

For Additional Resources

Unit Bibliography

Word Lists

Literature and Informational Text Charts

Web Sites

Resources

www.connected.mcgraw-hill.com

SCOPE & SEQUENCE

	K	1	2	3	4	5	6
READING PROCESS							
Concepts About Print/Print Awareness							
Recognize own name							
Understand directionality (top to bottom; tracking print from left to right; return sweep, page by page)	✔						
Locate printed word on page	✔						
Develop print awareness (concept of letter, word, sentence)	✔						
Identify separate sounds in a spoken sentence	✔						
Understand that written words are represented in written language by a specific sequence of letters	✔						
Distinguish between letters, words, and sentences	✔						
Identify and distinguish paragraphs							
Match print to speech (one-to-one correspondence)	✔						
Name uppercase and lowercase letters	✔						
Understand book handling (holding a book right-side-up, turning its pages)	✔						
Identify parts of a book (front cover, back cover, title page, table of contents); recognize that parts of a book contain information	✔						
Phonological Awareness							
Recognize and understand alliteration							
Segment sentences into correct number of words							
Identify, blend, segment syllables in words		✔					
Recognize and generate rhyming words	✔	✔					
Identify, blend, segment onset and rime	✔	✔					
Phonemic Awareness							
Count phonemes	✔	✔					
Isolate initial, medial, and final sounds	✔	✔					
Blend spoken phonemes to form words	✔	✔					
Segment spoken words into phonemes	✔	✔					
Distinguish between long- and short-vowel sounds	✔	✔					
Manipulate phonemes (addition, deletion, substitution)	✔	✔					
Phonics and Decoding /Word Recognition							
Understand the alphabetic principle	✔	✔					
Sound/letter correspondence	✔	✔	✔	✔			
Blend sounds into words, including VC, CVC, CVCe, CVVC words	✔	✔	✔	✔			
Blend common word families	✔	✔	✔	✔			

KEY	✔ = Assessed Skill Tinted panels show skills, strategies, and other teaching opportunities.

	K	1	2	3	4	5	6
Initial consonant blends		✔	✔	✔			
Final consonant blends		✔	✔	✔			
Initial and medial short vowels	✔	✔	✔	✔	✔	✔	✔
Decode one-syllable words in isolation and in context	✔	✔	✔	✔			
Decode multisyllabic words in isolation and in context using common syllabication patterns		✔	✔	✔	✔	✔	✔
Distinguish between similarly spelled words	✔	✔	✔	✔	✔	✔	✔
Monitor accuracy of decoding							
Identify and read common high-frequency words, irregularly spelled words	✔	✔	✔	✔			
Identify and read compound words, contractions		✔	✔	✔	✔	✔	✔
Use knowledge of spelling patterns to identify syllables		✔	✔	✔	✔	✔	✔
Regular and irregular plurals	✔	✔	✔	✔	✔	✔	✔
Long vowels (silent *e*, vowel teams)	✔	✔	✔	✔	✔	✔	✔
Vowel digraphs (variant vowels)		✔	✔	✔	✔	✔	✔
r-Controlled vowels		✔	✔	✔	✔	✔	✔
Hard/soft consonants		✔	✔	✔	✔	✔	✔
Initial consonant digraphs		✔	✔	✔	✔	✔	
Medial and final consonant digraphs		✔	✔	✔	✔	✔	
Vowel diphthongs		✔	✔	✔	✔	✔	✔
Identify and distinguish letter-sounds (initial, medial, final)	✔	✔	✔				
Silent letters		✔	✔	✔	✔	✔	✔
Schwa words				✔	✔	✔	✔
Inflectional endings		✔	✔	✔	✔	✔	✔
Triple-consonant clusters		✔	✔	✔	✔	✔	
Unfamiliar and complex word families				✔	✔	✔	✔
Structural Analysis/Word Analysis							
Common spelling patterns (word families)		✔	✔	✔	✔	✔	✔
Common syllable patterns		✔	✔	✔	✔	✔	✔
Inflectional endings		✔	✔	✔	✔	✔	✔
Contractions		✔	✔	✔	✔	✔	✔
Compound words		✔	✔	✔	✔	✔	✔
Prefixes and suffixes		✔	✔	✔	✔	✔	✔
Root or base words			✔	✔	✔	✔	✔
Comparatives and superlatives			✔	✔	✔	✔	✔
Greek and Latin roots			✔	✔	✔	✔	✔
Fluency							
Apply letter/sound knowledge to decode phonetically regular words accurately	✔	✔	✔	✔	✔	✔	✔
Recognize high-frequency and familiar words	✔	✔	✔	✔	✔	✔	✔
Read regularly on independent and instructional levels							
Read orally with fluency from familiar texts (choral, echo, partner, Reader's Theater)							
Use appropriate rate, expression, intonation, and phrasing		✔	✔	✔	✔	✔	✔
Read with automaticity (accurately and effortlessly)		✔	✔	✔	✔	✔	✔
Use punctuation cues in reading		✔	✔	✔	✔	✔	✔

	K	1	2	3	4	5	6
Adjust reading rate to purpose, text difficulty, form, and style							
Repeated readings							
Timed readings		✔	✔	✔	✔	✔	✔
Read with purpose and understanding		✔	✔	✔	✔	✔	✔
Read orally with accuracy		✔	✔	✔	✔	✔	✔
Use context to confirm or self-correct word recognition		✔	✔	✔	✔	✔	✔
READING LITERATURE							
Comprehension Strategies and Skills							
Read literature from a broad range of genres, cultures, and periods		✔	✔	✔	✔	✔	✔
Access complex text		✔	✔	✔	✔	✔	✔
Build background							
Preview and predict							
Establish and adjust purpose for reading							
Evaluate citing evidence from the text							
Ask and answer questions	✔	✔	✔	✔	✔	✔	✔
Inferences and conclusions, citing evidence from the text	✔	✔	✔	✔	✔	✔	✔
Monitor/adjust comprehension including reread, reading rate, paraphrase							
Recount/Retell	✔	✔					
Summarize			✔	✔	✔	✔	✔
Story structure (beginning, middle, end)	✔	✔	✔	✔	✔	✔	✔
Visualize							
Make connections between and across texts		✔	✔	✔	✔	✔	✔
Point of view		✔	✔	✔	✔	✔	✔
Author's purpose							
Cause and effect	✔	✔	✔	✔	✔	✔	✔
Compare and contrast (including character, setting, plot, topics)	✔	✔	✔	✔	✔	✔	✔
Classify and categorize		✔	✔				
Literature vs informational text	✔	✔	✔				
Illustrations, using	✔	✔	✔	✔			
Theme, central message, moral, lesson		✔	✔	✔	✔	✔	✔
Predictions, making/confirming	✔	✔	✔				
Problem and solution (problem/resolution)		✔	✔	✔	✔	✔	✔
Sequence of events	✔	✔	✔	✔	✔	✔	✔
Literary Elements							
Character	✔	✔	✔	✔	✔	✔	✔
Plot development/Events	✔	✔	✔	✔	✔	✔	✔
Setting	✔	✔	✔	✔	✔	✔	✔
Stanza				✔	✔	✔	✔
Alliteration						✔	✔
Assonance						✔	✔
Dialogue							
Foreshadowing						✔	✔

KEY
✔ = Assessed Skill
Tinted panels show skills, strategies, and other teaching opportunities.

	K	1	2	3	4	5	6
Flashback						✔	✔
Descriptive and figurative language		✔	✔	✔	✔	✔	✔
Imagery					✔	✔	✔
Meter					✔	✔	✔
Onomatopoeia							
Repetition		✔	✔	✔	✔	✔	✔
Rhyme/rhyme schemes		✔	✔	✔	✔	✔	✔
Rhythm		✔	✔				
Sensory language							
Symbolism							
Write About Reading/Literary Response Discussions							
Reflect and respond to text citing text evidence		✔	✔	✔	✔	✔	✔
Connect and compare text characters, events, ideas to self, to other texts, to world							
Connect literary texts to other curriculum areas							
Identify cultural and historical elements of text							
Evaluate author's techniques, craft							
Analytical writing							
Interpret text ideas through writing, discussion, media, research							
Book report or review							
Locate, use, explain information from text features		✔	✔	✔	✔	✔	✔
Organize information to show understanding of main idea through charts, mapping							
Cite text evidence	✔	✔	✔	✔	✔	✔	✔
Author's purpose/ Illustrator's purpose							
READING INFORMATIONAL TEXT							
Comprehension Strategies and Skills							
Read informational text from a broad range of topics and cultures	✔	✔	✔	✔	✔	✔	✔
Access complex text		✔	✔	✔	✔	✔	✔
Build background							
Preview and predict	✔	✔	✔				
Establish and adjust purpose for reading							
Evaluate citing evidence from the text							
Ask and answer questions	✔	✔	✔	✔	✔	✔	✔
Inferences and conclusions, citing evidence from the text	✔	✔	✔	✔	✔	✔	✔
Monitor and adjust comprehension including reread, adjust reading rate, paraphrase							
Recount/Retell	✔	✔					
Summarize			✔	✔	✔	✔	✔
Text structure	✔	✔	✔	✔	✔	✔	✔
Identify text features		✔	✔	✔	✔	✔	✔
Make connections between and across texts	✔	✔	✔	✔	✔	✔	✔
Author's point of view				✔	✔	✔	✔
Author's purpose		✔	✔				

	K	1	2	3	4	5	6
Cause and effect	✔	✔	✔	✔	✔	✔	✔
Compare and contrast	✔	✔	✔	✔	✔	✔	✔
Classify and categorize		✔	✔				
Illustrations and photographs, using	✔	✔	✔	✔			
Instructions/directions (written and oral)		✔	✔	✔	✔	✔	✔
Main idea and key details	✔	✔	✔	✔	✔	✔	✔
Persuasion, reasons and evidence to support points/persuasive techniques						✔	✔
Predictions, making/confirming	✔	✔					
Problem and solution		✔	✔	✔	✔	✔	✔
Sequence, chronological order of events, time order, steps in a process	✔	✔	✔	✔	✔	✔	✔
Writing About Reading/Expository Critique Discussions							
Reflect and respond to text citing text evidence		✔	✔	✔	✔	✔	✔
Connect and compare text characters, events, ideas to self, to other texts, to world							
Connect texts to other curriculum areas							
Identify cultural and historical elements of text							
Evaluate author's techniques, craft							
Analytical writing							
Read to understand and perform tasks and activities							
Interpret text ideas through writing, discussion, media, research							
Locate, use, explain information from text features		✔	✔	✔	✔	✔	✔
Organize information to show understanding of main idea through charts, mapping							
Cite text evidence		✔	✔	✔	✔	✔	✔
Author's purpose/Illustrator's purpose							
Text Features							
Recognize and identify text and organizational features of nonfiction texts		✔	✔	✔	✔	✔	✔
Captions and labels, headings, subheadings, endnotes, key words, bold print	✔	✔	✔	✔	✔	✔	✔
Graphics, including photographs, illustrations, maps, charts, diagrams, graphs, time lines	✔	✔	✔	✔	✔	✔	✔
Self-Selected Reading/Independent Reading							
Use personal criteria to choose own reading including favorite authors, genres, recommendations from others; set up a reading log							
Read a range of literature and informational text for tasks as well as for enjoyment; participate in literature circles							
Produce evidence of reading by retelling, summarizing, or paraphrasing							
Media Literacy							
Summarize the message or content from media message, citing text evidence							
Use graphics, illustrations to analyze and interpret information	✔	✔	✔	✔	✔	✔	✔
Identify structural features of popular media and use the features to obtain information, including digital sources				✔	✔	✔	✔
Identify reasons and evidence in visuals and media message							
Analyze media source: recognize effects of media in one's mood and emotion							

KEY	✔ = Assessed Skill Tinted panels show skills, strategies, and other teaching opportunities.

	K	1	2	3	4	5	6
Make informed judgments about print and digital media							
Critique persuasive techniques							
WRITING							
Writing Process							
Plan/prewrite							
Draft							
Revise							
Edit/proofread							
Publish and present including using technology							
Teacher and peer feedback							
Writing Traits							
Conventions		✔	✔	✔	✔	✔	✔
Ideas		✔	✔	✔	✔	✔	✔
Organization		✔	✔	✔	✔	✔	✔
Sentence fluency		✔	✔	✔	✔	✔	✔
Voice		✔	✔	✔	✔	✔	✔
Word choice		✔	✔	✔	✔	✔	✔
Writer's Craft							
Good topic, focus on and develop topic, topic sentence			✔	✔	✔	✔	✔
Paragraph(s); sentence structure			✔	✔	✔	✔	✔
Main idea and supporting key details			✔	✔	✔	✔	✔
Unimportant details							
Relevant supporting evidence			✔	✔	✔	✔	✔
Strong opening, strong conclusion			✔	✔	✔	✔	✔
Beginning, middle, end; sequence		✔	✔	✔	✔	✔	✔
Precise words, strong words, vary words			✔	✔	✔	✔	✔
Figurative and sensory language, descriptive details							
Informal/formal language							
Mood/style/tone							
Dialogue				✔	✔	✔	✔
Transition words, transitions to multiple paragraphs				✔	✔	✔	✔
Select focus and organization			✔	✔	✔	✔	✔
Points and counterpoints/Opposing claims and counterarguments							
Use reference materials (online and print dictionary, thesaurus, encyclopedia)							
Writing Applications							
Writing about text	✔	✔	✔	✔	✔	✔	✔
Personal and fictional narrative (also biographical and autobiographical)	✔	✔	✔	✔	✔	✔	✔
Variety of expressive forms including poetry	✔	✔	✔	✔	✔	✔	✔
Informative/explanatory texts	✔	✔	✔	✔	✔	✔	✔
Description	✔	✔	✔	✔			
Procedural texts		✔	✔	✔	✔	✔	✔
Opinion pieces or arguments	✔	✔	✔	✔	✔	✔	✔

	K	1	2	3	4	5	6
Communications including technical documents		✔	✔	✔	✔	✔	✔
Research report	✔	✔	✔	✔	✔	✔	✔
Responses to literature/reflection				✔	✔	✔	✔
Analytical writing							
Letters		✔	✔	✔	✔	✔	✔
Write daily and over short and extended time frames; set up writer's notebooks							
Penmanship/Handwriting							
Write legibly in manuscript using correct formation, directionality, and spacing							
Write legibly in cursive using correct formation, directionality, and spacing							
SPEAKING AND LISTENING							
Speaking							
Use repetition, rhyme, and rhythm in oral texts							
Participate in classroom activities and discussions							
Collaborative conversation with peers and adults in small and large groups using formal English when appropriate							
Differentiate between formal and informal English							
Follow agreed upon rules for discussion							
Build on others' talk in conversation, adding new ideas							
Come to discussion prepared							
Describe familiar people, places, and things and add drawings as desired							
Paraphrase portions of text read alone or information presented							
Apply comprehension strategies and skills in speaking activities							
Use literal and nonliteral meanings							
Ask and answer questions about text read aloud and about media							
Stay on topic when speaking							
Use language appropriate to situation, purpose, and audience							
Use nonverbal communications such as eye contact, gestures, and props							
Use verbal communication in effective ways and improve expression in conventional language							
Retell a story, presentation, or spoken message by summarizing							
Oral presentations: focus, organizational structure, audience, purpose							
Give and follow directions							
Consider audience when speaking or preparing a presentation							
Recite poems, rhymes, songs							
Use complete, coherent sentences							
Organize presentations							
Deliver presentations (narrative, summaries, research, persuasive); add visuals							
Speak audibly (accuracy, expression, volume, pitch, rate, phrasing, modulation, enunciation)							
Create audio recordings of poems, stories, presentations							
Listening							
Identify musical elements in language							
Determine the purpose for listening							

KEY	✔ = Assessed Skill Tinted panels show skills, strategies, and other teaching opportunities.

	K	1	2	3	4	5	6
Understand, follow, restate, and give oral directions							
Develop oral language and concepts							
Listen openly, responsively, attentively, and critically							
Listen to identify the points a speaker makes							
Listen responsively to oral presentations (determine main idea and key details)							
Ask and answer relevant questions (for clarification to follow-up on ideas)							
Identify reasons and evidence presented by speaker							
Recall and interpret speakers' verbal/nonverbal messages, purposes, perspectives							
LANGUAGE							
Vocabulary Acquisition and Use							
Develop oral vocabulary and choose words for effect							
Use academic language		✔	✔	✔	✔	✔	✔
Identify persons, places, things, actions		✔	✔	✔			
Classify, sort, and categorize words	✔	✔	✔	✔	✔	✔	✔
Determine or clarify the meaning of unknown words; use word walls		✔	✔	✔	✔	✔	✔
Synonyms, antonyms, and opposites		✔	✔	✔	✔	✔	✔
Use context clues such as word, sentence, paragraph, definition, example, restatement, description, comparison, cause and effect		✔	✔	✔	✔	✔	✔
Use word identification strategies		✔	✔	✔	✔	✔	✔
Unfamiliar words		✔	✔	✔	✔	✔	✔
Multiple-meaning words		✔	✔	✔	✔	✔	✔
Use print and online dictionary to locate meanings, pronunciation, derivatives, parts of speech		✔	✔	✔	✔	✔	✔
Compound words		✔	✔	✔	✔	✔	✔
Words ending in -er and -est		✔	✔	✔	✔	✔	
Root words (base words)		✔	✔	✔	✔	✔	✔
Prefixes and suffixes		✔	✔	✔	✔	✔	✔
Greek and Latin affixes and roots			✔	✔	✔	✔	✔
Denotation and connotation					✔	✔	✔
Word families		✔	✔	✔	✔	✔	✔
Inflectional endings		✔	✔	✔	✔	✔	✔
Use a print and online thesaurus			✔	✔	✔	✔	✔
Use print and online reference sources for word meaning (dictionary, glossaries)		✔	✔	✔	✔	✔	✔
Homographs				✔	✔	✔	✔
Homophones			✔	✔	✔	✔	✔
Contractions		✔	✔	✔			
Figurative language such as metaphors, similes, personification			✔	✔	✔	✔	✔
Idioms, adages, proverbs, literal and nonliteral language			✔	✔	✔	✔	✔
Analogies							
Listen to, read, discuss familiar and unfamiliar challenging text							
Identify real-life connections between words and their use							
Use acquired words and phrases to convey precise ideas							
Use vocabulary to express spatial and temporal relationships							

	K	1	2	3	4	5	6
Identify shades of meaning in related words	✔	✔	✔	✔	✔	✔	✔
Word origins				✔	✔	✔	✔
Morphology				✔	✔	✔	✔
Knowledge of Language							
Choose words, phrases, and sentences for effect							
Choose punctuation effectively							
Formal and informal language for style and tone including dialects							
Conventions of Standard English/Grammar, Mechanics, and Usage							
Sentence concepts: statements, questions, exclamations, commands		✔	✔	✔	✔	✔	✔
Complete and incomplete sentences; sentence fragments; word order		✔	✔	✔	✔	✔	✔
Compound sentences, complex sentences				✔	✔	✔	✔
Combining sentences		✔	✔	✔	✔	✔	✔
Nouns including common, proper, singular, plural, irregular plurals, possessives, abstract, concrete, collective		✔	✔	✔	✔	✔	✔
Verbs including action, helping, linking, irregular		✔	✔	✔	✔	✔	✔
Verb tenses including past, present, future, perfect, and progressive		✔	✔	✔	✔	✔	✔
Pronouns including possessive, subject and object, pronoun-verb agreement, indefinite, intensive, reciprocal; correct unclear pronouns		✔	✔	✔	✔	✔	✔
Adjectives including articles, demonstrative, proper adjectives that compare		✔	✔	✔	✔	✔	✔
Adverbs including telling how, when, where, comparative, superlative, irregular		✔	✔	✔	✔	✔	✔
Subject, predicate; subject-verb agreement		✔	✔	✔	✔	✔	✔
Contractions		✔	✔	✔	✔	✔	✔
Conjunctions				✔	✔	✔	✔
Commas			✔	✔	✔	✔	✔
Colons, semicolons, dashes, hyphens						✔	✔
Question words							
Quotation marks			✔	✔	✔	✔	✔
Prepositions and prepositional phrases, appositives		✔	✔	✔	✔	✔	✔
Independent and dependent clauses						✔	✔
Italics/underlining for emphasis and titles							
Negatives, correcting double negatives					✔	✔	✔
Abbreviations			✔	✔	✔	✔	✔
Use correct capitalization in sentences, proper nouns, titles, abbreviations		✔	✔	✔	✔	✔	✔
Use correct punctuation		✔	✔	✔	✔	✔	✔
Antecedents				✔	✔	✔	✔
Homophones and words often confused			✔	✔	✔	✔	✔
Apostrophes				✔	✔	✔	✔
Spelling							
Write irregular, high-frequency words	✔	✔	✔				
ABC order	✔	✔					
Write letters	✔	✔					
Words with short vowels	✔	✔	✔	✔	✔	✔	✔
Words with long vowels	✔	✔	✔	✔	✔	✔	✔

KEY	✔ = Assessed Skill Tinted panels show skills, strategies, and other teaching opportunities.

	K	1	2	3	4	5	6
Words with digraphs, blends, consonant clusters, double consonants		✔	✔	✔	✔	✔	✔
Words with vowel digraphs and ambiguous vowels		✔	✔	✔	✔	✔	✔
Words with diphthongs		✔	✔	✔	✔	✔	✔
Words with r-controlled vowels		✔	✔	✔	✔	✔	✔
Use conventional spelling		✔	✔	✔	✔	✔	✔
Schwa words				✔	✔	✔	✔
Words with silent letters			✔	✔	✔	✔	✔
Words with hard and soft letters			✔	✔	✔	✔	✔
Inflectional endings including plural, past tense, drop final e and double consonant when adding -ed and -ing, changing y to i		✔	✔	✔	✔	✔	✔
Compound words		✔	✔	✔	✔	✔	✔
Homonyms/homophones			✔	✔	✔	✔	✔
Prefixes and suffixes		✔	✔	✔	✔	✔	✔
Root and base words (also spell derivatives)				✔	✔	✔	✔
Syllables: patterns, rules, accented, stressed, closed, open				✔	✔	✔	✔
Words with Greek and Latin roots						✔	✔
Words from mythology						✔	✔
Words with spelling patterns, word families		✔	✔	✔	✔	✔	✔
RESEARCH AND INQUIRY							
Study Skills							
Directions: read, write, give, follow (includes technical directions)			✔	✔	✔	✔	✔
Evaluate directions for sequence and completeness				✔	✔	✔	✔
Use library/media center							
Use parts of a book to locate information							
Interpret information from graphic aids		✔	✔	✔	✔	✔	✔
Use graphic organizers to organize information and comprehend text		✔	✔	✔	✔	✔	✔
Use functional, everyday documents				✔	✔	✔	✔
Apply study strategies: skimming and scanning, note-taking, outlining							
Research Process							
Generate and revise topics and questions for research				✔	✔	✔	✔
Narrow focus of research, set research goals				✔	✔	✔	✔
Find and locate information using print and digital resources		✔	✔	✔	✔	✔	✔
Record information systematically (note-taking, outlining, using technology)				✔	✔	✔	✔
Develop a systematic research plan				✔	✔	✔	✔
Evaluate reliability, credibility, usefulness of sources and information						✔	✔
Use primary sources to obtain information					✔	✔	✔
Organize, synthesize, evaluate, and draw conclusions from information							
Cite and list sources of information (record basic bibliographic data)					✔	✔	✔
Demonstrate basic keyboarding skills							
Participate in and present shared research							
Technology							
Use computer, Internet, and other technology resources to access information							
Use text and organizational features of electronic resources such as search engines, keywords, e-mail, hyperlinks, URLs, Web pages, databases, graphics							
Use digital tools to present and publish in a variety of media formats							

INDEX

A

Key X = Unit X

B

C

Key X = Unit X

D

E

F

Key X = Unit X

H

Key X = Unit X

M

N

O

Key X = Unit X

P

 Key X = Unit X

S

Key **X** = Unit X

T

U

V

Key **X** = Unit X

CCSS

Common Core State Standards Correlations

English Language Arts

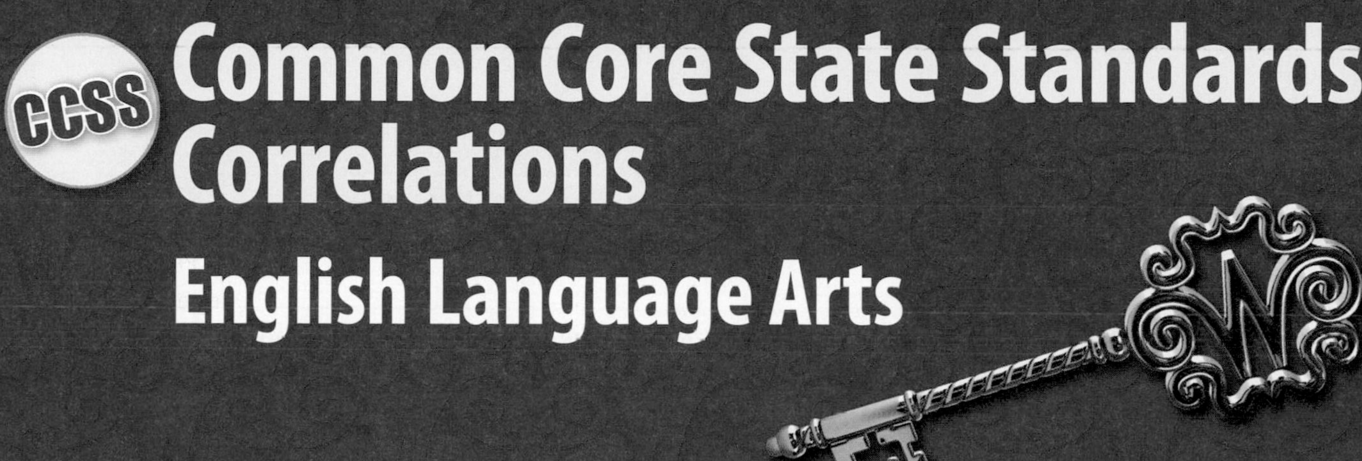

CCSS Common Core State Standards Correlations

College and Career Readiness Anchor Standards for READING

The K–5 standards on the following pages define what students should understand and be able to do by the end of each grade. They correspond to the College and Career Readiness (CCR) anchor standards below by number. The CCR and grade-specific standards are necessary complements—the former providing broad standards, the latter providing additional specificity—that together define the skills and understandings that all students must demonstrate.

Key Ideas and Details
1. Read closely to determine what the text says explicitly and to make logical inferences from it; cite specific textual evidence when writing or speaking to support conclusions drawn from the text.
2. Determine central ideas or themes of a text and analyze their development; summarize the key supporting details and ideas.
3. Analyze how and why individuals, events, and ideas develop and interact over the course of a text.
Craft and Structure
4. Interpret words and phrases as they are used in a text, including determining technical, connotative, and figurative meanings, and analyze how specific word choices shape meaning or tone.
5. Analyze the structure of texts, including how specific sentences, paragraphs, and larger portions of the text (e.g., a section, chapter, scene, or stanza) relate to each other and the whole.
6. Assess how point of view or purpose shapes the content and style of a text.
Integration of Knowledge and Ideas
7. Integrate and evaluate content presented in diverse media and formats, including visually and quantitatively, as well as in words.
8. Delineate and evaluate the argument and specific claims in a text, including the validity of the reasoning as well as the relevance and sufficiency of the evidence.
9. Analyze how two or more texts address similar themes or topics in order to build knowledge or to compare the approaches the authors take.
Range of Reading and Level of Text Complexity
10. Read and comprehend complex literary and informational texts independently and proficiently.

CCSS CORRELATIONS

Common Core State Standards
English Language Arts

Grade K

Each standard is coded in the following manner:

Strand	Grade Level	Standard
RL	K	1

Reading Standards for Literature

Key Ideas and Details		*McGraw-Hill Reading Wonders*
RL.K.1	With prompting and support, ask and answer questions about key details in a text.	**READING WRITING WORKSHOP BIG BOOK:** Unit 1, Week 3: 44-49 **LEVELED READERS: Unit 1, Week 2:** *Hop!* (A), *We Hop!* (O), *We Can Move!* (B) **Unit 2, Week 3:** *We Like Bugs!* (A), *The Bugs Run* (O), *I See a Bug!* (B) **Unit 3, Week 1:** *We Run* (A), *Go, Nat!* (O) **Unit 3, Week 2:** *A Noisy Night* (B) **Unit 4, Week 2:** *My Neighbors* (A), *Neighborhood Party* (O), *Parade Day* (B) **Unit 5, Week 1:** *My Garden* (A), *My Garden Grows* (O) **Unit 6, Week 2:** *The Rain* (A), *Weather Is Fun* (O), *Kate and Tuck* (B) **Unit 7, Week 3:** *We Want Water* (A), *A New Home* (O), *Bird's New Home* (B) **Unit 8, Week 3:** *Going Up* (A), *In the Clouds* (O), *How Sun and Moon Found Home* (B) **Unit 9, Week 1:** *Let Me Help You* (A), *How Can Jane Help?* (O), *I Used to Help Too* (B) **Unit 10, Week 1:** *Animal Band* (A), *We Want Honey* (O), *A Good Idea* (B) **YOUR TURN PRACTICE BOOK:** 29, 37, 45, 234 **READING WORKSTATION ACTIVITY CARDS:** 1, 2 **TEACHER'S EDITION: Unit 1:** T23, T106, T189 **Unit 2:** T177, T186-191 **Unit 3:** T25, T104-109 **Unit 4:** T35, T104-108, T142-143, T150-151, T186-191, T224-225, T232-233, T238-239 **Unit 5:** T61, T69, T238-239 **Unit 6:** T23-26, T61, T69, T75, T105-108, T143, T151, T186-191 **Unit 7:** T45, T107 **Unit 8:** T61, T69, T75, T105-108, T186-191 **Unit 9:** T22-26, T61, T69, T75, T104-109 **Unit 10:** T106-110, T145, T153, T159 **LITERATURE BIG BOOKS: Unit 1, Week 1:** *What About Bear?* **Unit 2 Week 3:** *I Love Bugs!* **Unit 3, Week 1:** *How Do Dinosaurs Go to School?* **Unit 4, Week 2:** *What Can You Do With a Paleta?* **Unit 6, Week 1:** *Mama, Is It Summer Yet?* **Unit 6, Week 2:** *Rain* **Unit 7, Week 2:** *The Birthday Pet* **Unit 7, Week 3:** *Bear Snores On* **Unit 8, Week 1:** *When Daddy's Truck Picks Me Up* **Unit 9, Week 2:** *Hen Hears Gossip* **Unit 10, Week 2:** *All Kinds of Families* **INTERACTIVE READ-ALOUD CARDS:** SS: "The Ugly Duckling", "Tikki Tikki Tembo" **Unit 1, Week 1:** "The Lion and the Mouse" **Unit 1, Week 2:** "The Tortoise and the Hare" **Unit 2, Week 1:** "Timimoto" **Unit 4, Week 1:** "Little Juan and the Cooking Pot" **Unit 4, Week 3:** "A Bundle of Sticks"
RL.K.2	With prompting and support, retell familiar stories, including key details.	**LEVELED READERS: Unit 1, Week 2:** *Hop!* (A), *We Hop!* (O, ELL), *We Can Move!* (B) **Unit 2, Week 3:** *I See a Bug!* (B) **Unit 3, Week 1:** *We Run* (A), *Go, Nat!* (O, ELL), *The Birdhouse* (B) **Unit 3, Week 2:** *City Sounds* (A), *Farm Sounds* (O, ELL), *A Noisy Night* (B) **Unit 4, Week 3:** *We Clean!* (A), *Can You Fix It?* (O, ELL), *Helping Mom* (B) **Unit 5, Week 1:** *The Mystery Seeds* (B) **Unit 6, Week 1:** *It Is Hot!* (A), *Little Bear* (O, ELL), *Ant and Grasshopper* (B) **Unit 6, Week 2:** *The Rain* (A), *Weather Is Fun* (O, ELL), *Kate and Tuck* (B) **Unit 8, Week 1:** *I Go Places* (A), *Run, Quinn!* (O, ELL), *Going to Gran's House* (B) **Unit 10, Week 2:** *My Box* (A), *Let's Make a Band* (O, ELL), *Going Camping* (B) **READING WORKSTATION ACTIVITY CARDS:** 5 **YOUR TURN PRACTICE BOOK:** 157, 167 **TEACHER'S EDITION: Unit 1:** T27, T109, T191 **Unit 2:** T75, T109, T143, T151, T157, T161, T186-191 **Unit 3:** T27, T109, T191 **Unit 4:** T109, T143, T151, T157, T225, T233, T239 **Unit 5:** T61, T69, T75, T79, T109, T143, T151, T157, T191, T225, T233, T239 **Unit 6:** T27, T61, T109, T191, T225 **Unit 7:** T109, T143, T144, T151, T157, T158, T191, T225, T233, T239 **Unit 8:** T61, T69, T75, T143, T151, T157, T191, T225, T233, T239 **Unit 9:** T27, T61, T69, T75, T79, T109, T143, T151, T159, T225, T233, T239 **Unit 10:** T29, T63, T71, T77, T81, T111, T145, T153, T157, T191, T227, T235, T241 **LITERATURE BIG BOOKS: Unit 1, Week 1:** *What About Bear?* **Unit 1, Week 2:** *Pouch!* **Unit 3, Week 1:** *How Do Dinosaurs Go to School?* **Unit 3, Week 2:** *Clang! Clang! Beep! Beep! Listen to the City* **Unit 6, Week 1:** *Mama, Is It Summer Yet?* **Unit 7, Week 2:** *The Birthday Pet*

Reading Standards for Literature

Key Ideas and Details		McGraw-Hill Reading Wonders
RL.K.3	With prompting and support, identify characters, settings, and major events in a story.	**LEVELED READERS:** Unit 1, Week 2: *Hop!* (A), *We Hop!* (O), *We Can Move!* (B) **Unit 2, Week 3:** *The Bugs Run* (O) **Unit 3, Week 2:** *A Noisy Night* (B) **Unit 3, Week 3:** *We Can Go* (A), *Going by Cab* (O), *Cal's Busy Week* (B) **Unit 4, Week 2:** *My Neighbors* (A), *Neighborhood Party* (O) **Unit 5, Week 1:** *My Garden* (A), *My Garden Grows* (O), *The Mystery Seeds* (B) **Unit 7, Week 2:** *My Cats* (A), *Their Pets* (O), *Will's Pet* (B) **Unit 8, Week 1:** *I Go Places* (A), *Run, Quinn!* (O), *Going to Gran's House* (B) **Unit 9, Week 2:** *Mike Helps Out* (A), *Clive and His Friend* (O), *Farmer White's Best Friend* **YOUR TURN PRACTICE BOOK:** 129, 217, 234 **READING WORKSTATION ACTIVITY CARDS:** 3, 4, 6, 7, 10, 11 **TEACHER'S EDITION:** Unit 1: T75, T108 **Unit 3:** T156-157, T186-191, T224-225 **Unit 4:** T104-109, T142-143, T150-151 **Unit 5:** T22-27, T60-61, T68-69, T74-75 **Unit 7:** T104-109, T142-143, T150-151, T156-157, T186-191, T224-225, T232-233, T238-239 **Unit 8:** T22-27, T60-61, T68-69, T75, T186-191 **Unit 9:** T22-29, T60-61, T68-69, T74-75, T104-109, T117, T142-143, T150-151, T156-157 **Unit 10:** T22-29, T62-63, T70-71, T76-77 **LITERATURE BIG BOOKS:** Unit 3, Week 3: *Please Take Me for a Walk* **Unit 4, Week 2:** *What Can You Do with a Paleta?* **Unit 7, Week 3:** *Bear Snores On* **Unit 8, Week 3:** *Bringing Down the Moon* **Unit 9, Week 1:** *Peter's Chair* **Unit 9, Week 2:** *Hen Hears Gossip* **Unit 10, Week 1:** *What's the Big Idea, Molly?* **INTERACTIVE READ-ALOUD CARDS:** SS: "The Ugly Duckling", "Tikki Tikki Tembo" **Unit 1, Week 1:** "The Lion and the Mouse" **Unit 1, Week 2:** "The Tortoise and the Hare" **Unit 3, Week 1:** "The Boy Who Cried Wolf" **Unit 4, Week 1:** "Little Juan and the Cooking Pot" **Unit 7, Week 3:** "Anansi: An African Tale" **Unit 9, Week 2:** "The Little Red Hen"
Craft and Structure		***McGraw-Hill Reading Wonders***
RL.K.4	Ask and answer questions about unknown words in a text.	**READING/WRITING WORKSHOP BIG BOOK:** Unit 1, Week 2: 32-37 **Unit 2, Week 1:** 8-13 **LEVELED READERS:** Unit 4, Week 3: *We Clean!* (A), *Can You Fix It?* (O, ELL), *Helping Mom* (B) **TEACHER'S EDITION:** Unit 1: T74 **Unit 4:** T127, T225, T238 **Unit 6:** T23, T189 **Unit 7:** T45 **Unit 9:** T45 **Unit 10:** T47
RL.K.5	Recognize common types of texts (e.g., storybooks, poems).	**LEVELED READERS:** Unit 6, Week 1: *Ant and Grasshopper* (B) **TEACHER'S EDITION:** Unit 1: T25, T208, T218 **Unit 4:** T126-127 **Unit 5:** T44-45, T54-55 **Unit 6:** T44, T74-75, T186 **Unit 7:** T44-45 **Unit 9:** T44-45, T126 **Unit 10:** T46 **LITERATURE BIG BOOK:** Unit 1, Week 3: *I Smell Springtime* **Unit 5, Week 1:** *Tommy* **Unit 6, Week 1:** *Covers* **Unit 7, Week 1:** *Kitty Caught a Caterpillar* **INTERACTIVE READ-ALOUD CARDS:** SS: "The Ugly Duckling", "Tikki Tikki Tembo" **Unit 1, Week 1:** "The Lion and the Mouse" **Unit 1, Week 2:** "The Tortoise and the Hare" **Unit 2, Week 1:** "Timimoto" **Unit 3, Week 1:** "The Boy Who Cried Wolf" **Unit 4, Week 3:** "A Bundle of Sticks" **Unit 5, Week 2:** "The Pine Tree" **Unit 6, Week 2:** "The Frog and the Locust" **Unit 6, Week 3:** "Rainbow Crow" **Unit 7, Week 3:** "Anansi: An African Tale" **Unit 8, Week 1:** "The King of the Winds" **Unit 9, Week 2:** "The Little Red Hen" **Unit 9, Week 3:** "Spider Woman Teaches the Navajo" **Unit 10, Week 1:** "The Elves and the Shoemakers"
RL.K.6	With prompting and support, name the author and illustrator of a story and define the role of each in telling the story.	**LEVELED READERS:** Unit 2, Week 3: *I See a Bug!* (B) **Unit 4, Week 2:** *Parade Day* (B), *Helping Mom* (B) **Unit 10, Week 1:** *A Good Idea* (B) **TEACHER'S EDITION:** Unit 1: T68, T94, T142 **Unit 2:** T176, T238-239 **Unit 3:** T12, T94, T176 **Unit 4:** T94, T156, T238 **Unit 5:** T12 **Unit 6:** T12, T94, T176 **Unit 7:** T94, T176 **Unit 8:** T12, T176 **Unit 9:** T12, T94-95 **Unit 10:** T12, T76, T96 **LITERATURE BIG BOOKS:** Unit 1, Week 1: *What About Bear?* **Unit 1, Week 2:** *Pouch!* **Unit 2, Week 3:** *I Love Bugs!* **Unit 3, Week 1:** *How Do Dinosaurs Go to School?* **Unit 5, Week 1:** *My Garden* **Unit 6, Week 2:** *Rain* **Unit 7, Week 2:** *The Birthday Pet* **Unit 8, Week 1:** *When Daddy's Truck Picks Me Up* **Unit 9, Week 2:** *Hen Hears Gossip* **Unit 10, Week 1:** *What's the Big Idea, Molly?* **READING WORKSTATION ACTIVITY CARDS:** 6

Reading Standards for Literature

Integration of Knowledge and Ideas		McGraw-Hill Reading Wonders
RL.K.7	With prompting and support, describe the relationship between illustrations and the story in which they appear (e.g., what moment in a story an illustration depicts).	**LEVELED READERS:** **Unit 5, Week 1:** *My Garden Grows* (O, ELL) **Unit 5, Week 3:** *Farm Fresh Finn* (B) **Unit 6, Week 1:** *It Is Hot!* **Unit 7, Week 3:** *Bird's New Home* (B) **READING WORKSTATION ACTIVITY CARDS:** 1, 4, 11 **TEACHER'S EDITION:** **Unit 1:** T25, T60-61, T108 **Unit 3:** T24, T60-T61, T68-T69 **Unit 5:** T22-27, T68-69, T238-239 **Unit 6:** T25, T60-61, T105, T188 **Unit 7:** T238-239 **Unit 8:** T25 **Unit 10:** T46-47 **LITERATURE BIG BOOKS:** **Unit 1, Week 1:** *What About Bear?* **Unit 2, Week 3:** *I Love Bugs!* **Unit 3, Week 1:** *How Do Dinosaurs Go to School?* **Unit 3, Week 2:** *Clang! Clang! Beep! Beep! Listen to the City* **Unit 5, Week 1:** *My Garden* **Unit 6, Week 3:** *Waiting Out the Storm* **Unit 8, Week 1:** *When Daddy's Truck Picks Me Up* **Unit 9, Week 1:** *The Clean Up!* **Unit 10, Week 1:** *The Variety Show* **Unit 10, Week 2:** *All Kinds of Families!* **INTERACTIVE READ-ALOUD CARDS:** **Unit 5, Week 2:** "The Pine Tree" **Unit 6, Week 2:** "The Frog and the Locust" **Unit 6, Week 3:** "Rainbow Crow"
RL.K.8	(Not applicable to literature.)	
RL.K.9	With prompting and support, compare and contrast the adventures and experiences of characters in familiar stories.	**LEVELED READERS:** **Unit 3, Week 1:** *Go, Nat!* (O, ELL) **READING WORKSTATION ACTIVITY CARD:** 15 **TEACHER'S EDITION:** **Unit 1:** S27, S51, S75, T35, T117, T136 **Unit 2:** T218-219 **Unit 3:** T35, T136, T218-219 **Unit 4:** T136-137 **Unit 6:** T54, T117, T136, T199, T218 **Unit 7:** T136-137, T199, T218 **Unit 8:** T35, T54, T218 **Unit 9:** T54, T117, T136 **Unit 10:** T37, T56, T138 **LITERATURE BIG BOOKS:** **Unit 1, Week 1:** *What About Bear?* **Unit 1, Week 2:** *Pouch!, Baby Animals on the Move* **INTERACTIVE READ-ALOUD CARDS:** **Unit 1, Week 1:** "The Lion and the Mouse" **Unit 1, Week 2:** "The Tortoise and the Hare" **Unit 2, Week 1:** "Timimoto" **Unit 7, Week 3:** "Anansi: An African Tale" **Unit 8, Week 1:** "The King of the Winds" **Unit 10, Week 1:** "The Elves and the Shoemakers"
Range of Reading and Level of Text Complexity		***McGraw-Hill Reading Wonders***
RL.K.10	Actively engage in group reading activities with purpose and understanding.	**READING/WRITING WORKSHOP BIG BOOKS:** SS: 36-41 **Unit 1:** 34-39, 46-51 **Unit 2:** 10-15, 28-33, 34-39 **Unit 3:** 10-15, 28-33, 46-51 **Unit 4:** 24-31, 38-45 **Unit 5:** 10-17, 38-45 **Unit 6:** 24-31, 38-45 **Unit 7:** 24-31, 38-45 **Unit 8:** 10-17, 24-31 **Unit 9:** 10-17, 24-31 **Unit 10:** 10-17, 24-31 **LEVELED READERS:** **Unit 5, Week 1:** *My Garden Grows* (ELL) **Unit 7, Week 2:** *Their Pets* (ELL) **Unit 7, Week 3:** *A New Home* (ELL) **TEACHER'S EDITION:** **Unit 1:** S12, S14, S17, S22, S24, S31, S36, S38, S41, S46, S48, S55, S62, S65, S70, S72, T22-27, T126-127 **Unit 2:** T30-31, T112-113, T130-131 **Unit 3:** T34-35, T94-95, T212-213 **Unit 4:** T112-113, T126-127, T130-131, T194-195, T199 **Unit 5:** T12-13, T48-49, T78-79, T117, T194-195 **Unit 6:** T12-13, T22-26, T94-95, T104-108, T117, T130-131, T176-177, T186-190, T194-195, T199 **Unit 7:** T112-113, T130-131, T160-161, T176-177, T194-195, T199, T212-213, T242-243 **Unit 8:** T12-13, T30-31, T34-35, T48-49, T112-113, T176-177, T212-213 **Unit 9:** T12-13, T30-31, T48-49, T94-95, T112-113, T117, T199, T212-213 **Unit 10:** T12-13, T32-33, T50-51, T96-97, T132-133 **INTERACTIVE READ-ALOUD CARDS:** SS: "The Ugly Duckling", "Tikki Tikki Tembo" **Unit 1, Week 1:** "The Lion and the Mouse" **Unit 1, Week 2:** "The Tortoise and the Hare" **Unit 3, Week 2:** "The Turtle and the Flute" **Unit 4, Week 1:** "Little Juan and the Cooking Pot" **Unit 4, Week 3:** "A Bundle of Sticks" **Unit 5, Week 2:** "The Pine Tree" **Unit 6, Week 2:** "The Frog and the Locust" **Unit 6, Week 3:** "Rainbow Crow" **Unit 7, Week 3:** "Anansi: An African Tale" **Unit 8, Week 1:** "The King of the Winds" **Unit 9, Week 2:** "The Little Red Hen" **Unit 9, Week 3:** "Spider Woman Teaches the Navajo" **Unit 10, Week 1:** "The Elves and the Shoemakers"

Reading Standards for Informational Text

Key Ideas and Details		McGraw-Hill Reading Wonders
RI.K.1	With prompting and support, ask and answer questions about key details in a text.	**READING/WRITING WORKSHOP BIG BOOKS:** Unit 2: 14-19 **LEVELED READERS: Unit 1, Week 3:** *The Beach* (A), *At School* (O), *See It Grow!* (B) **Unit 2, Week 1:** *We Need Tools* (A), *A Trip* (O), *What Can You See?* (B) **Unit 2, Week 2:** *Shapes!* (A), *Play with Shapes!* (O), *Use a Shape!* (B) **Unit 4, Week 1:** *You Cook* (A), *On the Job* (O), *The Neighborhood* (B) **Unit 8, Week 2:** *See This!* (A), *Places to See* (O), *My Trip to Yellowstone* (B) **Unit 9, Week 3:** *Look Where It Is From* (A), *What's for Breakfast?* (O), *Nature at the Craft Fair* (B) **Unit 10, Week 3:** *Help Clean Up* (A), *Let's Save Earth* (O), *Babysitters for Seals* (B) **YOUR TURN PRACTICE BOOK:** 53, 147 **READING WORKSTATION ACTIVITY CARDS:** 1 **TEACHER'S EDITION: Unit 1:** T126-127, T186-191, T225, **Unit 2:** T22-27, T44-45, T107 **Unit 4:** T22-27, T44-45, T61, T69, T75, T186-191, T208-209 **Unit 5:** T104-109, T151, T157, T186-191, T209 **Unit 6:** T23-26, T105-108, T187-188 **Unit 7:** T23, T25 **Unit 8:** T104-109, T126-127, T142-143, T151, T157, T209 **Unit 9:** T35, T127, T186-191 **Unit 10:** T188-193, T227, T241 **LITERATURE BIG BOOKS: Unit 1, Week 2:** *Baby Animals on the Move* **Unit 1, Week 3:** *Senses at the Seashore* **Unit 2, Week 1:** *The Handiest Things in the World, Discover with Tools* **Unit 4, Week 1:** *Whose Shoes?* "A Shoe for Every Job" **Unit 4, Week 3:** *Roadwork* **Unit 5, Week 2:** *A Grand Old Tree* **Unit 5, Week 3:** *An Orange in January* **Unit 7, Week 1:** *ZooBorns!* **Unit 9, Week 3:** *Bread Comes to Life* **Unit 10, Week 3:** *Panda Kindergarten* **INTERACTIVE READ-ALOUD CARDS:** SS: "Kindergarteners Can!" **Unit 1, Week 3:** "A Feast of the Senses" **Unit 2, Week 3:** "From Caterpillar to Butterfly" **Unit 4, Week 2:** "Cultural Festivals" **Unit 9, Week 1:** "Helping Out at Home" **Unit 10, Week 2:** "The Perfect Color"
RI.K.2	With prompting and support, identify the main topic and retell key details of a text.	**LEVELED READERS: Unit 1, Week 3:** *The Beach* (A), *At School* (O, ELL), *See It Grow!* (B) **Unit 2, Week 1:** *We Need Tools* (A), *A Trip* (O, ELL), *What Can You See?* (B) **Unit 5, Week 2:** *The Tree* (A), *Many Trees* (O, ELL), *Our Apple Tree* (B) **Unit 5, Week 3:** *The Farmers' Market* (A), *Let's Make a Salad!* (O, ELL) **Unit 9, Week 3:** *Look Where It Is From* (A) **READING WORKSTATION ACTIVITY CARDS:** 5 **TEACHER'S EDITION: Unit 4:** T191 **Unit 5:** T104-109, T126-127, T142-143, T150-151, T156-157, T186-T190, T208-209, T224-225 **Unit 8:** T104-109, T127, T160-161, T248-249 **Unit 9:** T127, T186-191, T224-225, T232-233, T248-249 **Unit 10:** T188-193, T211, T226-227, T240-241, T250-251 **LITERATURE BIG BOOKS: Unit 1, Week 3:** *Senses on the Seashore* **Unit 5, Week 2:** *A Grand Old Tree,* "From a Seed to a Tree" **Unit 5, Week 3:** *An Orange in January* **Unit 8, Week 2:** *Ana Goes to Washington, D.C.* **Unit 9, Week 3:** *Bread Comes to Life* **Unit 10, Week 3:** *Panda Kindergarten* **INTERACTIVE READ-ALOUD CARDS: Unit 1, Week 3:** "A Feast of the Senses" **Unit 2, Week 3:** "From Caterpillar to Butterfly" **Unit 4, Week 2:** "Cultural Festivals" **Unit 9, Week 1:** "Helping Out at Home" **Unit 10, Week 2:** "The Perfect Color"
RI.K.3	With prompting and support, describe the connection between two individuals, events, ideas, or pieces of information in a text.	**LEVELED READERS: Unit 7:** *Two Cubs* (A), *Animal Bodies* (O, ELL), *Two Kinds of Bears* (B); **Unit 9:** *Look Where It is From* (A), *What's for Breakfast?* (O, ELL) **READING WORKSTATION ACTIVITY CARDS:** 8, 9 **TEACHER'S EDITION: Unit 6:** T24, T25, T106 **Unit 7:** T22-26, T60-61, T68-69, T74-75, T208-209 **Unit 8:** T44-45, T95 **LITERATURE BIG BOOKS: Unit 2, Week 2:** *Shapes All Around* **Unit 7, Week 1:** *ZooBorns!* **Unit 7, Week 3:** "Animal Homes" **Unit 8, Week 1:** *Getting from Here to There* **Unit 8, Week 2:** *Ana Goes to Washington, D.C.* **Unit 9, Week 3:** *Bread Comes to Life* **INTERACTIVE READ-ALOUD CARDS: Unit 2, Week 3:** "From Caterpillar to Butterfly" **Unit 6, Week 1:** "A Tour of the Seasons" **Unit 8, Week 2:** "The Best of the West" **Unit 9, Week 1:** "Helping Out at Home" **Unit 10, Week 3:** "Protect the Environment"
Craft and Structure		***McGraw-Hill Reading Wonders***
RI.K.4	With prompting and support, ask and answer questions about unknown words in a text.	**LEVELED READERS: Unit 1, Week 3:** *At School* (O, ELL), *See It Grow!* (B) **Unit 2, Week 1:** *A Trip* (O, ELL) **Unit 4, Week 1:** *You Cook* (A), *On the Job* (O, ELL) **Unit 5, Week 2:** *The Tree* (A) **Unit 5, Week 3:** *The Farmers' Market* (A) **Unit 7, Week 1:** *Animal Bodies* (O, ELL) **Unit 9, Week 3:** *Nature at the Craft Fair* (B) **Unit 10, Week 3:** *Let's Save Earth* (O, ELL), *Babysitters for Seals* (B) **TEACHER'S EDITION: Unit 4:** T127 **Unit 5:** T107 **Unit 7:** T209 **Unit 8:** T127, T209 **Unit 10:** T234
RI.K.5	Identify the front cover, back cover, and title page of a book.	**READING/WRITING WORKSHOP: Unit 1:** 8-13, 26-31, 44-49 **Unit 2:** 8-13, 26-31, 44-49 **Unit 3:** 8-13, 26-31, 44-49 **Unit 4:** 8-15, 22-29, 36-43 **LEVELED READERS: Unit 10, Week 3:** *Help Clean Up* (A) **TEACHER'S EDITION: Unit 1:** T30-31, T176 **Unit 4:** T12 **Unit 5:** T94, T176, T232 **Unit 7:** T12, T60, T68, T74, T94 **Unit 8:** T87, T94 **Unit 9:** T176 **Unit 10:** T178, T226 **LITERATURE BIG BOOKS: Unit 1, Week 3:** *Senses at the Seashore* **Unit 2, Week 1:** *The Handiest Things in the World* **Unit 4, Week 1:** *Whose Shoes? A Shoe for Every Job*

Reading Standards for Informational Text

Craft and Structure		McGraw-Hill Reading Wonders
RI.K.6	Name the author and illustrator of a text and define the role of each in presenting the ideas or information in a text.	**LEVELED READERS:** Unit 5, Week 3: *Let's Make a Salad!* (O, ELL), **Unit 7, Week 1:** *Two Cubs* (A), *Animal Bodies* (O, ELL), *Two Kinds of Bears* (B) **READING WORKSTATION ACTIVITY CARDS:** 12 **TEACHER'S EDITION:** Unit 1: T176 **Unit 2:** T12 **Unit 4:** T12 **Unit 5:** T94, T176, T232 **Unit 6:** T12, T94, T176 **Unit 7:** T12, T60, T68, T74, T94 **Unit 8:** T94 **Unit 9:** T176 **Unit 10:** T178 **LITERATURE BIG BOOKS:** Unit 1, Week 3: *Senses at the Seashore* **Unit 2, Week 1:** *The Handiest Things in the World* **Unit 2, Week 2:** *Shapes All Around* **Unit 8, Week 2:** *Ana Goes to Washington, D.C.* **Unit 9, Week 3:** *Bread Comes to Life*
Integration of Knowledge and Ideas		**McGraw-Hill Reading Wonders**
RI.K.7	With prompting and support, describe the relationship between illustrations and the text in which they appear (e.g., what person, place, thing, or idea in the text an illustration depicts).	**READING/WRITING WORKSHOP BIG BOOK:** Unit 2, Week 1: 14-19 **LEVELED READERS:** Unit 1, Week 3: *The Beach* (A) **Unit 2, Week 1:** *We Need Tools* (A) **Unit 2, Week 2:** *Shapes!* (A), *Play with Shapes!* (O, ELL), *Use a Shape!* (B) **Unit 9, Week 3:** *What's for Breakfast?* (O, ELL) **READING WORKSTATION ACTIVITY CARDS:** 1 **TEACHER'S EDITION:** Unit 1: T126-T127, T186-191, T224-225 **Unit 2:** T24, T60-61, T124-T127, 143 **Unit 3:** T45, 127, T208-209 **Unit 4:** T22-27 **Unit 6:** T126-127, T209 **Unit 9:** T208-209, T232-233 **Unit 10:** T190, T244-245 **LITERATURE BIG BOOKS:** Unit 1, Week 3: *Senses at the Seashore*, pp. 4-34 **Unit 2, Week 1:** *The Handiest Things in the World* **Unit 2, Week 2:** *Shapes All Around* **Unit 3, Week 2:** *Sounds Are Everywhere* **Unit 3, Week 3:** *A Neighborhood* **Unit 4, Week 1:** *Whose Shoes? A Shoe for Every Job* **Unit 6, Week 2:** *Cloud Watch* **Unit 9, Week 3:** *Nature's Artists* **INTERACTIVE READ-ALOUD CARDS:** Unit 3, Week 3: "Field Trips" **Unit 6, Week 1:** "A Tour of the Seasons" **Unit 9, Week 1:** "Helping Out at Home"
RI.K.8	With prompting and support, identify the reasons an author gives to support points in a text.	**READING WORKSTATION ACTIVITY CARDS:** 12 **TEACHER'S EDITION:** Unit 2: T26, T108 **Unit 4:** T26, T190 **Unit 5:** T108, T190 **Unit 8:** T108 **Unit 9:** T190 **Unit 10:** T210-211 **LITERATURE BIG BOOKS:** Unit 1, Week 3: *Senses at the Seashore* **Unit 2, Week 1:** *The Handiest Things in the World* **Unit 2, Week 2:** *Shapes All Around* **Unit 4, Week 1:** *Whose Shoes? A Shoe for Every Job* **Unit 4, Week 3:** *Roadwork* **Unit 5, Week 2:** *A Grand Old Tree* **Unit 5, Week 3:** *An Orange in January* **Unit 8, Week 2:** *Ana Goes to Washington, D.C.* **Unit 9, Week 3:** *Bread Comes to Life* **Unit 10, Week 3:** *Save Big Blue!*
RI.K.9	With prompting and support, identify basic similarities in and differences between two texts on the same topic (e.g., in illustrations, descriptions, or procedures).	**READING/WRITING WORKSHOP BIG BOOK:** Unit 1, Week 3: A Feast of the Senses **READING WORKSTATION ACTIVITY CARDS:** 16 **TEACHERS EDITION:** Unit 1: T199 **Unit 2:** T54-55, T117, T126-127 **Unit 4:** T116-117, T218-219 **Unit 5:** T136-137, T198-199, T208-209, T218-219 **Unit 7:** T35, T54, T117 **Unit 8:** T136 **Unit 9:** T218 **Unit 10:** T128-129, T201, T220 **LITERATURE BIG BOOKS:** Unit 1, Week 3: *Senses at the Seashore* **Unit 2, Week 1:** *The Handiest Things in the World* **Unit 2, Week 2:** *Shapes All Around,* "Find the Shapes" **Unit 5, Week 3:** *An Orange in January,* "Farmers' Market" **Unit 10, Week 2:** *Good For You* **INTERACTIVE READ-ALOUD CARDS:** Unit 1, Week 3: "A Feast of the Senses" **Unit 2, Week 2:** "Kites in Flight" **Unit 5, Week 3:** "Farms Around the World" **Unit 7, Week 1:** "Baby Farm Animals" **Unit 7, Week 2:** "The Family Pet" **Unit 10, Week 3:** "Protect the Environment!"
Range of Reading and Level of Text Complexity		**McGraw-Hill Reading Wonders**
RI.K.10	Actively engage in group reading activities with purpose and understanding.	**READING/WRITING WORKSHOP BIG BOOKS:** Start Smart: 18-23, 53-58 **Unit 1:** 10-15, 28-33, 52-57 **Unit 2:** 16-21, 52-57 **Unit 3:** 34-39, 52-57 **Unit 4:** 10-17 **Unit 5:** 24-31 **Unit 6:** 10-17 **Unit 7:** 10-17 **Unit 8:** 38-45 **Unit 9:** 38-45 **Unit 10:** 38-45 **LEVELED READERS:** Unit 5, Week 2: *Many Trees* (ELL) **TEACHER'S EDITION:** Unit 1: S60, T112-113, T126-127, T199 **Unit 2:** T22-27, T44-45, T74-75, T186-191 **Unit 3:** T126-127, T198-199, T212-213 **Unit 4:** T12-13, T30-31, T116-117, T176-177 **Unit 5:** T34-35, T92-95, T160-161, T174-177, T198-199 **Unit 6:** T35, T126-127, T208-209 **Unit 7:** T12-13, T22-27, T30-31, T34-35, T48-49, T116-117 **Unit 8:** T94-95, T116-117 **Unit 9:** T34-35, T176-177, T194-195, T208-209 **Unit 10:** T118-119, T178-179, T201 **INTERACTIVE READ-ALOUD CARDS:** SS: "Kindergarteners Can!" **Unit 1, Week 3:** "A Feast of the Senses" **Unit 2, Week 3:** "From Caterpillar to Butterfly" **Unit 3, Week 3:** "Field Trips" **Unit 4, Week 2:** "Cultural Festivals" **Unit 5, Week 1:** "Growing Plants" **Unit 5, Week 3:** "Farms Around the World" **Unit 6, Week 1:** "A Tour of the Seasons" **Unit 7, Week 1:** "Baby Farm Animals" **Unit 7, Week 2:** "The Family Pet" **Unit 8, Week 2:** "The Best of the West" **Unit 8, Week 3:** "A View from the Moon" **Unit 9, Week 1:** "Helping Out at Home" **Unit 10, Week 2:** "The Perfect Color" **Unit 10, Week 3:** "Protect the Environment"

Reading Standards for Foundational Skills

These standards are directed toward fostering students' understanding and working knowledge of concepts of print, the alphabetic principle, and other basic conventions of the English writing system. These foundational skills are not an end in and of themselves; rather, they are necessary and important components of an effective, comprehensive reading program designed to develop proficient readers with the capacity to comprehend texts across a range of types and disciplines. Instruction should be differentiated: good readers will need much less practice with these concepts than struggling readers will. The point is to teach students what they need to learn and not what they already know—to discern when particular children or activities warrant more or less attention.
Note: In Kindergarten, children are expected to demonstrate increasing awareness and competence in the areas that follow.

Print Concepts		*McGraw-Hill Reading Wonders*
RF.K.1	Demonstrate understanding of the organization and basic features of print.	**TEACHER'S EDITION:** Unit 1: S10, S18, S23, S28, S29, S32, S37, S39, S42, S43, S47, S52, S53, S56, S61, S62, S63, S66, S71, S77, T12, T15, T16, T60, T97, T98, T180, T189, T192 **Unit 2:** T12, T15, T30, T97, T112, T179, T180, T212, T224 **Unit 3:** T15, T26, T94, T97, T106, T112, T130, T142, T176, T179, T211, T232 **Unit 4:** T12, T15, T23, T30, T47, T48, T60, T68, T94, T97, T105, T108, T112, T129, T130, T142, T150, T179, T187, T194, T211, T212, T224 **Unit 5:** T12, T15, T30, T47, T48, T60, T68, T94, T97, T112, T129, T130, T142, T150, T176, T179, T211, T212, T224, T232 **Unit 6:** T12, T15, T29, T37, T47, T97, T129, T179, T211 **Unit 7:** T15, T16, T47, T94, T97, T98, T129, T150, T176, T179, T180, T211, T212, T232 **Unit 8:** T12, T15, T47, T48, T68, T94, T97, T129, T142, T179 **Unit 9:** T12, T15, T25, T47, T60, T94, T97, T129, T142, T176, T179, T211 **Unit 10:** T12, T15, T49, T62, T96, T97, T13, T144, T178, T179, T213
RF.K.1a	Follow words from left to right, top to bottom, and page by page.	**READING/WRITING WORKSHOP:** Start Smart: 4-5, 22-23, 40-41 **LITERATURE BIG BOOK:** Start Smart, Week 3: *ABC Big Book* **Unit 4, Week 2:** *What Can You Do With a Paleta?* **TEACHER'S EDITION:** **Unit 1:** S10, S62, T12, T60, T189 **Unit 2:** T30, T112, T224 **Unit 3:** T26, T94, T176 **Unit 4:** T12, T23, T30, T48, T60, T68, T94, T105, T108, T112, T130, T142, T150, T187, T194, T212, T224 **Unit 5:** T68, T94, T112, T130, T142, T150, T176, T212, T224, T232 **Unit 6:** T12 **Unit 7:** T94, T150 **Unit 8:** T12, T68, T94, T142 **Unit 9:** T12, T25, T60, T94, T142 **Unit 10:** T12, T62, T96, T144, T178
RF.K.1b	Recognize that spoken words are represented in written language by specific sequences of letters.	**TEACHER'S EDITION:** **Unit 1:** S39, S63 **Unit 2:** T212 **Unit 3:** T47-129, T211 **Unit 4:** T47, T129, T211 **Unit 5:** T47, T129, T211 **Unit 6:** T29, T37, T47, T129, T211 **Unit 7:** T47, T129, T176, T211, T212 **Unit 8:** T47, T48, T129, T211 **Unit 9:** T47, T129, T176, T211 **Unit 10:** T49, T131, T213
RF.K.1c	Understand that words are separated by spaces in print.	**TEACHER'S EDITION:** **Unit 1:** S29, S39, S43, S53, S63, S77 **Unit 2:** T12, T180 **Unit 3:** T94, T106, T112, T130, T142, T232 **Unit 5:** T12, T30, T48, T60, T94 **Unit 7:** T232
RF.K.1d	Recognize and name all upper- and lowercase letters of the alphabet.	**YOUR TURN PRACTICE BOOK:** 3, 7, 8, 11, 15, 16, 20, 24, 34, 42, 50, 58, 66, 84, 92, 100, 108, 116, 134, 142, 143-144, 162, 172, 192, 202, 212, 222, 232 **TEACHER'S EDITION:** **Unit 1:** S23, S18, S23, S28, S32, S37, S42, S47, S52, S56, S61, S66, S71, T15, T16, T97, T98, T180, T192 **Unit 2:** T15, T97, T179 **Unit 3:** T15, T97, T179 **Unit 4:** T15, T97, T179 **Unit 5:** T15, T97, T179 **Unit 6:** T15, T97, T179 **Unit 7:** T15, T16, T97, T98, T179, T180 **Unit 8:** T15, T97, T179 **Unit 9:** T15, T97, T179 **Unit 10:** T15, T97, T179
Phonological Awareness		***McGraw-Hill Reading Wonders***
RF.K.2	Demonstrate understanding of spoken words, syllables, and sounds (phonemes).	**TEACHER'S EDITION:** **Unit 1:** S13, S18, S23, S42, S47, S52, S56, S61, S66, S71, T14, T36, T102, T118, T124, T184, T206 **Unit 2:** T14, T20, T42, T70, T96, T102, T124, T144, T178, T184, T206, T210, T226 **Unit 3:** T20, T36, T42, T62, T96, T102, T118, T124, T144, T184, T206, T226 **Unit 4:** T20, T28, T42, T56, T62, T70, T102, T118, T128, T138, T145, T152, T184, T192, T200, T206, T210, T220, T226 **Unit 5:** T14, T20, T28, T36, T42, T62, T63, T72, T102, T110, T118, T124, T138, T144, T145, T152, T184, T192, T206, T210, T226, T227, T234 **Unit 6:** T20, T28, T36, T42, T46, T56, T62, T63, T70, T102, T124, T138, T144, T152, T154, T184, T192, T206, T210, T220, T227, T234 **Unit 7:** T20, T28, T36, T42, T46, T62, T102, T110, T118, T124, T128, T138, T144, T145, T178, T184, T206, T210, T220, T226, T234 **Unit 8:** T20, T28, T42, T46, T56, T62, T63, T102, T110, T118, T124, T128, T138, T144, T145, T152, T184, T200, T206, T226, T227, T234 **Unit 9:** T14, T20, T42, T62, T102, T124, T144, T184, T206, T210, T220, T226, T227, T234 **Unit 10:** T20, T44, T48, T58, T64, T72, T104, T126, T130, T140, T146, T147, T154, T212, T222, T229, T236
RF.K.2a	Recognize and produce rhyming words.	**LITERATURE BIG BOOKS:** Start Smart, Weeks 1-3: *Big Book of Rhymes* **TEACHER'S EDITION:** **Unit 1:** S23, S42, S47, S52, T102, T124 **Unit 2:** T210 **Unit 3:** T20, T42, T62 **Unit 4:** T184, T206, T226 **Unit 5:** T184, T206, T226 **Unit 6:** T102, T124, T144 **Unit 7:** T102, T124, T144 **Unit 8:** T102, T124, T144 **Unit 9:** T102, T124, T144
RF.K.2b	Count, pronounce, blend, and segment syllables in spoken words.	**LITERATURE BIG BOOK:** Smart Start, Week 3: *Big Book of Rhymes* **TEACHER'S EDITION:** **Unit 1:** S56, S61, S66, S71 **Unit 2:** T184, T206, T226 **Unit 3:** T184, T206, T226 **Unit 5:** T20, T42, T62 **Unit 9:** T20, T42, T62, T184, T206, T226 **Unit 10:** T20, T44, T64

Reading Standards for Foundational Skills

Phonological Awareness		*McGraw-Hill Reading Wonders*
RF.K.2c	Blend and segment onsets and rimes of single-syllable spoken words.	**YOUR TURN PRACTICE BOOK:** 88, 96, 104, 112, 124, 130, 138, 148, 158, 168, 182, 183, 188, 198, 208, 228, 242, 243, 248, 256, 264, 272, 280, 293 **TEACHER'S EDITION: Unit 1:** T184, T206 **Unit 2:** T102, T124, T144 **Unit 3:** T102, T124, T144 **Unit 4:** T20, T42, T62 **Unit 5:** T102, T124, T144 **Unit 6:** T20, T42, T62 **Unit 7:** T20, T42, T62, T184, T206, T226 **Unit 8:** T20, T42, T62, T184, T206, T226 **Unit 10:** T104, T126, T146
RF.K.2d	Isolate and pronounce the initial, medial vowel, and final sounds (phonemes) in in three-phoneme (consonant-vowel-consonant, or CVC) words. (This does not include CVCs ending with /l/, /r/, or /x/.)	**YOUR TURN PRACTICE BOOK:** 80, 193 **TEACHER'S EDITION: Unit 1:** T14, T36, T118 **Unit 2:** T14, T70, T96, T178 **Unit 3:** T36, T96, T118 **Unit 4:** T28, T70, T110, T118, T128, T138, T145, T152, T192, T200, T210, T220 **Unit 5:** T14, T28, T36, T63, T72, T110, T118, T138, T145, T152, T192 **Unit 6:** T28, T36, T46, T56, T62, T63, T70, T138, T152, T154, T184, T192, T206 **Unit 7:** T28, T36, T110, T118, T178 **Unit 8:** T28, T46, T56, T63, T110, T118, T145, T152
RF.K.2e	Add or substitute individual sounds (phonemes) in simple, one-syllable words to make new words.	**TEACHER'S EDITION: Unit 5:** T210, T220, T227, T234 **Unit 6:** T210, T220, T227, T234 **Unit 7:** T128, T138, T145, T152, T210, T220, T227, T234 **Unit 8:** T128, T138, T145, T152, T200, T227, T234 **Unit 9:** T210, T220, T227, T234 **Unit 10:** T48, T58, T72, T130, T140, T147, T154, T212, T222, T229, T236
Phonics and Word Recognition		***McGraw-Hill Reading Wonders***
RF.K.3	Know and apply grade-level phonics and word analysis skills in decoding words.	**TEACHER'S EDITION: Unit 1:** S19, S43, S67, T28, T29, T97, T105, T121, T179, T181, T210, T211, T220, T245 **Unit 2:** T15, T39, T46, T97, T128-129, T179, T203, T221 **Unit 3:** T15, T38, T39, T46, T56, T97, T110, T111, T128, T179, T181, T210 **Unit 4:** T15, T17, T28-29, T30-31, T37 , T39, T46, T47, T48-49, T57, T66, T73, T76, T81, T97, T99, T110, T111, T112-113, T121, T128, T129, T130-131, T139, T148, T155, T158, T163, T179, T181, T193, T194-195, T203, T210, T211, T212-213, T221, T230, T237, T240, T245 **Unit 5:** T14, T17, T28, T29, T30-31, T36, T39, T47, T48-49,T56, T57, T66, T73, T76, T81, T99, T110-111, T112-113, T118, T119, T121, T128, T129, T130-131, T138, T139, T146, T148, T153,T155, T158, T163, T181, T192, T193, T194-195, T200, T203, T210, T211, T212-213, T220, T221, T228, T230, T237, T240, T245 **Unit 6:** T15, T17, T29, T30-31, T39, T46, T47, T48-49, T57, T66, T73, T81, T97, T99, T111, T112-113, T121, T128, T129, T130-131, T139, T148, T155, T158, T163, T178, T179, T181, T193, T194-195, T201, T203, T210, T212-213, T221, T230, T237, T240, T245 **Unit 7:** T15, T17, T28-29, T30-31, T37, T46, T47, T48-49, T56, T57, T64, T65, T66, T73, T76, T81, T96, T97, T99, T110, T112-113, T119, T121, T128, T129, T130-131, T139, T146, T148, T155, T158, T163, T178, T179, T181, T192, T193, T194-195, T201, T203, T210, T211, T212-213, T220, T221, T230, T237, T240, T245 **Unit 8:** T15, T17, T29, T30-31, T39, T46, T47, T48-49, T57, T66, T73, T76, T81, T97, T99, T111, T112-113, T121, T128, T129, T130-131, T139, T148, T155, T158, T163, T179, T181, T193, T194-195, T201, T203, T210, T211, T212-213, T220, T221, T230, T237, T240, T245 **Unit 9:** T15, T17, T29, T30-31, T37, T39, T46, T47, T48-49, T56, T57, T64, T65, T66, T71, 72, T73, T76, T81, T97, T99, T110-111, T112-113, T119, T120, T121, T128, T129, T130-131, T138, T139, T146, T147,T148, T153, T154, T155, T158, T163, T179, T181, T192-193, T194-195, T201, T202, T203, T210, T211, T212-213, T220, T221, T228, T229, T230, T235, T236, T237, T240, T245 **Unit 10:** T15, T17, T30-31, T32-33, T39, T40, T41, T48, T49, T50-51, T58, T59, T66, T67, T68, T74, T75,T83, T97, T99, T101, T110, T112-113, T114-115, T121, T123, T130, T131, T140, T141, T148, T149, T150, T156, T157, T160, T165, T179, T181, T182, T183, T191, T194-195, T196-197, T203, T204, T205, T212-213, T222, T223, T230, T231, T232, T238, T239, T242, T247
RF.K.3a	Demonstrate basic knowledge of one-to-one letter-sound correspondences by producing the primary or many of the most frequent sounds for each consonant.	**PHONICS/WORD STUDY WORKSTATION ACTIVITY CARDS:** 1, 2, 3, 4, 5, 6, 7, 8, 9, 10, 11, 12, 13, 14, 15, 16, 17, 18, 19, 20, 21, 22, 23, 24 **TEACHER'S EDITION: Unit 1:** T28, T179, T210, T220 **Unit 2:** T15, T97, T179 **Unit 3:** T97, T110, T179 **Unit 4:** T97, T110, T179 **Unit 5:** T14, T28, T36, T56, T118, T138, T192, T200, T220, T228 **Unit 6:** T15, T97, T179 **Unit 7:** T56, T96, T97, T110, T146, T178, T179, T192, T220 **Unit 8:** T15, T97, T179 **Unit 10:** T97, T110, T179

CCSS CORRELATIONS

Reading Standards for Foundational Skills

Phonics and Word Recognition		McGraw-Hill Reading Wonders
RF.K.3b	Associate the long and short sounds with the common spellings (graphemes) for the five major vowels.	**YOUR TURN PRACTICE BOOK:** 36, 62, 101-102, 135-136, 138, 246, 248, 254, 256, 262, 264, 270, 278 **PHONICS/WORD STUDY WORKSTATION ACTIVITY CARDS:** 2, 7, 10, 14, 19, 25, 26, 27, 28, 29, 30 **TEACHER'S EDITION:** **Unit 1:** T97, T105 **Unit 2:** T46, T128–T129, T221 **Unit 3:** T15, T38, T56 **Unit 4:** T15, T28-29, T37 **Unit 5:** T110-111, T119, T146, T153 **Unit 6:** T193, T201, T211 **Unit 7:** T15, T28-29, T37, T46, T64, T65, T119, T201 **Unit 8:** T201, T220 **Unit 9:** T15, T29, T37, T56, T64, T65, T71, 72, T76, T97, T110-111, T119, T120, T138, T146, T147, T153, T154, T179, T192-193, T201, T202, T220, T228, T229, T235, T236 **Unit 10:** T15, T30-31, T39, T40, T58, T66, T67, T74, T99, T112-113, T121, T140, T148, T149, T156, T181, T182, T191, T194-195, T203, T204, T222, T230, T231, T238
Phonological Awareness		***McGraw-Hill Reading Wonders***
RF.K.3c	Read common high-frequency words by sight (e.g., *the, of, to, you, she, my, is, are, do, does*).	**READING/WRITING WORKSHOP:** Start Smart: 9, 16-22, 27 **Unit 1:** 7-13, 14-19, 25-31 **Unit 2:** 7-13, 14-19, 25-31 **Unit 3:** 7-13, 25-31, 32-37 **Unit 4:** 7-15, 21-29, 35-43 **Unit 5:** 7-15, 21-29, 35-43 **Unit 6:** 7-15, 21-29, 35-43 **Unit 7:** 7-15, 21-29, 35-43 **Unit 8:** 7-15, 21-29, 35-43 **Unit 9:** 7-15, 21-29, 35-43 **Unit 10:** 7-15, 21-29, 35-43 **YOUR TURN PRACTICE BOOK:** 4, 9-10, 12, 17-18, 21, 25-26], 31-32, 39-40, 47-48, 55-56, 63-64, 71-72, 89-90, 97-98, 105-106, 113-114,121-122, 131-132, 139-140, 149-150, 159-160, 169-170, 179-180, 189-190, 199-200, 209-210, 219-220, 229-230, 239-240, 249-250, 257-258, 265-266, 273-274, 281-282, 291-292 **TEACHER'S EDITION:** **Unit 1:** S19, S43, S67, T29, T121, T181, T211, T245 **Unit 2:** T39, T129, T203 **Unit 3:** T39, T111, T181 **Unit 4:** T17, T29, T30-31, T39, T47, T48-49, T57, T66, T73, T76, T81, T99, T111, T112-113, T121, T129, T130-131, T139, T148, T155, T158, T163, T181, T193, T194-195, T203, T211, T212-213, T221, T230, T237, T240, T245 **Unit 5:** T17, T29, T30-31, T39, T47, T48-49, T57, T66, T73, T76, T81, T99, T111, T112-113, T121, T129, T130-131, T139, T148, T155, T158, T163, T181, T193, T194-195, T203, T211, T212-213, T221, T230, T237, T240, T245 **Unit 6:** T17, T29, T30-31, T39, T47, T48-49, T57, T66, T73, T81, T99, T111, T112-113, T121, T129, T130-131, T139, T148, T155, T158, T163, T181, T193, T194-195, T203, T211, T212-213, T221, T230, T237, T240, T245 **Unit 7:** T17, T29, T30-31, T39, T47, T48-49, T57, T66, T73, T76, T81, T99, T111, T112-113, T121, T129, T130-131, T139, T148, T155, T158, T163, T181, T193, T194-195, T203, T211, T212-213, T221, T230, T237, T240, T245 **Unit 8:** T17, T29, T30-31, T39, T47, T48-49, T57, T66, T73, T76, T81, T99, T111, T112-113, T121, T129, T130-131, T139, T148, T155, T158, T163, T181, T193, T194-195, T203, T211, T212-213, T221, T230, T237, T240, T245 **Unit 9:** T17, T29, T30-31, T39, T47, T48-49, T57, T66, T73, T76, T81, T99, T111, T112-113, T121, T129, T130-131, T139, T148, T155, T158, T163, T181, T193, T194-195, T203, T211, T212-213, T221, T230, T237, T240, T245 **Unit 10:** T17, T31, T32-33, T41, T49, T50-51, T59, T68, T75, T78, T83, T101, T113, T114-115, T123, T131, T141, T150, T157, T160, T165, T183, T195, T196-197, T205, T212-213, T223, T232, T239, T242, T247
RF.K.3d	Distinguish between similarly spelled words by identifying the sounds of the letters that differ.	**TEACHER'S EDITION:** **Unit 2:** T46, T128 **Unit 3:** T46, T128, T210 **Unit 4:** T46, T128, T210 **Unit 5:** T128, T210 **Unit 6:** T46, T128, T210 **Unit 7:** T46, T128, T210 **Unit 8:** T46, T128, T210 **Unit 9:** T46, T128, T210 **Unit 10:** T48, T130, T212

CCSS

CORRELATIONS

Reading Standards for Foundational Skills

Fluency		McGraw-Hill Reading Wonders
RF.K.4	Read emergent-reader texts with purpose and understanding.	**READING/WRITING WORKSHOP:** **Unit 1:** 32-37, 44-49, 50-55 **Unit 2:** 32-37, 44-49, 50-55 **Unit 3:** 8-13, 32-37, 50-55 **Unit 4:** 8-15, 22-29, 36-43 **Unit 5:** 8-15, 22-29, 36-43 **Unit 6:** 8-15, 22-29, 36-43 **Unit 7:** 8-15, 22-29, 36-43 **Unit 8:** 8-15, 22-29, 36-43 **Unit 9:** 8-15, 22-29, 36-43 **Unit 10:** 8-15, 22-29, 36-43 **LEVELED READERS:** **Unit 1, Week 1:** *Soup!* (A), *Mouse and Monkey* (O, ELL), *Come and Play!* (B) **Unit 1 Week 2:** *Hop!* (A), *We Hop!* (O, ELL) *We Can Move!* (B) **Unit 1, Week 3:** *The Beach* (A), *At School* (O, ELL), *See It Grow!* (B) **Unit 2, Week 1:** *We Need Tools* (A), *A Trip* (O, ELL), *What Can You See?* (B) **Unit 2, Week 2:** *Shapes!* (A), *Play with Shapes!* (O, ELL), *Use a Shape!* (B) **Unit 2, Week 3:** *We Like Bugs!* (A), *The Bugs Run* (O, ELL), *I See a Bug!* (B) **Unit 3, Week 1:** *We Run* (A), *Go, Nat!* (O, ELL), *The Birdhouse* (B) **Unit 3, Week 2:** *City Sounds* (A), *Farm Sounds* (O, ELL), *A Noisy Night* (B) **Unit 3, Week 3:** *We Can Go* (A), *Going by Cab* (O, ELL), *Cal's Busy Week* (B) **Unit 4, Week 1:** *You Cook* (A), *On the Job* (O, ELL), *The Neighborhood* (B) **Unit 4, Week 2:** *My Neighbors* (A), *Neighborhood Party* (O, ELL), *Parade Day* (B) **Unit 4, Week 3:** *We Clean!* (A) *Can You Fix It?* (O, ELL), *Helping Mom* (B) **Unit 5, Week 1:** *My Garden* (A), *My Garden Grows* (O, ELL), *The Mystery Seeds* (B) **Unit 5, Week 2:** *The Tree* (A), *Many Trees* (O, ELL), *Our Apple Tree* (B) **Unit 5, Week 3:** *The Farmer* (A), *Let's Make a Salad!* (O, ELL), *Farm Fresh Finn* (B) **Unit 6, Week 1:** *It Is Hot!* (A), *Little Bear* (O, ELL), *Ant and Grasshopper* (B) **Unit 6, Week 2:** *The Rain* (A), *Weather Is Fun* (O, ELL), *Kate and Tuck* (B) **Unit 6 Week 3:** *Bad Weather* (A), *Getting Ready* (O, ELL), *The Storm* (B) **Unit 7, Week 1:** *Two Cubs* (A), *Animal Bodies* (O, ELL), *Two Kinds of Bears* (B) **Unit 7, Week 2:** *My Cats* (A), *Their Pets* (O, ELL), *Will's Pet* (B) **Unit 7, Week 3:** *We Want Water* (A) *A New Home* (O, ELL), *Bird's New Home* (B) **Unit 8, Week 1:** *I Go Places* (A), *Run, Quinn!* (O, ELL), *Going to Gran's House* (B) **Unit 8, Week 2:** *See This!* (A), *Places to See* (O, ELL), *My Trip to Yellowstone* (B) **Unit 8, Week 3:** *Going Up* (A), *In the Clouds* (O, ELL), *How Sun and Moon Found Home* (B) **Unit 9, Week 1:** *Let Me Help You* (A), *How Can Jane Help?* (O, ELL), *I Used to Help, Too* (B) **Unit 9, Week 2:** *Mike Helps Out* (A), *Clive and His Friend* (O, ELL), *Farmer White's Best Friend* (B) **Unit 9, Week 3:** *Look Where It Is From* (A), *What's for Breakfast?* (O, ELL), *Nature at the Craft Fair* (B) **Unit 10, Week 1:** *Animal Band* (A), *We Want Honey* (O, ELL), *A Good Idea* (B) **Unit 10, Week 2:** *My Box* (A), *Let's Make a Band* (O, ELL), *Going Camping* (B) **Unit 10, Week 3:** *Help Clean Up* (A), *Let's Save Earth* (O, ELL), *Babysitters for Seals* (B) **TEACHER'S EDITION:** **Unit 1:** S14, S48, T48-49, T112-113, T150-151, T232-233 **Unit 2:** T48-49, T130-131, T224-225 **Unit 3:** T60-61, T130-131, T212-213 **Unit 4:** T30-31, T48-49, T60-61, T65, T68-69, T72, T74-75, T78-79, T112-113, T130-131, T142-143, T147, T150-151, T156-157, T160-161, T194-195, T212-213, T224-225, T229, T232-233, T236, T238-239, T242-243 **Unit 5:** T30-31, T48-49, T60-61, T65, T68-69, T72, T74-75, T78-79, T112-113, T130-131, T142-143, T147, T150-151, T156-157, T160-161, T194-195, T212-213, T224-225, T229, T232-233, T236, T238-239, T242-243 **Unit 6:** T30-31, T48-49, T60-61, T65, T68-69, T72, T74-75, T78-79, T112-113, T130-131, T142-143, T147, T150-151, T194-195, T212-213, T224-225, T229, T232-233, T236 **Unit 7:** T30-31, T48-49, T60-61, T65, T68-69, T72, T74-75, T78-79, T112-113, T130-131, T142-143, T147, T150-151, T156-157, T160-161, T194-195, T212-213, T224-225, T229, T232-233, T236, T238-239, T242-243 **Unit 8:** T30-31, T48-49, T60-61, T65, T68-69, T72, T74-75, T78-79, T112-113, T10-131, T142-143, T147, T150-151, T156-157, T160-161, T194-195, T212-213, T224-225, T229, T232-233, T236, T238-239, T242-243 **Unit 9:** T30-31, T48-49, T60-61, T65, T68-69, T72, T74-75, T78-79, T112-113, T130-131, T142-143, T147, T150-151, T156-157, T160-161, T194-195, T212-213, T224-225, T229, T232-233, T236, T238-239, T242-243 **Unit 10:** T32-33, T50-51, T62-63, T67, T70-71, T74, T76-77, T80-81, T114-115, T132-133, T144-145, T149, T152-153, T156, T158-159, T162-163, T196-197, T214-215, T226-227, T231, T234-235, T238, T240-241, T244-245

College and Career Readiness Anchor Standards for WRITING

The K–5 standards on the following pages define what students should understand and be able to do by the end of each grade. They correspond to the College and Career Readiness (CCR) anchor standards below by number. The CCR and grade-specific standards are necessary complements—the former providing broad standards, the latter providing additional specificity—that together define the skills and understandings that all students must demonstrate.

Text Types and Purposes
1. Write arguments to support claims in an analysis of substantive topics or texts, using valid reasoning and relevant and sufficient evidence.
2. Write informative/explanatory texts to examine and convey complex ideas and information clearly and accurately through the effective selection, organization, and analysis of content.
3. Write narratives to develop real or imagined experiences or events using effective technique, well-chosen details, and well-structured event sequences.
Production and Distribution of Writing
4. Produce clear and coherent writing in which the development, organization, and style are appropriate to task, purpose, and audience.
5. Develop and strengthen writing as needed by planning, revising, editing, rewriting, or trying a new approach.
6. Use technology, including the Internet, to produce and publish writing and to interact and collaborate with others.
Research to Build and Present Knowledge
7. Conduct short as well as more sustained research projects based on focused questions, demonstrating understanding of the subject under investigation.
8. Gather relevant information from multiple print and digital sources, assess the credibility and accuracy of each source, and integrate the information while avoiding plagiarism.
9. Draw evidence from literary or informational texts to support analysis, reflection, and research.
Range of Writing
10. Write routinely over extended time frames (time for research, reflection, and revision) and shorter time frames (a single sitting or a day or two) for a range of tasks, purposes, and audiences.

Common Core State Standards
English Language Arts

Grade K

Writing Standards

Text Types and Purposes		*McGraw-Hill Reading Wonders*
W.K.1	Use a combination of drawing, dictating, and writing to compose opinion pieces in which they tell a reader the topic or the name of the book they are writing about and state an opinion or preference about the topic or book (e.g., My favorite book is...).	**READING/WRITING WORKSHOP:** Unit 1: 38-39 Unit 3: 58 Unit 5: 32-33 Unit 6: 18-19 Unit 9: 18-19 Unit 10: 46-47 **TEACHER'S EDITION:** Unit 1: T87, T100, T114, T122 Unit 3: T196, T204, T214 Unit 5: T100, T114, T122-123, T132, T144 Unit 6: T32, T40, T41 Unit 9: T5, T18, T32, T40-41, T50 Unit 10: T17, T184, T198, T206, T216 **WRITING WORKSTATION ACTIVITY CARDS:** 5, 20
W.K.2	Use a combination of drawing, dictating, and writing to compose informative/explanatory texts in which they name what they are writing about and supply some information about the topic.	**READING/WRITING WORKSHOP:** Unit 2: 20-21 Unit 4: 44 Unit 5: 44-45 Unit 6: 44 Unit 7: 16-17, 44 Unit 8: 30-31 Unit 9: 44 **TEACHER'S EDITION:** Unit 1: S15, S33, S53, S67, S77, T182, T196, T204 Unit 2: T100, T122, T164 Unit 3: T18, T32, T40 Unit 4: T18, T32, T40, T114, T122, T196, T204 Unit 5: T182, T196, T204 Unit 6: T52-53, T135 Unit 7: T18, T32, T40, T100, T114, T122 Unit 8: T53, T100, T114, T122, T135 Unit 9: T182, T196, T204, T214 Unit 10: T18, T34, T42-43, T52 **WRITING WORKSTATION ACTIVITY CARDS:** 18, 23
W.K.3	Use a combination of drawing, dictating and writing to narrate a single event or several loosely linked events, tell about the events in the order in which they occurred, and provide a reaction to what happened.	**READING/WRITING WORKSHOP:** Unit 3: 38-39, 56 Unit 5: 44 Unit 6: 30 Unit 8: 16, 46-47 Unit 9: 30 Unit 10: 16 **TEACHER'S EDITION:** Unit 2: T196, T204, T246 Unit 3: T114, T122, T164 Unit 5: T32, T40, T82, T164, T246 Unit 6: T114, T123, T164, T246 Unit 8: T32, T40, T82, T196, T204 Unit 9: T82, T100, T114, T122-123, T132 Unit 10: T18, T34, T42, T43, T52, T84, T116, T166, T248 **WRITING WORKSTATION ACTIVITY CARDS:** 1, 4, 5, 7, 15

Writing Standards

Production and Distribution of Writing		McGraw-Hill Reading Wonders
W.K.4	(Begins in grade 3.)	
W.K.5	With guidance and support from adults, respond to questions and suggestions from peers and add details to strengthen writing as needed.	**TEACHER'S EDITION: Unit 1:** T32, T40 (Go Digital: Writing), T50, T58 (Go Digital: Writing), T122 (Go Digital: Writing), T132, T140 (Go Digital: Writing), T204 (Go Digital: Writing), T214, T222 (Go Digital: Writing) **Unit 2:** T40 (Go Digital: Writing), T50, T58 (Go Digital: Writing), T122 (Go Digital: Writing), T132, T140 (Go Digital: Writing), T204 (Go Digital: Writing), T214, T222 (Go Digital: Writing) **Unit 3:** T40 (Go Digital: Writing), T50, T58 (Go Digital: Writing), T122 (Go Digital: Writing), T132, T140 (Go Digital: Writing), T204 (Go Digital: Writing), T222 (Go Digital: Writing) **Unit 4:** T40 (Go Digital: Writing), T50, T58 (Go Digital: Writing), T122 (Go Digital: Writing), T132, T140 (Go Digital: Writing), T204 (Go Digital: Writing), T214, T222 (Go Digital: Writing) **Unit 5:** T40 (Go Digital: Writing), T50, T58 (Go Digital: Writing), T122 (Go Digital: Writing), T132, T140 (Go Digital: Writing), T204 (Go Digital: Writing), T214, T222 (Go Digital: Writing) **Unit 6:** T40 (Go Digital: Writing), T50, T58 (Go Digital: Writing), T122 (Go Digital: Writing), T132, T140 (Go Digital: Writing), T204 (Go Digital: Writing), T214, T222 (Go Digital: Writing) **Unit 7:** T40 (Go Digital: Writing), T58 (Go Digital: Writing), T122 (Go Digital: Writing), T140 (Go Digital: Writing), T164, T204 (Go Digital: Writing), T222 (Go Digital: Writing) T246 **Unit 8:** T40 (Go Digital: Writing), T50, T58 (Go Digital: Writing), T122 (Go Digital: Writing), T132, T140 (Go Digital: Writing), T164, T204 (Go Digital: Writing), T214, T222 (Go Digital: Writing), T246 **Unit 9:** T40 (Go Digital: Writing), T50, T58 (Go Digital: Writing), T122 (Go Digital: Writing), T132, T140 (Go Digital: Writing), T204 (Go Digital: Writing), T214, T222 (Go Digital: Writing) **Unit 10:** T42 (Go Digital: Writing), T52, T60 (Go Digital: Writing), T124 (Go Digital: Writing), T134, T142 (Go Digital: Writing), T166, T206 (Go Digital: Writing), T224 (Go Digital: Writing), T248 **WRITING WORKSTATION ACTIVITY CARDS:** 10, 11, 12, 13, 14, 16
W.K.6	With guidance and support from adults, explore a variety of digital tools to produce and publish writing, including in collaboration with peers.	**TEACHER'S EDITION: Unit 1:** T134 **Unit 2:** T216 **Unit 6:** T248-249 **Unit 7:** T52, T134, T216, T248-249 **Unit 8:** T52, T134, T216, T248-249 **Unit 9:** T216, T248-249 **Unit 10:** T218, T250-251 **ConnectED Digital Resources:** My Binder (My Work)
Research to Build and Present Knowledge		***McGraw-Hill Reading Wonders***
W.K.7	Participate in shared research and writing projects (e.g., explore a number of books by a favorite author and express opinions about them).	**TEACHER'S EDITION: Unit 1:** T52, T134, T216 **Unit 2:** T52, T134, T216 **Unit 3:** T52, T134, T216 **Unit 4:** T52, T134, T216 **Unit 5:** T52, T100, T114, T122-123 **Unit 6:** T52, T134, T216 **Unit 7:** T52, T134, T216, T248-249 **Unit 8:** T52, T134, T216 **Unit 9:** T52, T134, T216 **Unit 10:** T54, T136, T218 **WRITING WORKSTATION ACTIVITY CARDS:** 20, 23 **ConnectED Digital Resources:** Collaborate (Projects)
W.K.8	With guidance and support from adults, recall information from experiences or gather information from provided sources to answer a question.	**READING/WRITING WORKSHOP:** Unit 7: 44 **TEACHER'S EDITION: Unit 1:** T32, T40, T100 **Unit 2:** T52, T134, T216 **Unit 3:** T100, T214 **Unit 4:** T18, T52, T100, T134, T182, T216 **Unit 5:** T18, T52, T134, T216 **Unit 6:** T52, T100, T134, T216 **Unit 7:** T50, T52, T132, T134, T196, T204, T214, T216 **Unit 8:** T52, T134, T216 **Unit 9:** T52, T134, T216 **Unit 10:** T54, T102, T136, T218
W.K.9	(Begins in grade 4.)	
Range of Writing		***McGraw-Hill Reading Wonders***
W.K.10	(Begins in grade 3.)	

College and Career Readiness Anchor Standards for SPEAKING AND LISTENING

The K–5 standards on the following pages define what students should understand and be able to do by the end of each grade. They correspond to the College and Career Readiness (CCR) anchor standards below by number. The CCR and grade-specific standards are necessary complements—the former providing broad standards, the latter providing additional specificity—that together define the skills and understandings that all students must demonstrate.

Comprehension and Collaboration
1. Prepare for and participate effectively in a range of conversations and collaborations with diverse partners, building on others' ideas and expressing their own clearly and persuasively.
2. Integrate and evaluate information presented in diverse media and formats, including visually, quantitatively, and orally.
3. Evaluate a speaker's point of view, reasoning, and use of evidence and rhetoric.
Presentation of Knowledge and Ideas
4. Present information, findings, and supporting evidence such that listeners can follow the line of reasoning and the organization, development, and style are appropriate to task, purpose, and audience.
5. Make strategic use of digital media and visual displays of data to express information and enhance understanding of presentations.
6. Adapt speech to a variety of contexts and communicative tasks, demonstrating command of formal English when indicated or appropriate.

Common Core State Standards
English Language Arts

Grade K

Speaking and Listening Standards		
Comprehension and Collaboration		***McGraw-Hill Reading Wonders***
SL.K.1	Participate in collaborative conversations with diverse partners about kindergarten topics and texts with peers and adults in small and larger groups.	**TEACHER'S EDITION:** Unit 1: S10-11, S44, S58, T11, T54-55, T117, T134, T136-137, T216 **Unit 2:** T34, T51, T52, T134, T222 **Unit 3:** T20, T33, T45, T175, T216 **Unit 4:** T11, T20, T52, T54, T58, T93, T134, T136, T140, T175, T216, T218 **Unit 5:** T11, T20, T52, T93, T120, T136, T174, T175, T216, T222 **Unit 6:** T11, T52, T54, T93, T136, T140, T216, T218 **Unit 7:** T10-11, T52, T54, T55, T93, T134, T136, T137, T175, T218, T219 **Unit 8:** T11, T54, T58, T80, T92, T93, T134, T136, T140, T175, T218, T222 **Unit 9:** T10-11, T52, T54, T93, T136, T140, T175, T218, T222 **Unit 10:** T11, T20, T56, T60, T95, T104, T136, T138, T142, T177, T186, T220, T224
SL.K.1a	Follow agreed-upon rules for discussions (e.g., listening to others and taking turns speaking about the topics and texts under discussion).	**READING/WRITING WORKSHOP:** Unit 1: 6-7, 24-25 **Unit 2:** 24-25 **Unit 3:** 6-7, 24-25, 42-43 **Unit 4:** 6-7, 20-21, 34-35 **Unit 5:** 6-7, 20-21, 34-35 **Unit 6:** 6-7, 20-21, 36-43 **Unit 7:** 6-7, 20-21, 34-35 **Unit 8:** 6-7, 20-21 **Unit 9:** 6-7, 8-15, 20-21, 34-35 **Unit 10:** 6-7, 20-21 **YOUR TURN PRACTICE BOOK:** 31-32, 45, 68, 70-71, 81-82, 93 **READING WORKSTATION ACTIVITY CARDS:** 1, 6, 18, 19 **WRITING WORKSTATION ACTIVITY CARDS:** 1, 11, 13, 21+D89 **TEACHER'S EDITION:** Unit 1: T11, T134, T216 **Unit 2:** T52, T134, T222 **Unit 3:** T175, T216 **Unit 4:** T11, T52, T58, T93, T134, T140, T216 **Unit 5:** T11, T52, T93, T175, T216 **Unit 6:** T11, T52, T93, T140, T216 **Unit 7:** T11, T52, T55, T93, T134, T137, T219 **Unit 8:** T11, T58, T93, T134, T140, T222 **Unit 9:** T11, T52, T93, T140, T175, T222 **Unit 10:** T11, T60, T95, T142, T224
SL.K.1b	Continue a conversation through multiple exchanges.	**READING/WRITING WORKSHOP:** Unit 1: SS4-SS5, SS22-SS23, SS40-SS41, 6-7, 24-25, 42-43 **Unit 2:** 6-7, 8, 14-19, 24, 25, 42-43, 46, 47, 48, 51, 54, 55, 58 **Unit 3:** 6-7, 14-19, 24-35, 42-43 **Unit 4:** 6-7, 20-21, 34-35 **Unit 5:** 6-7, 20-21, 34-35 **Unit 6:** 8-15 **Unit 7:** 6-7, 8-15, 20-21, 22-29, 34-35, 36-43 **Unit 8:** 6-7, 8-15, 20-21, 22-29, 34-35, 36-43 **Unit 9:** 6-7, 8-15, 20-21, 22-29, 34-35 **Unit 10:** 6-7, 8-15, 20-21, 22-29, 34-35, 36-43 **YOUR TURN PRACTICE BOOK:** 29, 45, 53, 61, 68 **READING WORKSTATION ACTIVITY CARDS:** 1, 6, 17, 18 **WRITING WORKSTATION ACTIVITY CARDS:** 1, 9, 11 **PHONICS/WORD STUDY WORKSTATION ACTIVITY CARDS:** W11, W12, R2, R3 **SCIENCE/SOCIAL STUDIES WORKSTATION ACTIVITY CARDS:** W4, W26, R10 **LITERATURE BIG BOOKS:** Smart Start: *Animals in the Park* **Unit 2, Week 1:** *The Handiest Things in the World* **Unit 2, Week 2:** *Shapes All Around* **Unit 3, Week 2:** *Clang! Clang! Beep! Beep! Listen to the City* **Unit 4, Week 1:** *Whose Shoes? A Shoe for Every Job* **Unit 4, Week 2:** *What Can You Do with a Paleta?* **Unit 4, Week 3:** *Roadwork* **Unit 5, Week 3:** *An Orange in January* **Unit 6, Week 1:** *Mama, Is It Summer Yet?* **Unit 6, Week 2:** *Rain* **Unit 7, Week 1:** *ZooBorns!* **Unit 7, Week 2:** *The Birthday Pet* **Unit 8, Week 1:** *When Daddy's Truck Picks Me Up* **Unit 8, Week 2:** *Ana Goes to Washington, D.C.* **Unit 9, Week 3:** *Bread Comes to Life* **Unit 10, Week 3:** *Panda Kindergarten* **TEACHER'S EDITION:** Unit 1: S10-S11, S21, S26-S27, S34-S35, S44-S45, S54, S58-S59, S64, S68-S69, S74-S75, T11, T34, T35, T52, T53, T54-55, T81, T84, T93, T101, T117, T123, T133, T134, T135, T136-137, T162, T175, T183, T197, T199, T215, T216, T217, T218 **Unit 2:** T11, T19, T33, T41, T51, T52, T64, T93, T134, T136, T137, T175, T204, T215, T216, T217, T218 **Unit 3:** T11, T19, T54-55, T58, T93, T117, T134, T135, T136-137, T175, T216, T217, T218 **Unit 4:** T11, T54, T93, T134, T136, T175, T216, T218 **Unit 5:** T11, T52, T54, T93, T136, T175, T216, T218 **Unit 6:** T11, T52, T54, T136, T218 **Unit 7:** T10-11, T52, T54, T93, T134, T136, T175, T218 **Unit 8:** T11, T54, T58, T80, T92, T93, T136, T140, T175, T218, T222 **Unit 9:** T10-11, T54, T93, T136, T140, T175, T218 **Unit 10:** T11, T56, T95, T136, T138, T177, T220 **INTERACTIVE READ-ALOUD CARDS:** Smart Start, Week 1: "The Ugly Duckling" **Smart Start, Week 2:** "Tikki Tikki Tembo" **Smart Start, Week 3:** "Kindergarteners Can!" **Unit 1, Week 1:** "The Lion and the Mouse" **Unit 1, Week 2:** "The Tortoise and the Hare" **Unit 1, Week 3:** "A Feast of the Senses" **Unit 2, Week 1:** "Timimoto" **Unit 2, Week 2:** "Kites in Flight" **Unit 2, Week 3:** "From Caterpillar to Butterfly" **Unit 3, Week 1:** "The Boy Who Cried Wolf" **Unit 3, Week 2:** "The Turtle and the Flute" **Unit 3, Week 3:** "Field Trips" **Unit 4, Week 1:** "Little Juan and the Cooking Pot" **Unit 4, Week 2:** "Cultural Festivals" **Unit 4, Week 3:** "The Bundle of Sticks" **Unit 5, Week 1:** "Growing Plants" **Unit 5, Week 2:** "The Pine Tree" **Unit 5, Week 3:** "Farmers Around the World" **Unit 6, Week 1:** "A Tour of the Seasons" **Unit 6, Week 1:** "The Frog and the Locust" **Unit 6, Week 3:** "Rainbow Crow" **Unit 7, Week 1:** "Baby Farm Animals" **Unit 7, Week 2:** "The Family Pet" **Unit 7, Week 3:** "Anansi, An African Tale" **Unit 8, Week 1:** "The King of the Winds" **Unit 8, Week 2:** "The Best of the West" **Unit 8, Week 3:** "A View From the Moon" **Unit 9, Week 1:** "Helping Out at Home" **Unit 9, Week 2:** "The Little Red Hen" **Unit 9, Week 3:** "Spider Woman Teaches the Navajo" **Unit 10, Week 1:** "The Elves and the Shoemakers" **Unit 10, Week 1:** "Good for You!" **Unit 10, Week 1:** "Help Save Big Blue!"

Speaking and Listening Standards

Comprehension and Collaboration		McGraw-Hill Reading Wonders
SL.K.2	Confirm understanding of a text read aloud or information presented orally or through other media by asking and answering questions about key details and requesting clarification if something is not understood.	**READING/WRITING WORKSHOP:** **Unit 1:** 6-7, 26-31, 33, 35, 37, 42-43, 45, 47, 49, 51, 53, 55 **Unit 2:** 6-7, 8, 9, 10, 13, 14-19, 24-25, 27, 28, 30, 33, 34, 35, 46, 47, 48, 51, 54, 55, 58 **Unit 3:** 6-7, 9, 12, 13, 16, 17, 19, 33, 34, 37, 42-43, 46, 47, 49, 51, 53, 55 **Unit 4:** 6-7, 9-15, 20-21, 23-25, 28-29, 34-43 **Unit 5:** 8-15, 23-28 **Unit 6:** 8-15, 22-29 **Unit 7:** 8-15, 18-19, 20-21, 22-29, 34-35, 36-43 **Unit 8:** 6-7, 8-15, 20-21, 22-29, 34-35, 36-43 **Unit 9:** 6-7, 8-15, 20-21, 22-29, 34-35, 36-43 **Unit 10:** 6-7, 8-15, 20-21, 22-29, 34-35, 36-43 **LEVELED READERS:** **Unit 1, Week 3:** *The Beach* (A), *See It Grow!* (O, ELL), *At School* (B) **Unit 2, Week 1:** *We Need Tools* (A), *A Trip* (O, ELL), *What Can You See?* (B) **Unit 3, Week 1:** *We Run* (A), *Go, Nat!* (O, ELL), *The Birdhouse* (B) **Unit 4, Week 2:** *My Neighbors* (A), *Neighborhood Party* (O, ELL), *Parade Day* (B) **Unit 5, Week 1:** *My Garden* (A), *My Garden Grows* (O, ELL), *The Mystery Seeds* (B) **Unit 5, Week 3:** *The Farmer* (A), *Let's Make a Salad!* (O, ELL), *Farm Fresh Finn* (B) **Unit 6, Week 1:** *It Is Hot!* (A), *Little Bear* (O, ELL), *Ant and Grasshopper* (B) **Unit 7, Week 2:** *My Cats* (A), *Their Pets* (O, ELL), *Will's Pet* (B) **Unit 7, Week 3:** *We Want Water* (A), *A New Home* (O, ELL), *Bird's New Home* (B) **Unit 8, Week 2:** *See This!* (A), *Places to See* (O, ELL), *My Trip to Yellowstone* (B) **Unit 8, Week 3:** *Going Up* (A), *In the Clouds* (O, ELL) *How Sun and Moon Found Home* (B) **Unit 9, Week 2:** *Mike Helps Out* (A), *Clive and His Friend* (O, ELL), *Farmer White's Best Friend* (B) **Unit 9, Week 3:** *Look Where It Is From* (A), *What's for Breakfast?* (O, ELL), *Nature at the Craft Fair* (B) **Unit 10, Week 2:** *My Box* (A), *Let's Make a Band* (O, ELL), *Going Camping* (B) **Unit 10, Week 3:** *Help Clean Up* (A), *Let's Save Earth* (O, ELL) *Babysitters for Seals* (B) **YOUR TURN PRACTICE BOOK:** 29-30, 35-38, 45-46, 53, 59-61, 68, 79-80, 85-86, 93-94, 99, 101-103, 107, 109-111, 115, 118, 123, 127-128, 129, 137, 141, 143-144, 147, 153-154, 164-165, 174, 187, 207, 217, 221, 227, 231, 234 **READING WORKSTATION ACTIVITY CARDS:** 7, 8, 16, 20 **WRITING WORKSTATION ACTIVITY CARDS:** 4, 6, 9 **TEACHER'S EDITION:** **Unit 1:** T11, T22-26, T186-191 **Unit 2:** T35, T186-191, T244 **Unit 3:** T104-108, T137, T175 **Unit 4:** T11, T55, T92, T137, T175, T219, T244 **Unit 5:** T11, T52, T93, T175, T186 **Unit 6:** T11, T20, T26, T93, T175 **Unit 7:** T11, T52, T55, T93, T137, T175, T219, T242 **Unit 8:** T11, T55, T78, T92-93 **Unit 9:** T11, T52, T55, T80, T93, T137, T162, T175, T219, T242 **Unit 10:** T11, T57, T80, T95, T139, T221, T244 **LITERATURE BIG BOOKS:** **Unit 1, Week 1:** *What About Bear?* **Unit 1, Week 2:** *Pouch!* **Unit 1, Week 3:** *Senses at the Seashore* **Unit 2, Week 1:** *The Handiest Things in the World* **Unit 2, Week 2:** *Shapes All Around* **Unit 3, Week 1:** *How Do Dinosaurs Go to School?* **Unit 3, Week 2:** *Clang! Clang! Beep! Beep! Listen to the City* **Unit 3, Week 3:** *Please Take Me for a Walk* **Unit 4, Week 1:** *Whose Shoes? A Shoe for Every Job* **Unit 4, Week 2:** *What Can You Do with a Paleta?* **Unit 4, Week 3:** *Roadwork* **Unit 5, Week 1:** *My Garden* **Unit 5, Week 2:** *A Grand Old Tree* **Unit 6, Week 3:** *Waiting Out the Storm* **Unit 7, Week 3:** *Bear Snores On* **Unit 8, Week 3:** *Bringing Down the Moon* **Unit 9, Week 1:** *Peter's Chair* **Unit 9, Week 2:** *Hen Hears Gossip* **Unit 10, Week 1:** *What's the Big Idea, Molly?* **Unit 10, Week 2:** *All Kinds of Families* **INTERACTIVE READ-ALOUD CARDS:** **Smart Start, Week 1:** "The Ugly Duckling" **Smart Start, Week 2:** "Tikki Tikki Tembo" **Smart Start, Week 3:** "Kindergarteners Can!" **Unit 1, Week 1:** "The Lion and the Mouse" **Unit 1, Week 2:** "The Tortoise and the Hare" **Unit 1, Week 3:** "A Feast of the Senses" **Unit 2, Week 1:** "Timimoto" **Unit 2, Week 2:** "Kites in Flight" **Unit 2, Week 3:** "From Caterpillar to Butterfly" **Unit 4, Week 1:** "Little Juan and the Cooking Pot" **Unit 4, Week 2:** "Cultural Festivals" **Unit 4, Week 3:** "The Bundle of Sticks" **Unit 5, Week 1:** "Growing Plants" **Unit 5, Week 2:** "The Pine Tree" **Unit 6, Week 1:** "A Tour of the Seasons" **Unit 6, Week 2:** "The Frog and the Locust" **Unit 6, Week 3:** "Rainbow Crow" **Unit 8, Week 1:** "The King of the Winds" **Unit 8, Week 2:** "The Best of the West" **Unit 8, Week 3:** "A View From the Moon" **Unit 9, Week 1:** "Helping Out at Home" **Unit 9, Week 2:** "The Little Red Hen" **Unit 9, Week 3:** "Spider Woman Teaches the Navajo" **Unit 10, Week 1:** "Help Save Big Blue!"

Speaking and Listening Standards

Comprehension and Collaboration		McGraw-Hill Reading Wonders
SL.K.3	Ask and answer questions in order to seek help, get information, or clarify something that is not understood.	**READING/WRITING WORKSHOP:** Unit 1: 6-7, 26-31, 33, 36, 37, 42-43, 45, 47, 49, 51, 53, 55 Unit 2: 6, 7, 14-19 Unit 3: 8-13, 14-19, 42-43 Unit 4: 6-7, 9, 11, 14, 20-29, 34-43 Unit 5: 6-7, 9, 11, 14, 20-29, 34-43 Unit 6: 6-7, 9, 11, 14, 20-29, 34-43 Unit 7: 6-7, 20-21 Unit 8: 6-7, 20-21 Unit 9: 6-7, 20-21 Unit 10: 6-7 **LEVELED READERS:** Unit 2, Week 1: *We Need Tools* (A), *What Can You See?* (O, ELL), *A Trip* (B) Unit 4, Week 1: *You Cook* (A), *On the Job* (O, ELL), *The Neighborhood* (B) Unit 4, Week 3: *We Clean!* (A), *Can You Fix It?* (O, ELL), *Helping Mom* (B) Unit 5, Week 1: *My Garden* (A), *My Garden Grows* (O, ELL), *The Mystery Seeds* (B) Unit 5, Week 3: *The Farmer* (A), *Let's Make a Salad!* (O, ELL), *Farm Fresh Finn* (B) Unit 6, Week 1: *It Is Hot!* (A), *Little Bear* (O, ELL), *Ant and Grasshopper* (B) Unit 6, Week 3: *Bad Weather* (A), *Getting Ready* (O, ELL), *The Storm* (B) Unit 7, Week 1: *Two Cubs* (A), *Animal Bodies* (O, ELL), *Two Kinds of Bears* (B) Unit 8, Week 2: *See This!* (A), *Places to See* (O, ELL), *My Trip to Yellowstone* (B) Unit 9, Week 1: *Let Me Help You* (A) *How Can Jane Help?* (O, ELL), *I Used to Help Too* (B) Unit 10, Week 1: *Animal Band* (A), *We Want Honey* (O, ELL), *A Good Idea* (B) Unit 10, Week 3: *Help Clean Up* (A), *Let's Save Earth* (O, ELL) *Babysitters for Seals* (B) **READING WORKSTATION ACTIVITY CARDS:** 7, 16, 20 **WRITING WORKSTATION ACTIVITY CARDS:** 4, 6, 9 **TEACHER'S EDITION:** Unit 1: T13, T216, T233 Unit 2: T95, T131, T137 Unit 3: T31, T49 Unit 4: T11, T55, T93, T137, T216, T219 Unit 5: T11, T52, T134, T216 Unit 6: T11, T93 Unit 7: T52, T93, T134, T182, T196, T205 Unit 8: T11, T93, T175 Unit 9: T13, T22, T52, T55 Unit 10: T11, T95, T97 **LITERATURE BIG BOOKS:** Unit 1, Week 1: *What About Bear?* Unit 1, Week 2: *Pouch!* Unit 1, Week 3: *Senses at the Seashore* Unit 2, Week 1: *The Handiest Things in the World* Unit 2, Week 2: *Shapes All Around* Unit 3, Week 1: *How Do Dinosaurs Go to School?* Unit 3, Week 2: *Clang! Clang! Beep! Beep! Listen to the City* Unit 3, Week 3: *Please Take Me for a Walk* Unit 4, Week 1: *Whose Shoes? A Shoe for Every Job* Unit 4, Week 2: *What Can You Do with a Paleta?* Unit 4, Week 3: *Roadwork* Unit 9, Week 1: *Peter's Chair* Unit 9, Week 2: *Hen Hears Gossip* Unit 10, Week 2: *All Kinds of Families!* Unit 10, Week 3: *Panda Kindergarten* **INTERACTIVE READ-ALOUD CARDS:** Unit 1, Week 1: "The Lion and the Mouse" Unit 1, Week 2: "The Tortoise and the Hare" Unit 1, Week 3: "A Feast of the Senses" Unit 2, Week 1: "Timimoto" Unit 2, Week 2: "Kites in Flight" Unit 2, Week 3: "From Caterpillar to Butterfly" Unit 3, Week 1: "The Boy Who Cried Wolf" Unit 3, Week 2: "The Turtle and the Flute" Unit 4, Week 1: "Little Juan and the Cooking Pot" Unit 4, Week 2: "Cultural Festivals" Unit 9, Week 2: "The Little Red Hen"
Presentation of Knowledge and Ideas		***McGraw-Hill Reading Wonders***
SL.K.4	Describe familiar people, places, things, and events and, with prompting and support, provide additional detail.	**READING/WRITING WORKSHOP BIG BOOK:** Unit 1: 6-7, 42-43 Unit 2: 6-7, 24-25, 42-43 Unit 3: 6-7, 24-25, 42-43 Unit 4: 6-7, 20-21, 34-35 Unit 5: 6-7, 20-21, 34-35 Unit 6: 6-7, 20-21, 34-35 Unit 7: 6-7, 20-21, 34-35 Unit 8: 6-7, 20-21, 34-35 Unit 9: 6-7, 20-21, 34-35 Unit 10: 6-7, 20-21, 34-35 **YOUR TURN PRACTICE BOOK:** 27-28, 35-38, 51-52, 61, 67, 68, 83, 85-86, 93-94, 103, 107, 109-110, 115, 117, 118, 141, 157, 167, 174, 193, 221, 231 **READING WORKSTATION ACTIVITY CARDS:** 10, 12, 14, 16 **WRITING WORKSTATION ACTIVITY CARDS:** 1, 2, 8, 16, 19, 22 **TEACHER'S EDITION:** Unit 1: S58, S74-75, T19, T33, T134, T183, T197, T205 Unit 2: T175, T182 Unit 3: T11, T93, T175, T177 Unit 4: T10-11, T18-19, T92, T114-115, T132-133, T135, T175, T182-183, T197, T214-215 Unit 5: T54, T136, T175, T218 Unit 6: T11, T13, T52, T54, T136, T175, T218 Unit 7: T54, T136, T163, T175, T218 Unit 8: T54, T175, T216 Unit 9: T11, T93, T136, T175, T183 Unit 10: T102, T116, T136, T177 **LITERATURE BIG BOOKS:** Smart Start: *Animals in the Park* Unit 1, Week 1: *What About Bear?* Unit 1, Week 2: *Pouch!* Unit 1, Week 3: *Senses at the Seashore* Unit 2, Week 3: *I Love Bugs!* Unit 4, Week 1: *Whose Shoes? A Shoe for Every Job* Unit 4, Week 2: *What Can You Do with a Paleta?* Unit 4, Week 3: *Roadwork* Unit 5, Week 1: *My Garden* Unit 5, Week 2: *A Grand Old Tree* Unit 5, Week 3: *An Orange in January* Unit 6, Week 1: *Mama, Is It Summer Yet?* Unit 6, Week 2: *Rain* Unit 7, Week 1: *ZooBorns!* Unit 7, Week 2: *The Family Pet* Unit 7, Week 3: *Bear Snores On* Unit 8, Week 1: *When Daddy's Truck Picks Me Up* Unit 8, Week 2: *Ana Goes to Washington, D.C.* Unit 9, Week 1: *Peter's Chair* Unit 9, Week 2: *Hen Hears Gossip* Unit 9, Week 3: *Bread Comes to Life* Unit 10, Week 1: *What's the Big Idea, Molly?* Unit 10, Week 2: *All Kinds of Families!* **INTERACTIVE READ-ALOUD CARDS:** Smart Start, Week 2: "Tikki Tikki Tembo" Smart Start, Week 3: "Kindergarteners Can!" Unit 1, Week 1: "The Lion and the Mouse" Unit 1, Week 2: "The Tortoise and the Hare" Unit 1, Week 3: "A Feast of the Senses" Unit 2, Week 1: "Timimoto" Unit 2, Week 2: "Kites in Flight" Unit 2, Week 3: "From Caterpillar to Butterfly" Unit 3, Week 1: "The Boy Who Cried Wolf" Unit 3, Week 2: "The Turtle and the Flute" Unit 4, Week 3: "The Bundle of Sticks" Unit 5, Week 3: "Farms Around the World" Unit 6, Week 3: "Rainbow Crow" Unit 7, Week 3: "Anansi: An African Tale" Unit 8, Week 3: "A View From the Moon" Unit 9, Week 3: "Spider Woman Teaches the Navajo" Unit 10, Week 1: "The Elves and the Shoemakers" Unit 10, Week 1: "Good for You!"

Speaking and Listening Standards

Presentation of Knowledge and Ideas		McGraw-Hill Reading Wonders
SL.K.5	Add drawings or other visual displays to descriptions as desired to provide additional detail.	**YOUR TURN PRACTICE BOOK:** 27-28, 30-32, 35-38, 43-46, 51-53, 59-60, 61, 62, 67-70, 77-80, 83, 85-86, 88, 93-94, 99, 101-102, 103-104, 107, 109-112, 115, 117-118, 123, 127-128, 129, 130, 133, 135-136, 137, 138, 141, 143-144, 147, 148, 151, 153-154, 157, 158, 164-165, 167, 168, 174, 187, 193, 207, 217, 221, 227, 231, 234 **READINGWORK STATION ACTIVITY CARDS:** 1, 6, 12, 15, 16, 20 **WRITING WORKSTATION ACTIVITY CARDS:** 1, 2, 4, 9, 17, 20, 23 **TEACHER'S EDITION: Unit 1:** T32, T41, T123, T214 **Unit 2:** T40-41, T123, T132 **Unit 3:** T41, T134, T217 **Unit 4:** T32, T41, T52, T123, T134, T205 **Unit 5:** T53, T134, T217 **Unit 6:** T53, T122-123, T135, T140, T163, T197, T205, T222 **Unit 7:** T33, T41, T114, T123 **Unit 8:** T53, T132, T134, T216 **Unit 9:** T41, T53, T123, T205, T214, T241 **Unit 10:** T43, T137, T216
SL.K.6	Speak audibly and express thoughts, feelings, and ideas clearly.	**READING/WRITING WORKSHOP: Unit 1:** 6-7, 8-13, 14-19, 24-25, 26-31, 42-43 **Unit 2:** 6-7, 8, 9, 10, 13, 14-19, 24-25, 33, 34, 35, 42-43, 46, 47, 48, 51, 54, 55, 58 **Unit 3:** 6-7, 13, 26, 27, 30, 31, 42-43, 44-49 **Unit 4:** 6-8, 22-29, 34-35 **Unit 5:** 6-7 **Unit 6:** 6-7 8-15, 22-29 **Unit 7:** 6-7 **Unit 8:** 20-21, 34-35 **LEVELED READERS: Unit 1, Week 2:** *Hop!* (A), *We Hop!* (O, ELL), *We Can Move!* (B) **Unit 2, Week 3:** *We Like Bugs!* (A), *The Bugs Run* (O, ELL), *I See a Bug* (B) **Unit 3, Week 1:** *We Run* (A), *Go, Nat!* (O, ELL), *The Birdhouse* (B) **Unit 5, Week 3:** *The Farmer* (A), *Let's Make a Salad!* (O, ELL), *Farm Fresh Finn* (B) **Unit 6, Week 1:** *It Is Hot!* (A), *Little Bear* (O, ELL), *Ant and Grasshopper* (B) **Unit 6, Week 2:** *The Rain* (A), *Weather Is Fun* (O, ELL), *Kate and Tuck* (B) **YOUR TURN PRACTICE BOOK:** 29, 37, 39-40, 43-44, 45, 47-48, 53, 61, 68, 71-72, 81-82, 83, 89-90, 97-98, 103, 105-106, 107, 113-114, 115, 121-122, 129, 131-132, 137, 141, 147, 149-150, 151, 187, 221, 227, 231 **READING WORKSTATION ACTIVITY CARDS:** 1, 3, 12, 17 **WRITING WORKSTATION ACTIVITY CARDS:** 1, 2, 6, 20, 25 **TEACHER'S EDITION: Unit 1:** T134, T175, T222 **Unit 2:** T58, T175, T222 **Unit 3:** T58, T140, T222 **Unit 4:** T58, T140, T175, T222 **Unit 5:** T11, T58, T140, T222 **Unit 6:** T11, T58, T140, T175, T222 **Unit 7:** T52, T58, T140, T175, T222 **Unit 8:** T11, T58, T93, T40, T175, T222 **Unit 9:** T11, T52, T58, T140, T222, T245 **Unit 10:** T11, T95, T142, T177, T224 **LITERATURE BIG BOOKS: Unit 1, Week 1:** *What About Bear?* **Unit 1, Week 2:** *Pouch!* **Unit 1, Week 3:** *Senses at the Seashore* **Unit 2, Week 1:** *The Handiest Things in the World* **Unit 2, Week 2:** *Shapes All Around* **Unit 2, Week 3:** *I Love Bugs!* **Unit 3, Week 2:** *A Grand Old Tree* **Unit 3, Week 3:** *An Orange in January* **Unit 5, Week 1:** *My Garden* **Unit 6, Week 1:** *Mama, Is It Summer Yet?* **Unit 8, Week 2:** *Ana Goes to Washington, D.C.* **INTERACTIVE READ-ALOUD CARDS: Unit 1, Week 1:** "The Lion and the Mouse" **Unit 1, Week 2:** "The Tortoise and the Hare" **Unit 1, Week 3:** "A Feast of the Senses" **Unit 2, Week 1:** "Timimoto" **Unit 2, Week 2:** "Kites in Flight" **Unit 2, Week 3:** "From Caterpillar to Butterfly" **Unit 3, Week 1:** "The Boy Who Cried Wolf" **Unit 3, Week 2:** "The Turtle and the Flute" **Unit 3, Week 3:** "Field Trips" **Unit 4, Week 1:** "Little Juan and the Cooking Pot" **Unit 4, Week 2:** "Cultural Festivals" **Unit 4, Week 3:** "The Bundle of Sticks" **Unit 5, Week 1:** "Growing Plants" **Unit 7, Week 2:** "The Family Pet"

College and Career Readiness Anchor Standards for LANGUAGE

The K–5 standards on the following pages define what students should understand and be able to do by the end of each grade. They correspond to the College and Career Readiness (CCR) anchor standards below by number. The CCR and grade-specific standards are necessary complements—the former providing broad standards, the latter providing additional specificity—that together define the skills and understandings that all students must demonstrate.

Conventions of Standard English
1. Demonstrate command of the conventions of standard English grammar and usage when writing or speaking.
2. Demonstrate command of the conventions of standard English capitalization, punctuation, and spelling when writing.
Knowledge of Language
3. Apply knowledge of language to understand how language functions in different contexts, to make effective choices for meaning or style, and to comprehend more fully when reading or listening.
Vocabulary Acquisition and Use
4. Determine or clarify the meaning of unknown and multiple-meaning words and phrases by using context clues, analyzing meaningful word parts, and consulting general and specialized reference materials, as appropriate.
5. Demonstrate understanding of figurative language, word relationships, and nuances in word meanings.
6. Acquire and use accurately a range of general academic and domain-specific words and phrases sufficient for reading, writing, speaking, and listening at the college and career readiness level; demonstrate independence in gathering vocabulary knowledge when encountering an unknown term important to comprehension or expression.

Common Core State Standards
English Language Arts

Grade K

CORRELATIONS

Language Standards

Conventions of Standard English		McGraw-Hill Reading Wonders
L.K.1	Demonstrate command of the conventions of standard English grammar and usage when writing or speaking.	**TEACHER'S EDITION: Unit 1:** T16, T19, T32-33, T41, T36, T98, T101, T114-115, T122-123, T125, T133, T141, T165, T180, T183, T197, T205, T214-215, T223, T247 **Unit 2:** T16, T18-19, T32-33, T40-41, T50-51, T59, T83, T98, T101, T115, T123, T133, T141, T165, T180, T183, T185, T197, T205, T215, T223 **Unit 3:** T16, T98, T180, T183, T197, T215 **Unit 4:** T16, T18-19, T32-33, T40-41, T47, T51, T59, T98, T101, T114-115, T122-123, T129, T133, T139, T141, T180, T182-183, T196-197, T204-205, T211, T215, T221, T223 **Unit 5:** T16, T21, T43, T83, T98, T103, T180, T196, T247 **Unit 6:** T16, T19, T33, T41, T44, T47, T51, T53, T59, T83, T98, T101, T114, T115, T123, T129, T133, T141, T180, T183, T185, T197, T205, T207, T211, T215, T223, T247 **Unit 7:** T16, T19, T33, T41, T47, T51, T83, T98, T114-115, T123, T129,T133, T139, T141, T165, T180, T182, T183, T196, T197, T204-205, T211, T215, T223, T247 **Unit 8:** T16, T19, T21, T33, T41, T47, T50-51, T83, T98, T101, T115, T123, T129,T133, T141, T180, T182-183, T196-197, T205, T211, T215, T223 **Unit 9:** T16, T19, T21, T32-33, T41, T47, T51, T59, T83, T98,T101, T103, T114-115, T123, T133, T141, T165, T129, T180, T183, T185, T197, T205, T211, T215, T223, T247 **Unit 10:** T16, T21, T34, T42, T49, T85, T100, T131, T182, T187, T198, T213, T249
L.K.1a	Print many upper- and lowercase letters.	**TEACHER'S EDITION: Unit 1:** T16, T98, T180 **Unit 2:** T16, T98, T180 **Unit 3:** T16, T98, T180 **Unit 4:** T16, T47, T98, T129, T139, T180, T211, T221 **Unit 5:** T16, T98, T180 **Unit 6:** T16, T47, T98, T129, T180, T211 **Unit 7:** T16, T47, T98, T129, T139, T180, T211 **Unit 8:** T16, T47, T98, T129, T180, T211 **Unit 9:** T16, T47, T98, T129, T180, T211 **Unit 10:** T16, T49, T100, T131, T182, T213 **YOUR TURN PRACTICE BOOK:** 34, 42, 50, 58, 66, 76, 84, 92, 100, 108, 116, 126, 134, 142, 152, 162, 172, 184, 192, 202, 212, 222, 232, 244, 252, 260, 268, 276, 284
L.K.1b	Use frequently occurring nouns and verbs.	**TEACHER'S EDITION: Unit 1:** T19, T32-33, T41, T36, T101, T114-115, T122-123, T125, T133, T141, T165, T183, T197, T205, T214-215, T223, T247 **Unit 2:** T18-19, T32-33, T40-41, T50-51, T59, T83, T101, T115, T123, T133, T141, T165, T183, T185, T197, T205, T215, T223 **Unit 5:** T103 **Unit 6:** T19, T33, T44, T51, T53, T83, T114, T223, T247 **Unit 7:** T19, T33, T41, T51, T83, T114-115, T123, T133, T141, T165, T183, T197, T205, T215, T223, T247 **Unit 8:** T10, T18, T114, T115 **Unit 9:** T21, T103, T185 **Unit 10:** T187 **YOUR TURN PRACTICE BOOK:** 23, 41, 65, 73, 83, 107, 115, 141, 151, 161, 191, 201, 211, 221, 241, 251, 259, 267, 295
L.K.1c	Form regular plural nouns orally by adding /s/ or /es/ (e.g., *dog, dogs; wish, wishes*).	**TEACHER'S EDITION: Unit 5:** T21, T43 **Unit 6:** T33, T41, T51, T59, T101, T115, T123, T133, T141, T183, T197, T205, T215
L.K.1d	Understand and use question words (interrogatives) (e.g., *who, what, where, when, why, how*).	**TEACHER'S EDITION: Unit 3:** T183, T197, T215 **Unit 6:** T185, T207 **Unit 7:** T182, T196, T204-205 **Unit 9:** T103, T125 **Unit 10:** T21
L.K.1e	Use the most frequently occurring prepositions (e.g., *to, from, in, out, on, off, for, of, by, with*).	**TEACHER'S EDITION: Unit 3:** T29, T47 **Unit 5:** T193, T211 **Unit 7:** T29, T47 **Unit 8:** T19, T33, T41, T50-51, T83, T101, T115, T123, T133, T141, T183, T197, T205, T223
L.K.1f	Produce and expand complete sentences in shared language activities.	**TEACHER'S EDITION: Unit 4:** T18-19, T32-33, T40-41, T51, T59, T101, T114-115, T122-123, T133, T141, T182-183, T196-197, T204-205, T215, T223 **Unit 5:** T83, T196, T247 **Unit 8:** T182-183, T196-197, T215, T223; **Unit 9:** T19, T32-33, T41, T51, T59, T83, T101, T114-115, T123, T133, T141, T165, T183, T197, T205, T215, T223, T247 **Unit 10:** T34, T42, T85, T198, T249

Language Standards

Conventions of Standard English		McGraw-Hill Reading Wonders
L.K.2	Demonstrate command of the conventions of standard English capitalization, punctuation, and spelling when writing.	**TEACHER'S EDITION:** **Unit 1:** T16, T72, T129, T211, T221 **Unit 2:** T47, T57, T129, T139, T211, T221 **Unit 3:** T19, T47, T50-51, T53, T57, T59, T83, T101, T115, T120, T123, T132-133, T139, T141, T183, T196-197, T205, T211, T214-215, T221, T223, T247 **Unit 4:** T16, T47, T57, T98, T129, T139, T211, T221 **Unit 5:** T16, T47, T57, T98, T101, T115, T123, T139, T180, T211, T221 **Unit 6:** T12, T16, T47, T57, T98, T129, T139, T176, T211, T221 **Unit 7:** T16, T47, T57, T98, T129, T139, T180, T211, T214, T221 **Unit 8:** T16, T32, T47, T98, T101, T114, T129, T132, T164, T211, T221 **Unit 9:** T47, T129, T211 **Unit 10:** T49, T53, T103, T116, T131, T213, T216
L.K.2a	Capitalize the first word in a sentence and the pronoun *I*.	**TEACHER'S EDITION:** **Unit 3:** T19, T50-51, T53, T59, T83, T115, T123, T132-133, T197, T223 **Unit 5:** T101, T115, T123 **Unit 8:** T32, T101, T114, T132 **Unit 10:** T53, T103, T116, T216
L.K.2b	Recognize and name end punctuation.	**TEACHER'S EDITION:** **Unit 3:** T101, T115, T123, T132-133, T141, T183, T196-197, T205, T214-215, T223, T247 **Unit 6:** T12, T176 **Unit 7:** T214 **Unit 8:** T32, T101, T114, T132, T164
L.K.2c	Write a letter or letters for most consonant and short-vowel sounds (phonemes).	**TEACHER'S EDITION:** **Unit 1:** T16, T72, T129, T211 **Unit 2:** T47, T129, T211 **Unit 3:** T47, T120, T211 **Unit 4:** T16, T47, T98, T129, T139, T211, T221 **Unit 5:** T16, T47, T98, T180, T211 **Unit 6:** T16, T47, T98, T129, T211 **Unit 7:** T16, T47, T57, T98, T129, T139, T180, T211 **Unit 8:** T16, T47, T98, T129, T211 **Unit 9:** T47, T129, T211 **Unit 10:** T49, T131, T213 **YOUR TURN PRACTICE BOOK:** 34, 42, 50, 58, 51-52, 62, 66, 76, 84, 85, 86, 88, 92, 100, 104, 108, 116, 126, 130, 134, 138, 142, 148, 158, 162, 164-165, 168, 172, 192, 202, 212, 222, 232 **PHONICS AND WORD STUDY WORKSTATION ACTIVITY CARDS:** 1, 2, 3, 4, 5, 6, 7, 8, 9, 10, 11, 12, 13, 14, 15, 16, 17, 18, 19, 20, 21, 22, 23, 24
L.K.2d	Spell simple words phonetically, drawing on knowledge of sound-letter relationships.	**TEACHER'S EDITION:** **Unit 1:** T221 **Unit 2:** T57, T139, T221 **Unit 3:** T57, T139, T221 **Unit 4:** T47, T57, T129, T139, T211, T221 **Unit 5:** T57, T139, T221 **Unit 6:** T57, T139, T221 **Unit 7:** T47, T57, T129, T139, T211, T221 **Unit 8:** T47, T129, T139, T211, T221 **YOUR TURN PRACTICE BOOK:** 30, 38, 46, 54, 62, 74, 75, 80, 88, 96, 104, 112, 124, 125, 130, 138, 148, 158, 168, 182, 183, 188, 198, 208, 228, 242, 243, 256, 264, 272, 280, 293, 294
Knowledge of Language		***McGraw-Hill Reading Wonders***
L.K.3	(Begins in grade 2.)	
Vocabulary Acquisition and Use		***McGraw-Hill Reading Wonders***
L.K.4	Determine or clarify the meaning of unknown and multiple-meaning words and phrases based on *kindergarten reading and content*.	**TEACHER'S EDITION:** **Unit 4:** T127 **Unit 5:** T45, T46, T108, T187 **Unit 6:** T21, T23, T33, T41 **Unit 7:** T24, T45, T189, T209 **Unit 9:** T21, T24, T25, T43, T185, T189, T207 **Unit 10:** T25, T187, T209
L.K.4a	Identify new meanings for familiar words and apply them accurately (e.g., knowing *duck* is a bird and learning the verb to *duck*).	**TEACHER'S EDITION:** **Unit 5:** T108, T185, T187 T207 **Unit 6:** T21, T189 **Unit 7:** T24, T45, T189 **Unit 8:** T21 **Unit 9:** T25, T45, T185, T207 **Unit 10:** T25, T47
L.K.4b	Use the most frequently occurring inflections and affixes (e.g., *-ed, -s, re-, un-, pre-, -ful, -less*) as a clue to the meaning of an unknown word.	**TEACHER'S EDITION:** **Unit 5:** T45, T46, T187 **Unit 6:** T23, T33, T41 **Unit 9:** T21, T24, T43, T189 **Unit 10:** T187, T209

Language Standards

Vocabulary Acquisition and Use		McGraw-Hill Reading Wonders
L.K.5	With guidance and support from adults, explore word relationships and nuances in word meanings.	**TEACHER'S EDITION: Unit 1:** T10-11, T34, T43 **Unit 2:** T10, T43, T103, T116, T125, T135, T175, T185, T207, T245 **Unit 3:** T10, T116, T175 **Unit 4:** T10-11, T12-13, T21, T34, T43, T44-45, T54, T67, T80, T81, T83, T92-93, T94-95, T103, T116, T125, T126-127, T133, T136, T141, T149, T165, T174-175, T176-177, T183, T185, T188, T198, T207, T208-209, T218, T231, T245, T247 **Unit 5:** T10-11, T12-13, T21, T34, T43, T54, T67, T80, T81, T92-93, T94-95, T116, T149, T174-175, T185, T195, T207, T218, T245 **Unit 6:** T10-11, T20, T34, T35, T42, T43, T44, T67, T81, T92-93, T103, T108, T116, T125, T126-127, T136, T149, T163, T174-175, T176-177, T185, T198, T208-209, T218, T231, T245 **Unit 7:** T10-11, T12-13, T21, T25, T34, T43, T54, T67, T81, T92-93, T94-95, T103, T116, T126-127, T136, T149, T163, T174-175, T185, T190, T207, T208-209, T218, T231, T245 **Unit 8:** T10-11, T12-13, T21, T23, T34, T43, T44-45, T54, T67, T81, T92-93, T94-95, T103, T116, T125, T126-127, T136, T149, T163, T174-175, T185, T198, T207, T208-209, T218, T231, T245 **Unit 9:** T10-11, T12-13, T34, T44-45, T54, T67, T81, T92-93, T103, T116, T126-127, T136, T149, T163, T174-175, T176-177, T185, T198, T207, T208-209, T218, T231, T245 **Unit 10:** T10-11, T25, T36, T46-47, T56, T69, T83, T94-95, T96-97, T105, T106-111, T118, T127, T128-129, T136-137, T138, T151, T165, T176-177, T178-179, T187, T189, T190, T200, T209, T210-211, T220, T233, T247
L.K.5a	Sort common objects into categories (e.g., shapes, foods) to gain a sense of the concepts the categories represent.	**TEACHER'S EDITION: Unit 2:** T43, T103, T125, T135 **Unit 4:** T103, T183 **Unit 5:** T21, T185, T207 **Unit 6:** T43 **Unit 8:** T43 **Unit 10:** T127, T129, T136-137
L.K.5b	Demonstrate understanding of frequently occurring verbs and adjectives by relating them to their opposites (antonyms).	**YOUR TURN PRACTICE BOOK:** 241, 283 **TEACHER'S EDITION: Unit 6:** T44 **Unit 7:** T25 **Unit 8:** T23, T185, T207 **Unit 9:** T189 **Unit 10:** T25, T105, T127, T189, T190
L.K.5c	Identify real-life connections between words and their use (e.g., note places at school that are colorful).	**READING/WRITING WORKSHOP: Unit 1: Smart Start:** 4-5, 22-23, 40-41; 6-7, 24-25, 42-43 **Unit 2:** 6-7, 24-25, 42-43 **Unit 3:** 6-7, 24-25, 42-43 **Unit 4:** 6-7, 20-21, 34-35 **Unit 5:** 6-7, 20-21, 34-35 **Unit 6:** 6-7, 20-21, 34-35 **Unit 7:** 6-7, 20-21, 34-35 **Unit 8:** 6-7, 20-21, 34-35 **Unit 9:** 6-7, 20-21, 34-35 **Unit 10:** 6-7, 20-21, 34-35 **YOUR TURN PRACTICE BOOK:** 23, 33, 41, 49, 57, 65, 73, 83, 107, 115, 133, 141, 151, 161, 171, 191, 201, 211, 221, 241, 251, 259, 267, 275, 283, 295 **TEACHER'S EDITION: Unit 1:** T10-11, T34, T43 **Unit 2:** T10, T116, T175 **Unit 3:** T10, T116, T175 **Unit 4:** T10-11, T12-13, T21, T34, T43, T44-45, T54, T67, T80, T81, T83, T92-93, T94-95, T103, T116, T125, T126-127, T133, T136, T141, T149, T165, T174-175, T176-177, T183, T185, T198, T207, T208-209, T218, T231, T245, T247 **Unit 5:** T10-11, T12-13, T21, T34, T43, T54, T67, T80, T81, T92-93, T94-95, T116, T149, T174-175, T185, T198, T218, T245 **Unit 6:** T10-11, T20, T34, T35, T42, T67, T81, T92-93, T103, T116, T125, T126-127, T136, T149, T163, T174-175, T176-177, T185, T198, T208-209, T218, T231, T245 **Unit 7:** T10-11, T12-13, T21, T25, T34, T43, T54, T67, T81, T92-93, T94-95, T103, T116, T126-127, T136, T149, T163, T174-175, T185, T207, T208-209, T218, T231, T245 **Unit 8:** T10-11, T34, T81, T92-93, T102, T116, T124, T136, T149, T163, T174-175, T185, T198, T207, T208-209, T218, T231, T245 **Unit 9:** T10-11, T12-13, T20, T34, T42-43, T54, T67, T92-93, T103, T116-117, T124-125, T136, T149, T174-175, T176-177, T185, T198, T206-207, T218, T231 **Unit 10:** T10-11, T25, T36, T46-47, T56, T69, T83, T94-95, T96-97, T106-111, T118, T128-129, T138, T151, T165, T176-177, T178-179, T187, T190, T200, T209, T210-211, T220, T233, T247 **INTERACTIVE READ-ALOUD CARDS: SS:** "The Ugly Duckling", "Kindergarteners Can!", "Tikki Tikki Tembo" **Unit 1, Week 1:** "The Lion and the Mouse" **Unit 1, Week 2:** "The Tortoise and the Hare" **Unit 2, Week 3:** "From Caterpillar to Butterfly" **Unit 3, Week 2:** "The Turtle and the Flute" **Unit 4, Week 1:** "Little Juan and the Cooking Pot" **Unit 4, Week 2:** "Cultural Festivals" **Unit 4, Week 3:** "A Bundle of Sticks" **Unit 6, Week 3:** "Rainbow Crow" **Unit 7, Week 3:** "Anansi: An African Tale" **Unit 9, Week 2:** "The Little Red Hen" **Unit 9, Week 3:** "Spider Woman Teaches the Navajo" **Unit 10, Week 1:** "The Elves and the Shoemakers" **ConnectED Digital Resources:** Visual Glossary

Language Standards

Vocabulary Acquisition and Use		*McGraw-Hill Reading Wonders*
L.K.5d	Distinguish shades of meaning among verbs describing the same general action (e.g., *walk, march, strut, prance*) by acting out the meanings.	**TEACHER'S EDITION: Unit 2:** T185, T207, T245 **Unit 4:** T188 **Unit 6:** T35, T108 **Unit 7:** T185, T190, T207
L.K.6	Use words and phrases acquired through conversations, reading and being read to, and responding to texts.	**READING/WRITING WORKSHOP:** Smart Start: 4-5, 22-23, 40-41 **Unit 1:** 6-7, 24-25, 42-43 **Unit 2:** 6-7, 24-25, 42-43 **Unit 3:** 6-7, 24-25, 42-43 **Unit 4:** 6-7, 20-21, 34-35 **Unit 5:** 6-7, 20-21, 34-35 **Unit 6:** 6-7, 20-21, 34-35 **Unit 7:** 6-7, 20-21, 34-35 **Unit 8:** 6-7, 20-21, 34-35 **Unit 9:** 6-7, 20-21, 34-35 **Unit 10:** 6-7, 20-21, 34-35 **TEACHER'S EDITION: Unit 1:** S26, S34, S44 **Unit 2:** T20-21, T93, T198 **Unit 3:** T20, T93, T198 **Unit 4:** T10-11, T12-13, T20-21, T22-27, T34, T42-43, T44-45, T54-55, T67, T80, T81, T92-93, T94-95, T176-177, T184-185, T186-191, T198, T205, T206-207, T208-209, T215, T218-219, T223, T218-219, T231, T244, T245 **Unit 5:** T10-11, T12-13, T20-21, T22-27, T34, T42-43, T44-45, T54-55 , T117, T162-163, T174-175, T176-177, T184-185, T186-191, T198, T199, T206-207, T208-209, T218-219, T231, T244-245 **Unit 6:** T10-11, T20-21, T34-35, T42-43, T44-45, T54-55, T67, T80, T81, T92-93, T94-95, T102-103, T104-109, T116, T124-125, T126-127, T136-137, T149, T231, T244 **Unit 7:** T10-11, T12-13, T20-21, T22-27, T34-35, T42-43, T44-45, T54-55, T67, T80, T81, T92-93, T94-95, T102-103, T104-109, T116, T124-125, T126-127, T136-137, T149, T231, T244, T245 **Unit 8:** T10-11, T12-13, T20-21, T22-27, T34-35, T42-43, T44-45, T54-55, T67, T80, T81, T92-93, T94-95, T102-103, T104-109, T116, T124-125, T126-127, T136-137, T149, T231, T244, T245 **Unit 9:** T10-11, T12-13, T20-21, T22-27, T34-35, T42-43, T44-45, T54-55, T162, T163, T174-175, T176-177, T184-185, T186-191, T198, T199, T206-207, T208-209, T218-219, T231, T244, T245 **Unit 10:** T10-11, T12-13, T20-21, T22-29, T36, T44-45, T46-47, T56-57, T69, T82, T83, T94-95, T96-97, T104-105, T106-111, T118, T126-127, T128-129, T138-139, T151, T179, T233, T246, T247 **LITERATURE BIG BOOKS: Unit 1, Week 2:** *Pouch!* **Unit 2, Week 2:** *Shapes All Around* **Unit 2, Week 3:** *I Love Bugs!* **Unit 3, Week 1:** *How Do Dinosaurs Go to School?* **Unit 4, Week 1:** *Whose Shoes? A Shoe for Every Job* **Unit 4, Week 2:** *What Can You Do with a Paleta?* **Unit 5, Week 2:** *A Grand Old Tree* **Unit 5, Week 3:** *An Orange in January* **Unit 6, Week 1:** *Mama, Is It Summer Yet?* **Unit 7, Week 1:** *ZooBorns!* **Unit 7, Week 2:** *The Birthday Pet* **Unit 8, Week 2:** *Ana Goes to Washington, D.C.* **Unit 8, Week 3:** *Bringing Down the Moon* **Unit 9, Week 3:** *Bread Comes to Life* **Unit 10, Week 1:** *What's the Big Idea, Molly?* **Unit 10, Week 2:** *All Kinds of Families!* **INTERACTIVE READ-ALOUD CARDS: SS:** "The Ugly Duckling", "Kindergarteners Can!", "Tikki Tikki Tembo" **Unit 1, Week 1:** "The Lion and the Mouse" **Unit 1, Week 2:** "The Tortoise and the Hare" **Unit 2, Week 3:** "From Caterpillar to Butterfly" **Unit 3, Week 2:** "The Turtle and the Flute" **Unit 4, Week 1:** "Little Juan and the Cooking Pot" **Unit 4, Week 2:** "Cultural Festivals" **Unit 4, Week 3:** "A Bundle of Sticks" **Unit 6, Week 3:** "Rainbow Crow" **Unit 7, Week 3:** "Anansi: An African Tale" **Unit 9, Week 2:** "The Little Red Hen" **Unit 9, Week 3:** "Spider Woman Teaches the Navajo" **Unit 10, Week 1:** "The Elves and the Shoemakers"